JAPANESE SINGERS OF TALES

To Miyama and Nowaki

In memory of
John Miles Foley (1947–2012)

Japanese Singers of Tales
Ten Centuries of Performed Narrative

ALISON McQUEEN TOKITA
Kyoto City University of Arts, Japan

LONDON AND NEW YORK

First published 2015 by Ashgate Publishing

2 Park Square, Milton Park, Abingdon, Oxfordshire OX14 4RN
52 Vanderbilt Avenue, New York, NY 10017

Routledge is an imprint of the Taylor & Francis Group, an informa business

First issued in paperback 2020

Copyright © 2015 Alison McQueen Tokita

Alison McQueen Tokita has asserted her right under the Copyright, Designs and Patents Act, 1988, to be identified as the author of this work.

All rights reserved. No part of this book may be reprinted or reproduced or utilised in any form or by any electronic, mechanical, or other means, now known or hereafter invented, including photocopying and recording, or in any information storage or retrieval system, without permission in writing from the publishers.

Notice:
Product or corporate names may be trademarks or registered trademarks, and are used only for identification and explanation without intent to infringe.

Bach musicological font © Yo Tomita

British Library Cataloguing in Publication Data
A catalogue record for this book is available from the British Library.

The Library of Congress has cataloged the printed edition as follows:
Tokita, Alison, 1947–
    Japanese singers of tales : ten centuries of performed narrative / by Alison McQueen Tokita.
        pages cm. – (SOAS musicology series)
    Includes bibliographical references and index.
    ISBN 978-0-7546-5379-0 (hardcover : alk. paper)
  1. Vocal music – Japan – History and criticism. 2. Narrative poetry, Japanese – History and criticism. I. Title.

ML1451.J3T65 2015
782.00952–dc23
                                                                    2014027129

ISBN 978-0-7546-5379-0 (hbk)
ISBN 978-0-367-59955-3 (pbk)

Contents

List of Tables		*vii*
List of Music Examples		*ix*
Contents of Accompanying Compact Disc		*xi*
Preface and Acknowledgements		*xiii*
Periods of Japanese History		*xv*
1	Singing the Story: Continuity and Change in Japanese Performed Narratives	1
2	Musical Buddhist Preaching: Kōshiki Shōmyō	25
3	Heike Narrative: The Musical Recitation of *The Tale of the Heike*	53
4	Dance and Narrative: Kōwaka and Nō	91
5	Jōruri and the Puppet Theatre	133
6	Sung Narratives and Kabuki Dance: Bungo-kei Jōruri	171
7	Sung Narratives and Kabuki Dance: Nagauta and Ōzatsuma-bushi	233
Epilogue		*263*
References		*269*
Index		*283*

List of Tables[1]

2.1	Performances of kōshiki today	27
2.2	Outline of *Nehan kōshiki* Dan 1	41
3.1	A comparison of kataribon and yomihon texts	58
3.2	Vertical structure of heike narrative	64
3.3	Fushimono and hiroimono	65
3.4	The principal heike pattern types classified according to hypothesized origin	66
3.5	Comparison of kōshiki and heike musical structure and patterns	67
3.6	The principal heike substyles	67
3.7	Outline of *Yokobue*	71
3.8	Outline of *Nasu no Yoichi*	78
3.9	Contrasting features of *Yokobue* and *Nasu no Yoichi*	89
4.1	The eight kōwaka pieces transmitted in Ōe, Kyūshū	101
4.2	The structure of kōwaka	103
4.3	The substyles of kōwaka narrative and their sequencing	104
4.4	Araki's analysis of kōwaka melodies	106
4.5	Outline of kōwaka *Togashi*	107
4.6	Structural levels of nō	121
4.7	Outline of nō *Ataka*	124
5.1	Vertical structure of gidayū-bushi	145
5.2	Outline of the play *Kanadehon Chūshingura*	152
5.3	Outline of Act VI 'Kanpei seppuku no dan'	154
6.1	Structural analysis of itchū, tokiwazu, tomimoto, kiyomoto, shinnai	180
6.2	Types of piece in four bungo-kei genres: itchū, tokiwazu, kiyomoto, shinnai	181
6.3	Kabuki dance form	184
6.4	Comparison of basic soft reiterative patterns and declamatory rōshō kakari patterns	192
6.5	Comparison of substyles in itchū and bungo-kei	194
6.6	Senritsukei across the transcribed examples	194
6.7	Outline of itchū *Wankyū michiyuki*	196
6.8	Outline of tokiwazu *Seki no to*	203
6.9	Outline of shinnai *Ranchō*	216
6.10	Outline of kiyomoto *Kasane* (CD track 12)	224
7.1	The named patterns of ōzatsuma-bushi	238

---

[1] Where given as a heading in tables, FMM denotes formulaic musical material.

7.2	Outline of ōzatsuma *Ya no ne*	243
7.3	Outline of nagauta-ōzatsuma *Kanjinchō* (CD Track 14)	253

List of Music Examples

2.1	Shojū	35
2.2	Nijū	35
2.3	Sanjū	35
2.4	Chūon	37
2.5	Shojū-kutsu-shojū	37
2.6	Kōshiki tonal material	38
2.7	*Nehan kōshiki* Dan 1	46
3.1	*Yokobue*: kudoki-orikoe	75
3.2	*Nasu no Yoichi*: hiroi	81
3.3	*Nasu no Yoichi*: sanjū	85
4.1	Kōwaka, *Togashi* (1)	112
4.2	Kōwaka, *Togashi* (2)	117
5.1	Gidayū, 'Kanpei seppuku no dan' (1)	158
5.2	Gidayū, 'Kanpei seppuku no dan' (2)	160
5.3	Gidayū, 'Kanpei seppuku no dan' (3)	162
5.4	Gidayū, 'Kanpei seppuku no dan' (4)	165
6.1	Itchū, *Wankyū michiyuki*	199
6.2	Tokiwazu, *Seki no to* (1)	208
6.3	Tokiwazu, *Seki no to* (2)	210
6.4	Tokiwazu, *Seki no to* (3)	211
6.5	Shinnai, *Ranchō*	219
6.6	Kiyomoto, *Kasane*	227
7.1	Ōzatsuma, *Ya no ne* (1)	246
7.2	Ōzatsuma, *Ya no ne* (2)	250
7.3	Nagauta-ōzatsuma, *Kanjinchō*	257

Contents of Accompanying Compact Disc

Track title	Source	Length of track
(1) Chinese prosimetric narrative	Iguchi Junko, *Chūgoku hoppō nōson no kōshō bunka* (Chinese edition) (1999), accompanying CD	2'19"
(2) Japan: *Goze uta*	*Goze uta*. Goze narrative. From *Jōetsu-shi Hossoku 20-shūnen kinen*. ACD-908 (CD) (1991). Track 2, selection from 'Kuzu no ha: kowakare no dan'	1'36"
(3) Kōshiki, *Nehan kōshiki*, selection from the first dan	Aoki Yūkō, *Shiza Kōshiki*. Columbia GL-7003-08 (LP) (1978). *Nehan Kōshiki*, 1st dan. GL-7003 B (Disc I, side B)	7'45"
(4) Heike, *Yokobue*	Imai Tsutomu, *Heike Biwa*. EBISU-13~19 (CD) (2009)	5'57"
(5) Heike, *Nasu no Yoichi*	Imai Tsutomu, *Heike Biwa*. EBISU-13~19 (CD) (2009)	6'43"
(6) Kōwaka, *Togashi*	Kyoto City University of Arts Japanese Traditional Music Research Centre, *Kōwakamai* (DVD) (2010)	8'55"
(7) Nō, *Ataka*	*Kanze-ryū Yōkyoku Hyakuban-shū*, no. 87. King CNT-815 (cassette) (n.d.)	5'11"
(8) Gidayū, *Kanadehon Chūshingura*, 'Kanpei seppuku no dan'	*Kanadehon Chūshingura*, King Records KICH 2148~54 (CD) (1994). CD4: Rokudanme: Kanpei seppuku no dan	10'50"
(9) Itchū, *Wankyū michiyuki*	Miyako Ichiiki, *Itchū-bushi Koten Meisakusen*. Teichiku GM-6019~6024 (LP) (1982)	3'39"
(10) Tokiwazu, *Seki no to*	*Nihon Koten Ongaku Taikei* VII. Kōdansha (LP) (1983)	3'42"
(11) Shinnai, *Ranchō*	*Nihon Koten Ongaku Taikei* VII. Kōdansha (LP) (1983)	4'50"
(12) Kiyomoto, *Kasane*	*Kiyomoto Shizudayū Zenshū*. Victor SJ-3025 (LP) (1970), VZCG-8094 (CD) (2000)	5'11"
(13) Ōzatsuma, *Ya no ne*	*Ōzatsuma-bushi*. Victor SJ-3018-9 (LP) (1968)	5'57"
(14) Nagauta, *Kanjinchō*	*Nihon Koten Ongaku Taikei* IV. Kōdansha (LP) (1983)	4'07"

Preface and Acknowledgements

This book is the product of many years of stumbling and fumbling to understand the nature of Japan's musical narratives. It has taken far too long, and in the end I have not got very far. Having written a whole monograph on one genre, kiyomoto-bushi, it has been challenging to cover several genres in a single comparative study. As my understanding of each genre has limitations, I have relied heavily on the work of many other researchers. Hence, I owe an intellectual debt to many whose work is found in the list of references. On the conceptual side, these include Yokomichi Mario, Machida Kashō, Okamoto Bun'ya, Milman Parry and Albert Lord, and one who assumed their mantle, John Miles Foley, to whose memory this volume is dedicated. I have benefited from the support and guidance of many mentors and colleagues, including Gamō Satoaki, Gamō Mitsuko, Satō Michiko, Hyōdō Hiromi and Tokumaru Yosihiko. I have been blessed with wonderfully helpful research colleagues, including Komoda Haruko, Yamada Chieko, Tanaka Yumiko, Fujita Takanori, Hugh de Ferranti and members of innumerable research gatherings. In particular, I benefited from the opportunity to lead a year-long team research project at the International Research Centre for Japanese Studies (Nichibunken) in 1998, when I was most fortunate to have Mitsuta Kazunobu as my manager and my link with the administration, and Komoda Haruko who graciously agreed to be co-editor of the resulting volume in Japanese. I am most grateful to them, and to all members of that project.

For producing the master of the accompanying CD, I am truly indebted to Fujimoto Sō, director of the Japan Traditional Cultures Foundation in Tokyo.

Funding to assist the production of the CD was generously given by Monash University's Faculty of Arts. A further year spent as a visiting researcher at the International Research Centre for Japanese Studies in 2008 enabled substantial progress towards completing the research for this project; my thanks to Hosokawa Shūhei for being my counterpart during that time. I have also been supported with research funding from the Tokyo Institute of Technology and Doshisha University.

For moral and editorial support over many years, I express my sincere gratitude to Teresa Anile in Melbourne. For typesetting the musical examples, Peggy Polias and Mariko Okubo have given excellent support.

At Ashgate, I am grateful to several generations of editorial personnel since first being awarded a contract, who have patiently waited for me to finish. David Hughes and Keith Howard of the SOAS Ashgate Musicology Series board have been most supportive and patient during the gestation of the book.

Finally, my biggest debt is to my life companion, Masahiro, for his intellectual stimulus, his constant moral support and his patient and loving solicitude.

Our children, to whom this volume is dedicated, have cheerfully put up with years of forbearance towards my slow research progress.

Kyoto

Periods of Japanese History

Nara	710–794
Heian	794–1185
Kamakura	1185–1333
Nanbokuchō	1333–1392
Musomachi	1392–1568
Momoyama	1568–1600
Edo (Tokugawa)	1600–1867
Meiji	1868–1912
Taishō	1912–1926
Shōwa	1926–1988
Heisei	1989–

Chapter 1

Singing the Story: Continuity and Change in Japanese Performed Narratives

Itinerant bards travelling the length and breadth of the Japanese archipelago over a long period of time were instrumental in circulating a body of narratives. The narratives they performed were continually re-told and recycled in different versions and formats, contributing to a sense of a shared Japanese identity that extended spatially – because it defined the geographical extent of 'Japan' – and temporally – because it created a sense of history as 'Japanese' and a connection with the past. Thus the wide circulation of oral narratives in medieval Japan contributed to the creation of what can be called an incipient 'national literature' (Ruch 1977). Shared cultural practices enable people to feel part of an 'imagined community' (Anderson 1983), extending beyond their face-to-face daily contacts. Whereas Anderson emphasized the role of the print media in early modern European society in this regard, in Japan performed narratives have provided a similar shared cultural heritage, giving people a sense of belonging to an extended community.

This is the enduring power of many specific narratives such as *The Tale of the Heike* and *The Tale of the Soga Brothers*, which began as orally transmitted tales (episodes), and coalesced into quasi-epic cycles. Such narratives became part of the literary canon, but continued to be re-created in various performance traditions. In addition, the circulation of narratives through all regions by itinerant bards generated a common language with literary features, even in texts with clear indications of oral composition. The language of the performed narratives was not the colloquial regional languages of folktales.

The Japanese have shown a strong preference for stories with music, to judge by the large number of genres of musical storytelling. By adding music to narrative, memorability is enhanced, but also an element of artificiality. At the same time, the possibility of creating emotional and dramatic nuances is increased through musical expression.

The study of Japanese performed narratives opens up the possibility of an alternative cultural history of Japan. It allows us to hear the voice of the people whose socially determined role it was to tell these stories professionally, often by virtue of their blindness. It can also give us an understanding of the world view of those who listened to and patronized these performing arts, since these narratives convey ideas about how people saw themselves, what ideal types they revered, what they aspired to, what behaviours were admired and what despised – in short, the values of the common people.

A great deal of scholarly attention has been paid to Japanese pre-modern literature and drama, but traditions of oral narrative are seldom mentioned, despite their importance to the development of both literature and theatre. A world-wide revolution since the 1960s in the study of oral literature has occurred as a result of Parry and Lord's work (Lord 1960; Foley 1988), and this has begun to introduce a new paradigm in Japan for understanding received 'literary' works such as *The Tale of the Heike* (McCullough 1988; Tyler 2012b) and *The Tale of the Soga Brothers* (Cogan 1987). Instead of trying to determine the original author of *The Tale of the Heike* (which has over a dozen highly divergent textual variants, as well as being a performed musical genre), many scholars now see it as oral literature, or at least 'oral-connected' (Foley 1999: xiv) or 'oral-derived' (ibid.: 31), in addition to having a complex textual tradition of reception (Tokita 2003).

This book is a study of Japanese narratives which are sung in performance, commonly known as katarimono. It is a journey through ten centuries of Japanese history using extant performed narratives as signposts. Of the many genres of performed narrative, this study focuses on one particular group of narratives with a strong musical element, which can be traced as a single tradition defined by both thematic and formal continuities.

I will argue that, despite the apparently discrete nature of the individual genres, it is possible to identify a continuous tradition of musically performed narrative in Japan from the tenth to the twentieth centuries. The elements of change relate to the move away from oral narrative to text-based performance, and from a simple narrative situation by one performer to complex theatrical narratives with dancers, puppeteers, singers and other musicians. The resulting complexity led to the foregrounding of the musical aspects in some cases, and of dramatic or dance aspects in others. Musical and textual analysis of these extant performance traditions reveals points of divergence in both form and content, while also stressing continuities.

These genres have a highly developed musical aspect, which differentiates them from most oral narrative. Their orality is not 'composition in performance', because they have been textualized and their texts are largely fixed. Their music, however, has retained oral features and it is to this aspect that orality theory can be applied.

In Europe, oral narrative arts belonged to a pre-literate stage of society, or pre-literate segments of society, and ceased to be relevant as literacy became widespread. Indeed, sung narratives had probably given way to literature, drama and opera by the end of the medieval era. In contrast, in Japan, even as literacy rates grew remarkably from the seventeenth century, performed narratives continued to thrive in the increasingly literate culture of the Edo period (1603–1867) and into the modern period.

The vitality of performed narratives in pre-modern Japan can be seen in the urban arts of kabuki and bunraku, in didactic and witty storytelling in small theatres, and in the street performance of satiric ballads and broadsides, as well as folk and regional narrative arts. The urbanites of the Edo period spent a lot of leisure time and money on learning to perform these arts from professional performers. In the period of modernization performed narratives lost their place at the pinnacle of both popular and officially patronized culture. The old working classes of cities such as Tokyo and Osaka continued to enjoy genres such as gidayū-bushi, kiyomoto and shinnai until the 1950s, but television was the death knell to the practice on any wide scale.

Even in the modern period, despite the prioritization of Western music over Japanese music from 1868, indigenous music including performed narratives remained vigorous until the Second World War, since which there has been a steady erosion of Japanese pre-modern forms. Instead, in the period of rapid economic growth in the 1960s and 1970s, enka (a ballad with a definite narrative element) emerged (Yano 2002), there was a min'yō boom (Hughes 2008), and from the 1970s karaoke developed (Mitsui and Hosokawa 1998). The non-musical narrative arts of rakugo and kōdan continue to occupy a significant though limited space in contemporary popular culture, maintaining a strong following in small theatres and on television. It is remarkable that performed narratives have retained their popularity for so long.

The narrative arts with a strong musical component are now regarded as 'traditional' or 'classical', which is code for fossilized, or worse, almost defunct. One fateful event leading to their downfall was the disestablishment of the traditional class system in 1871, which took away the officially supported professions of blind artists (Groemer 2001: 374). Whereas heike narratives performed by blind musicians had been supported by the military government, the modern nation state had no use for them.

As the title *Japanese Singers of Tales* suggests, this study is situated in a body of research about oral narrative, inspired by the work of Parry and Lord, which was published under the title *Singers of Tales* (Lord 1960). Marshall Pihl used this phrase in his study of pan'sori in *Korean Singers of Tales* (Pihl 1994). It considers centrally the issues of orality and literacy. The sub-title of the book, *Ten Centuries of Performed Narrative*, indicates the diachronic aspect of the study. It focuses on genres in one particular stream of Japanese narrative, and points out the continuity of grand narratives which endured over several centuries.

The concept of a continuous tradition overarching discrete genres is congruous with Foley's concept of 'traditional referentiality' (Foley 1999). The thematic continuity occurs in the use and development of specific stories and characters, as well as the use of certain consistent story patterns and stock expressions. The formal continuity occurs in both verbal and musical narrative structuring and expressive devices. I will point to a heritage of formulaic expression in both verbal and musical aspects of the narratives: the accumulation of a stock of verbal and musical formulaic material.

This book will examine four extant genres dating from the medieval period: kōshiki, heike, nō and kōwaka; followed by a selection from the large number of jōruri musical narratives dating from the Edo period. These form a stream that can be traced back to the tenth century. This study will demonstrate the fundamental aspects of continuity between the separately named highly musicalized narratives, that is, the role of tradition, and through the case studies will point to political, social and cultural changes at various points that stimulated innovation, development and transformation, and the emergence of new genres from old ones. The later genres show an awareness of preceding genres and traditions, resulting in quotation and intertextuality.

Later genres did not always supplant earlier ones, but developed alongside them, hence the survival of the medieval genres into the Edo period, and further into the twentieth century. Many older genres have continued to be performed and appreciated well after newer ones emerged, leading to a complex interplay of mutual influence, and strong linkages between old and new. All the genres dealt with in this study are in the twenty-first century still being performed by both professionals and amateurs, and still being appreciated by audiences.

Continuity and Change: Historical Overview

The remarkable continuity in Japan's culture gives an excellent opportunity for a diachronic study of the dynamics of cultural change, with the creation and transmission of a number of performance genres over ten centuries. At historical junctures of social and political upheaval, we note major epistemic shifts, where there occurs attrition of performing art forms and the emergence of new forms, in a burst of cultural creativity. Often these points of disjuncture involve major stimulus from outside. In the more stable periods, such as the Heian and Edo periods, consolidation and elaboration of introduced elements and innovations occurs. The transitional periods see big changes in social and cultural praxis; they produce change in dominant philosophy and ideology, and generate new stories purveyed by new media.

From Myth to History

With the introduction of writing from China between the Kofun period (fifth to seventh centuries) and the Nara period (eighth century), the Japanese archipelago changed from a primarily oral society to a literate society. More than just a change of medium from oral to written communication, it was a major change in episteme. This involved the shift from the court's oral custodians of genealogy, ritual and procedure using oral narrative, to scribes making written records of all matters in Chinese. Many aspects of Chinese culture were introduced, including the administrative system, court music and Buddhism.

The mythic age is partially known through Japan's oldest extant book, the *Kojiki* (712), which records Japan's pre-Buddhist, pre-Chinese indigenous oral culture compiled from earlier accounts which were written from the oral lore transmitted by the narratorial caste, the kataribe. The book was written in a hybrid Japanese-Chinese style, in an attempt to retain the orally transmitted culture.

Chinese characters were used both for meaning and for sound, the latter especially for noting place names and personal names, and in transcribing songs. The *Kojiki* was a compilation of myths and legends, purporting to be the history of the Yamato clan, and of genealogies of the major clans (see Philippi 1968; Lurie 2011). One of its most famous myths is the account of the sun goddess, Amaterasu, who, offended by her brother's obnoxious behaviour, shut herself in a cave and thus plunged the world into darkness (perhaps symbolizing a solar eclipse, or the winter solstice). The other gods put on a bawdy amusing show to entice her out, and their laughter piqued her curiosity enough to make her emerge from the cave (Lu 1997: 6). The description of that performance suggests it is regarded as ritual and a prototype of theatrical performance. Written in a complex variety of adaptations of Chinese characters to Japanese phonology (manyōgana), the *Kojiki* became difficult to read after the Japanese writing system evolved with the development of the two kana syllabaries. When the ancient narratives were invoked by later writers, such as Zeami in his writings about nō (Zeami and Hare 2008, 14 and 47), it was the companion volume the *Nihongi*, compiled in pure Chinese in 720, that was more accessible (Miner et al. 1985: 186). On the whole, the *Kojiki* and *Nihongi* narratives have not been major sources of material for later performance genres, one exception being the kōwaka piece, *Nihongi* (Araki 1964: 112, 144). However, they are significant as evidence of a formalized system of indigenous oral narrative by a professional caste.

Salvation Narratives

The introduction of Buddhism led to the practice of preaching (sekkyō) by highly literate ordained priests in temples, and also to proselytizing (shōdō) by a variety of priest-like figures on the streets, in which context storytelling flourished. Towards the end of the Heian period, the musical liturgy of kōshiki as a devotional and teaching practice for the elite class appears, and its musical development continued over the Kamakura period (see Chapter 2). The rhetorical art of preaching called on local and imported legends and moral tales to illustrate paths to achieve salvation, or tales about saintly people. The impact of preaching on storytelling culture was profound. The practice of teaching Buddhism with pictures (etoki) in temples and in market places grew, and popular preaching developed into a musical storytelling called sekkyō-bushi, although this genre (sermon music, musical sermons, sermon ballads) as it flourished in the sixteenth and seventeenth centuries had little to do with the world of Buddhism. A syncretic fusion of many folk beliefs, sekkyō-bushi became an entertainment performed with shamisen and puppets in the seventeenth century, and was subsumed into jōruri (Kimbrough 2013).

Tales (Setsuwa)

Kamakura-period Buddhism developed fund-raising (kanjin) practices by itinerant holy men (hijiri) and women (miko, later nuns, especially the Kumano bikuni) to raise money for religious and public works, by telling stories on themes of salvation. There emerged a body of many types of legends of the origins of shrines and temples (engitan), the original gods associated with Buddhist entities (honjitan), confession narratives (zange monogatari), and journeys through hell (jigoku meguri). Many groups of people, women and men, blind and sighted, purveyed stories that circulated widely, and these orally circulating stories were collected and compiled by literati as setsuwa tales. The earliest collections seem to have been for the use of Buddhist priests for sermon material.[1] These collections were then further drawn on as sources for nō, kōwaka, jōruri and kabuki plays in later generations. The abiding circulation of oral performance in the medieval period by illiterate outcast groups casts doubt on their access to written sources, but instead suggests a fund of oral lore freely exchanged. It seems most likely that setsuwa stories continued to be generated and elaborated orally. This is an area outside the scope of this study that requires careful future research.

The English terms of oral narrative, performed narrative and epic are not necessarily easily matched with the Japanese terms of katari (performed narrative), monogatari (literary tales) and katarimono (musicalized performed narratives). Scholars in Japan commonly distinguish the act of telling (kataru) from that of singing (utau). In the twentieth century long-lasting debates took place about whether Japan had an epic tradition: quasi-historical tales of glory, of legendary heroes, known by all the community – the 'grand narratives' of the nation. The most likely candidate was *The Tale of the Heike*, but it differs from many other epic traditions in its elegiac tone and the marked differences between variant texts.

Scholars such as Yanagita Kunio and Orikuchi Shinobu were concerned to understand the fundamental nature of Japanese culture in the era when it seemed that Japan was in danger of becoming fully westernized. Thus they spearheaded a profound reaction against westernization and modernization in the first half of the twentieth century, and attempted various re-definitions of Japanese tradition. Yanagita was influential on later generations of literary scholars, including Hyōdō Hiromi (1997, 2000) and Fukuda Akira. Hyōdō (2000), for example, discusses the dilemmas created with the equation of kōshō bungei with oral literature, noting in particular that it failed to notice the currently popular urban oral art of naniwa-bushi.

War Tales (Gunkimono) and Revenge Narratives

The earliest war tale was *Shōmonki* (trans. Rabinovitch 1986), a chronicle of a rebellion that took place in 935. War tales have been studied by Varley (1994) as a source of information about warrior history and culture. Originating as separate tales, they came to form sequences and cycles, leading to the extended narratives

---

[1] Examples of setsuwa collections include *Nihon ryōiki* (Nara period), *Konjaku monogatari-shū* (late Heian period), *Shintō-shū* (fourteenth century), *Otogi zōshi* (sixteenth to seventeenth century) and many others.

of the Heike clan, the Soga Brothers and the Minamoto warrior hero, Yoshitsune (*Gikeiki*; see McCullough 1966). At the end of the twelfth century the wars between two warrior clans, the Heike and the Genji, gave rise to the narratives which came to be called *The Tale of the Heike* and the related performance tradition of heike narrative by blind monks playing the biwa lute (see Chapter 3). The heike narratives were subsequently drawn on by nō, kōwaka mai and then jōruri (in both bunraku and kabuki). Another smaller scale incident, a revenge feud of the same era, gave rise to *The Tale of the Soga Brothers*, which similarly provided abundant material for later genres. These tales also had a religious element, but not fundamentally of a Buddhist kind. Their earliest function seems to have been as a propitiatory ritual narrative to appease angry spirits of those who suffered unnatural deaths.

Nō and mai

Nō drew on many precedents, including ritual placatory rites, and the dance and oracle narratives of shamanistic women (miko). The latter developed into women entertainers who danced solo in mai style, and sang while playing a drum. In the fourteenth century, a turbulent transition period between the Kamakura and Muromachi periods (the Nanbokuchō divided court from 1333 to 1392), the nō drama was formalized and reached its present form under Kannami and Zeami. It has a rich combination of dramatic, musical and dance elements. Its singing is closely related to the musical narrative of heike and kōwaka.

The era of the divided courts was chronicled in the *Taiheiki* which was 'read' (see Hyōdō 1995 [2005]; Varley 1994: 171). Although some extant texts have musical indications, it did not become an ongoing musical performance tradition, but may be linked to the non-musical kōdan and rakugo storytelling. Although not ascribed to a single author, it seems to have been formed as a written chronicle and, unlike *The Tale of the Heike* and *The Tale of the Soga Brothers*, does not have myriad variants. A diary of the time mentions a Kojima Hōshi, a biwa hōshi who may have been the compiler. (See McCullough's partial translation, 1959.)

Closely related to nō are the performing arts of mai, of which the latest is the still extant kōwaka. Kōwaka narrative is a simple version of nō. Where earlier mai was performed by women (shirabyōshi, kusemai, maimai), later boys' mai (chigo mai), and then mai by mature males developed. Kōwaka is men's mai. It was popular with the military class in the sixteenth century.

Jōruri

The earliest references to jōruri narrative come from the early fifteenth century. The period of civil war from 1466 to the end of the sixteenth century eventually subsided and the peaceful Edo period dawned from 1600. Shamisen was the central instrument of Edo-period music. Generally thought to have been introduced to Japan via Ryukyu by the 1570s, the shamisen was a major stimulus to musical development at the plebeian level and in bourgeois settings. Very soon, shamisen music became differentiated into a myriad of genres, including popular song, theatre and narrative. Jōruri narrative was elaborated into a large number of related but competing styles, each with a separate identity and musico-social system. The jōruri genres developed first in the puppet theatre and later in kabuki.

The Modern Period

The modern period saw the adoption of Western music, but also the generation of the neo-traditional genres, kindai biwa and naniwa-bushi. From the margins of pre-modern Japan (Kyūshū) sprang the Meiji revolutionaries and kindai biwa, redolent of modern nationalism, singing conservative anti-modern tales to the accompaniment of the biwa. Meanwhile in the poorest quarters, street performers who through the Edo period had sung satirical narratives (saimon, chobokure, chongara) developed naniwa-bushi accompanied by shamisen, and this too became a vehicle for nationalist sentiment through the musical recitation of tales of valour and romance.

The 'heike-jōruri' Stream of Narratives

In Japan, we should distinguish initially between two broad categories of storytelling genres of performed narrative: first those with no musical aspect whatsoever, such as rakugo, kōdan and manzai, and secondly those with a musical delivery. In the latter we can further distinguish between narratives with simple musical delivery, with one basic melody only (stichic narrative; see below), and narratives with a more complex musical structure, that use multiple melodies. The latter type, the focus of this book, includes the alternation of sung and spoken delivery, the sung passages employing a number of different melodies and styles. The spoken passages are in most cases dramatic dialogue. The narrative is therefore incipiently dramatic.

This study focuses on the most musically-developed stream of performed narratives: kōshiki, heike, nō, kōwaka and the several genres of jōruri. As a convenient shorthand, I will refer to this as the heike-jōruri stream (some scholars call this the biwa hōshi stream). While moving through the various selected genres within this stream, we will make many comparisons, diachronic and synchronic. This study excludes folk or regional narrative genres, such as oku jōruri, saimon types, goze, kudoki, ondo, deroren saimon and a later style of musical preaching called fushidan sekkyō. It also excludes the remarkable new sung narratives of the twentieth century: naniwa-bushi or rōkyoku, and two modern biwa styles originating from the provinces of Satsuma and Chikuzen. They are of a different lineage and work on different musical principles, and require a separate study.

Thematic Continuities: Fictional / Narrative Worlds

The heike-jōruri narratives show a remarkable degree of both thematic and formal continuity.

Oral origins are undisputed for the heike narratives by biwa hōshi, for the narrative of the Soga Brothers, for the moral or didactic tales compiled as setsuwa bungaku and otogi zōshi, for the tale of Lady Jōruri, and for the sekkyō narratives. However, literate and oral cultures coexisted, constantly interacting and cross-fertilizing each other. Hence, narrative and dramatic creations often derived from literary works, just as oral narratives provided materials for written vernacular works. The latter describes the dominant direction; indeed, many of the early Heian literary monogatari drew on oral sources.

The stock of thematic material in theatrical forms such as nō, bunraku and kabuki originates in early sources that are continually re-invented in new media and new forms. In kabuki and bunraku this is articulated as sekai versus shukō – world and contrivance – or, to put it more abstractly, tradition and innovation (Parker 2006).

Hard and Soft Narrative Worlds

In heike-jōruri narratives a number of broad narrative strands ('grand narratives') that have continued over the centuries, in oral, performed and written forms, are identifiable. These can be found in the world of storytelling and its interpenetrating worlds of history, literature, proselytizing and begging. Such narrative worlds exist as verbal constructs and have created meaning for many communities of people in many eras. The diffusion of narratives over the geographical extent of the Japanese archipelago contributed from early on towards the formation of a community or a society at the national level, through the shared reception of narratives.

There are two broad narrative strands: the 'soft' one of salvation, suffering and self-sacrifice, with a strong Buddhist flavour, later evolving to include tales of romantic suffering; and the 'hard' one focusing on valorous warrior exploits, with a strong Shintō flavour, and also auspicious, life-affirming elements.

Salvation and romantic narratives share many formal aspects of expression. The soft narrative mode led to the love suicide plays of Chikamatsu and other jōruri authors, the major new type of narrative in the Edo period. The narrative world of battle tales developed different expressive means and can be called hard narrative. This led to the historical jōruri plays. Both modes are deeply connected: for example, the battle tale often ends with a warrior undergoing a spiritual awakening (hosshin) and turning to monastic life.

Another stream of narratives can be identified in most genres, whose purpose is primarily of a ritual nature (Shintō, not Buddhist). They are auspicious in nature – for example, nō's *Okina*, kabuki's *Sanbasō* and jōruri's shūgi auspicious pieces, and follow the tradition of seeking ritual appeasement or good fortune. Auspicious expression tends to draw on hard narrative music resources.

The distinction between hard and soft narrative relates to the issue of formal continuities of structure and formulaic expression. Thus, although this is a loose and broad way of talking about different styles of musical narrative, it is nonetheless productive in the conceptualization of heike-jōruri narrative music and its development over ten centuries. In the broadest sense it asserts that differentiated and specific narrative musical styles or substyles are available to suit the content of a narrated story. It also provides a clue as to the provenance and lineage of many aspects of musical formulaism.

The predominantly hard genres that focus on military themes, historical tales of warrior families and feuds are heike, kōwaka, gidayū-bushi and ōzatsuma-bushi. They typically portray a masculine, warrior culture. Other genres, such as itchū-bushi and bungo-bushi, are predominantly soft, focusing on salvation narratives, repentance, romance, love suicides and so on. However, constant influence between genres has led to increasing complexity and hybridity, so that most genres have both hard and soft elements. In heike narrative some pieces (hiroimono) feature battle scenes and use particular melodies, whereas scenes about romance and religious awakening are melodic (fushimono) and feature other particular melodies. Kōwaka is usually classified as military (gunkimono) but a substantial part of its traditional repertoire is mythic and salvation oriented and can be considered to comprise setsuwa pieces (Squires 2001). Nō (utai) comprises a wide variety of plays, one whole category being shura or warrior plays, which feature a lot of 'strong singing' (tsuyogin), another being women plays or third-act plays (sanbanme mono), which feature only 'soft singing' (yowagin).

Orality, Literacy and Textualization

Oral narrative is characteristic of people who for various reasons do not rely on written texts. It could be that writing is not yet known to them, or that only the elite groups of their society have access to the technology of writing. Orality is one of the central issues to have been addressed by researchers of performed narrative. In particular, the narratives of living traditions of the South Slavs (in the Balkans, former Yugoslavia), of Africa and of India have been the object of extensive fieldwork, documentation and analysis. The field of oral literature studies was firmly established by Parry and Lord (Lord 1960 [2000]), who collected data in the Balkans to demonstrate the characteristics of performed narrative. However, the musical element, although an integral part of the narrative, receives little attention in the influential structural model that they created. Their model is based on the formulaic nature of the line and phrase (the *formula*), and the formulaic nature of the section or scene, or group of lines (the *theme*).

A lot of textual criticism has been done from the perspective of oral narrative theory on narratives which are known now only as written texts, such as the Homeric epics, the Bible and medieval European texts such as Beowulf,

Robin Hood and King Arthur.[2] There are also plenty of studies on still-performed oral literature: Clunies-Ross (2000) for Iceland; Reichl (2000) for Turkmen, India, China and others; Pihl (1994) for Korea; Børdahl (1999) and McLaren (1998) for China. Many apply the Parry-Lord model. Few, however, deal with musical issues. Similar studies have been published for Japan: kiyomoto (Tokita 1999), zatō biwa (de Ferranti 2009) and the area of comic storytelling (rakugo) (Morioka and Sasaki 1990).

The concept of oral narrative is generally applied to the verbal aspect of narratives which use 'oral composition', and have a high degree of verbal formulaism. In such narratives, the musical aspect is simple, and there is only one performer who both sings and plays an instrument. This kind of oral narrative applies to the Japanese Ainu yukar, goze uta and zatō biwa, in the sense that the Ainu practised oral composition as theorized by Parry-Lord. Furthermore, these traditions do not have performance texts (although ethnologists may have collected the narratives and made texts for research purposes). They therefore relied totally on oral transmission. Goze uta and zatō biwa were the preserve of the blind.

The narratives introduced in this book are not oral narratives in the sense of being newly composed each performance (oral composition). However, they have orality, because they are performed rather than read; the role of texts is limited and that of notation even more limited. We can say that these genres have deliberately avoided written texts in the process of transmission of certain or all aspects of the art, and even if the narrated verbal text is written down, its musical and kinetic realizations are not.

To look at issues of orality and literacy in regard to these performed narratives helps to establish the most appropriate model for understanding their structure. This includes the 'residual orality' of formulaic expression (Ong 1982). As all the genres have a strong element of textuality, we will also place them in the framework of the textualization of oral epics proposed by Honko (2000).

Orality theory has been applied to the study of *The Tale of the Heike*, which, until the impact of oral studies, had primarily been studied as literature. The first to apply the Parry-Lord oral-formulaic theory to Japan was Kenneth Butler (1966), with his work on the oral origins of the heike narrative and the interaction between oral performance and literate texts. This led nearly 20 years later to its take-up by Yamamoto Kichizō who applied the theory to goze, kōwaka and sekkyō narratives, thereby introducing it to pre-modern literary scholars (Yamamoto 1988). Hyōdō and many others saw its relevance especially to debates about the origins of heike narrative, but there has not been a full acceptance of the orality position in literary studies, rather a division into two camps seems to have become entrenched.

Oral culture is prone to being romanticized when it is seen as dichotomous with literate culture. Ong's powerful exposition of the intrinsic value of orality

---

[2] Ivan Illich's study of the foundations of bookish culture in Europe draws on Parry-Lord and related work to examine the moment of shift from oral to written culture in Europe around the thirteenth century (Illich 1993).

was instrumental in achieving a swing from the exclusive valorization of the written text to the valuing of oral texts (Ong 1982). Subsequent research has shown that rarely are orality and literacy mutually exclusive, but that there is vigorous interaction between the two. Indeed, it is virtually impossible to investigate a 'pure' oral culture. Japan began to use the Chinese writing system from at least the fifth century. By the ninth century two syllabaries had been developed, and the hiragana syllabary in particular fostered the growth of a vernacular literature, which flowered spectacularly in the tenth and eleventh centuries with imperial poetry anthologies (chokusen waka-shū), and with women's prose fiction, epitomized by Lady Murasaki's *The Tale of Genji*.

Thus Japanese literacy has been defined by the use of Chinese characters, so that writing in the vernacular using the phonetic kana scripts is closer to orality, and captures the sounds of the spoken Japanese language.

> People in lower levels of society had access to literate knowledge through professional scribes without knowing how to read and write themselves ... orality and literacy mutually interact, support and influence each other in many ways. (Judith Fröhlich on literacy in premodern Japan, *Premodern Japanese Studies*, 18 January 2007. See also Fröhlich 2007)

The use of a written script by ruling elites affects all levels of society. However, even performance genres which generate written texts are linked through their lineage of development with earlier 'pure' oral narratives, and show traces of 'residual orality' in their verbal and musical formulaic expression. The written texts of heike and jōruri, for example, are realized musically in performance on the basis of unsystematic and limited musical notation. Their orality is maintained in both their performance and in their transmission process.

Factors that Distance heike-jōruri from Oral Narrative

As narrative performance arts developed over the centuries, many factors affected the degree to which they could be termed oral. One factor was the influence of literacy, first in the form of Chinese characters. Early on, the advent of Chinese literate culture, especially as carried to Japan by Buddhism, led to the creation of a literate court elite, and literate monks in the temples. As literacy was an importation from China and carried by men, it was superimposed on an oral culture which became the domain of women and the blind (Pollack 1986). A second factor which brought musical narratives out of the purely oral domain was the increasing elaboration of the musical aspect. A third factor was the kinetic realization of narrative in theatrical contexts: nō, kōwaka, jōruri. As narrative was incorporated into theatrical performance, the complexity of having multiple performers – musicians, actors, puppeteers, dancers, singers – meant that more had to be determined in advance and less could be left to the discretion of a single performer. This type of contextual change also led to further development of the musical aspect of the narrative performance, and the extensive incorporation of lyric songs into the narrative text, which affected narrative structure.

With these changes, the blind ceased to be the only practitioners. In early narrative practice, the blind were given sole right to control the performance of some narratives, but after the marriage of jōruri narrative with shamisen and puppet performance around the turn of the seventeenth century, it became the realm of sighted males. This coincided with the general shift from a single performer who sang and accompanied himself (as in heike) to a separation of the roles of narrator and shamisen (as in jōruri), together accompanying the kinetic representation of the narrative by puppets or live actors.

Each genre represents a stage in the development of Japanese musical narratives from simple to complex: from closer to oral expression to the greater incorporation of literary narrative elements; the amplification of narrative's dramatic capability by going on stage, with kinetic illustration; and by increasingly complex musical expression. Other aspects of change included the moving away from religious and ritual intent to secular entertainment. Furthermore, whereas women had a more active input into ancient Japanese performing arts, increasingly men came to control artistic performance, culminating in the banning of women from the public stage in 1629, a ban which remained in force until 1879 (Kano 2001).

Situating Japanese Musical Narratives in a Global Context

Models of Performed Narrative: Cross-cultural Comparisons

A cursory survey of performed narratives in several cultures suggests at least three forms of narrative, yielding the following structural models: *strophic*, like the Scottish ballad, many folksongs and enka; *stichic*, like Southern Slav epics (Erdely 1995; 2000); and *prosimetric*, like many Chinese musical narratives, including Chinese opera.

Strophic model
The strophic form features stanzaic rhyme and a regular metre and is found not only in folk song, art song, most Japanese school songs, and contemporary popular songs and hymns, but also in ballads (such as Scottish border ballads and country and western music) which tell a story but musically function like songs. The number of verses and hence the length of the narrative is flexible, but usually is limited to a performance time of no longer than 10 minutes. It consists of a number of stanzas or strophes, all of which follow the same metric pattern and melody, with the possibility of a refrain. There is no spoken delivery. The ballad may or may not be accompanied by an instrument. Narrative has taken on the musical dimensions of song.

Stichic model

In stichic ('one line') narrative, the text is made up of metrically uniform lines, with a fixed number of syllables / morae. Basically only one melody is applied to each line. Sections are marked by a descending melody with a different rhythm (usually slower), and an instrumental interlude. In contrast to strophic form, sections are variable in length: there is no fixed number of lines. Not only is the number of lines in a section varied (and hence the length of a section), neither is the number of sections fixed by any particular formal requirement. There is no spoken delivery. It is typical of long epic narratives in poetic metre. This type can be seen in South Slavic narratives (Lord 2000), in Russian bylina and in Japanese goze narratives (CD Track 2).

South Slav stichic case

The purpose of most English language research on this has been to provide a case study to illumine the nature of Homeric epic narrative (known as text only), and has not been concerned particularly with the musical aspect of the narrative. Because the music seems very simple and repetitive, it is paid lip service to, but not analysed or theorized (and not included in the Parry-Lord theory as such). Lord, for example, provides one musical example. Significant exceptions are Herzog (1951) and Erdely (1995). Herzog's brief paper manages to show that there is a subtle but significant variation in the basic melody of the Slavic narratives depending on the position in the section, which contributes towards the narrative impetus; he argues that the music has its own logic as a system (Herzog 1951). It is not a simple or mechanical repetition. A narrative climax may also be musically reinforced. Erdely's transcriptions of five complete narratives is prefaced with an insightful introduction. His study takes care to show the minute variations of the basic melody within one performance, and the variations between performers, in contrast to the Lord book, which has only one musical example to represent the entire musical corpus.

The South Slavic narrative performer accompanies himself with the one-stringed bowed lute, the gusle. He is called a guslar (lute player). In some regions the accompanying instrument is a two-stringed fiddle, or a tamboura with anything from two to six strings. The performer is a sighted male, who both sings and plays. Typically illiterate, the guslar learnt his repertory orally from a teacher, and later by listening to other guslars' songs (Lord 2000: 20). Written texts started to be collected from the eighteenth century, but until recently did not form part of the learning process. The guslar practises oral composition; each performance is different, in length, in number and detail of episodes, and in actual verbal phrasing. The number of lines forming a section is not at all set, so section length is highly variable. Sections are marked by the playing of an instrumental interlude, while the narrative is only accompanied briefly between phrases. The opening and closing lines are musically different in character, as shown by both Herzog and Erdely (examples can be heard at: http://chs119.chs.harvard.edu/mpc/songs/mp_songs.html).

The musical element of the South Slavic narratives has been given little attention by researchers. Clearly, there is only one basic line-length melody, quite different from the multiple-melody nature of heike-jōruri narratives. However, the key element of the Parry-Lord theory is its structural analysis in terms of the formulaic nature of the phrase (*formula*) and the formulaic nature of the story element (*theme*). This is suggestive for the understanding of formulaic expression in this study.

Prosimetric model
Prosimetric (or chantefable) literature is a dominant form in world oral narrative, found in China, Mongolia, Turkey, Arabia, India and many other cultures, as demonstrated in the case studies in Harris and Reichl (1997) and Reichl (2000). Prosimetric narrative is generally understood to mean the alternation of sections of explanatory, expository prose in spoken delivery, and metric sections in verse with melodic delivery. Harris and Reichl (1997), in presenting many cross-cultural case studies, argue for a broader, more flexible definition, calling it simply 'the mixture of verse and prose, in particular in narrative' (1997: 3), while noting that the 'change between narrating in prose and singing in verse is characteristic of a great number of oral prosimetric genres in world literature' (ibid.: 6). However, they continue, the definition of both verse and prose is not so simple when seen cross-culturally: 'When it comes to defining prose, a more radical view has been proposed, namely that all prose in oral narrative is rhythmic, patterned, and poetically structured' (ibid.: 7). Prose is only relevant to written language on the printed page.

Prosimetric Narrative in China

There are said to be over 300 extant long performed narrative genres in China, and many more must have existed, but are no longer extant, in a known tradition going back at least 1,000 years. Naturally, much variation must be expected between these genres, but the broad and generally accepted definition of the very widespread form of Chinese oral narrative called shuochang (Jp. sesshō) is the alternation of prose (spoken) sections called shuo and verse (sung) sections called chang (Bender 2003; Børdahl 1999, Børdahl 2013) (CD track 1).

Prose sections are presented in spoken delivery, close to vernacular speech, but still stylized. These sections are not accompanied by musical instruments. They are flexible, free and open to improvisation, expansion and contraction in performance. For verse sections in sung delivery, the text is more fixed, not subject to change in performance. There are various possible metric forms, but regular line lengths are maintained in one narrative. These sections are accompanied by an instrumental ensemble, whose composition varies with different genres and different regions. Typically, the ensemble includes a drum or drums, and melody instruments such as flute or lute – pi'pa or sanxian.

Early in the twentieth century large quantities of 'transformation texts' (pienwen; Jp. henbun) were discovered in the Dun Huang caves in northwest China. These prosimetric written narratives had their origin in oral preaching modes in the early Tang period. Scholars point out that they originated with Buddhist preaching, whose Indian origins derived from Buddhist sutras featuring explanatory prose interpolated with verses (gatha) (McLaren 1998: 78; Mair 1997: 366; Idema 1986). The kernel of the teaching is encapsulated in the verses with their memorable formal features, and is further explained for the listeners in a commentary form, with greater flexibility and variation. Idema suggests, however, that some kind of prose-verse alternating style may have pre-existed the introduction of Buddhism in China (Idema 1986: 85).

This prosimetric style of oral narrative and preaching led to secular narratives, both oral and written, and also formed the basis for theatrical forms such as so-called Chinese opera (Idema 1986: 87; Mair 1997: 368–9). Iguchi's study of liaoting dagu (1999) shows that the same prosimetric model applies to that particular contemporary genre. Bender presents a case study of contemporary performed narrative in Suzhou (Bender 2003).

The key difference between these prosimetric Chinese oral and musical narratives and Japanese heike-jōruri genres would seem to be that in Japan we do not see the alternation of prose and poetry as the basic form. The metric parts in Chinese narratives are lyrical song rather than narrative, and are actually sung, whereas in the Japanese musical narratives the expository narrative sections are delivered musically, not spoken. Some genres are in metric style, and some in non-metrical 'prose' (for want of a better word), but both are delivered musically. Non-musical delivery is with few exceptions limited to dramatic speech.

Kōshiki might be expected to reveal the influence of Chinese Buddho-Indian prosimetric narrative. However, it shows this Japanese characteristic, that the metric verses in Chinese (kada; Sanskrit gatha) in between sections of prose are in typical shōmyō melismatic melodic style, whereas the main expository parts in prose are delivered melodically, and furthermore this melodic delivery exhibits variety and musical development, and is not just a straight chant. No part of kōshiki is spoken.

Heike musical narrative (formed in the same period as kōshiki) is not in poetic metre, apart from some florid 'poetic' sections, and the occasional presence of waka poems as part of the exchange between characters in the story. The whole tale is delivered musically, except for shirakoe sections. I will argue in Chapters 2 and 3 that kōshiki and heike can be linked not to a continental prosimetric model, but to the pre-Buddhist indigenous tradition of narrative in Japan.

Jōruri, like heike, delivers narrative musically, but is more like nō utai in that most of the narrative has the metric form of lines of 12 (7 + 5) syllables. The spoken sections represent the dramatic dialogue of the characters in the story or drama, not narrative. The sung narrative of jōruri is realized through the liberal use of a variety of types of formulaic musical materials, or melodic formulas.

The non-narrative musical parts of jōruri are diegetically interpolated (quoted) songs whose music and text are taken from various sources: folksong, popular songs from the entertainment districts, or quotations of other narrative musical genres, both past and contemporary. The music for these quotation sections imitates the style of the quoted song or genre. This tendency gets stronger with the later forms of jōruri in the context of kabuki dance.

Incidentally, the Korean musical narrative, pan'sori, might be included in the prosimetric model because its form is the alternation of sung sections called chang and spoken delivery sections called aniri.

The present study attempts to elucidate the nature of Japanese musical narrative in a global context. Based on the above, it is clear that the Japanese narratives of the heike-jōruri type do not fit the prosimetric model characteristic of many Chinese oral narratives. If we take the broader definition of prosimetric narrative as proposed by Harris and Reichl, we can include Japanese narratives under this rubric as they alternate sections of spoken and musicalized delivery. It will be necessary to clarify how the poetry and prose are realized musically, and to identify all varieties of the sung, that is, the narrative substyles. Most important is the centrality of multiple styles of delivery, and multiple melodies for different sections of the narrative.[3]

Form and Structure of Japanese Musical Narratives: Adopting an Analytical Framework

All three models of performed narrative – strophic, stichic, and prosimetric if broadly defined as the alternation of spoken and sung delivery – can be found in Japan. The prosimetric model is the most relevant to our present study of heike-jōruri narratives, which are characterized more than anything else by the use of a number of styles of musical delivery (substyle or katarikuchi) for different parts of the narrative. The alternation of varied types of delivery gives rise to the possibilities of a formal structural development, and to expressive devices through music.

Within each genre in this study exists a basic style which while flexible can look like the repeated melody (stichic) type. Indeed it is probable that the multi-melodic narratives studied here all originated in the stichic model, the simple basic melody used again and again, like shojū and nijū in kōshiki, and kudoki in heike. Their diversification came about gradually, first by transposing the basic melodic contour to a register one fourth higher, and then another fourth and so on, following the tonal framework of the music. Thus, by moving through the different

---

[3] Intriguingly, Helen McCullough's chapter on verse-prose in the volume *Prosimetrum* (Harris and Reichl 1997) did not address issues of performance, but only written narratives. This was a missed opportunity to place the heike and other Japanese performed narratives in a global context.

pitch registers using the same melodic contour the variant patterns developed in the basic style of each genre.

In Chapter 2 we will see how kōshiki moves through different melodic types, further elaborated in heike (Chapter 3) and jōruri (Chapters 5, 6 and 7). This feature gradually diversified into a set of different melody types which were used for different narrative purposes. By calling on different types of delivery (musical substyles), including spoken delivery, a whole range of expressive possibilities emerge. Some melodies have a purely formal function, such as providing musical variety, creating a musical climax, or indicating closure (cadential); others relate to specific narrative content. Rhythmic diversification also occurred, especially with the advent of the shamisen in jōruri.

Inter-genre research of katarimono has barely begun, though there is much excellent research on individual genres. The difficulty in viewing the whole of the katarimono tradition, spanning many centuries and many genres, lies first in the lack of agreement among scholars about the overall meaning and function of what I will call formulaic musical expression, and second, in the resulting conundrum of finding common terminology in order to define concepts, levels and units of analysis (Tokita 2000: 108–10).

My research methodology is based on a structural model inspired initially by Yokomichi (1986) on the one hand, and by oral-formulaic theory on the other. In addition, the work of Machida Kashō (1982) has provided essential guidance in the cross-genre research of shamisen music (phrase level analysis), and Okamoto Bun'ya's (1972) analysis of the formulaic musical expression of shinnai was illuminating (at phrase, section and substyle level). My model applies the overarching concept of formulaic musical material at the structural levels of piece, section and phrase.

Formulaic Musical Material and Formulaic Verbal Expression

As already indicated, the Parry-Lord theory suggests that the use of formulaic material in the verbal aspect of the narrative indicates orality (or residual orality). Verbal formulaism can be analysed using the Parry-Lord concepts of the *theme*, which occupies a group of lines, and the *formula*, which occupies one phrase or line only. Japanese musical narratives of the heike-jōruri type are indeed characterized by formulaic expression, both in the verbal and (especially) in the musical aspects of the narrative. Narratives in which the musical aspect is dominant have lost most of their verbal orality, but some residual oral features can be identified. An example of a verbal *formula* is the phrase 'saru hodo ni' ('and so it came to pass' or 'in the meantime'), a ubiquitous opening phrase in older types of katarimono (heike, kōwaka, ōzatsuma). It meets the conditions of metrical consistency, as it fits the five-syllable requirement of the opening line of a style which tends to maintain the alternation of seven and five syllables. An example of a verbal *theme* is that of the kudoki, or any number of similar stock scene types used in jōruri, called shukō in gidayū-bushi (see Chapter 5). A section-length theme of this type has a predictable type of style and content and can be brought into a variety of stories.

Is Parry-Lord theory with its structural model of formula and theme applicable to the musical aspect of the narrative, in which we find abundant evidence of formulaic musical expression? Can oral-formulaic theory help in understanding the meaning and function of the musical formulas used in these narratives? Does formulaic musical material indicate orality? What does orality mean at the musical level? The parallels between language and music are always fascinating, but have limitations. The studies in this book will suggest that the formulaic expression in the verbal and musical aspects of the narrative is analogical, but not directly parallel.

The musical analogy for themes and formulas can be proposed thus: the Parry-Lord *formula* is equivalent to the formulaic musical phrase; the Parry-Lord *theme* is equivalent to the formulaic section or musical substyle.

The heike-jōruri musical narratives are all structured in clearly-defined sections, each section characterized by a unified narrative substyle; the section is often identified and named as a particular type of section, such as the gidayū-bushi narrative opening section (makura) the bungo-kei jōruri oki. A section consists of an indeterminate number of phrases or musical lines, many of which are musical formulas (such as cadential patterns) analogous to the verbal formula. These are frequently called senritsukei or melody patterns.

These formulas are analogous to the verbal formulas that are a part of the oral-formulaic theory. However, musical formulaism does not always have a close correspondence to verbal formulaism. Musical narrative has a certain degree of autonomy from verbal narrative.

Vertical and Horizontal Structure

Performed narrative tends to be rather amorphous and flexible, until the formalized aspects of poetic metre, music and dance movement become more dominant. Compared with musical form, or with dramatic structure, the structure of storytelling is loose. The more closely it becomes associated with drama and dance, or with musically elaborate performance, the more formalistic elements come to the fore.

Yokomichi's model of the structure of nō has been adapted by researchers of musical narrative. It identifies several levels, displaying a vertically layered structure:

>piece or play
>section (dan)
>sub-section (shōdan)
>phrase or line (ku)

Each of these levels tends to have formulaic elements.

At the same time, because narrative is a linear progression through time, a horizontal structure, which accounts for different types of narrative in one performance, is also identifiable. Narrative essentially lacks a clear structure.

It is linear and unfolds through performance time. There are no repeats or refrains, and the length of the whole and the parts is flexible. We need to see how the elements of the vertical structure relate to each other in time, and how, within one level, the narrative progresses through the use of varied melodies and substyles.

Structural Units and Levels of Analysis: Section, Phrase, Substyle

All the genres in this study are made up of a succession of small sections, each finished off with a recognizable cadential formula (Tokita 2000: 108).

Each piece usually has a sense of progression; the beginning is different from the end in terms of substyle, type of section, and phrase length patterns used. In some genres, within sections, a horizontal progression from speech, through non-metric musical narrative, to metric musical narrative is observable.

A section of narrative (shōdan) is a relatively independent unit having a unified character in terms of musical style, and which is closed off with a cadential formula. At the structural level of the section, despite stylistic musical unity, music and text may not always match.

The formulaic phrase is a line of text delivered musically usually in one breath and has some textual unity. In kōwaka and jōruri the line or phrase tends towards the predominant Japanese poetic metre of 12 syllables, grouped as 7 + 5, but in kōshiki and heike this is not the case. The formulaic musical phrase, often named, is most conspicuous in cadences and openings, but there are other such phrases that function to define the substyle of a section.

My musical analysis focuses on these two basic structural units of section and phrase, in conjunction with the concept of substyle, which unites the two: the key concept of melodic patterns, and their combination (cumulation) in well-defined sections that have a unified style.

My definition of substyle is the internal structure and/or style of narrative in the section. It is defined by musical parameters, such as a pitch area, tempo, rhythm, style of delivery: syllabic, melismatic or a combination of the two. Substyles can consist of patterned phrases as well as non-patterned or loosely-patterned material.

A substyle does not consist entirely of a sequence of named formulaic phrases. It is not so predictable or prescribed, but can respond to the demands of the text, to the creative impulse of the composer. The composer in oral narratives may of course be the performer; in text-based jōruri narratives, the composer is usually the shamisen player.

We can note here Hirano's (1990 and 1993) model of three types of vocal delivery in sung narrative style: ginshō (stylized speech), rōshō (syllabic singing) and eishō (melismatic singing). These concepts have been widely applied in discussions of performed narrative. At the most general level, the concept of substyle can be discussed in terms of these three styles of delivery: there is a continuum from a chant-like style, very close to speech, through a more melodic style, to a highly expressive, melismatic style. However, each genre has its own clearly defined substyles, characterized by several musical parameters, to be analysed in the following chapters. While useful and appropriate for most medieval genres, Hirano's concept does not go far enough towards defining the different types of musical substyles to be found, especially in jōruri, because he does not refer to the element of rhythm nor of pitch register or melodic patterns – in short, most of the musical parameters mentioned above under substyle.

A set of narrative substyles allows the composer-narrator to convey the meaning of the text more effectively. It enables more than the selection of ready-made melodies and phrases, but the creative use of a loosely defined style. Some substyles have extremely broad, loose parameters within which the musical narrative operates, allowing great flexibility and variety, rather than the use of fixed melodies. Unlike in prosimetric narrative, in heike-jōruri sung delivery is used throughout, except when the characters deliver dramatic speech.

In medieval narratives, such as heike, non-metric narrative, close to prose, is dominant, and the substyles tend to take the form of extended melodic patterns. In jōruri narratives, we see the establishment of the 12 (7+5) syllable line (7-5 chō) as the dominant form for the narrative text, and this coincides with a more regular use of phrase-length patterns. These formulaic phrases are not necessarily tied to a verbal formula. So, while we can say that in jōruri where there is a verbal formula there will also be a musical formula, the reverse is not necessarily true.

Each narrative genre has a variety of substyles at its disposal for various parts in the progression of the piece. This is important at the formal level as a structural device, to achieve variety in the narrative. It is important also in order to express the verbal content effectively; often a substyle has an expressive purpose tied to textual content, related to the needs of the narrative. The use of varied substyles for expressive more than for formal purposes increased radically in jōruri.

As jōruri developed, it shook off verbal formulaism and used more literary expression and poetic imagery. It was, however, at this stage, it seems, that the phrase length formula (senritsukei) was elaborated, associated with the more consistent use of 7-5 chō. It can be said that genres which are almost entirely non-metrical, such as kōshiki and heike, have mostly substyles; in contrast, 7-5 metrical genres such as gidayū-bushi feature more phrase-length formulas.

It can also be argued that named patterns, as systematized in many genres of Japanese music in the Edo period (such as the *Heike mabushi*, and the ōzatsuma-bushi jōruri patterns), are the musical equivalent of the movement patterns, or kata, that exist in acting, dance and martial arts, all of which are characterized by control by the iemoto (family head) system. The creation of compendia of melodic patterns (fushi-zukushi) in gidayū and ōzatsuma from the Edo period is a conspicuous result of the function of names given to formulaic phrases. While they have some links with the formulas of oral narrative, the Edo-period tendency to systematize cannot be ignored. Such systematization occurs particularly in periods of stasis, of threat and of strict social control.

Structure of the Book

The narratives introduced in this book are exciting and engaging. Their continuity lies in the referencing of the received tradition, which is not just a tired recycling of content, but creative development. Furthermore, their continuity is formal and structural, despite the changes in genres over time. The analysis shows that there is a strong thread of structural continuity between genres which originated in different eras.

For each genre, we discuss the historical factors which led to the emergence of the narrative, the people who contributed to its formation, those who performed it, the social context, patronage, audiences, and the relation between orality and textuality. Generic musical analysis is followed by discussion of the textual content and musical structure of a select example piece as a case study, an extract from which can be followed visually with a transcription and by listening to audio examples contained in the attached CD. The outline of the whole piece is followed by the text in Japanese and English of the recorded extract, and then by the musical transcription of the CD extract.

Each chapter is organized so that readers interested in only literary aspects can pick these up easily from chapter to chapter, while those interested in musical aspects can follow the musical sections.

In the discussion of kōshiki (Chapter 2, 'Musical Buddhist Preaching: Kōshiki Shōmyō'), to illustrate the initial soft salvation narratives associated with preaching, I analyse the large-scale work *Shiza kōshiki*, which consists of four movements, each focusing on an aspect of the Buddha's life, death and teachings. In kōshiki, although we do not find such a wide range of musical expression as in subsequent genres related to different narrated content, the basic feature of moving through three substyles, which are in fact three pitch regions, is already evident.

To explicate heike narrative (Chapter 3, 'Heike Narrative: The Musical Recitation of *The Tale of the Heike*') as a mix of warrior tale and romance, I introduce two of the best-known pieces: *Nasu no Yoichi*, as an example of hard battle narrative, and *Yokobue*, as an example of soft narrative which combines the themes of romance and religious awakening.

To discuss the application of narrative art to stage arts in nō and kōwaka mai (Chapter 4, 'Dance and Narrative: Kōwaka and Nō'), I discuss the kōwaka piece *Togashi* and the nō play *Ataka*. Both originated about the same time, and the story appears in *The Chronicle of Yoshitsune* (*Gikeiki*), in at least three nō plays and in a number of setsuwa. It appears again in kabuki and in nagauta as *Kanjinchō* (see Chapter 7).

In Chapter 5 ('Jōruri and Puppet Theatre'), moving to the jōruri narratives which dominated the Edo period, I briefly discuss the originary eponymous jōruri narrative, the romance of Lady Jōruri, then the emblematic jōruri puppet play of revenge and loyalty, *Kanadehon Chūshingura*, one of the most powerful plays in the gidayū-bushi repertoire.

To present the other major group of jōruri narratives, the so-called bungo-kei jōruri genres, Chapter 6 ('Sung Narratives and Kabuki Dance: Bungo-kei Jōruri') focuses on the itchū piece *Maboroshi wankyū*, the tokiwazu piece *Seki no to*, in which hard narrative dominates, the shinnai piece *Ranchō*, and the kiyomoto piece *Kasane*. These examples illustrate historical, love suicide and poetic journey types of plot and corresponding musical resources.

Just as nō drama cannot strictly be classified as a narrative genre, so in Edo kabuki nagauta is categorized as a lyric, not a narrative genre. However, its style has absorbed so much from jōruri that it should be treated alongside jōruri. Chapter 7 ('Sung Narratives and Kabuki Dance: Nagauta and Ōzatsuma-bushi') demonstrates these dual features of nagauta through a discussion of the pieces *Ya no ne*, originally an 'old jōruri' ōzatsuma narrative on the Soga theme, and *Kanjinchō*, which contains large portions of ōzatsuma-bushi-derived narrative. The latter is a kabuki dance version of the kōwaka *Togashi* and nō *Ataka*, introduced in Chapter 4.

Case studies have been chosen in order to underline the continuities of content as well as form, and to extend Parker's view of plot development in the world of Japanese theatre to the wider sphere of musically performed narrative.

The story really begins in the mists of time with the age of the gods, whose oral narratives are preserved in the *Kojiki* and later collections of tales (Plutschow 1990). However, for the purposes of this study, our journey through Japanese cultural history via sung narratives starts with the narratives of Buddhism in the Heian period, then moves on to the tales of warriors of the medieval period, then the stories of samurai and commoners in the Edo period. Each age had its narratives, mediated by voice and instrument, whose musical element raised the verbal text up out of the realm of the prosaic, just as poetic language does. The coexistence of verbal and musical arts makes for a complex performance situation, but for the listener of every age the story is a familiar one subject to both infinite repetition and infinite variation and development. The repetition and recreation of familiar stories 'known to all Japanese' reinforces the sense of community and group identity, even the national identity of the Japanese, while providing aesthetic pleasure in music and dance.

This book traces the coming and going of different kinds of stories together with a growing complexity of musical presentation. This selection of extant genres and pieces represents only a small sample of the sung narratives that flourished over the centuries, but will serve to show the vitality of narrative arts, which, I argue, have enough continuity between genres in successive periods to be called one large tradition. Let us embark on this journey of sung narrative.

Chapter 2
Musical Buddhist Preaching: Kōshiki Shōmyō

Introduction

Buddhism first entered Japan in the sixth century CE, initially from the Korean peninsula and later from China. Japan's first formal contacts with Buddhism were gifts to the court from the King of Paekche: a gold and copper statue of Shakyamuni Buddha, banners and canopies, and several volumes of sutras and treatises (Bowring 2005: 15). After the consolidation of Buddhism as a state religion in the Korean kingdoms of Paekche and Silla, there followed a steady flow to Japan of monks and artisans from the Peninsula, who contributed to the construction of temple buildings and statues, the training and ordination of priests, and to ritual practice. From the time of Prince Shōtoku (574–622), China became Japan's main source of knowledge, and Japanese priests had contact with Korean priests there.[1]

Early in the transmission process the Japanization of Buddhism began. Neither the Koreans nor the Japanese translated the sutras, but intoned them in Chinese for their ritual value as much as for their meaning. However, preaching was carried out in the vernacular language. The continental practice of musical liturgy (which came to be called shōmyō in Japan) was intoned in Chinese and developed in parallel with popular preaching (sekkyō or shōdō). Sekiyama (1973: 60) writes of two streams of sekkyō practices: the hyōbyaku (musicalized) and the enzetsu (spoken) types. Clearly, kōshiki services with their narrative preaching mode and melodious style of delivery emerged from the musicalized stream; however, their purpose of preaching to the laity shares the overall intent of preaching and teaching (shōdō). Kōshiki originated as part of the proselytizing of the laity, rather than the priestly practice of shōmyō. It gradually became more musicalized and was eventually absorbed into shōmyō. Kōshiki services were an elaborate ritual popular among the Japanese nobility from the tenth century and, combining with court music and literary culture, often took on a strong element of entertainment. Kōshiki is the most musically developed of the so-called narrative shōmyō genres, in terms of its elaborate, extended structures, and its expressive musical capability.

Kōshiki musical preaching is introduced in this chapter for its intrinsic interest, but also for its historical importance: all the genres of musical narrative discussed in this book – heike, kōwaka and jōruri – show an affinity with kōshiki and share basic formal characteristics. The chapter problematizes the claim that kōshiki is the foundational

---

[1] The *Nihon shoki* (comp. 720) (Aston 1972, vol. 2: 75) states that this occurred in 552, but Bowring suggests that documents of the Gangōji Temple giving 538 are more reliable, and that even earlier informal contacts are likely (2005: 15–19).

genre of Japan's tradition of musical narrative. An important issue for both kōshiki and heike (Chapter 3) is what input there might have been from the indigenous tradition of oral narrative, especially the kataribe reciters of the oral lore preserved in the *Kojiki* (see Chapter 1), vis-à-vis the influence of forms of continental origin. I argue for the influence of indigenous narrative practices in the development of both kōshiki and heike narrative. Furthermore, in considering the connection between kōshiki and the formation of the heike epic, I demonstrate the hybridity of kōshiki as a genre within shōmyō, due to its interaction with indigenous Japanese performance traditions.

Although kōshiki is performed from texts written in Chinese, it uses a Japanese musical system. This chapter shows that the musical principles of kōshiki are quite different from those of shōmyō proper. Its minimal musical notation did not appear until the early fourteenth century, contemporary with, not prior to, heike. The musical analysis in this chapter argues for the fluidity of the musical aspect of kōshiki, which links it with oral narrative.

The chapter first defines and briefly limns kōshiki in contemporary practice. Second, the historical development of kōshiki is traced. Third, the texts of kōshiki are discussed in terms of their authorship, language, style and content. Fourth, a generic musical analysis of kōshiki is presented, and finally, an analysis of the first part of *Nehan kōshiki* is carried out.

What is kōshiki?

Kōshiki is a Buddhist liturgy centring on the interpretation of sutras (Guelberg 1999: 29–32). It is a form of preaching and teaching, performed musically by a solo cantor. The etymology of the term indicates that it is a public lecture (kō) to explain sutras, leading to ceremonial worship (shiki), enhancing faith for participants (Yamada 1995: 13).[2] The kōshiki explains, often quite prosaically, and simplifies the import of canonical texts; kōshiki texts are often based on specific sutras. But as well as teaching they tend towards the personally devotional and emotional.

A kōshiki is situated in a Buddhist service, framed by other shōmyō pieces such as saimon, jinbun, shōrei, wasan and kyōke to make up the service (Guelberg 1999: 38). The kōshiki itself forms the centre-piece, defining the nature of a particular service (Satō 1984: 39–40). Kōshiki are comparable to oratorio in their alternation of scriptural narrative (recitative) and devotional hymns (Abe 2007 likens them to cantata). They also contain the element of personal devotion which is a feature of popular Christian hymns, which tend to use the first person.

The kōshiki is a lengthy liturgy usually lasting at least an hour. It is made up of a number of large sections or movements, the first being the explanatory hyōbyaku, followed by the kōshiki proper, which consists of a variable number of movements (dan), most commonly three or five. Each section ends with one or more hymn-like verses called kada (Skt. gatha), mostly taken from a sutra, in lines

---

[2] This is similar to jiang jing (Jp. kōgyō) in China; see Bender (2001).

of five or seven words (characters) as classical Chinese poetry. The kōshiki ends with a short 'transfer of merit' (ekō), like a prayer for others, in spoken delivery.

Kōshiki Performance Today[3]

Performances of kōshiki today take place as in Table 2.1.

Table 2.1   Performances of kōshiki today

Temple	Place	Ceremony	Date	Kōshiki
Hōryūji	Nara	Shari kō	January 1–3	*Shari kōshiki*
		O-eshiki	March 21	*Shōtoku Taishi kōshiki*
			March 22	*Shōtoku Taishi santan shiki*
Yakushiji	Nara	Nehan-e	February 15	*Shari kōshiki*
		Urabon-e	August 15	*Shari kōshiki*
Tōshōdaiji	Nara	Nehan-e	February 15	*Nehan kōshiki*
		Urabon-e	August 14	*Rakan kōshiki*
		Nenbutsu-e	October 19–25	*Shiza kōshiki*
Tōdaiji	Nara	Kanshin kō	6th of every month	*Kanshi kōshiki*
		Kannon kō	17th of every month	*Kannon kōshiki*
		Chishiki kō	April 24	?
Kongōbuji	Kōyasan	Jōraku-e	February 14–15	*Shiza kōshiki*
		Myōjin kō	Not fixed	*Myōjin kōshiki*
Chishakuin	Kyoto	Jōraku-e	February 15	*Shari kōshiki*
Enryakuji	Hieizan	Eshin kō	June 10	*Rokudō kōshiki*
Nishihonganji	Kyoto	Hōon kō	January 16	*Chion kōshiki*

Source: Satō Michiko, personal communication 1995.

---

[3] I have had the privilege of observing and documenting a number of services in which kōshiki are the focus. However, the material I have relied on principally for the analysis in the present chapter is the studio recording of *Shiza kōshiki* by Aoki Yūkō, issued by Columbia in 1978.

I hereby record my gratitude to Professor Satō Michiko for providing information about the whereabouts and nature of current kōshiki performance. I carried out field work by attending and recording the *Shari kōshiki* at Chishakuin, 15 February 1995; *Eshin kōshiki*

Table 2.1 indicates that at present, *Shari kōshiki* is the most prevalent, with four individual performances per year; it is also one of the four-part *Shiza kōshiki*, of which there are two full performances. *Nehan kōshiki* and *Rakan kōshiki* are also performed individually, as well as in the *Shiza kōshiki*. Myōe's *Shiza kōshiki* clearly has had enduring influence. Other examples appear only once a year.

Previous Research

Kōshiki has been researched as literature, as language, as ritual performance and as music. Most research is conducted from the perspective of Buddhist literature (see Yamada Shōzen, Guelberg and others; kōshiki kenkyūkai). The linguist Kindaichi Haruhiko (1974) looked to kōshiki as material for researching the history of Japanese pitch accent, and provides detailed musical analysis including some musical transcriptions.

Kōshiki seems to be a marginal genre of Buddhist music. It has been anthologized by recording companies as Buddhist ritual, and studies of shōmyō by Buddhist music specialists usually include some analysis of kōshiki (Ōyama 1989; Iwata 1999; Amano 2000; Yokomichi 1984). The most solid study of kōshiki in a Western language is based on texts rather than on performance (Guelberg 1999 and Guelberg's linked online database[4]).

Musicological research has looked to kōshiki as a foundational genre in the history of Japanese music: it has been asserted since Tanabe Hisao (1883–1984) and other pioneering musicologists that kōshiki was the most important influence on the music of heike narrative, nō, jōruri, kōwaka (that is, all the genres in this book), and introduced the use of the written text with a basic means of notation. Many musicologists have in recent decades given attention to the musical structure of kōshiki and its musical patterning (Sawada, M. Gamō, Hirano, Komoda, Nelson, Tokita).

The two major recordings available are *Shiza kōshiki* by Aoki Yūkō, issued by Columbia in 1978, and several examples in the *Shōmyō Taikei* (Hōzōkan 1984). Masumoto's essay in the notes for the *Shiza kōshiki* record collection is an approachable overview including transcriptions in Western staff notation of patches of *Nehan kōshiki*. In the same collection, Kanazawa's English overview of the historical development of kōshiki is useful. The record notes in *Shōmyō Taikei* are extensive; in addition a valuable reference work was published as a companion volume to the record set: *Shōmyō Jiten* (Yokomichi 1984). Satō Michiko's brief account in the *Shōmyō Jiten* contains a useful table of the outline of selected kōshiki services (1984: 39–41).

---

at Enryakuji, Hieizan, 10 June 1995, and again in 2010; and *Shiza kōshiki* (*Nehan, Rakan, Yuiseki, Shari*) as part of the Jōraku-e at Kongōbuji, Kōyasan, February 1999. I hereby record my gratitude to Professor Sawada Atsuko for arranging the latter.

[4] http://www.f.waseda.jp/guelberg/koshiki/datenb-j.htm (accessed 6 December 2014).

Historical Development of kōshiki

After Buddhism entered China from the first century CE, teams of Indian and Chinese translators worked together to translate the bulk of the by-then extensive scriptural canon from Pali and Sanskrit. As Buddhism spread through active proselytizing by lay and clerical preachers from India, Buddho-Indian narrative techniques were transferred to China, and eventually influenced secular vernacular narrative. This was the prosimetric (or chantefable) form of alternating prose and verse. By the eighth century, these narratives became a written form called pienwen (Jp. henbun), as attested by the stacks of examples found in the Dun Huang caves (Mair 1988; He 1999: 40–44).

Ōyama (1989: 6) writes that in China there were two types of Buddhist liturgy: sung liturgy and preaching-teaching. The sung liturgies consisted of chantings of the sutras (tendoku) and melismatic renditions of text, including some residual fragments of Sanskrit text (bonnon or bonbai). The preaching aspect was adapted into vernacular Sinitic language, specifically for teaching the common people, using illustrative stories, parables and colourful examples (Mair 2004: 154–7).

Japan imported and has continuously practised and developed bonnon and the metrical intoning of sutra texts. As for the popular preaching part, the concept was imported, but not the actual practice (Sawada 2002: 182). A large number of Korean and Chinese Buddhist monks, teachers and artisans came to Japan and taught and trained monks; however, it was local Japanese monks who went out on the streets to teach the masses as missionaries.[5]

Neither the Koreans nor the Japanese translated the sutras from Chinese into the vernacular, because neither had developed a vernacular writing at that stage, but intoned them in Chinese for their ritual value as much as studying them for their meaning. Japanese shōmyō used texts as transmitted in Chinese (with fragments in Sanskrit; like the Greek phrase *kyrie eleison* in the Latin mass). Visual expressions of the Buddhist faith were thus vital: the impressive temples, images and statues, and the impact of increasingly elaborate rituals (Bowring 2005: 68). Gradually a full knowledge of teachings and practices was realized. It was some time before the institution of monastic life was fully established, but priests and nuns were ordained after a fashion, and functioned somewhat as public servants in the new administrative structure centred on the imperial court. Rituals developed more complex forms over time, including the musical intonation of sutras and other liturgies.

The practice of shōmyō is first documented in detail in the elaborate 'eye-opening' ceremony of the Great Buddha statue at the dedication of the Tōdaiji temple in 752 (Sawada 1994: 39), but some form of musical chanting must have gradually become established in Japan after the introduction of Buddhism from Korea in the sixth century. In adopting continental Buddhist musical liturgy,

---

[5] Musicalized sekkyō led to sekkyō-bushi (fourteenth century), then sekkyō jōruri (seventeenth century) and later fushidan sekkyō (nineteenth century).

Japanese shōmyō absorbed the principles of Chinese music theory (scale, mode, rhythm), as did gagaku. It was essentially an imported foreign form.

Influence of Indigenous Practices on shōdō and sekkyō: Literacy and Orality

As Buddhism was first transmitted to Japan at the state level it was inextricably embedded with politics and power, and was patronized by the court and other powerful families as a protective and legitimizing power. The authority and prestige of Chinese culture and of Buddhism inevitably had a negative impact on the indigenous religion that came to be called Shintō, which had to fight back, at first literally, in the seventh century, and over the following centuries by compromising doctrinally with Buddhism. This led to the fusion or synthesis of Buddhism and Shintō.

After the establishment of Buddhism as state religion, Buddhist liturgy flourished in an elite social and political context, but the oral narratives of indigenous storytellers continued to be practised and to develop, albeit in contexts of lesser influence, by itinerant women and men who were connected only tenuously, if at all, with the Buddhist establishment. The public places of medieval Japan were awash with the musicalized storytelling of itinerant 'singers of tales' such as the biwa hōshi, aruki miko, shirabyōshi, maimai, holy men from Mount Kōya (Kōya hijiri), nuns from Kumano (Kumano bikuni) and many others.

Kōshiki emerged as a facet of the popularization of Buddhism, but in an upper-class context. It was just one part of the nexus between Buddhist preaching and storytelling, and one of a large variety of modes of preaching and teaching, including sekkyō (preaching) and the more generic term shōdō, or proselytizing.

Kōshiki today is counted as part of shōmyō, Buddhist vocal music. However, its historical relation with other Buddhist music, and its role as the source of Japanese vocal music, cannot be stated with certainty. Guelberg casts doubt on claims made in earlier research that kōshiki represents the origin of Japanese vocal music (such as Kindaichi 1974; *Ongaku Daijiten*, vol. 3, 1982: 1227a), offering as circumstantial evidence the fact that the earliest kōshiki notations date only from the fourteenth century (Guelberg 1999: 33–4). It is easy to imagine the impact of indigenous oral narrative practice on musical kōshiki services, and that, in adopting the Japanese language in preference to Chinese, the preachers also applied a familiar musical style of delivery, not that of continental shōmyō.

Kōshiki emerged at the same time as a rise of Buddhist personal devotionalism, or the Pure Land faith and belief in the power of Amida to save the believer who intoned his name (see Bowring 2005: 196–216). One of the key figures in this was the prelate Genshin (942–1017; also known as Eshin), who wrote the influential treatise *Essentials of Salvation* (Ōjō yōshū) (Reischauer 1930).

Some large-scale kōshiki ceremonies were staged accompanied by gagaku, to show the glories of the Pure Land (Nelson 1998: 461–2). Yamada Shōzen (1995) mentions also quasi-theatrical performances with Bodhisattvas appearing.

Even today the visual focus is strong, with a picture or statue of the object of devotion being displayed.

Functionally deriving from sekkyō, kōshiki as a means of teaching lay people had predecessors in musical liturgies called kyōge (teaching) from the early Heian period, and hyōbyaku (plain speech), first documented as part of a service held in 703 (Amano 2000: 76–7); both were musically delivered in Japanese.

The so-called narrative genres of shōmyō include hyōbyaku – which was used in a number of ceremonies – and rongi, saimon, jinbun and kōshiki. This 'made in Japan' music is often dubbed by scholars 'katarimono shōmyō' or narrative shōmyō. The main reason for this naming seems to be the genres' communicability: they are quite syllabic in nature, in contrast to most continental shōmyō chants in Sanskrit and Chinese, which call for highly melismatic delivery, aiming at a mantra-like magical effect, whose virtue lies in the intonation itself, rather than in the content being understood, especially in esoteric Buddhism. Furthermore, kōshiki in particular makes extensive use of anecdotes and narrative illustrations to underline Buddhist teachings, and aims to make a direct emotional appeal to the listeners. Sekiyama argues that the sekkyō preachers excelled at depictions of hell, an integral part of the Pure Land world view. A further reason is the a posteriori knowledge that there are strong links with the musical and textual structure of later katarimono genres.

Kōshiki Texts

The physical texts are actually written in Chinese (kanbun), but are performed with Sino-Japanese pronunciation, and in Japanese word order, that is, yomikudashi kanbun.[6] Yomikudashi kanbun is a type of written Japanese which developed from kanbun. This was closer to the vernacular language, presumably easier for ordinary, lay people to understand, and thus facilitated the explanation and teaching of difficult Buddhist texts and doctrines in graphic terms, using illustrations and stories.

Hundreds of examples of kōshiki texts have come down to us, although only a few are still performed and those performances are few and far between (see Table 2.1). Guelberg provides a comprehensive list of all known authors and their works (Guelberg 1999: 43–79, 215–25), and documents about 306 in his on-line

---

[6] Kornicki (2008, Second Lecture) calls this 'bluffing your way in Chinese', using strategies developed for translation, adaptation and simplification of a Chinese text, trying to read Chinese as if it was your own language (ibid.: 7). Punctuation systems were used in Korea first, then transmitted to Japan. This started before the development of vernacular scripts, but anticipated and perhaps stimulated their development. Early systems were greatly improved after the development of kana syllabic script in the ninth century, using numerals on the left of Chinese characters and Japanese inflections and particles on the right (ibid.: 13).

database,[7] but only half have authors ascribed to them. It is significant in the context of the history of katarimono that even some of the authors of the kōshiki texts are known; however, the music is not 'composed' in the modern sense, but was delivered in a conventionalized way, as will be explained below.

The texts were written from the late Heian period to the Muromachi period by prominent upper-class prelates. Guelberg singles out the three most important authors as Genshin, Myōe and Yōkan. Genshin, the previously mentioned author of *Ōjō yōshū*, is credited as having written the first kōshiki, *Nijūgo sanmai shiki* (see the full translation of this into German in Guelberg 1999). Later reformulated into the *Rokudō kōshiki*, it is still performed annually on Hieizan (Table 2.1). Myōe (1173–1232) was author of *Shiza kōshiki*, and Yōkan (1033–1111: also read as Eikan), the author of *Ōjō kōshiki*. It is notable that Genshin and Yōkan were known as outstanding preachers (Sekiyama 1973). The connection between kōshiki and sekkyō is also underscored by the inclusion of Chōken (1126–1203) – the most famous preacher of the medieval era and founder of the Agui school of sekkyō – in Guelberg's longer list as the author of some kōshiki.

Yamada's classification of types of kōshiki is based on the object of devotion, that is, on textual content (1995: 38):

a. Buddha types (Amida, Shaka …), Buddhist deities (Bosatsu, Jizō, Kannon …), Ten (Benzaiten, Myō-onten = music, Bishamonten, Tamonten, Getten, Daikokuten …);
b. venerable historical figures, for example Shōtoku Taishi, Kōbō Daishi, Kakinomoto;
c. Shintō deities, for example Hachiman;
d. sutras, for example Lotus sutra;
e. others, for example stupa.

Some, however, are more private in nature, for example the priest Jōkei's *Hosshin kōshiki*, commissioned by retired emperor Gotoba in 1200 as a thanksgiving for his salvation (Guelberg 1999).

Kōshiki Textual Features

Kōshiki literary texts, written in kanbun, were, as noted above, performed in Japanese yomikudashi style, the oralization of a written text, following the by-then well-established Japanese practice of annotating a Chinese text and when reading 'mentally converting it into their own language(s) all the time' (Kornicki 2008, Second Lecture: 23). Kōshiki performance was a 'reading' for an assembled gathering, who needed to hear the message clearly. Although at a kōshiki service these days one can purchase a copy of the text and follow it through the liturgy,

---

[7] See note 4.

it can be assumed that in the Kamakura period this was not the case and that attendees relied on auditory perception for the verbal message, aided by visual illustrations.

Because the bulk of the kōshiki text is unmetered, though with some rhetorical flourishes, the verbal phrases, and consequently also musical phrases, are variable in length. Sung phrases are delineated primarily by the taking of a breath, as in reading out a text or in speech, and are shaped through ornamentation.

Although kōshiki features consciously literary language of a poetic nature, in comparison with most shōmyō, the language of the kōshiki is a kind of vernacular Japanese that is easy for the listeners to understand. However, it is still heavily Sinitic and uses Buddhist terms freely.[8] It is rather opaque if one is not familiar with the sutra being referred to. This is perhaps why some parts of the text are straightforward, even prosaic and explanatory: the opening and closing phrases of a section always say what is being done; they are performative speech acts. These parts are conversational and explanatory, replete with formulaic verbal expression. They directly address the interlocutor (whether human or divine). The older and simpler hyōbyaku form begins with an invocation of the object of veneration: 'Uyamatte (respectfully) ... ni mooshite moosaku'; or 'Tsutsushimi uyamatte ...', and ends with '... no mune o arawasu' (expresses the meaning of ...). A list of the beginnings of each section to follow appears, like a table of contents, at the end of the hyōbyaku. The purpose of the hyōbyaku is to make clear the significance of the ceremony for the participants and for the principal object of reverence. The Pali sutras also have this explanatory feature.

The subsequent sections of the kōshiki proper follow logically from the hyōbyaku. The opening phrase verbally announces the section with a number or an indication of sequence: Firstly (Dai ichi ni), Secondly (Dai ni ni), In the first place (mazu) / next (Tsugi ni) / afterwards (nochi ni). Then the theme is developed. The sections are signalled verbally rather than musically, in the absence of an accompanying instrument.

The closing phrase of the dan is usually an exhortation to sing a kada: 'Kada o tonaete, raihai subeshi' (Let us intone a kada and sing praise). For example, at the end of the first dan of *Nehan kōshiki*: 'Yotte hiryū wo nogoi, shutan wo osamete, kada wo tonae raihai wo gyōzu beshi' (So, we should wipe away our tears, put our grief aside, and sing praise intoning a kada hymn). In Tendai, instead of the kada, a nenbutsu is inserted between the movements.

The hymn-like units interpolated between the dan provide a strong musical and textual contrast to the kōshiki with its expository nature. The kada is in metrical Chinese, delivered in a highly melismatic way in typical shōmyō manner. These verses are reminiscent of chorales in a cantata or oratorio.

---

[8] Kornicki notes that even 'reading Chinese in such a way that it resembled their own language', key Chinese terms remained in Chinese. The Japanese had no translations of Buddhist and Confucian texts, but had to 'follow all the glosses so as to reconstruct the Chinese as a Japanese text' (2008, Second Lecture: 25). Kornicki further speaks of annotated kanbun as 'the act of deconstructing Chinese as Japanese' (ibid.: 26).

Generic Musical Analysis

Kōshiki is fundamentally different from other 'normal shōmyō' (hon-shōmyō), not only linguistically but also musically: it shows the same basic structural and musical principles as heike, utai, kōwaka and jōruri. Instead of the octave-based scalar structure of gagaku and shōmyō proper, it is based on the framework of conjunct and disjunct fourths, and melodic progression through three pitch territories. Although its use of named ornamental figures (such as yuri) are the same as in shōmyō proper, the larger-scale named formulaic musical materials are unique to kōshiki, and it is this feature which is shared with other katarimono genres. This shift from the octave framework to the melodic structure based on units of the fourth is evidence of the influence of indigenous narrative and musical practice, so clearly seen in heike, nō and kōwaka.

Iwata distinguishes 'foreign' (gairai-kei) shōmyō (1999: 253–70) from Japanese (nihon-kei) shōmyō (ibid.: 270–80), and sees kōshiki as belonging to the latter, along with hyōbyaku and other so-called katarimono shōmyō, and wasan. His musical analyses emphasize how different the Japanese genres are from continental-origin shōmyō. According to Iwata, foreign shōmyō uses the same scales and modes and rhythmic concepts as gagaku, both deriving from Chinese musical theory. Japanese shōmyō on the other hand is based on Japanese indigenous scales and tonal structure (ibid.: 272).

Amano (2000: 75) asserts that the basic tone of kōshiki is shojū (f-g in the transcriptions). He points out (ibid.: 81–5) that kōshiki does not use the five-tone scale of other shōmyō, but the terms ge, otsu, nijū / chū, sanjū (at intervals of a fourth). Sawada states that kōshiki went *beyond* the Chinese theory of hon-shōmyō (2002: 191). She emphasizes the divergence between theory and practice, and states that considerable variation exists depending on sect, branch, genre and individual performer. She affirms that the pitch system, musical structure and notation system of katarimono genres are distinct from other shōmyō. Furthermore, the progression from one pitch territory (jū) to another is almost unique to kōshiki, whereas rongi and hyōbyaku stay in shojū almost exclusively.

Sectional Structure, Substyles and Patterns: Fluidity and Fixity

One kōshiki consists of a number of large sections or movements (dan), the first being the explanatory hyōbyaku, followed by the kōshiki proper, which consists of a variable number of movements, most commonly three or five.[9] Each dan is separated by a 'song of praise' (kada).

A dan is further made up of smaller sections (shōdan), each marked off musically with a cadential phrase and sometimes by a longer transitional sub-section.

---

[9] The number of sections (in addition to the hyōbyaku) varies: 3 sections (103 works), 4 (3 works), 5 (99 works), 6 (13 works), 7 (10 works), 8 (2 works), 9 (2 works), 10 (1 work), 12 (1 work) (Guelberg 1999: 29–30).

The length of the sections is highly variable, from a couple of lines to several dozen lines.

Kōshiki has three main melody types, each generated from a pitch area or territory: low (shojū), medium (nijū) and high (sanjū). Examples 2.1 to 2.3 show representative versions of these melodic types. Shojū literally means 'first level', nijū means 'second level', and sanjū means 'third level'. These terms, referring to pitch areas, by extension refer also to the melodic realizations of movement between two or more nuclear tones. The melodic pattern can be called an extended melody, applied for an indeterminate length of time, depending on the amount of text allocated.

Example 2.1 Shojū

Example 2.2 Nijū

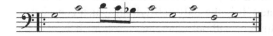

Example 2.3 Sanjū

In shōmyō musical theory as a whole, the range of one octave is traditionally called jū; three jū are identified (from low to high) as shojū (first level), nijū (second level) and sanjū (third level). In practice, however, kōshiki has less than two octaves (Nelson 1998: 466).

Each section features just one of the three named melody types: shojū, nijū or sanjū. The section is a structural unit, but because the whole section is delivered in only one of these melody types or substyles, it also designates the musical content. (The Japanese theoretical term kyokusetsu is ambiguous because it signifies both these meanings.)

The melodic structure of kōshiki is thus based on the sequencing of these named pitch areas or territories, which also represent formulaic melodies. Moving through these three tonal territories, kōshiki occupies a total range of one and a half octaves, including the lower cadential pattern for shojū (ge). However, the actual pitch shifts in performance from dan to dan, and even within one dan, because there is no instrumental accompaniment: the pitch is relative to the comfort of the singer's voice. There tends to be a gradual rise in pitch through the dan, and sometimes a radical shift in tonal centre at the start of a new section. So the actual range might be somewhat broader than one and a half octaves.

Shojū and nijū are the simplest melodic types, while sanjū has more melodic movement and complexity. Its length as a section is also more fixed, tending towards only four phrases. See Example 2.7 for an extended example.

Shojū and nijū are stichic musical substyles, featuring one and the same melodic pattern for every line of text. Centred on one particular pitch area or territory, they move back and forth between two pitches: a major second in the case of shojū and a fourth in the case of nijū. The highly fluid realization in performance of shojū and nijū, changing to match the requirements of a line of text and quite flexible in length, indicates that they are types of delivery rather than melody patterns. The number of syllables on each note is variable, necessarily since the lines are not of a fixed syllable length. Variation is achieved by the ornamental motives of yuri and other embellishments. It is believed that the movement between the lower and higher tones reflects the pitch accent of Japanese speech in the medieval period (Kindaichi 1974).

Shojū or 'first level' is the basic style of kōshiki. It is used the most extensively, can be used almost exclusively and occupies the largest amount of text. Each phrase takes the same melodic contour, but the number of syllables on each tone is variable, and the application of yuri ornamentation is mostly arbitrary. Shojū sections can be accumulated. It is the only substyle in which consecutive sub-sections can continue indefinitely without changing substyle. It is also the only substyle or style of delivery for hyōbyaku, jinbun and most other so-called katarimono shōmyō. The hyōbyaku dan consists only of a number of shojū sections.

Nijū or 'second level' style of delivery is a transposed variation of the basic shojū style, occupying the middle territory between shojū and sanjū. Its melody alternates between g, the upper pitch of shojū, and c, the lower pitch of sanjū, a major fourth interval apart rather than a major second. Although like shojū it can be assigned to large tracts of text (but not in cumulative sections), occupying a higher register it serves as variation and emotional highlight. It is used more sparingly than shojū, but still several times in every dan. It is primarily syllabic in its delivery, but is more consistently ornamented than shojū. It is also a stichic kind of narrative, each phrase taking the same melodic contour. Each nijū phrase consists of two balanced parts, the second part having a consistent pattern of ornament and melisma, giving a sense of closure at the end of each line. See Example 2.7, lines 11–20 and 28–31.

The cadence of nijū is the transitional melody of chūon (Example 2.7, lines 21 and 22), preceded by a pre-cadence. At the end of some nijū sections a sense of cadence is felt with the appearance of an intermediate note between the two nuclear tones, forming a min'yō tetrachord: G-b♭-C.

Sanjū or 'third level' moves up to the highest pitch register and focuses on the upper pitch of nijū (c). This relatively fixed melodic pattern is applied to passages usually of four lines in poetic metre and tends to emphasize particularly important segments of text which should touch the emotions of the listener. It functions to create a musical and textual climax of a dan. There is plenty of melismatic treatment of the text, and the yuri ornament is added frequently.

Sanjū is used the least frequently, never more than once in a dan (not at all in some dan), and a maximum of two or three times per piece, usually towards the end. It finishes not with a particular cadential pattern but by returning to nijū, where it settles.

Transitional sub-sections

Example 2.4 Chūon

Example 2.5 Shojū-kutsu-shojū

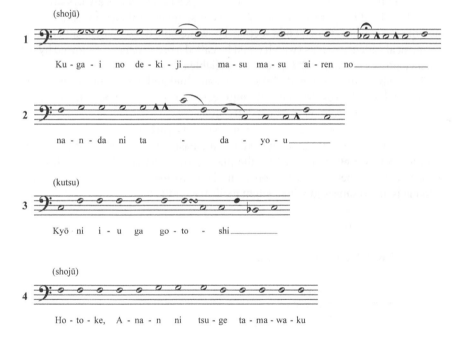

In addition to the three main melody types are transitional sections. The melody type chūon ('middle sound') is a short sub-section of only one or two phrases (Example 2.4; Example 2.7, lines 21 and 22). Musically very simple, it iterates just one tone, g, the lower tone of nijū, and functions as the transition from nijū to the next section. It can be called a cadential pattern of nijū, which barely has a cadential motive, while chūon has a substantial cadential pattern.

Kutsu is a cadential phrase or sub-section used in between some shojū sections (Example 2.5). It seems to have a tendency to certain types of text: proclaiming the authoritative voice of the sutra or similar.

These two named patterns should not be seen as structural units on the same level as shojū, nijū and sanjū. They have a bridging function rather than being sections in their own right.

Cadential phrases

The cadence at the end of shojū rises from f, to g, then to upper c, and then down to f – lower c – f – c (final tone) (Example 2.7, line 10). This cadential figure is very similar to the bridging pattern kutsu which occasionally appears in between sections of shojū (Example 2.5, lines 2 and 3).

The cadential patterns at the end of shojū and chūon do not seem to be especially named (Example 2.1; Example 2.7, line 10). (Sometimes the shojū cadence is marked as ge.) Although the final (usually fourth) line of the sanjū section is distinct from the preceding lines, sanjū does not have a true cadential phrase, but moves seamlessly into the following section which is always nijū.

Although all the phrases in the substyles of shojū and nijū are much the same melodically, towards the end of a section a new melodic development anticipating the musical cadence occurs (which could be called a pre-cadence), followed by the cadence proper (Example 2.7, line 9, the syllable ni).

The body of the shojū and nijū sections are fluid and elastic, unlike the fixity of the cadential phrases. In contrast, sanjū sections use the 7-5 poetic metre, as do some parts of nijū sections (Sawada 2002: 189).

A few named motives and ornaments, such as yuri (literally 'shake', it is a tremolo or turn), are also evident. Even in the basic melodic styles of shojū and nijū, melodic variety is created by the placing of ornamentation, as well as by the different number of syllables on each pitch (Yoshida 1954). The name of the Buddha is always marked with a slight melismatic inflection.

Jū and Tetrachords

Example 2.6 Kōshiki tonal material

The three main patterns – shojū, nijū, sanjū – clearly reflect the tetrachordal structure of Japanese scales with nuclear tones in a framework of conjunct and disjunct fourths, underscoring their affinity with indigenous musical practice. Example 2.6 shows the relation between the three pitch territories (jū) and the tetrachordal structure according to Koizumi theory (Koizumi 1977; Tokita 1996). The tetrachords correspond to the three pitch territories (jū). Shojū oscillates between its strongest, basic pitch, f, and g, and then moves to e♭, then descends to c for the cadential phrase. This forms the (min'yō) tetrachord C-e♭-F, and can be identified as the low jū or shojū. (In practice, however, the central melodic movement of shojū is between the upper tone of the tetrachord and the lower nuclear tone of the nijū tetrachord.)

Nijū occupies the middle (min'yō) tetrachord, G-b♭-C (disjunct from the shojū tetrachord); its strongest, basic pitch is G, and its melody alternates between G and upper C, touching on neighbouring b♭ and d in ornamental figures.

Sanjū is located in the upper (ritsu) tetrachord C-d-F (whose lower nuclear tone is conjunct with the nijū tetrachord), though its melodic movement for the most part centres on c and its neighbouring tones, b♭, which it leans on heavily, and touches on d more or less in passing. The upper note of the tetrachord, f, is only reached in the last phrase of a section, and very occasionally upper g.

For most of its duration, shojū style of delivery straddles the lower and middle tetrachords, maintaining the alternation between the two tones f (the central tone) and g (the upper tone), only going down to the lower leading note e♭ to signal the impending cadence.

In contemporary Tendai performance of *Rokudō kōshiki* the intervallic structure is less clear.

As the basic style of delivery in kōshiki, shojū has the same function as heike kudoki or kōwaka kotoba. It occurs the most frequently, and is used for the longest stretches. It is syllabic, and the melodic movement alternates between two nuclear tones, in a low pitch area. It can be applied to any number of lines, many or few, before being concluded with its own elaborate cadential phrase.

Nehan kōshiki

Nehan kōshiki is one of four individual kōshiki ('pieces') that constitute the *Shiza kōshiki*. The *Shiza kōshiki* is unusually large in scale among kōshiki.[10] Indeed, the larger work format is only found in the *Shiza kōshiki* ('four sessions of kōshiki'). The four individual kōshiki, each of which can be performed separately, that together make-up this almost symphonic, extensive suite are *Nehan* (Entering nirvana), *Rakan* (Arhats), *Yuiseki* (Holy sites) and *Shari* (Buddha's remains). It is performed in full at Kongōbuji Temple (at Kōyasan) as part of the service Jōraku-e on the eve of Buddha's death day, 14–15 February every year. It lasts all night. The component pieces are performed independently in other venues (see Table 2.1). Aoki Yūkō's performance, on which my analysis is based, was, however, a studio recording.

Each kōshiki movement is prefaced with a hyōbyaku dan. The text of this preliminary movement states the purpose of the whole service. It expresses reverence to the Buddha, the chief object of devotion, and his virtues, and briefly mentions the main point of each movement to follow,

---

[10] The notes to the recording stress its uniqueness as a major large-scale work and suggest that its literary quality expresses Myōe's yearning for the Buddha, as a substitute for his mother, and a compensation for not being able to make a pilgrimage to India.

the five kōshiki dan. This movement is intoned throughout using only the basic shojū pattern of delivery, and comprises eight sub-sections of irregular phrase length, each marked by the usual shojū cadential pattern.[11]

The first dan after the introductory hyōbyaku dan is based on the Mahāyāna Mahāpari nivāna sutra (Jp. Nehan kyō) and describes the scene of the dying Buddha on the fifteenth day of the second month. Wracked in pain, he lies on his right side, and speaks. All 52 species of beings gather to hear his last teachings. His body takes on heavenly colour as he enters a state of samadhi and dies (enters nirvana). The earth shakes, the mountains crumble and all creatures weep in grief at the pain of separation. However, tears must be wiped away, and all join in singing a kada.

The second dan describes the grief felt as the Buddha is cremated. After dying between the Sala trees, his body was wrapped in white cloth and put in a gold coffin. The strong ones tried to carry the coffin to the cremation ground on the other side of the river, but it refused to be moved. Instead, it levitated into the air and flew around over Kuśinagara city, then took itself to the cremation ground. The people tried to light the funeral pyre, but it would not ignite. At that time, Mahākāśyapa, one of the ten chief disciples, who had arrived too late for the death, now arrived at the cremation and the lid of the coffin opened of itself. The white cloth unwound and revealed the golden body. The cloth was then rewound and the coffin closed. Mahākāśyapa expressed grief by intoning a kada and weeping. The coffin then opened again, and the cloth unwound. The feet stuck out of the coffin. The lid was closed again, and Mahākāśyapa again intoned a kada and wept, and the feet went back into the coffin. Then Buddha produced fire from his chest, and the pyre was finally lit. It took seven days for the coffin and body to burn. The relics (shari) were divided into eight portions.

In the third dan the reasons why Buddha had to die are explicated. Drawing on Mahāyāna Buddhism's discourse of the Lotus, Kegon and Nehan sutras concerning the view of the Buddha's body, this movement explains how the Buddha's Dharma body never dies, but lives forever. He did not die to abandon living creatures, only to chasten the inverted hearts of humble people, and to evoke in them the emotion of sorrow or pity.

Drawing on Xuanzang's (Jp. Genjō; 602–664) pilgrimage to India, as recorded in Dà Táng Xīyù Jì (Jp. Daitō Saiiki-ki; The Great Tang Records on the Western Regions; source of the Ming novel *Journey to the West*), the fourth dan teaches about the sites of the place of Buddha's death, and the cremation, from a latter-day perspective. Buddha died among the Sala trees, on the west bank of the Hirannavati River, north of Kuśinagara. There were four Sala trees, one for each direction, each of which divided into two trunks. The Buddha was lying down between these four trees. The movement describes a number of sites, including the place nearby where his mother Lady Maya descended from heaven and mourned, and the place where the Deva king fell down and threw his vajra to the ground. The cremation ground is located across the river, a distance of 300 paces.

---

[11] A full transcription of Tendai performance is provided in Kindaichi (1974: 19–23).

The fifth dan is a short movement that expresses the wish that all people will feel longing for Shakyamuni, meet Buddha and listen to his teaching. The Dharma body of the Buddha is always present in the same way that the sun, the moon, the stars and the day and night are always with us. Even in the imperfect Latter Day of the Law (Jp. mappō), the Buddha is present wherever people carry out the practice of the Dharma. Putting aside the sadness of longing for the Buddha, if people turn their attention to following the Dharma, they will be with the Buddha.

CD Track 4 starts at the beginning of section (4) of the first dan, going through shojū, nijū, chūon, sanjū, nijū. The text is given only up to this point. The recording continues, omitting lines five to 24 of this very long 27-line nijū, then proceeds to chūon, and finishes the section with shojū; the recording finishes with the first eight lines of the next shojū at the beginning of section (5).

Nehan kōshiki First Dan

Table 2.2   Outline of *Nehan kōshiki* Dan 1

Sections	Text (number of phrases)	FMM*
(1) Introduction	Daiichi ni nyūmetsu no aishō o ... ... namida ni tadayou (16)	shojū cadence
	Kyō ni iu ga gotoshi. (1)	kutsu
(2) Buddha announces he will enter Nirvana	Hotoke, Anan ni tsugetamawaku ... ... ge o toite moosaku. (13)	shojū cadence
	Seson kinjiki kōmyō no mi ... (6) ... mata motte kaku no gotoshi. (1)	**nijū** **chūon**
	Sakidatte Nehan hittei no (7) ... tsui ni sunawachi (1)	shojū cadence
(3) The gathering of the 52 species	Rikishi shoji ... ... sono shōbō to iha iwayuru (21)	shojū cadence
	Shōmon Engaku onajiku ikka ni ... (9) ... tsuiren iyoiyo masu. (1) Menmen ni yūhi no iro o fukumi ... ... kitawashitamau. (35)	**nijū** **chūon** shojū cadence
(4) The grieving of the 52 species at the entering of Nirvana	Nyorai mata morotomo no taishū ni ... ... myōhō o toku iwayuru (11)	shojū cadence
	Mumyō honsai shōbon gedatsu ... (12) ... sunawachi daiyon zentei ni haitte (2)	**nijū** **chūon**
	Shōren no me tojite ... (4) Kono toki ni morifuyu no rakan wa (27) ... oyoso daichi shindō shi ... (4)	**SANJŪ** **nijū** **chūon**
	Kimoku shōrin kotogotoku ... ... kyō ni shue hikan no sō wo toite iwaku. (3)	shojū cadence

continued

Table 2.2   continued

Sections	Text (number of phrases)	FMM*
(5) Conclusion	Aruiha Hotoke ni shitagatte ... (15) ... amaneku issai sekai ni furuu' (1)	shojū cadence
	Makoto ni omonmireba ... (4) ... netsunō nanimono wo ka tatoe to senya (1)	**nijū** **chūon**
	Yotte hiryū o nogui ... (4) ... kada wo tonae raihai o gyōzubeshi (1)	shojū cadence

* Bold type indicates the more musical nijū-chūon substyle; capital letters indicate the most musically striking sanjū substyle, creating a climax.
Adapted from Gamō 1989: 126.

Text 2.1   *Nehan kōshiki* (extract) (CD Track 3)

4) The grieving of the 52 species
初重   **shojū**
1. 如来復、諸の大衆に   Nyorai turns again to the assembled
Nyorai mata moromoro no daishū ni   masses
2. 告げて言わく。   and speaks.
tsugete notamawaku
3.「我今、遍身疼痛む。   'My whole body is racked with severe
'Ware ima henshin hiiraki itamu   pain;
4. 涅槃時到れり」。   the time of nirvana has come.'
nehan toki itareri.'
5. この語を作し已って、   As he finished these words
kono kotoba o nashi owatte
6. 順逆超越して、   bypassing the normal order
jungyaku chōesshite
7. 諸の禅定に入る。   he entered the various states of samadhi.
moromoro no zenjō ni iru
8. 禅定より起ち已って、   Awakening from these states
zenjō yori tachi owatte
9. 大衆のために   he proclaimed a great teaching
daishū no tame ni
(Cadence)
10. 妙法を説く。所謂   to the assembled masses. This is what he said:
myōhō o toku. Iwayuru

(二重)   **nijū**
11.「無明本際、性本解脱   'Ignorance and absolute truth are one.
mumyō honzai shōhon gedatn
12.我今安住常寂滅光   I am now peacefully residing in the
gakon anjū jōjaku mekkō   absolute realm;

13.名大涅槃」と myō dainehan to	'This is called the great enlightenment.'
14.大衆に示し已って、 daishū ni shimeshi owatte	Finishing his words to the assembled masses,
15.遍身漸く傾き、 henjin yōyaku katabuki	he leaned over and
16.右脇にして臥す。 ukyō ni shite fusu	lay on his right side,
17.頭北方を枕とし、 kōbe hoppō o makura to shi	his head to the north,
18.足は南方を指す。 miashi wa nanbō o sasu	his feet to the south
19.おもてを西方に向え、 omote o saihō ni mukae	facing the west,
20.後東方を背けり。 ushiro tōbō o somukeri	and his back to the east.

中音 — **chūon**

21.即ち第四禅定に入って、
sunawachi daishi zenjō ni itte
22.大涅槃に帰したまいぬ。
dainehan ni kishi tamainu.

Then he entered the fourth stage of samadhi
and finally the state of Great Nirvana.

三重 — **sanjū**

23.青蓮の眼閉じて、
shōren no manako tojite
24.永慈悲の微笑を止め、
nagō jihi no mishō o yame
25.丹菓の
tanka no
26.唇黙して終に大梵の
kuchibiru modashite tsui ni daibon no
27.哀声を絶ちき。
aisei o tachiki

He closed his clear lotus eyes,
and lost forever his smile of compassion;
his red lips,
like the fruit of the bimbā tree, were shut;
his beautiful voice was never to be heard again.

二重 — **nijū**

28.この時に、漏尽の羅漢は、
Kono toki ni, rojin no rakan wa
29.梵行已立の歓喜を忘れ、
Bongyō iryu no kangi o wasure,
30.登地の菩薩は、
Tōji no Bosatsu wa
31.諸法無生の観智を捨つ。
Shohō mushō no kanchi o sutsu.

At this time, the arhat who had left behind all illusions
forgot the delights of carrying out the established Brahmacharya (pure life)
The Bodhisattva at the tenth level
abandoned the wisdom of no-birth and no-death ...
(CD extract and transcription end here)

The translation of the text omitted on CD track 3 is given here.

> ...threw away his vajra, shouted at heaven, threw his jeweled net and banner, and fell to the ground. The eighty billion demon kings protruded their tongues and convulsed in agony. The twenty billion lion kings prostrate themselves and cry out. The birds all feel sadness. Poisonous snakes and scorpion tribes all without exception are engulfed with grief. Lion and tiger, boar and deer, gather on their hoofs and forget their grievances. The monkeys and dogs lick each other for consolation. The sound of the waves on the Ajitavati River...

CD resumes here for the final three lines of the nijū sub-section, but there is no transcription.

1.別離の歎を催し、　　　　　　　　bring forth a lament of separation.
betsuri no nageki wo moyōshi
2.娑羅林の風の声も、　　　　　　　The voice of the wind in the Sararin tree
Sararin no kaze no koe mo
3.哀恋の思を勧む。　　　　　　　　inspires the memory of longing (for the
Airen no omoi wo susumu.　　　　　Buddha)

中音　　　　　　　　　　　　　　**chūon**
1.凡そ大地振動し、　　　　　　　　The earth quaked
Oyoso daichi shindō shi
2.大山崩裂す。　　　　　　　　　　Great mountains collapsed
Daisen hōretsu su.
3.海水沸涌し、　　　　　　　　　　The sea water churned
Kaisui hiyu shi
4.江河涸竭す。　　　　　　　　　　The rivers dried up.
Gōga kokatsu su.

初重　　　　　　　　　　　　　　**shojū**
1.卉木叢林悉く　　　　　　　　　　Flowers, grasses, trees, forests all
Kimoku sōrin kotogotoku
2.憂悲の声を出し、　　　　　　　　raised voices of mourning.
uhi no koe wo idashi,
3.山河大地皆痛悩の語を唱う。　　　Mountains and rivers, all the earth, utter
Senga daiji mina tsūnō no kotoba wo tonau.　words of agony
4.経に衆会悲感の相を説いて云く。　As it is written in the sutra, describing the
Kyō ni shue hikan no / Sō wo toite iwaku.　grief of the congregation:　　(Cadence)

初重　　　　　　　　　　　　　　**Shojū** (beginning of section 5)
1.「或は仏に随って滅する者あり。　'Some die following the Buddha
'Aruiha Hotoke ni shitagatte messuru mono ari.

2. 或は失心の者あり。 Aruiha shisshin no mono ari.	Others lose their heart.
3. 或は身心戦く者あり。 Aruiha shinjin wananaku mono ari	There are some who tremble body and soul;
4. 或は互相に手を執って、哽咽して涙を流す者あり。 Aruiha tagai ni te wo totte kōwetsu shite namida wo nagasu mono ari.	Others who take each other's hands and wail and sob
5. 或は常に胸を搥って、大きに叫ぶ者あり。 Aruiha tsune ni mune wo utte ōki ni sakebu mono ari.	Some beat keep beating their breast, and wail loudly.
6. 或は手を挙げて、頭を拍って、自ら髪を抜く者あり。 Aruiha te wo agete kōbe wo utte mizukara kami wo nuku mono ari.	Others raise their hand, hit their head, and pull out their own hair.
7. 或は遍体に血現れて、 Aruiha hentai ni chi arawarete	With some, blood appears over their whole body
8. 地に流れ灑ぐ者あり。 Ji ni nagaresosogu mono ari.	and pours onto the ground. (CD track 3 finishes here)
9. かくの如くの異類の殊音一切大衆の哀声、 Kaku no gotoku no irui no shuon issai daishu no aisei	In this way, the sound of sadness of all creatures together
10. 普く一切世界に震う。」 Amaneku issai sekai ni furū'	makes all worlds tremble'. (Cadence)

The text can be divided into five narrative sections (Table 2.2, first column), all opening and closing with a shojū sub-section.

There is no regularity in the number of lines allocated to each melody type; the shojū sections, for example, consist of 16, 12, 7, 21, 35, 11, 3, 8 and 9 lines respectively. The performance time of the sections is thus irregular, not only because of the different number of lines / phrases, but also due to different delivery styles; 4 lines of sanjū take 1 minute and 8 seconds, whereas 27 lines of nijū take 4 minutes and 20 seconds, and 15 lines of shojū take 1 minute and 17 seconds. This irregularity is typical of katarimono structure.

Occasionally there is a textual enjambement, where the musical cadence of a section has a textual break in the middle: the final few notes being for the opening words of the next musical section.

In the studio performance by Aoki Yūkō, in which tonal shifts occur between the sections in each pitch area, there is no apparent tonal link to the kada, which is musically and textually distinct from the kōshiki. After the first dan, the tonal centres of the kada are (d) – f – g (central tone) – a, whereas the central tone of the kōshiki part was f. They are tonally and stylistic quite contrasting.

Example 2.7 *Nehan kōshiki* Dan 1

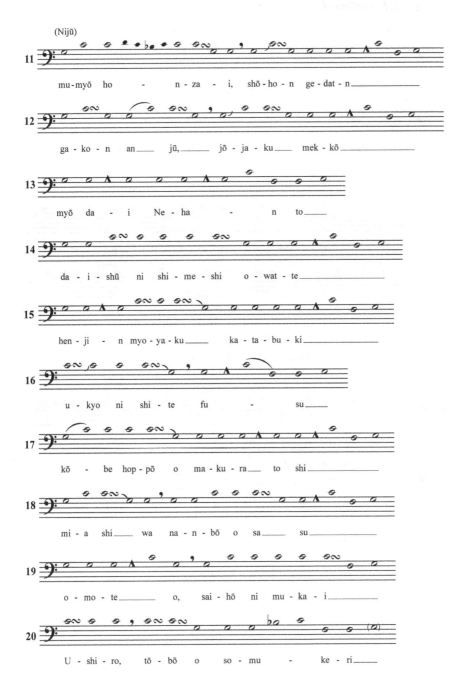

Example 2.7 *continued*

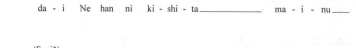

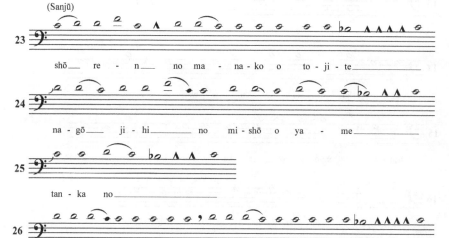

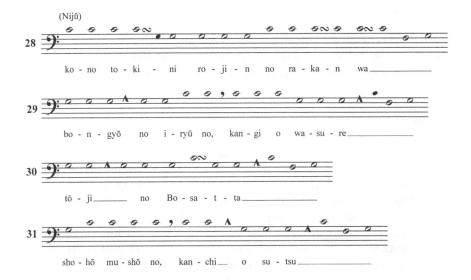

Frequency and Distribution of Melodic Material

The substyle of shojū is used most frequently in the first dan (nine times), in a sequence of two shojū sections four times; only the last is single. Nijū is used four times, always followed by chūon, the transitional pattern leading back into shojū or on to sanjū.

The musically climactic high register sanjū is used only once in the dan, for a run of only four lines of text. It is preceded by nijū – chūon. Section 4 of the first dan is structured around the sanjū section in a rising-falling contour: shojū – nijū – sanjū – nijū – chūon – shojū. The expressive, even sensuous sanjū gives musical interest, but is used in only the first, third and fifth dan of *Nehan kōshiki*. In *Rakan kōshiki* (5 dan), sanjū is in dan 2 and 5; in *Yuiseki kōshiki* (5 dan), in dan 1 and 5 (5th is very brief); in *Shari kōshiki* (3 dan), in dan 2 and 3. This sparing use of the most musically elaborate melody, in contrast to shojū and nijū, is effective in creating a musical and narrative climax. It is reserved for short segments of text to be highlighted, and no more than once in a movement, serving as a musical climax.

The pattern kutsu is used once in every hyōbyaku dan, but less regularly elsewhere. In *Shiza kōshiki* it is most prominent in *Nehan kōshiki*. Kutsu is inserted as a spacing device between two shojū sections. Again very sparingly used, rather than a musical highlight, the texts are suggestive of a declamatory function. In *Nehan*, it appears twice in the hyōbyaku dan ('Kore ni shinnu' and 'Kore ni yotte'); and once in each of the following shiki dan:

I: Kyō ni iu ga gotoshi
III: Masa ni shirubeshi

IV: Kyō ni iwaku
IV: Aru ki ni iwaku

Kutsu appears again in the hyōbyaku dan of the *Rakan kōshiki* ('Kore ni yotte'), *Yuiseki kōshiki* ('Tsui ni sunawachi') and *Shari kōshiki* ('Yotte deshi-ra'). In addition, it appears in the third dan of *Yuiseki kōshiki* ('Kono yue ni').

Conclusion

What is narrative about kōshiki? It is true that kōshiki favours a syllabic recitative style in the Japanese vernacular, since the purpose is to instruct and enlighten the lay congregation of believers (albeit upper-class ones) in a manner similar to storytelling. On the other hand, the performance is directed towards the object of devotion, rather than to an audience.

When Japanese commentaries refer to it as 'narrative' (katarimono shōmyō), this suggests its affinities with other narrative music genres, that is, its formal stylistic features, not its content. Kōshiki and Japanese indigenous narrative music starting from heike have similar musical structure, and some textual similarities. Most importantly, kōshiki is structured musically around clearly defined formulaic musical material: its named formulaic substyles focus on pitch territories one fourth apart, and contain some formulaic phrases, especially cadences. The cadences stand out from the main substyles through their melodic descent, and their slower melismatic delivery, exactly as in all other katarimono genres.

The range of substyles in kōshiki is, however, narrow, and there is no differentiation between hard and soft narrative, unlike in the other genres we will discuss. Perhaps kōshiki narrative is all soft, which would be consistent with its religious nature.

Kōshiki as a liturgy carried out in a literate environment had an influence on the later practice of singing from a written text-score, alongside which were indicated the melodic contour, with neumes (hakase) indicating pitch and ornamentation, and the musical structure, with the names of patterns (moji-fu). The practice of writing these alongside texts brought musical literacy into narrative performance. This elementary form of notation went into nō, jōruri and other narratives, even into heike narrative by the Edo period, despite it being the province of blind performers.

What is not narrative about kōshiki? Clearly no stories with characters in the normal sense are evident; it is a form of preaching, appealing to the emotions, in order to engender devotion. It does not 'tell a story', but it 'preaches a message', and performs a ritual function. Of course anecdotes and illustrations are inserted into the narrative text, but they are not part of a continuous epic plot with consistent narrative unities. Kōshiki is indeed not performed *to* the listeners face to face, but towards the object of devotion.

This chapter has demonstrated that kōshiki is not derived from Chinese prosimetric narrative, that is, the alternation of spoken prose and sung verse.

This melodically delivered, non-metred text interspersed with melismatically sung verse in Chinese could be seen as prosimetric form, but there is no spoken delivery in kōshiki, except that some dan are followed instead of a kada by a spoken group of phrases for the 'transfer of merit' (ekō). This is not, however, expository prose.

The formulaic terms and concepts of kōshiki correspond closely to the heike terms shojū (first level), chūon (middle sound) and sanjū (third level). Furthermore, the term sanjū was passed on through heike into all branches of jōruri. For this reason in particular it has been said that kōshiki was the origin of this tradition of narrative music.

We can point to circumstantial evidence for the indigenous origin of the music of both kōshiki and heike. The musical structure of katarimono shōmyō is quite different from that of continental shōmyō. All katarimono shōmyō (genres such as rongi and hyōbyaku), not just kōshiki, use only the shojū melodic type, indicating that shojū came earlier than nijū and sanjū, and suggesting that the musical elaboration of the latter two originated in Japan.

Guelberg suggests that in Myōe's time kōshiki performance was not yet musically developed, meaning that shojū dominated, and that kōshiki was not seen as part of shōmyō, but rather as part of preaching and teaching. This implies that kōshiki's musical development was not contemporaneous with Genshin (tenth century), or even Myōe (twelfth century), but could have developed at the same time as heike musical narrative (thirteenth and fourteenth centuries). This means that kōshiki became musicalized around the same time as the formation of heike musical narration. Even earlier than this, the influence of biwa hōshi style narrative is fully possible, as biwa hōshi were active from the Heian period before the emergence of heike (Sawada 1994: 55–6).

The argument that kōshiki was earlier and therefore was the origin of heike musical form is not a foregone conclusion. It is quite possible that the three levels of musical delivery were influenced rather by indigenous Japanese approaches to narrative than continental shōmyō. However, the interpolation of poetic musical sections in Chinese between the long expository sections may show the influence of continental prosimetric practice: they are 'pure shōmyō'. This situates the narrative in a shōmyō liturgical context and gives it its hybrid character.

Whatever the direction and paths of influence may be, it is clear that kōshiki, and by extension, heike, jōruri and other related genres, do not adhere to the Chinese model of alternating sections of sung metrical verse and spoken non-metric prose. On the contrary, the sung narrative of kōshiki and heike, and many parts of other genres is not in poetic metre. In the next chapter we turn to heike as the first extant musical narrative of Japan.

Chapter 3
Heike Narrative: The Musical Recitation of *The Tale of the Heike*

Introduction

The musical recitation of *The Tale of the Heike* (*Heike monogatari*) is the most significant of all the Japanese performed narratives to survive to the present from medieval times.

The heike narrative began with war tales recited and circulated by priests and nuns, and passed into the hands of the blind, biwa (lute)-playing beggar priests called biwa hōshi. The tales eventually coalesced to form a continuous narrative, and were written down and edited by literati, to become the massive work that forms part of Japan's literary canon.

The core content of heike narrative was formed around historical events of the late twelfth century, and is a mixture of historical chronicle and interpolated material from setsuwa tales that have little historical basis. It served a ritual function to pacify the dead or to lead to salvation, but it was also a form of entertainment for many groups of people in the medieval period. *The Tale of the Heike* was a foundation narrative of the victorious Minamoto clan's shogunate, and subsequently the Ashikaga lineage. It was used for political legitimization by the Ashikaga bakufu, leading to elite patronage and control by the shogun.

Heike narrative could not remain under the control of the biwa hōshi, but crossed genre boundaries into nō, kōwaka and jōruri (Tokita 2003). Its popular highlights provided a wealth of content for subsequent narrative, theatre and literature, and in formal terms was foundational for subsequent music and theatrical narratives, namely nō, kōwaka and jōruri; also for folk ritual practices, such as the Daimokutate in Nara Prefecture (Oyler 2006a).

Heike established a highly productive musical idiom, a means of narrative expression through music which was elaborated in later contexts. We can only speculate on the exact nature of its formative musical influences, but it has clear structural and expressive links with later forms. Like kōshiki it seems to have developed from the musical practices of indigenous narrative performance.

The apocryphal tales or spin-offs (kōjitsudan) of heike led to *The Chronicle of Yoshitsune* (*Gikeiki*; see McCullough 1966; Oyler 2006b; Parker 2006) and the original eponymous jōruri narrative, then the take-up of these tales in nō, kōwaka, kabuki as well as in mature jōruri, displaying a 'malleability of episodes' (Oyler 2006b: 6).

There is no single 'author' of the heike narrative: from oral origins it became a text-based literary tradition as well as a performance tradition. In performance, whose continuous tradition is documented from the thirteenth century, the solo singer-narrator accompanies himself on the biwa, and the sung narrative is interspersed with instrumental interludes. The written *Tale* has come down to the modern period in a number of variant textual recensions.[1] The relation between these two forms has been the object of a great deal of intense debate, the key question being whether text preceded performance, or vice versa.

Originating around the same time was another epic narrative, the *Soga monogatari* (Oyler 2006b: 115–37), about a family revenge that also had political repercussions (see Chapter 5 for its links with the Chūshingura narrative and Chapter 7 for a kabuki version). This also originated as performed narrative – possibly performed by female reciters – and like the heike narrative provided a vast stock of material for later narrative and theatrical genres. Both these narrative cycles from the medieval period were foundational for later narrative and theatre. It was the heike, however, that had the greatest and lasting musical impact.

The Chūshingura stories and plays of the eighteenth century (see Chapter 5) also hark back to the Soga revenge narrative. Oyler urges us to question the autonomy of all these overlapping narratives, arguing that they do not just display intertextuality but that they actively feed on each other (2006b: 24). This suggests that over the centuries performed narratives and literary traditions were highly integrated. The intertextuality evident in the overlap of *The Tale of the Heike* with *Gikeiki* and *The Tale of the Soga Brothers* is akin to that of oral composition (ibid.: 17). Both the Heike and the Soga tales were concerned with revenge and warrior ethics. Revenge for one's lord was at times permitted, but family revenge was legally outlawed by the military government; it remained powerful, however, in the popular imagination.

As with kōshiki, the study of heike narrative is valuable in itself, but also because of its foundational importance for later narratives. This chapter outlines the historical events behind the *Tale*, and discusses the less historical religious and romantic elements, and the themes that emerge from the narrative. The generation of multiple versions in oral narrative performance is mirrored by the multiplicity of written versions of the *Tale*, making this a rich field for study of the reception and 'ownership' of a narrative. The chapter also examines debates about the origins ('authorship') of the *Tale* and contesting views concerning its orality and textualization. Thereafter, the generic musical analysis demonstrates the nature of heike's formulaic musical material. Two of the extant eight pieces in the Nagoya repertoire are analysed.

---

[1] The most widely read *Kakuichibon* version has 12 volumes, plus the 'Initiates' volume. Other versions have six, 20 and 48 volumes.

The Narrated Content: History and Legend

The Tale of the Heike tells of historical events which took place in Japan in the late twelfth century whereby the imperial institution lost its power (while retaining cultural authority) to the military houses or clans (the so-called 'samurai' class). *The Tale of the Heike* is a chronicle of the power struggle between the Taira (Heike) warrior house and the Minamoto (Genji) house, who established the shogunate, the military institution which governed Japan from 1192 to 1867. The central narrative concerns the destruction of the Heike clan, which had held near absolute power in the name of the emperor. Its defeat by the Genji clan marked the end of the Heian period (794–1185) and of direct court rule. The narrative both reported and helped make sense of the events by interpreting and re-interpreting them over a long period of time.

The Genji had been defeated by the Taira in the Hōgen (1156) and Heiji (1160) uprisings (following disputes over imperial succession), ushering in the era of the Taira's apogee (Oyler 2006b: 18–19). Already in 1132 Taira Tadamori had been granted access to the court and had acquired political influence. The culmination of Taira ascendancy came in the time of Tadamori's son Kiyomori, who ultimately rose to the rank of premier and appointed members of his family to major imperial posts.

Imperial politics used the two warrior houses to achieve individual aims and ambitions, ostensibly to protect the court against its enemies. The most manipulative was the retired (later cloistered) sovereign, Go-Shirakawa (1127–1192; r. 1155–1158), a significant but ambiguous figure throughout the conflict. Initially Kiyomori's patron until Kiyomori became too powerful and overweening, Go-Shirakawa utilized general dissatisfaction with the Taira domination to instigate a plot to get rid of Kiyomori in 1177. The plot to rebel at Shishigatani failed; Kiyomori found out and exiled the main perpetrators, Shunkan and two others.

In 1180 Go-Shirakawa encouraged his third son Mochihito to rise against the Taira with the military support of the Genji. This re-emergence of the Genji warriors as a force initiated the Genpei War (1180–1185).

After Kiyomori died in 1181, his son Munemori led the Taira in battle against the rebellion of Genji Yoshinaka in 1183. When the victorious Yoshinaka entered the capital, the courtiers fled from Kyoto with the young Emperor Antoku and took to ships on the Inland Sea, creating a floating court in exile, drifting to Shikoku, then Kyūshū. The Genji attack was led by Yoshitsune in 1184 and 1185. The Taira were defeated in key battles at Ichinotani (near Kobe), then at Yashima (Shikoku), and met final defeat at Dannoura (Kyūshū).

In the end, the matter of who won and who lost is ambiguous. History knows that the victor, Yoritomo, did not retain power into the next generation but was taken over by the Hōjō regents.

The Tale of the Heike as a Romantic and Religious Tale

The Tale of the Heike (*Heike monogatari*) was viewed as a historical chronicle up to the late Edo period. However, as the title 'Tale' (monogatari) indicates, it is not just a chronicle concerned with historical events – indeed, there are many discrepancies between the *Tale* and other historical sources.[2] It became an expression of the culture of the military elite, but was also redolent of court culture, since the defeated Taira had become closely associated with the court. Furthermore, it has a strong religious message of Buddhist resignation and contains many salvation narratives. Over its formative stages, *The Tale of the Heike* incorporated stand-alone setsuwa stories and framed them in the discourse of a salvation narrative. These stories, often with an element of romance, were drawn from the oral tales that were circulated in early medieval Japan by itinerant preacher-storytellers such as the Kōya hijiri (Gorai 1975), and by groups of nuns (Hyōdō 2011: 154). Anecdotes from Chinese literature were also included in the *Tale* to forge the heike narrative world.

The *Tale* thus brings out various themes through the narration of the central events and the numerous side-plots. For example, the Buddhist doctrine of impermanence and evanescence, that all who rise must fall, is expressed in the opening lines about Gion shōja:

The Jetvana Temple bells	Gion shōja no kane no koe
ring the passing of all things.	Shogyō mujō no hibiki ari.
Twinned sal trees, white in full flower	Shara sōju no hana no iro
declare the great man's certain fall.[3]	jōsha hissui no kotowari o arawasu.

By depicting Kiyomori, head of the Taira clan, as a despot, the *Tale* passes judgement on Taira arrogance, and upholds the legitimacy of the Genji ascendancy. At the same time, clear sympathy for the defeated Taira after Kiyomori's downfall is evident; the fall of the proud becomes a moral lesson against pride and vanity, emphasizing the Buddhist teaching of evanescence and impermanence. The court, too, is not immune from criticism in this regard (Hyōdō 2009: 100–101).

Some versions (notably Kakuichi's) in particular convey a strong message reflecting the Pure Land doctrine whereby salvation was considered to be within easy reach for those who called on the name of Amida Buddha when dying. Prominent elements of religious teaching reveal strong affinities with sekkyō preaching by high-ranking priests (for example Chōken, 1126–1203) and by both male and female itinerants; it has already been pointed out that some parts are strongly reminiscent of kōshiki texts.

---

[2] Compare for example Kujō Kanezane's diary, *Gyokuyō*, the historical tale, *Azuma kagami*, and Jien's *Gukanshō*. Discrepancies also exist between heike textual variants.

[3] Royall Tyler's translation (Tyler 2012b: 3).

In the formative stages of the performed narrative, the most significant function is believed, by literary scholars influenced by folklore research, to have been the ritual appeasement (chinkon) of angry spirits (goryō). They argue that the performance of the battle tales functioned as a requiem or a propitiation for the troubled souls of those who were defeated or killed in battle, especially the Taira who were systematically liquidated by the victorious Genji. Through the performing of these stories by blind, lute-playing priests (biwa hōshi), the souls of the dead were propitiated and rendered nonthreatening for the living (Fukuda 1981).

Origins and Transmission

Even as the modern academic discipline of historiography brought into question its historical credibility, the *Tale* has continued to be highly valued as national literature, and scholars have put an enormous amount of effort into studying the various extant texts and the relations between them (see Bialock 2000). The question as to how the *Tale* came into being has vexed scholars for the past 100 years, and still the answer is hotly debated. A corollary question is *why* it came into being. After all, why would blind minstrels have needed a written text?[4]

This debate has to be waged on the basis of very limited materials, starting with a brief account in the *Tsurezuregusa* (see below), a collection of essays written in the fourteenth century, 200 years after the events. Having little more than this to go on, Meiji period scholars were convinced that there was a single author whose identity only had to be ascertained. This view was confirmed by western concepts of literary authorship, which were introduced into Japan in the nineteenth century. By the postwar period, the multiple versions of the *Tale* started to be systematically scrutinized, and the idea of composite authorship took hold. There followed a search for the original or oldest surviving text, an ur-text, relying partly on internal textual evidence, and partly on references to the *Tale* in other early written documents which had come to light (Yamashita 1993; Konishi 1991: 343–9).

The Existence of Multiple Texts

Transmission of texts and transmission (denshō) of oral performance are two different dimensions; and yet, there was interaction between the two. Hyōdō has raised the issue of ownership and control of the narrative by different groups, including the biwa hōshi guild (shoku yashiki, later the Tōdō) headed by Kakuichi.

---

[4] Hyōdō explains that of course the many blind minstrels who made a living reciting the *Heike monogatari* had no idea of the existence of a text, until they were brought under the control of the Tōdō guild whose head had connections with and patronage of the military government, leading to the creation of the authoritative text by Kakuichi in 1371 (Hyōdō 2009: 143).

The existence of dozens of variant texts attests to the power of the heike narrative itself, but ultimately many parallel versions came into being and were transmitted.[5]

The fact that the heike narrative exists in multiple written versions supports the view that it is not a single 'work of literature' with a single clearly identifiable author (or editor, compiler). Broadly, there are three types of text: yomihon ('reading texts', with the most variants); kataribon ('reciting texts'); and from the Edo period, fuhon, score-texts with musical notations. Although the texts are conventionally categorized as either performance texts or reading texts, this is not an absolute division (Table 3.1).

Table 3.1   A comparison of kataribon and yomihon texts

'Kataribon' (for performance)	'Yomihon' (for reading)
e.g. *Yashirobon* *Kakuichibon* *Nagatobon; Genpei tōjōroku* (Oyler 2006b: 16)	e.g. *Genpei jōsuiki* *Enkeibon*
In Japanese	In Chinese (kanbun)
Focus on Heike defeat	Focus on Genji takeover

The kataribon group of texts, also called tōdōkei – meaning connected with the Tōdō guild of blind performers – were produced by blind biwa hōshi. They are written in vernacular Japanese, but, although supposedly for performance, have been polished and influenced by literary editorship. Having been worked on and re-edited many times, a lot of strong oral features have been eliminated: for example, the narrator does not have a persona directly addressing his listeners. The *Yashirobon* was connected with the now defunct Yasaka-ryū performance lineage. The *Kakuichibon*, however, is the most representative example of kataribon, dictated at the behest of Kakuichi – in 1371, according to the colophon (okugaki) – in order to resolve any disputes about a correct version (Hyōdō 2000: 10–11). It is the most widely reprinted and read heike text in the twentieth century, and has been the basis for three complete English translations. It displays strong influence from the Jōdo Buddhist sect doctrine of salvation. It is unique in being followed by a five-chapter epilogue, the 'Kanjō no maki' ('The Initiates Book'), that focuses on a retelling of the events of Heike downfall by Kenreimon'in, the mother of the drowned boy Emperor Antoku and daughter of Kiyomori. They are a guide to the path to salvation for the Taira dead, and are reminiscent of kōshiki preaching, expounding the doctrine of transmigration and salvation.

The yomihon group of texts are written in Chinese (kanbun). They are more prosaic and less lyrical in style, and focus on the Genji take-over of power.

---

[5] The *Soga monogatari* has nothing like this number of variant texts, but is also indisputably of oral origin without a specific author.

They include some very long versions of the text, such as the *Genpei jōsuiki* and the *Enkeibon*, a short version (the *Ryakubon*), and the *Shibu kassenjō-bon*, a compilation of four war tales: Hōgen, Heiji, Heike and Jōkyūki, all recently translated by Tyler (2012a and 2012b). The set of four tales was copied around 1446–1447, but was probably compiled in 1323–1324, the earliest known full version.

When commercial printing developed in the early 1600s, rufubon (popular versions or vulgate) texts were printed. The most commonly printed version was based on the *Kakuichibon* and was widely circulated.

Texts with Musical Notations

In the Edo period, musical notations (fuhon) were developed. This is when heike narrative became a musical form (heikyoku), according to Hyōdō (1994). The 1737 *Heike ginpu* and the 1776 *Heike mabushi* both systematized the musical setting of the narrative, creating an orthodox or correct musical realization, making it consistent from one performance to another. This clinches the loss of orality from heike performance. The most significant example of the third group of texts, the musical scores (fuhon), is the *Heike mabushi*. It is very close to the *Kakuichibon*, but instead of the chapters being arranged in chronological order, they appear in the order that they were to be learnt (maki dōshi style). The episodes early in the book show greater musical variation and more formal structuring in comparison with the later ones, suggesting that they were more popular and therefore performed more frequently as independent pieces (Komoda 2003: 187ff.).

Performance Traditions: Singing the Tale

The Tale of the Heike is also a story told, or rather sung. Traditions of performed narrative can be seen to follow several stages of development, through rise and decline; clearly heike performance is now in decline. Komoda (1998) outlines four stages of heike's musical development. With the attrition of the repertoire, the eight surviving episodes in Nagoya do not really tell the 'grand narrative' of Taira defeat and Genji ascendancy.

Of the different performance lineages from the medieval era, the best documented ones are the Yasaka and the Ichikata. The Ichikata later gave rise to Maeda, and to Hatano (active until the Taishō period). Maeda was prominent in Kyoto, Nagoya, Edo and eventually Tsugaru and is the only surviving lineage.

The Accompanying Instrument

Any performance of *The Tale of the Heike* is a musical one, accompanied by the biwa (pi'pa in Chinese), a pear-shaped lute originating in western Asia. There are several types of biwa in Japan. The one used for heike narrative (the heike biwa) derived from the gagaku biwa (Komoda 2003: 314–29; Komoda 2008; de Ferranti 2000), with which it shares its rounded shape and the (bent) design of the peg box. While larger than the various so-called mōsō ('blind priest') biwa of the Kyūshū zatō, it is smaller than the gagaku biwa; furthermore the plectrum (bachi) has a distinctive shape, the instrument has five frets instead of four, and the playing technique is '[u]nlike [that for the] *gaku-biwa*, [as] left-hand pressure is applied between the frets, and is used to produce pitches raised by a major 2nd or less at some frets' (de Ferranti in *Grove Music Online*: Biwa). These features are common to all other biwa in Japan (sometimes called the katarimono biwa) apart from the gagaku biwa (de Ferranti 2009).

Who Were the biwa hōshi?

The origins of the *Heike monogatari* are hotly contested, particularly since the advent of orality theory, and yet they are still shrouded in mystery. Issues that have engaged researchers in the modern era include: authorship and identifying an urtext; an epic on the European model; oral origins as conceived for a Homeric epic on the Parry-Lord model; the identity of the narrator. A key factor in this debate is the role of the biwa hōshi.

The blind biwa hōshi (lute priests) were first documented in the tenth century before the heike events occurred, but it is not known what they performed then (Hyōdō 2009: 31–6). Their origins remain shadowy and subject to speculation. Fukuda (1981), for example, builds up a pre-Buddhist picture of the biwa hōshi as the descendants of the kataribe and the asobi-be, hereditary ritual narrators of the early proto-historical period, who are depicted in the *Nihon shoki* (Aston 1972: 389; Book XXX.8, AD 688, 7th month, 11th day) as performing funeral rites for the ruler. Their performance involved, as well as song and dance, a recitation of the deeds of previous generations of rulers, serving to legitimize the new regime. These pre-Buddhist ritual specialists, blind shamans who performed funeral rites, Fukuda believes, became attached to major temples after the advent of Buddhism, and adopted the biwa when it entered Japan from the continent.

History of the Performance Tradition

The idea that the *Tale* originated as an oral narrative became more widespread from the 1970s, under the influence of the Parry-Lord theory of oral narratives and introduced to heike studies by Kenneth Butler (Butler 1966). This view sees the originators of the heike narrative as the biwa hōshi who recited war tales for the sake of the dead and the bereaved at funeral rites for those who died in battle. Other performers of narratives of Buddhist content, as part of popular Buddhist evangelism in temples and on the streets, may also have contributed episodes to the *Tale*. Against the background of the cataclysmic events that marked the end of the ordered Heian period, the storytelling of such people served to interpret these events for the common people in a Buddhist framework. Eventually, this gave rise to an epic literature in the tradition of war tales (gunkimono). (See Varley 1994 for a study of war tales before and after the heike narrative.) Hyōdō gives a more complex view: episodes about figures such as Ariō, Kumagai, Kagekiyo tell us that they returned to monasteries where they entered religious life and circulated their stories through a network of itinerant ascetics; it was from such people that the biwa hōshi learned the heike stories (Hyōdō 2011).

At the same time, chronicles of the Heike wars were written in the established literary genre of the historical tale (rekishi monogatari, for example *Masu kagami*, covers 1183–1333, and the chronicle of the Kamakura bakufu, *Azuma kagami*) and as battle tales (gunki monogatari, for example *Shōmonki, Heiji, Hōgen*). According to the *Tsurezuregusa*, the first such history appeared 35 years after the wars, between 1218 and 1221, the work of the lay priest and courtier Yukinaga:

> During the reign of the Emperor Go-Toba, a former official from Shinano named Yukinaga ... wrote the *Heike Monogatari* and taught a blind man named Shōbutsu to recite it ... He wrote about Yoshitsune with a detailed knowledge, but omitted many facts about Noriyori, perhaps because he did not know much about him. Shōbutsu, a native of the Eastern Provinces, questioned the soldiers from his part of the country about military matters and feats of arms, then got Yukinaga to write them down. *Biwa* entertainers today imitate what was Shōbutsu's natural voice. (Keene 1967: 186)

It is important to note that Yukinaga's father, Fujiwara Yukitaka features in the *Tale* (Tyler 2012b: 27–8). It seems that Yukinaga based his chronicle, written in Chinese, on existing historical records of the battles and events, perhaps the *Chishō monogatari* (*Tale of the Chishō Era*), referring to the era when the battles between the Heike and the Genji took place (Konishi 1991: 345–6). He also, however, incorporated much material dictated to him by oral storytellers. This method was not entirely new, since oral material seems to be present in the earliest military tale, *Shōmonki* (Rabinovitch 1986). Yukinaga's text then passed back into the hands of the storytellers, who reworked it into a style closer to true oral storytelling. Finally in 1371, the biwa hōshi Akashi Kakuichi dictated a version which incorporated the best of the oral revisions (Butler 1966), and this version, the *Kakuichibon*, written down nearly 200 years after the events, has become the most familiar version.

Hyōdō argues that *The Tale of the Heike* was too important to be left as popular culture of the streets. It was the history of the regime shift from the Taira (Heike) to the Minamoto (Genji) clan, and hence of the founding of the shogunate; it was a legend of legitimizing authorization. Yoshimitsu sought a differen kind of succession from that of the emperor and powerful families, so he used heike, the new art form, to add to his prestige and underline his power (Hyōdō 2000: 25).

From the late sixteenth century, heike narrative became an amateur art form of dilettantes, practised together with other popular pursuits of the military class: tea ceremony, renga and haiku. The Tokugawa shogunate renewed the official patronage of the blind guilds after the hiatus of the period of decentralization and the warring states (Katō 1974: 146), and made heike their official music, performed on ceremonial occasions such as just before the New Year, accessions and funerals (Hyōdō 2009: 160). Hence, the high-ranking members of the Tōdō guild hierarchy (kengyō and kōtō) were privileged with higher incomes than those lower in rank, and enjoyed high social status; some received official stipends (Groemer 2001: 357). So affluent was the Tōdō guild that it developed a money-lending business from the seventeenth century (ibid.: 357–78).

The involvement of sighted amateurs led to the development of musically annotated performance versions such as the *Heike mabushi* (1776). In this way, the biwa hōshi performance became reduced to one fixed musical realization, in contrast to the medieval period.

Extant heike Performance Traditions

Two traditions of heike recitation survive: the Tsugaru lineage based in Sendai and the Nagoya lineage. The previous generation of Nagoya musicians had three active transmitters, but now only one active blind professional (kengyō) remains who has inherited the tradition orally, Imai Tsutomu (b. 1958), possessing a remaining repertoire of only eight pieces. In collaboration with the musicologist Komoda Haruko he created a revived version of the piece in 1990 (*Kaidō Kudari*; Nippon Columbia 1991) and later a partial revival of *Gion shōja*, relying on the basic notation of the *Heike mabushi* (Komoda 2009 CD set).

The Sendai transmission derives from heike as the amateur pastime (tashinami) of bushi dilettantes in the Edo period. The Sendai branch of heike narrative came into existence after a retainer of the Tsugaru Domain, Kusumi Taiso (1815–1882), studied heike in the mid-nineteenth century. He stipulated in his will that heike should continue to be transmitted (Komoda 2003: 7). His son, Tateyama Zennoshin, and grandson, Tateyama Kōgo (1894–1989), both preserved this tradition through conducting historical research, performance, recording and teaching. This Tsugaru tradition has recently flowered into a viable practice with performers such as Tokyo-based Hashimoto Toshie. Because they are sighted and use as their score the *Heike mabushi* text-notation, they can perform any episode or piece of the *Tale*.

In 1871, abolition of the feudal class structure meant that the biwa hōshi (the Tōdō) lost their patronage and their status as official musicians, and with their loss of status, support for their performance was taken away (Katō 1974 [1984]: 465–73), leaving the two remnants of heike performance in Nagoya and Sendai.

It should be noted too that heike narrative was preserved in tandem with the development of the lyrical chamber music, jiuta-sōkyoku, as the same blind performers of heike also played koto and shamisen, the two new main instruments of the Edo period. It was they who developed this art music, which has become perhaps the most representative genre of Japanese music. This multi-skill talent must have contributed to the musical elaboration and refinement of heike as well as its preservation through expanding the economic viability of music for the blind. It became part of Japan's art music (kinsei hōgaku).

Orality and Musicality in heike Narrative

The oral-formulaic theory, or the Parry-Lord theory, is concerned with two concepts: that of the *formula*, a group of words (a line or phrase) which is regularly employed under the same metrical conditions to express a given essential idea, and the *theme*, an idea regularly used in telling a tale (Lord 1960 [2000]: 30 and 68). The heavily edited *Kakuichibon* differs in many significant ways from the material which gave rise to the Parry-Lord theory. Because of its considerable interaction with upper-class literate culture, the narrative came to rely to a degree on written texts and notations for its transmission so that the performance has become fixed, without improvisation. In addition, as we have seen, the texts gave rise to an independent literary tradition, and even the so-called performance texts (kataribon) have been worked over by literary editors.

The *Kakuichibon* yet retains vestiges of orality. There are examples of verbal formulas such as the phrase 'saru hodo ni' which begins many episodes in *The Tale of the Heike*, including *Nasu no Yoichi* (see Watson 2003: 107–14). It is also found frequently in kōwaka and in ōzatsuma narrative. Examples of the narrative theme also abound: the description of the dress or armour of the hero (see *Nasu no Yoichi*); lists of warriors; ritual name-calling before engaging in combat. Furthermore, the episodic nature of the compilation strongly reflects the way oral sources were drawn on for individual episodes.

The most conspicuous indicator of orality is the musical formulaism in the form of fixed melody types, commonly called kyokusetsu, which I call substyles, and patterns, that constitute the musical aspect of heike performance.

Oral-formulaic theory suggests that the use of formulaic material (in the verbal aspect of the narrative) indicates orality, or residual orality. In heike narrative, the orality of the musical aspect of the narrative has persisted longer, since musical notations have not played a major role in its performance or transmission. More significant than written notations has been the use of named melodic patterns as a means of preserving and transmitting the musical tradition. Melodic patterns acquired some of the functions of notation, and can be called oral notation, that subsequently came to be used alongside the texts to indicate what melody to use.

Historically, the elaboration of these extended melodic patterns seems to have post-dated the era of 'composition in performance' of purely oral narrative, which forms the basis of the oral-formulaic theory. The function of formulaic musical material cannot be assumed to be the same as that of verbal formulas, but analogous to it.

Generic Musical Analysis

Analysis here is based on the eight main pieces in the current Nagoya transmission. The attrition of the blind performance tradition, especially in the modern era, has left only those pieces that are in greatest demand.

Table 3.2   Vertical structure of heike narrative

Contexts	Various; one (blind male) performer self-accompanied with biwa; book-length textual renditions
Larger work	Approximately 200 chapters
Piece	The chapter or piece (ku or kyoku)
Section	Extended melodic patterns (shōdan or kyokusetsu)
Phrase	Cadential melodies
	Biwa preludes and interludes

Table 3.2 shows the vertical structure of heike narrative, the top level of which is the whole narrative, the chapter level being equivalent to a piece for one performance, and variable levels of sections and sub-sections, according to different researchers: Komoda identifies 'scenes' (daidan and dan) as well as kyokusetsu, the latter being equivalent to the shōdan ('small section'), the most important level for musical analysis. These small sections (kyokusetsu) have traditional names, such as kudoki, sanjū and so on, that appear in the text-scores.

The Tale of the Heike has approximately 200 chapters or titled sections (called ku in the performance tradition), the number differing in variant texts. The whole 'work' did not always divide the same way into 200 chapters. Moreover, the ku was not a stable unit of performance until textual chapter division came to dictate performance. As a performance unit, in some textual versions, different cut-off points and combinations of episodes formed a ku (Hyōdō 2000). Many of the ku consist of more than one episode, sometimes only loosely linked, sometimes neatly embedded in analeptic (flashback) style. *Nasu no Yoichi* is one unified episode consistent with the ku. *Yokobue*, on the other hand, is an embedded narrative, framed by a narrative only loosely connected. It has several scenes spanning many years. However, the framing narrative has not been transmitted in the performance tradition, only the embedded narrative, which stands alone as a performance item.

Watson (2003: 116–18) cites evidence from the fifteenth century diary *Kanmon gyoki* to suggest that the heike was rarely performed as a continuous complete narrative, although this format did exist (ichibu heike), however unrealistic for both performer and listener. In performance, typically one episode forms a performance unit, but performances of several ku together, and even performances of the whole have occurred in the past, lasting several days. Another mode involved two performers (tsure heike), which Hyōdō argues is a throwback to the ritual performances of the manzai and saizō, ideas of duality and balance to find a proper level of auspicious energy. It also enabled the apprentice to perform with the master and be trained (see Hyōdō 2011: 169).

There are several different categories of piece, including read documents (yomimono) and secret pieces (hiden). Fushimono 'melodic pieces' are elegant, courtly and feature the pattern orikoe (Table 3.3). Hiroimono 'valiant pieces' are martial, and feature the hiroi pattern. The Nagoya tradition has shrunk, even since the early twentieth century, and now transmits eight of these pieces, not all of them in their entirety. Four of the remaining eight pieces in the Nagoya transmission are 'melodic pieces' (fushimono), and four are 'valiant pieces' (hiroimono). It is interesting to note that these pieces appear in the first three volumes of the *Heike mabushi* (Komoda 2003: 283) and that most are interludes featuring characters peripheral to the main narrative. They are also the most musically interesting and varied pieces (ibid.: 277).

Table 3.3   Fushimono and hiroimono

Fushimono 'melodic pieces'	Hiroimono 'valiant pieces'
Sotoba nagashi	Suzuki
Kōyō	Ikezuki
Chikubushima mōde	Ujigawa
Yokobue	Nasu no Yoichi

Sections and Substyles

Each piece consists of sections or paragraphs (scenes or narrative sections) according to narrative content.

Like kōshiki, heike narrative uses multiple melodies, or multiple styles of delivery. The musical aspect of heike recitation is made up of a succession of formulaic musical sections, all of which are named. Each such section is characterized by an extended melody type – that is, it has one main style of musical delivery and ends with a cadential formula. These are narrative substyles (see Chapter 1). These heike melody types are the equivalent of the substyles of kōshiki. Some have more internal development and structure; however, they are not fixed melodies. Their length is not predetermined, but varies according to the needs of the text.

The sense of a distinction between the beginning and the end of a piece is relatively weak, and sections can be piled up indefinitely without any difficulty, but a number of pieces show a tendency towards a dramatic climax, since certain melodies function to produce a musical climax, like sanjū in kōshiki. There are, however, no special melodies which can only be used as opening or closing formulas for a piece. The narrative structure is thus relatively loose.

Most sections are introduced by, and hence separated by a biwa prelude corresponding to the substyle or extended melodic pattern of the section.

The names of the formulaic melodies eventually came to be written as a shorthand for the musical realization of a passage. This 'letter notation' (moji-fu) was used in conjunction with neumes (hakase) which indicated melodic movement, and with some symbols indicating pitch, such as jō, chū, ge and so on.

The only spoken delivery in heike is shirakoe. However, it is not used for dramatic speech; it is only another type of narrative delivery.

Within the typical piece, several substyles or musical patterns can be called on. There are over 40 such named musical units, which Komoda classifies into 13 groups of patterns (1993: 165). Further, she attempts to see back into the mists of time to trace the historical development of heike musical narrative. She identifies two groups of kyokusetsu. The first group she calls the biwa hōshi type: kudoki, hiroi; the second group she calls the kōshiki type: shojū, chūon, sanjū, orikoe, sashikoe (Komoda 1998: 263).

Table 3.4 summarizes the principal groups of melody types and their possible alignment with different sources, as hypothesized by Komoda. Whether the heike patterns should be viewed in this way is still not conclusive, but deserves serious consideration.

Table 3.4 The principal heike pattern types classified according to hypothesized origin

biwa hōshi tradition	kudoki
	hiroi
Buddhist music (kōshiki) tradition	shojū
	chūon
	sanjū
	orikoe (developed from sanjū)
	sashikoe (developed from shojū)

Source: After Komoda (1993 and 1998).

Nijū and chūon have basically the same meaning in this context: the second or middle register. Komoda quotes Gamō in noting that kōshiki nijū ends with the transitional phrase chūon. The heike chūon is the equivalent of kōshiki nijū.

The principal melodies used in the eight pieces in the Nagoya transmission
In comparing kōshiki and heike we confront the issue of the transmission of terminology that changes in meaning or musical content (Table 3.5).

The principal melody types (Table 3.6) are preceded by a biwa prelude, called 'bachi'. There is no 'bachi' before the 'dependent' patterns – such as kowarisage and kudari (actually cadential patterns) – only before major melody types. Although sashikoe is similar in function to kudoki and shirakoe, of these three, only kudoki has the punctuating bachi.

Table 3.5   Comparison of kōshiki and heike musical structure and patterns

Kōshiki	Heike
(no equivalent)	shirakoe
shojū	kudoki hiroi
nijū	chūon shojū
sanjū	sanjū orikoe
chūon	(no equivalent)

Source: After Sawada (2002).

Table 3.6   The principal heike substyles

Name of substyle	Function	Examples in transcriptions
Kudoki	Basic narrative	Example 3.1
Shirakoe	Basic narrative (spoken)	
Sashikoe	Basic narrative (melodic)	
Shojū	Melodic narrative	
Chūon	Melodic narrative	
Sanjū	Melodic narrative	Example 3.3
Hiroi	Content-related	Example 3.2
Orikoe	Content-related	Example 3.1

Kudoki   Kudoki is one of the most extensively used patterns in heike. It is the 'basic style' and appears in all pieces. The name implies the sense of 'explaining at great length'. It is a simple narrative style close to natural speech delivery, used to get through a lot of text quickly, with the stichic-like repetition of the same simple melodic movement between two main tones one fourth apart over a long narrative section, with the occasional inclusion of the pitch one semitone above the lower tone. The upper tone is nuanced in its approach and in leaving often touches on the note above. Kudoki can be used for an indefinite amount of text, short or long. All eight pieces open with this. This term as the name of formulaic musical material appears in nō and jōruri, but with a different meaning and function. In jōruri it is the emotional highlight of a piece, similar to sanjū in kōshiki and heike (see Chapter 6).

Shirakoe   Shirakoe appears in seven of the eight pieces. It is not sung delivery but spoken quietly and rapidly. Even more than kudoki, it can dispose of a large amount of text in a short period. Although not sung, its intonation is notated in the

Heike mabushi, indicating the shape that phrases should take. It concludes with a spoken cadence called hazumi.

Sashikoe Sashikoe functions similarly to kudoki and shirakoe, but is more melismatic and uses a different scalar structure, because it developed from shojū (Komoda 1998).

Shojū, chūon, sanjū As shown in Chapter 2, the melodic structure of kōshiki is based on three named pitch areas set in a framework of intervals of a fourth: shojū (first level = low), nijū (second level = middle), sanjū (third level = high); each represents formulaic melodies or substyles. Similarly, heike has melodies called shojū (first level), chūon (middle sound) and sanjū (third level), each representing both pitch areas and formulaic melodies. See Table 3.5 for their corresponding kōshiki terms. Komoda argues that these heike melodies, which are all melismatic and musical, originate from kōshiki, whereas kudoki and hiroi originate from biwa hōshi singing.

Shojū appears in seven of the eight pieces, and as the final melody of three (*Ikezuki*, *Ujikawa kassen*, *Sotoba nagashi*). It has a variety of applications and is used in any category of piece. It occupies a low pitch area, and is melismatic and melodic.

Chūon appears in the four fushimono pieces, and at the end of *Kōyō* and *Yokobue*, and in the sequence shojū-chūon in *Chikubushima mōde*. It starts in syllabic delivery, then becomes melismatic; it is focused in the pitch area of middle b for the greater part of its duration, descending to the lower pitch areas in the last very drawn-out phrases of the section.

All eight pieces except *Nasu no Yoichi* end with either shojū or chūon or both in sequence (shojū-chūon).

Sanjū appears as a musical climax in seven of the eight pieces. It is not necessarily tied to any particular type of narrative content, or any particular type of piece, though nearly half of the examples in the whole *Heike mabushi* relate to identifying the month and day of the action (Suzuki 2007). For example, the sanjū section in *Yokobue* begins 'Koro wa nigatsu tōka amari no ...' and in *Nasu no Yoichi*, 'Koro wa nigatsu jūhachinichi ...' (but see Suzuki's cautioning against concluding that this is the only text type). Musically, sanjū is the most elaborate of the formulaic melodies, melismatic and at a high pitch register. It sits in the fourth between top e and top a, touching occasionally on top b. It has two parts, separated by a biwa interlude, the second part descending to the two adjacent fourths below, finishing with its own quite long cadential pattern, sanjū kudari. In *Yokobue* this comprises six phrases.

Hiroi and orikoe   Hiroi and orikoe are unique in heike music as being linked with specific narrative content.

Hiroi appears as a musical climax in the four hiroimono pieces. It is used for valiant battle scenes or other military-related description and is delivered in a forceful, emphatic, mainly syllabic manner. In *Suzuki* it is used for Kiyomori's auspicious experience, in *Nasu no Yoichi*, for describing the armour of the main character. Compared with kudoki, its melody is of a complex type, containing other formulaic melodies often in a set sequence, such as the sequence ryo – ge – jō. Pieces containing lots of this are hiroimono. *Nasu no Yoichi* features hiroi in two separate sections (4 and 16). Komoda says it is the equivalent of kudoki at a higher pitch range. It would seem that kōshiki nijū is close to heike hiroi, both being placed in the middle tetrachord.

Orikoe appears as a musical climax in the four fushimono pieces. So named because it uses the ornamental vocal technique called oru (break) at its beginning, the melody centres on the alternation between the tones upper b and middle e, that is, the middle of the vocal range, with some internal development, starting with syllabic delivery and ending with more melismatic delivery. It is used for sections with lyrical, romantic or religious narrative content. *Yokobue* features this melody twice (in sections 2 and 10).

Other melodies   Kamiuta and shimouta are used for waka exchanged between characters, as in *Yokobue*. Kamiuta is very similar to chūon. If there are two, the second is called shimouta, which uses a lower pitch register (see section 7 of the *Yokobue* structural diagram in Table 3.7). The waka can be considered quotations, textually and musically, as they are distinct from the bulk of heike narrative. Other quotations include the occasional imayō song and read documents or letters.

Phrases
Heike text is not metric, but neither could it be called simple prose.[6] In some sections, for example sanjū sections, the text tends to be 'poetic', arranged in couplet style after Chinese poetry (tsuiku) or in lines more or less close to the 7-5 syllable system after Japanese poetry. The phrases, whether tending towards some metric pattern or, as is most common, of irregular length, are punctuated by a couple or a few strokes of the biwa. Only rarely does the biwa play during the delivery of the narrative.

Musical phrases are an integral part of the substyle melodies. The cadential phrases of each section are more melismatic, and descend to a lower pitch region. This applies even to the pattern sage, the cadence of the syllabic kudoki. Some finals, such as kudari, which follows sanjū, comprise more than one phrase, and function like a sub-section.

---

[6] Partly for this reason, Tyler chose to divide the more musically delivered parts of the text into lines in his translation (Tyler 2012b).

Discussion and Analysis of Two Pieces: *Yokobue* and *Nasu no Yoichi*

These two contrasting pieces, one a fushimono and the other a hiroimono, have remained in the extant repertoire of the biwa hōshi tradition – that is, the Nagoya transmission – to the present day. Neither is a crucial part of the fight between the two major parties in the conflict. They are episodes of romance which have an appeal independent of the major events of the story, both portraying a minor figure, not the major players. *Yokobue* highlights the pathos and suffering caused by unrequited love and the way it necessitates Buddhist resignation. It is not directly connected to the war, but relates to the broader elegiac Buddhist theme of the *Tale*. *Nasu no Yoichi* illustrates a delight in the shooting prowess of a young otherwise unknown warrior.

Loosely linked to the major concerns of the *Tale*, each episode possibly represents separate oral narrative traditions woven into the larger more complex narrative that grew, and was eventually formed by educated courtiers, into a literary work. Hyōdō argues that such stories were generated and circulated by those residing at various religious centres around Kyoto and that they soon found their way into the repertoire of the biwa hōshi. Several people involved in the conflict retired to such centres and devoted themselves to Buddhist devotion, and their accounts of events were told by others at those centres. For example, the Kōya hijiri were no doubt responsible for the circulation of the *Yokobue* tale (Hyōdō 2011: 147–8). *Nasu no Yoichi*, on the other hand, portrays the warrior ethic, culture and belief in the god Hachiman, and would appear to originate from the earliest biwa hōshi battle tales. It is typical of the earlier war tales.

Yokobue

Table 3.7   Outline of *Yokobue*

Sections	Text (number of phrases)	FMM*
(1) Koremori's journey from Yashima to Kōyasan. (No longer performed)	Saruhodo ni Komatsu no sanmi	**kudoki** sage
	Waka, Fukiage, Sotōrihime no kami	**chūon**
(2) Koremori, resigned to not rejoining wife and child in the capital, journeys to Kōyasan. (No longer performed)	Kore yori yamazutai	**shojū**
	Kono mi sae torawarete	**shojū-chūon**
(3) Takiguchi's love for Yokobue; his father's disapproval. Takiguchi counters his father's disapproval by quoting two Chinese figures, who though famous are dead and gone, no different from the spark of a flint.	Kōya ni toshigoro shiritamaeru hijiri ari (12)	(kudoki bachi) **kudoki**
	(Anagachi ni) isamekereba Takiguchi moushikeru wa	sage
	Seiōbo to iishi hito (8) (Sekika no hikari ni kotonarazu.)	(orikoe bachi) **orikoe**
(4) He replies to his father that life is too short to put up with a partner one does not love, and resolves to takes vows.	Tatoi hito jōmyō to iedomo (4)	(sashikoe bachi) **sashikoe**
	Yume maboroshi no (3)	(chūon bachi) **chūon I**
	Omowashiki mono nō (8)	**chūon II**
(5) Yokobue is upset to have been abandoned, and journeys to Saga to look for Takiguchi.	Yokobue kono yoshi o tsutaekiite (5)	(kudoki bachi) **kudoki**
	Dairi o ba magire idete	sage
	Saga no kata e zo akogarekeru	
	Koro wa nigatsu tōka amari no (5)	(sanjū bachi) **sanjū**
	Hitokata naranu awaresa mo (6)	(kudari)

continued

Table 3.7   continued

Sections	Text (number of phrases)	FMM*
(6) Takiguchi refuses to meet Yokobue. Takiguchi doubts he could refuse her if she came again, so he removes to Kōyasan.	Sumi-arashitaru sōbō ni	(shirakoe bachi) **shirakoe**
	... kaeshikeru.	(hazumi)
	Yokobue nasake nō urameshikeredomo (2)	(kudoki bachi) **kudoki**
	(Sono nochi Takiguchi Nyūdō) dōjuku no sō ni katarikeru wa	(sage)
	Kore mo yo ni shizuka ni te (7)	(orikoe bachi) **orikoe**
	Itoma mōshite to te (3)	**shojū**
(7) Yokobue is resigned and enters the Hokkeji temple in Nara. Exchange of waka between Yokobue and Takiguchi. She dies soon after.	Sono nochi Yokobue mo (3)	**sashikoe**
	Soru made wa (5)	(uta bachi) **kamiuta**
	Yokobue no henji ni	(hansage)
	Soru to te mo (5)	**shimouta**
	Sono nochi Yokobue wa (3)	(chūon ryaku bachi) **chūon I**
	Takiguhi kono yoshi o tsutaekiite (6)	**chūon II**
(8) Meeting between Koremori and Takiguchi. (No longer performed)		**shojū**
		shojū-chūon
		shojū

* Bold type indicates the main substyles; parentheses indicate biwa introductory phrases.
Note: Only sections 3 to 7 continue to be performed.
Source: Book 10, Chapter 8 of *Heike monogatari* (Fujii 1966: 71–92).

Text 3.1   *Yokobue* (CD Track 4)

Kudoki

1. 高野にとしごろ知り給える聖あり Kōya ni toshigoro shiritamaeru hijiri ari 2. 三条の斎藤左衛門茂頼が子に Sanjō no Saitōzaemon Mochiyori ga ko ni 3. 斎藤滝口時頼とて Saitō Takiguchi Tokiyori to te 4. 元は小松殿の侍なり Moto wa Komatsudono no saburai nari 5. 十三の年本所へ参りたりしが Jūsan no toshi Honjo e mairitarishi ga 6. 建礼門院の雑仕に横笛といふ女あり Kenreimon'in no zōshi ni Yokobue to iu ona ari 7. 滝口かれに最愛す Takiguchi kare ni saiaisu 8. 父この由を伝へ聞いて Chichi kono yoshi o tsutaekiite 9. いかならん世にある人の婿にもなして 'Ika naran, yo ni aru hito no muko ni mo nashite 10. 出仕なんどをも心安せさせんと思ひ居たれば Shusshi nando o mo kokoro yasusesasen to omoiitareba 11. 由なき者を見初めてなんど Yoshi naki mono o misomete' nando 12. あながちに諌めければ Anagachi ni isamekereba 13. 滝口申しけるは Takiguchi moushikeruwa	On Mount Kōya there lived a priest whom Koremori had known many years before. He was a son of Saitō Mochiyori of the Left Gate Watch. His name was Saitō Takiguchi Tokiyori. He had once been a retainer of Lord Komatsu (Koremori's father). When he was 13, he moved to the palace where a girl called Yokobue was in attendance upon Kenreimon'in. Takiguchi fell in love with her. When his father heard about this, he said 'What are you doing? I've been planning to have you marry into an influential family, to help you get on in the world. You shouldn't fall for such a low person!' Thus his father admonished him severely. Takiguchi replied,

Heike Narrative: The Musical Recitation of The Tale of the Heike   73

Orikoe

14. 西王母といひし人	'A person known as Queen Mother of
Seiōbo to iishi hito	the West
15. 昔はあって今はなし	used to live in China, but she is no more.
Mukashi wa atte ima wa nashi	
16. 東方逆と聞こえし者も	There was also a hermit called
Tōbō Saku to kikoeshi mono mo	Dong-fang Shuo,
17. 名をのみ聞きて目には見ず	but only his name remains.
Na o nomi kikite me ni wa mizu	
18. 老少不定の世の中はただ	In this world, whether we die old or
Rōshō fujō no yo no naka wa tada	young is uncertain;
19. 石火の光に	Life is like the spark of a flint,
Sekika no hikari ni	
20. 異ならず	nothing more.'
Koto narazu	

Translation adapted from Tyler (2012b: 548) and Kitagawa and Tsuchida (1975: 609–10).

The *Yokobue* episode must have originated as a Buddhist tale told by itinerant religious teachers to inspire devotion. It was retold in many later forms (see Pigeot's French translation of the otogi zōshi tale in Pigeot 1972). It is the tragic love story of Yokobue, a girl in service to the empress, and Takiguchi Tokiyori, son of an imperial court guard, and is carefully embedded into the main historical chronological narrative. Taira Koremori (a grandson of Kiyomori) has left the Heike camp at Yashima, ostensibly to return to his family in the capital, travelling via Kōyasan. There he took the tonsure, that is, he became a monk, and then committed suicide by entering the sea at Kumano, with two of his retainers. This is a feminine act of despair, not taken under immediate threat of personal defeat as is usual with warriors. (Hyōdō 2011 discusses Koremori's 'sin' of attachment at some length.)

Interpolated into this narrative is the story that took place several years prior to Koremori's visit. Tokiyori is the link to the heike narrative: he was known to Koremori who sought him out for spiritual and mental sustenance and support. The reputation of Tokiyori as an ascetic who gave up the world is brought out by the tale of his romance with Yokobue. In a mere 40 minutes a whole life drama unfolds. The story illustrates the pathos and suffering caused by unrequited love and the way it necessitates Buddhistic resignation. The theme is only loosely connected to the broader elegiac theme of vanity and transiency in the Buddhist context. It is irrelevant whose side Takiguchi is on.

Heike Narrative: The Musical Recitation of The Tale of the Heike 75

Example 3.1 *Yokobue*: kudoki-orikoe[7]

---

[7] Transcriptions in this chapter have been made to follow the CD tracks 4 and 5, with reference to the published transcriptions of the Nagoya repertoire by Fujii Seishin (Fujii 1966), and adapting them according to the style used by Komoda Haruko (Komoda 2003).

76 *Japanese Singers of Tales: Ten Centuries of Performed Narrative*

Example 3.1 *continued*

Heike Narrative: The Musical Recitation of The Tale of the Heike

The CD excerpt (Track 4) is taken from the opening of the piece as transmitted in current performance, with kudoki and orikoe sections. The *Heike mabushi* and the Kakuichi book begin with the framing narrative of Koremori escaping from Yashima (kudoki, chūon, shojū, shojū-chūon). The piece now begins with the story of Takiguchi and his love for Yokobue. Similarly, the last section, section 8, picks up the narrative present again (shojū, shojū-chūon, shojū), which is no longer performed.

The musical highlights are the sections featuring orikoe (sections 3 and 6), and sanjū (section 5), the latter being a poetic description of Yokobue's journey (michiyuki) to Saga to seek Takiguchi. The exchange of waka between them after both have renounced the world in section 7 is profoundly moving.

Nasu no Yoichi

Table 3.8   Outline of *Nasu no Yoichi*

Sections	Text (number of phrases)	FMM*
(1) The scene is set. Appearance of a small boat, and a young woman beckons to hit the fan. The gesture is interpreted as a challenge to the Genji.	Saruhodo ni, Awa Sanuki ni (15)	(kudoki bachi) **kudoki**
	(Fune no) segai ni hasamitate, kugae muite zo, manekikeru	kowari sage
	Hōgan Gotō Byōe Sanemoto	**shirakoe**
	mōsu.	Hazumi
(2) Yoshitsune enquires who in their ranks would be able to shoot it. Yoichi is summoned, and is described.	Hōgan, 'Shōko wa ikani' to notamaeba (3)	(kudoki bachi) **kudoki**
	(sourou to) mōsu, Hōgan 'saraba Yoichi yobe' to te, mesarekeri.	kowari sage
	Yoichi sono koro wa imada ... (14) (nodameno kabura ...)	**hiroi**
(3) Dialogue of Hōgan and Yoichi. Yoichi's internal monologue.	Hōgan 'Ika ni Yoichi ... (8)	(kudoki bachi) **kudoki**
	mōshikereba Hōgan ooki ni ikatte	kowari sage
	Kondo Kamakura o tatte (4)	**kō no koe** (high voice)
	Sore ni sukoshi mo shisai o	**shirakoe**
	... ayumasekeru.	(hazumi)

Heike Narrative: The Musical Recitation of The Tale of the Heike

Sections	Text (number of phrases)	FMM*
(4) The scene at Yashima: tension on both sides, expectation of an interesting event.	Mikata no tsuwamonodomo (8)	(kudoki bachi) **kudoki**
	... shichitan bakari mo aruran to zo mieshi	kowari sage
	Koro wa nigatsu jūhachinichi (9)	(sanjū bachi) **sanjū**
	Fune wa yuriage ...	**kō** = a type of sanjū; goes down to low e, lower than sanjū
	Oki ni wa Heike fune o ichimen ni narabete kenbusu Kugai ni wa Genji kutsubami o soroete kore o misu Izure mo izure mo Hare narazu to (5)	**kudari**
(5) Yoichi's prayer to Hachiman.	iu koto nashi Yoichi	**ro**
	me o fusaide (3)	**ge**
	Nikkō no Gongen (10)	**jō-on**
(6) He shoots the fan. His action is applauded by both sides.	... nari ni kere. Yoichi	**ro**
	... kabura o totte (4)	**ge-on**
	... yumi wa tsuyoshi (6)	**jō-on**
	Hitomomi	Hashiri sanjū
	Futamomi momarete (6) (kanjitari. Kuga ni wa Genji, ebira o tataite, doyomekikeri.) (2)	**jō-on** (melismatic cadence)

* Bold type indicates the main substyles; parentheses indicate biwa introductory phrases.
Source: Book 11, Chapter 4 of *Heike monogatari* (Fujii 1966: 9–31) Hiroimono.

Text 3.2   *Nasu no Yoichi* (CD Track 6)

Hiroi

1. 与一、そのころはいまだ Yoichi sono koro wa imada	Yoichi was at that time
2. 二十ばかりの男なり。 Nijū bakan onoko nari	just 20 years old.
3. 褐に赤地の錦をもって Kachi ni akaji no nishiki o motte	His deep blue robe was edged with red brocade
4. 大領端袖いろへたる直垂に Ōkubi hatasode iroetaru hitatare ni	on collar and sleeves.
5. 萌黄匂の鎧着て Moyogi nioi no yoroi kite	His armour was laced with light green silk
6. 足白の太刀をはき Ashijiro no tachi o haki	His sword hung at his side from a silver ring.
7. 二十四さいたる切斑の矢負ひ Nijūshi saitaru kiriu no ya oi	In his quiver were the few black and white eagle-feathered arrows remaining
8. 薄切斑に鷹の羽割り合はせてはいだりける Usugiriu ni taka no ha wariawasete haidarikeru. (CD to here)	from the day's fighting, together with a humming arrow tipped with stag horn and fletched with hawk's feathers.
9. のた目の鏑をぞ Notame no kabura o zo	These could be seen sticking up
10. さし添へたる Sashisoetaru (CD track ends here)	from behind his head.
11. 滋藤の弓脇に挟み Shigedō no yumi waki ni hasami	Under his arm he clutched a rattan- bound bow.
12. 甲をば脱いで Kabuto o ba nuide	He took off his helmet,
13. 高紐にかけ Tamahimo ni kake	and slung it on his back,
14. 判官のお前に畏まる。 Hōgan no mae ni kashikomaru.	and knelt respectfully before Yoshitsune.

Translation adapted from Tyler 2012b and Kitagawa and Tsuchida 1975.

Example 3.2 *Nasu no Yoichi*: hiroi

continued

Example 3.2 *continued*

Heike Narrative: The Musical Recitation of The Tale of the Heike

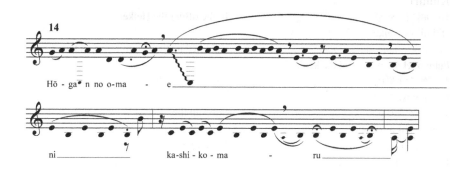

Text 3.3 *Nasu no Yoichi*: sanjū (CD Track 5 continued)

Sanjū

1. 頃は二月、十八日	It was the eighteenth day of the second month,
Koro wa ningatn jiuhachinichi	
2. 酉の刻ばかんの、ことなれば	at the hour of the cock [6:00 pm].
Tori no koku bakan koto nareba	
3. 折節北風、激しくて	The north wind was blowing hard,
Orifushi kitakaze hageshikute	
4. 磯打つ波も	and the waves breaking on the beach
Iso utsu nami mo	
5. 高かりけり	were very high.
Takakarikeri.	
(CD track 5 ends here)	
6. 船はゆり上げゆりすゑて	As the boat now rocked and now was still,
Fune wa yuriage yurisuete	
7. ただよえば	adrift,
Tadayoeba	
8. 扇も串に、定まらなで	the fan on the pole
Ōgi mo kushi ni sadamarade	
9. ひらめいたり	kept fluttering.
Hirameitari	

Translation adapted from Tyler (2012b: 594) and Kitagawa and Tsuchida (1975: 659).

Kudari

10. 沖には平家	In the offing the Heike
Oki ni wa Heike	
11. 船を一面に並べて見物す	had lined up their ships to watch the show.
Fune o ichimen ni narabete kenbusu	
12. 陸には源氏	On the shore the Genji
Kuga ni wa Genji	
13. くつばみを揃えて	lined up their horses neck to neck.
Kutsubami o soroete	
14. これを見る	Looking on,
Kore o miru	
15. いづれもいづれも	both sides
Izure mo izure mo	
16. 晴ならずと、いふことなし	were in fine spirits.
Harenarazu to iu koto nashi.	

Translation adapted from Tyler (2012b: 5494–5) and Kitagawa and Tsuchida (1975: 659–60).

After the defeat and further retreat of the Heike at the battle of Ichinotani, there is a lull in the fighting at twilight (Table 3.8). The Heike challenge the Genji to shoot a fan pinned to the mast of their boat, and the challenge is taken by Yoichi, a young warrior from an eastern province. The narrative delights in celebrating the breathtaking and romantic prowess of the young, otherwise unknown hero, not the Genji strength as such. Both the Heike and the Genji applaud his feat when his arrow hits the target. This episode celebrates military values, but is non-partisan. There is no battle and no death, in strong contrast to the following ku, in which Yoichi is ordered to shoot the Heike warrior who danced in celebration on the boat, following which several nasty skirmishes ensued.

Hyōdō (2011: 169) puts this scene in the context of rituals of tests of strength, quoting Orikuchi Shinobu's essay on Yashima-gatari no kenkyū (1934). The long tradition of two-way ritual performances he saw as the background for the widespread acceptance of war tales. Hyōdō argues that the biwa hōshi tales were a subsidiary part of their ritual work that became the main part. In this tale we can agree that the shooting of the fan is not part of the battle, but is a test of strength of a young Genji warrior, challenged, incited, provoked by the Heike in their ships. Implicitly, it predicts the Genji victory.

CD Track 5 contains the first eight lines of the hiroi section from dan 2 and the first five lines of the sanjū section from dan 4.

Nasu no Yoichi is one of the shorter ku in *The Tale of the Heike*, and is transmitted entirely. It is the most frequently performed of the Nagoya pieces. In contrast to *Yokobue*, it has the unity of just one scene and one incident, narrating in 35 minutes what must have taken only a few minutes to happen. However, with the shifting narrative focus, there are several mini-scenes in this close-up treatment of a dramatic tense moment (Table 3.9).

Example 3.3 *Nasu no Yoichi*: sanjū

continued

Example 3.3 *continued*

Example 3.3   *concluded*

Table 3.9   Contrasting features of *Yokobue* and *Nasu no Yoichi*

Yokobue	Nasu no Yoichi
lady = courtly values	warrior = military values
Buddhist faith: renunciation	Shintō faith: celebrates physical prowess
setsuwa Buddhist tale: female, soft	war tale: male warrior mood, hard
focal formulaic musical material: orikoe and sanjū	focal formulaic musical material: hiroi and sanjū

Conclusion

The above discussion indicates how the vicissitudes of the performance history of *The Tale of the Heike* gave it different meanings in different eras and for different groups of people. The earliest formative years of its development are still a mystery. Those who fashioned the tales of the biwa hōshi and other storytellers brought these episodes out of the realm of funeral ritual to the service of official chronicle. The appropriation of the biwa hōshi performance by the shogunate from the fourteenth century shows that it was to them more than a simple romance to entertain the common folk in temple and marketplace, but a narrative legitimizing a change of dynasty. Once held in the straitjacket of official control, heike performance functioned as a high-class hobby for the Edo-period intelligentsia.

In addition to changes in heike narrative as a performance tradition outlined above, the narrative was selectively adopted by many other artistic forms, such as nō, kōwaka and jōruri. Furthermore, local narrative traditions in Kyūshū in which blind males performed sutras and religious rites to an accompaniment, with secular storytelling as a sideline, included many episodes from the heike narrative in their repertoire. These Kyūshū narratives were the forebears of new narrative styles accompanied by the biwa in the modern period: Satsuma biwa and Chikuzen biwa. In addition, *The Tale of the Heike* provided material for visual arts, in the form of picture scrolls (emaki), and for new media such as the modern novel, cinema and television. Its enduring popularity is indicated by the frequency with which it forms the stuff of television dramas.[8]

As a research field, Heike studies are not as popular as Genji studies; however, there are now two monographs in English that deal substantially with the heike narrative (Oyler 2006b; Bialock 2007), three complete English translations, translations into French, Czech and Russian, and a handful of research articles. It is an exciting area of research, because it is not a 'work of literature' in the modern sense, and accommodates the challenge of orality studies. It demands

---

[8]   NHK Taiga dramas: 1966, *Minamoto Yoshitsune*; 1972, *Shin-Heike monogatari* (Kiyomori; based on Yoshikawa Eiji's novel); 1979, *Kusa moeru* (Yoritomo and Hojo Masako); 2006, *Yoshitsune*; 2012, *Taira Kiyomori*.

rigorous hermeneutical scrutiny. This involves understanding the connection between oral and literate culture, the issues of transmission throughout the centuries of performance and written versions, and the reception of the narrative in a variety of contexts.

The *Tale* retains an important place in Japanese cultural history, even to the present, when it can help us to understand the traditional underpinnings of contemporary culture and society.

Chapter 4
Dance and Narrative: Kōwaka and Nō

Introduction

The narrative arts (katari no geinō) made an inestimable contribution to all three of Japan's major dramatic forms of nō, bunraku and kabuki. Any study of the katarimono tradition from heike to jōruri cannot bypass these dramatic theatrical forms.

Whereas heike could be called one-dimensional, an art to be listened to rather than watched, nō and kōwaka were recited and danced by troupes of sighted performers, thus bringing visual (kinetic) and rhythmic dance elements to the fore. The combination of narrative with dance movement was the mode of women entertainers (shirabyōshi, imayō, kusemai and maimai). Kōwaka mai is a masculine development of these women's performances. Mai performance genres used the formal movements of dance to articulate narrative and song, but the movement did not necessarily represent or illustrate narrated or sung content. Only nō created the mimetic enactment and portrayal of narrative, including the use of dramatic costumes, masks and props (but falling short of scenery).

Preceding chapters established a framework within which to understand early musical narratives as the combination of indigenous oral culture and continental elite culture. This is linked to an underlying concern with orality and formulaic expression in the narrative performing arts. In each genre, there are discernible links with oral culture. The emergence of kōshiki and heike narrative shows the early development of a syntax and a modus operandi for performed narrative with some melodic complexity. In the nō theatre, the principles established in kōshiki and heike were generalized to become the fundamental structure of vocal music in the medieval period (Gamō 1989). This congruity made possible the applicability of Yokomichi's analysis of nō to heike, gidayū and kiyomoto (Yokomichi 2011).

This chapter argues that both nō and kōwaka have narrative at their core, and that they are thus closely related to heike narrative. The chapter analyses the verbal-musical narrative (katari) and visual-kinetic dance (mai) structures shared by nō and kōwaka mai, and the mimetic (monomane) which only nō features. A historical survey is followed by the implications of mai when combined with narrative. A discussion follows of how narrative is danced in kōwaka, which is then contrasted with the mimetic nō with its flute and drum ensemble (hayashi), its central place of songs, and its pure dance sections. Texts and orality are then discussed, and finally music. The structural congruence between nō and kōwaka and the differences between them are shown in a comparative analysis of a piece that has a counterpart in both genres (*Ataka* and *Togashi*).

Social Context and History

Like the blind minstrels who recited the heike narrative, the performers of nō and mai were of outcaste social status by virtue of their birth and place of abode: they were fellows of the ritualists called shōmonji and lived in designated areas (sanjo) on the outskirts of certain villages. All three arts eventually came under the protection and patronage of the bushi class, and of the shogun in particular, despite the original humble status of the performers.

Kōwaka mai

Kōwaka mai is narrative recited and sung to formalized dance movements, accompanied by a drum (tsuzumi). Although a stage art whose main mode of movement is mai dance, kōwaka is more like a recital, situated between heike story-singing and nō drama. It has a place in the katarimono lineage because of its strong narrative focus on war tales (gunkimono). It flourished in the fifteenth to seventeenth centuries, sharing similar characteristics of content and form with early jōruri, sekkyō-bushi, and of course nō. Fujita argues that kōwaka mai can show us much about what nō might have been like before the Edo period (Fujita 2009).

Mai has its origins in the ancient shamanistic practices and utterances of the miko, who performed rituals involving Shintō prayers (norito), oracles or the words of a god (takusen). They were also called yūjo and asobime (medium-prostitute), as itinerant ritual specialists who also entertained. With the marginalization of women religious practitioners from the late Heian to early medieval periods, miko (both the itinerant aruki miko and those who lived in village settlements) evolved into entertainers called shirabyōshi. A shirabyōshi performed solo and dressed in male court costume; she sang and danced, while accompanying herself with a tsuzumi drum, and often formed sexual liaisons with influential patrons. Shirabyōshi seem to have lived in matrilineal communities of women. Much of what is known about shirabyōshi are the examples of dancer-singers Giō, Hotoke Gozen and Senju no Mae in the *Heike monogatari* (Strippoli 2006). We also know that shirabyōshi were the performers of the imayō songs loved and collected by Cloistered Emperor Go-Shirakawa, a key figure in *The Tale of the Heike* (Kwon 1988).

The shirabyōshi were the predecessors of the fourteenth-century kusemai female performers (Wakita 2001: 185–91). Zeami's writings provide some of the few documentary sources for kusemai: he writes that his father Kannami learned kusemai from one Otozuru in Nara, and incorporated her art into nō; this is still evident in the narrative kuse section with its unique rhythm (see Wakita 2006; Nishino 1987: 122–3; Zeami and Hare 2008: 483).

In the fifteenth century, kusemai was wildly popular. It was a simple art, singing a story while performing mai dance movements to the accompaniment of the drum. In the fifteenth and sixteenth centuries, female performers called maimai are mentioned in various diaries. Troupes of boy dancers (chigo mai) were also in evidence. This art is coeval with sekkyō and jōruri, and like them focuses on romantic and religious tales, the world of otogi zōshi (Araki 1981). Another related women's performing art at that time was onna sarugaku (women's nō), one of the precursors of women's kabuki (Hattori 1968: 77).

It is during the same period that the term kōwaka mai first appears.[1] Although the exact lineage of mai as a male performing art is not clear, by the sixteenth century its popularity exceeded that of nō. The kōwaka mai repertoire retained a few romantic and religious themed narratives. However, it is unique among mai performing arts in its incorporation of a large number of pieces with military themes, from the Soga, Genpei and Yoshitsune cycles. Together with Heiji, Hōgen and heike, it is usually classified as part of the tradition of gunkimono narratives (Suda et al. 1990). This repertoire focus was related to their particular form of patronage by upper-class bushi, particularly the military leaders, even as highly placed as the hegemons Oda Nobunaga and Toyotomi Hideyoshi. Hand-written collections of kōwaka texts (mai no hon) start to appear towards the late sixteenth century, and printed texts burgeoned and were widely circulated as popular reading matter from the 1620s.

During the Edo period, kōwaka mai continued to secure shogunal patronage, but as an art it became fossilized. It survives vestigially in Kyūshū today: it is performed as a shrine ritual once a year. It was 'discovered' and made widely known by song collector and theatre researcher Takano Tatsuyuki (1876–1947) in the late Meiji period, and can still be appreciated in an annual performance on 20 January in Ōe village in Setaka, Fukuoka Prefecture. Whether or not the current performance accurately reflects the style of kōwaka mai in its heyday, it does give us some idea of what it might once have been like.

The Origins of the nō Drama

Over six centuries of transmission, nō became highly refined and systematized. It was formed most decisively by Zeami in the early fifteenth century, on the basis of his father Kannami's achievements, notably the latter's incorporation of the rhythmic kusemai from the women's performance of mai. Zeami was responsible for the literary refinement and the creation of mugen nō. He brought to nō aesthetic and philosophical concepts, especially that of yūgen (profound and mysterious beauty) which became a central aspect of mugen nō (dream nō).

When Kannami's troupe performed in front of the young shogun Yoshimitsu in 1375 at the Imakumano Temple, the 12-year-old Zeami was taken into Yoshimitsu's court and was educated in classical literature, which he learned to incorporate into the nō drama. The influence of court poetry is thus strong in the

---

[1] The first documentary mention of kōwaka appears in 1442 in the Kankenki diary (one year before Zeami died, aged 81). The occasion was a performance in the garden of the Saionji residence: the diarist expresses being deeply impressed by the music and the dance. Many similar entries follow, ushering in the peak of kōwaka's popularity (Muroki 1998: 1).

poetic diction of mature nō drama, whose texts are replete with poetic quotation and allusion to the Chinese and Japanese classics. Zeami's acquired aesthetic and philosophical knowledge is expressed eloquently in his numerous writings about nō, which show him to have been a major thinker of his day.[2]

Kannami's Yamato sarugaku was primarily straight drama (monomane), whereas a rival troupe, Ōmi sarugaku, emanated the quality of yūgen with their emphasis on song and dance. Zeami's desire to vie with them for aristocratic patronage led to a much greater emphasis on song (Quinn 2005). Monomane or straight acting remained the basic form of the comic kyōgen plays, in which occasional songs function diegetically as part of the drama. The musicalization of nō meant that the bulk of the play was delivered musically.

Hyakuman is an 'old nō' (kosaku nō), probably created by Kannami and 'revised' (completed and polished) by Zeami. This play shows us the narrative nature of nō.[3] It provides a portrait of a kusemai performer named Hyakuman. It has many narrative-type sections, including an extended kuse. This became the prototype of the kuse section in the mature nō.

The structure of nō was probably still fluid in Kannami's time, open to influences from ritual performances in temples and shrines (such as the piece *Okina*), and by itinerant artists. Under Zeami and the influence of court aesthetics and the literary tradition, nō changed, but after Zeami suffered a change in political fortune and was exiled, the earlier non-courtly elements of straight drama reasserted themselves. Rather than the mugen nō perfected by Zeami, his successors preferred the more straightforward plays which unfold in chronological order (genzai nō). Many of the most popular plays in the current repertoire date from the fifteenth and sixteenth centuries, such as *Ataka* and *Funa Benkei* (both written by Kanze Kojirō Nobumitsu, Zeami's grandson [or grand-nephew?] [1450?–1535]).Virtually no new plays were written after about 1600 until the twentieth century, but the Edo period saw developments in mode of performance, most notably the differentiation of the soft chant, yowagin, and the strong chant, tsuyogin (see Fujita 2012), and a systematization of the formulaic standardized movements called kata.

Performance Elements of kōwaka and nō

The performative elements of musically delivered narrative (katari), visual and kinetic representation embodied in dance (mai), and mimetic representation (monomane) respectively characterize the performance genres of heike, kōwaka and nō. In all three genres, the musically delivered verbal narrative is central.

---

[2] These theoretical writings have only been generally known since 1908 (Zeami and Hare 2008: 451).

[3] Translated as 'One Million' by Royall Tyler in *Granny Mountains: A Second Cycle of Nō Plays* (Tyler 1978). It is a Category Four play, a mad woman play, and a taiko-mono.

By analysing the formal differences between narrative, drama and dance, we can ascertain what was gained and what was lost in the process of transposing the narrative from heike to stage performance. Put another way, we can ascertain how the formal and performative requirements of each genre dictated and manipulated the selection and arrangement of narrated content. Saya's work helps us understand this in the case of the *Atsumori* legend (Saya 2002: 43–139), as does Kobayashi's (2001: 384–99), Squires' (2001) and Anzako's (2000: 37–96) for *Manjū*.

The following sections discuss first the kinetic and visual (mai), then the mimetic (monomane), then the verbal and textual, and finally the musical aspects.

Mai

At its most basic, the art of mai involves a dancer who plays the drum (tsuzumi) as she sings and/or narrates. This use of the drum as the principal accompaniment by all mai genres underlines the centrality of rhythm in this form, in contrast to the melodic accompaniment of plucked lutes, the biwa in heike and shamisen in jōruri. According to the *Engeki Hyakka Daijiten* (1960/1983, vol. 5: 215), the meanings of the word 'mai' have varied a lot in different contexts and in the hands of different users, and it is not always clearly distinguished from other types of dance.[4]

Originally, mai involved an abstract circling movement with minimal raising of the foot from the ground or stage, and a sedate, slow tempo. Mai was connected with ritual, a deliberate movement which according to Gunji developed into monomane to express the meaning of narrative. Gunji further defines kusemai as 'narration delivered melodically while dancing' (Gunji 1970: 88). Fujita (2009: 1) insists that the verbal form, mau, is equivalent to narrating (kataru), again suggesting the intimate connection between mai and the act of narration. Perhaps mai should not be defined purely as a dance movement.[5]

---

[4] Mai, odori and furi are the three principal Japanese dance modes. As we have seen, mai is the principal form of movement in nō and kōwaka. In contrast, what was new about early kabuki was its incorporation of odori into a women's performance tradition which had had mai at its core, for example, onna sarugaku, maimai, shirabyōshi. Previously a communal group dance, odori became a staged dance by professional performers. The other style of dance which became the core of kabuki dance is furi, literally 'pretence'. Furi is associated with mature kabuki dance after the Genroku period. It is mimetic, the kabuki equivalent of what in nō is called monomane (also shikata-banashi). The dance dramas of kabuki (shosagoto) are identifiable from this time. It would seem that mai was also present in early kabuki as well as odori. Furi developed most strongly from the era of mature men's kabuki (yarō kabuki) when drama came to be emphasized over song and dance. Certainly, the reliance of early kabuki on the music of the nō drum and flute ensemble (hayashi) (shamisen only entering kabuki from the mid-seventeenth century), suggests that the kouta (short song) odori dances were not so different from kouta mai.

[5] Many types of mai are known to have been part of the Heian court's annual ceremonies (nenchū gyōji). Mai was also the term applied to dance in bugaku (bu is the

Muroki (1992: 126) believes that there was a disjuncture between mai performing arts and long narratives around 1500, because it proved difficult for a dancer to maintain the vocal narrative while dancing, and that this is why the Ōe kōwaka transmission relegated dance to a subsidiary role. Muroki further states that originally kusemai was *sung* while dancing (utainagara mau), and that the pieces were relatively short (1998: 12).

In both nō and kōwaka, mai is a relatively sedate circling movement, or rather a movement that geometrically describes a square, a part circle, a triangle, with occasional emphatic stomps, which contribute to the rhythmic work of the percussion accompaniment. The almost square nō stage facilitates these geometric circles and divisions thereof. The foot-sliding movement (suriashi) of nō is always performed in tabi socks, while the long formal trousers covering the feet in kōwaka similarly facilitate sliding the foot.

In kōwaka, all mai movement is accompanied by sung narrative, but mai in nō falls into two basic types: the type which is performed together with utai and hayashi, and the maigoto type which is performed to the rhythmic accompaniment of hayashi only without utai. The sung utai is taken partly by the shite (dancer), but most of it devolves to the chorus, to allow the dancer to concentrate on movement. Utai-dance sections include mimetic as well as abstract movement, but the purely instrumental maigoto sections express a mood or feeling: the emotion of a character, often in the nature of an epiphany or a revelation of true nature or identity, or celebration, lament, anger or torment. The maigoto are usually 'the highlight of a nō performance. In these, the shite or main actor of the play does not portray realistic movements or gestures. Instead, he expresses abstractly the mood and the emotions that are the central theme to that particular play by performing standard dance patterns' (Emmert 1983: 5).

Bethe and Brazell make clear the distinction of the formal abstract mai patterns from the mimetic movements in terms of figure and ground, or design patterns against ground patterns:

> The abstract nature of the ground patterns allows them to function both as a part of the formal structure and as a vehicle for meaning, a meaning dependent largely on the context in which the patterns appear. The versatility of these patterns makes them the solid groundwork of nō dance on which more dynamic patterns stand out. This second type of pattern we label 'design patterns'. These two large categories of patterns – ground and design – may be distinguished not only in terms of the frequency and context of their occurrences (design patterns are sparsely used and are not essential parts of the model sequences), but also in terms of their relationship to referential meaning. Whereas ground patterns can be performed without reference to anything other than the dance itself (the purest example is the long instrumental dance), a design pattern almost always

---

Sino-Japanese reading of mai). Mai features in many folk ritual performances (minzoku geinō); daikokumai was a significant precursor of kabuki dance.

refers to something mentioned in the text, that something varying with the context. (Bethe and Brazell 1982, vol. 1: 53)

The principal instrumental dance types of nō are:

chū no mai – mostly woman's role; the most basic dance
jo no mai – mostly woman's role; very slow tempo
otoko mai – man's dance; fast tempo; actor does not wear a mask
kami mai – (male) god dance; fast tempo
kagura – (female) deity dance
gaku – play set in China, supernatural character or musician

Dances for female, divine or exotic characters predominate, but mai was an important form of expression for men too in medieval Japan, and male characters at least have the otoko mai (for example Benkei's dance in nō *Ataka* and nagauta *Kanjinchō*). Many bushi wanted to dance the shite role in amateur nō performances; whereas Nobunaga (1534–1582) danced kōwaka pieces, Hideyoshi (1537–1598) danced in nō plays. Nō developed as a theatre of male actors, and kōwaka grew out of the male desire to perform narrative with mai. In this way, both paved the way for the all-male theatre forms of the Edo period, after the ban on women's public performance in 1629.

Mai in kōwaka, by contrast, is not differentiated by role or character; it is described dismissively by Araki: 'the physical movements in the kōwaka are strikingly simple, comprising only four items – a stylized bow, two stationary poses, and a rhythmic strut. Only the last can be termed choreographic' (Araki 1978 [1964]: 87). The stage on which kōwaka is performed in Ōe village today, built in 1901, is 'approximately twenty feet square and stands three feet above the ground. Thatch-roofed and enclosed on three sides, it is dark even at midday' (ibid.: 88). Araki describes both the movement (ibid.: 92–9) and the melodies (ibid.: 99–108). Actually, the dancers use the nō basic posture called kamae, and the same hour-glass movement pattern as nō mai.

The mai dance movement was a means of articulating vocalized narrative rhythmically. Fujita (2009: 1) sees kōwaka as the 'origin' (genryū) of nō. He quotes Zeami on mai: 'Mai wa koe o ne to nasu; mai wa neiro yori idezuba kan arubekarazu' (Mai has its root in the voice; if mai does not come from sound, it cannot produce deep emotion. From Zeami's treatise *Kakyō* [A Mirror to the Flower], 1424) arguing that the mai movement is based on 'moving on the stage in circling movements'. In the Muromachi period, he argues, the shite always performed the singing at the same time as mai, as happens in kōwaka, because the role of the chorus had not been established. He also shows that the dance movements of mai (in the kuse in particular) are basically the same as in kōwaka today. In the medieval performing arts, mai and dance-music (bukyoku) were synonymous and mutually supporting; mai grew out of the singing ('from voice to mai'). He points out that similar scenes of singing together with mai can be found in kyōgen today. Fujita shows that the nō kuse (which used to be called kusemai) and kōwaka mai are similar in three aspects: the dancer sings and moves around the stage simultaneously; the movements are an alternation of left-right-left-right circling; and rhythm is delineated by occasional foot-stamping during the movement (2009: 6–7).

Arguably, one of the major appeals of mai as a female art (shirabyōshi and kusemai) and as a boys' art (chigo mai) was the physical beauty of the dancer-singer-narrator. It would seem that much of the appeal of kōwaka too was in youthful male beauty, overlapping with chigo mai. This feature continues through to the later wakashū kabuki in the seventeenth century. The nō on the other hand was monopolized by mature male performers, who had to rely more on acting and dancing skill and developed the aesthetic of mask and costume to compensate for the lack of appeal offered by women performers (Wakita 2006: 127). This did not mean that nō ceased to rely on physical appeal of a certain kind, as we can tell by the shogun Yoshimitsu's attraction to and adoption of the 12-year-old Zeami. Zeami also writes in *Kadensho* (*Fūshi Kaden*) that hana (flower) is the supreme beauty of nō, and that young boy actors did not need to have skill, because of their natural appeal (Zeami and Hare 2008: 480). This may have been one reason for having child actors (kokata) take some of the major roles (for example Yoshitsune in *Ataka*).

Mimesis / monomane

The mai tradition of shirabyōshi and maimai, and the later kōwaka mai, seems to have had no mimetic elements. The formalized movements of kōwaka mai as transmitted in Ōe village in Kyūshū do not mirror textual meaning. Dramatic dialogue between characters is not delivered by different performers. Neither masks nor costumes are worn, only the formal dress of the samurai of the sixteenth century. So we can call kōwaka mai narrative on stage with movement and drum accompaniment, but it cannot be called drama, although Araki calls it ballad drama.

While nō's mimesis is limited in comparison with bunraku and kabuki, compared with kōwaka, it is decidedly mimetic. From the moment the actor enters along the hashigakari, he is in dramatic costume, and some shite characters also wear a mask (female, old and non-human characters, such as divine beings). Most characters carry a fan, which is more generic than mimetic, functioning as an extension of the arm in abstract dance movements, but on occasion representing a prop such as a cup. As for specifically mimetic movement, there is a limited number of realistic actions.

The nō drama draws so heavily on narrative musical and verbal elements that it can be considered narrative which became dramatized. It is a powerful dramatized storytelling medium with mimetic elements as well as formalized movements, but without losing the elements of narrative. The nō theatre is not usually considered part of the narrative tradition, but as contemporary performing art forms of the medieval period, nō and kōwaka share many structural features, and also in a lot of their content (Kobayashi 2001: 1–6). Nō is a spectacular visualization and kinetic embodiment of narrative. The whole nō text is a combination of first and third person narrative; spoken dialogue (mondō) and sung dialogue or antiphonal singing (kakeai, rongi), usually the waki (priest) questioning the shite; song (ageuta, sageuta); sung narrative sections with dance (kuse), and so on.

The utai of early sarugaku-nō had as its basic singing style the pattern of 7-5 syllable lines in an 8-beat framework. Kannami brought the music and rhythm of kusemai into the structure. Musically, it seems to have been the same basic style of singing as other medieval genres, including imayō, kusemai, sōga. The basic metrical form of alternating phrases of seven and five syllables, forming an indeterminate number of lines of 12 syllables, goes back to the longer poems (chōka) of the eighth century poetry collection, *Manyōshū*.

Nō actually has three verbal styles: archaic speech of an earlier age (sōrotai), the language of written stories in literary Japanese (nari style), and the metric language of poetry, revealing that nō is a mixture of drama, narrative and poetry (Yokomichi 1986: 30). The main character (shite) in a nō drama *tells* more than *acts*. The music itself is not always distinctly narrative, but it is based on the same broad formulaic structure as kōshiki, heike and jōruri. Although Keene stated that a nō play is better understood as a poem than a drama, it can equally be said that narrative is central to the nō theatre. In 'dream nō' (mugen nō) in particular, when 'time flows in reverse', the use of narrative by the shite is a central device. There is very little dramatic interaction in these plays; rather there is the narrating, relating or (re-)telling of the drama by a character. Embedded narrative (narrative within a narrative), when a character becomes the narrator to another character, is very common in oral narrative. Dramatic dialogue, such as the mondō, functions to elicit such narratives. Verbal narrative is amplified by the dramatic, mimetic and kinetic elements of dramatis personae, the chorus, the instrumental accompaniment of the hayashi ensemble, dance, kyōgen dramatic interludes, as well as mask, costume and props.

While nō is a theatrical form, it has never shaken off many aspects of narrative performance. Every play has clearly identified narrative features, even a section called 'narrative' (katari), and another called kudoki (where a character appeals to the listener's sympathy in a lament), and most famously the kuse.

The persona of the narrator is sometimes ambiguous. In what might be called self-narration, the actor recites any lines which relate to that character, not just his dramatic speech (Fujita 2000: xiii–xix). So the actor playing Yoshitsune says 'Yoshitsune did this and that'. Famous, for example, are Yoshitsune's lines in *Funa Benkei*: the child actor declaims 'At that time, Yoshitsune did not lose his cool one bit' (Omote and Yokomichi 1963/81: 161). In nō, the narrator is on stage; the characters are the narrators.

We can point to numerous other narrative elements in nō. Perhaps the two most important utai sections are the ageuta (high song) and sageuta (low song). While their formal features and their content mark them as lyrical and musical, functioning to express a character's feelings or describe scenery, they are also used for most journey descriptions (michiyuki), a prominent feature of performed narratives. The arriving words (tsukizerifu) at the end of a character's entrance (shidai or issei sections) narrate his arrival at his destination. The waki narrates his self-introduction (nanori) to the audience in prosaic language (sōrōbun). *Ataka* is a genzai nō, so it is more dramatic and less poetic than the mugen nō, but the narrative elements are strongly present.

The Texts of kōwaka and nō

Thematically, nō draws on a wide range of the narrative worlds of its time. Its warrior plays (shuramono) in particular overlap with kōwaka. The bulk of the kōwaka repertoire (47 of 52 pieces in extant texts) derives from the heike, Soga and Yoshitsune (*Gikeiki*) story cycles. For this reason, kōwaka is conventionally positioned in a lineage of gunkimono military narratives, though some pieces are also derived from sekkyō source books and setsuwa and take the structure of medieval myth (Squires 2001).

As an art flourishing most vigorously in the era of warring states (sixteenth century), this heroic content suited the cultural climate of the time, and the tastes of its principal patrons. However, as Araki points out (1964: 111–20), it abounds in poetic passages such as michiyuki, poetic journeys. Kobayashi (2009: 2–3) states that kōwaka texts belong to the world of gunkimono; however, even the setsuwa tales are part of the warrior culture (Anzako 2000). Of the extant texts, approximately 85 per cent can be called gunkimono (Suda et al. 1990: 470). Many variant kōwaka texts have been well-preserved and extensively researched.[6]

Fujita has argued that many aspects of nō drama can be attributed to high-class patrons who wanted to perform the main parts in private performances (2008: 128–9). The chorus developed to make it easier for a non-professional to perform without having to dance and sing at the same time. In kōwaka, there is no chorus, but being much simpler than nō, it was well within the reach of noble amateurs, and we know that Oda Nobunaga loved to perform kōwaka, and Hideyoshi had pieces created especially for him (Araki 1964: 148–9; *Miki* and *Honnōji*), and also nō plays.

Of over 50 known pieces (based on texts preserved in various sources), eight have been transmitted in Ōe village (Table 4.1). These reflect the groupings of the broader repertoire as known through extant texts and other sources.

---

[6] The Bukyoku (kōwaka mai) Kenkyūkai produced ten volumes of edited texts and research essays on kōwaka. See Agō et al. (ed.) (1979–2004).

Table 4.1   The eight kōwaka pieces transmitted in Ōe, Kyūshū

	Source	Suda classification
Nihongi	*Nihongi*	Setsuwa-monogatari
Togashi	*Gikeiki*	Yoshitsune-mono
Izumi ga jō	*Gikeiki*	Yoshitsune-mono
Nasu no Yoichi (Ōgi no mato)	*Heike*	Genpei-mono
Hamaide	*Heike*	Genpei-mono
Takadachi	*Gikeiki*	Yoshitsune-mono
Youchi Soga	*Soga*	Soga-mono
Yashima	*Gikeiki*	Yoshitsune-mono

Of the eight, only three, *Nihongi*, *Ōgi no mato* and *Hamaide*, are preserved in full (Gamō and Kumada 1990: 18). *Atsumori* has been revived, based on text and notations, and on the performers' sense of what musical types to put where. It was first performed in January 2007, again in Kyoto in February 2009, and was one of the pieces performed in January 2013.

The surviving texts (mai no hon) date from the late sixteenth and early seventeenth century. Manuscript texts appeared earlier and seem to be performance texts (daihon) because they have mojifu notation to distinguish various types of delivery. Printed texts in moveable type (kokatsuji-bon) with illustrations proliferated slightly later and circulated widely as popular reading matter. The first printed books of kōwaka and jōruri appeared between the 1590s and the 1640s (Muroki 1982: 106). In the 1620s to 1640s whole anthologies containing 20 to 30 pieces were published with illustrations and were bestsellers of the time (Suda et al. 1990: 472). Muroki writes that in the early seventeenth century, people were familiar with kōwaka aurally and with its musical delivery, and the kōwaka repertoire at the time of its greatest popularity was very large. Performers would be asked to perform a certain piece on a particular occasion and they most likely did not have time to go and study the text, nor did they probably have the literacy skills to do so. They could not get by with a repertoire of even 30 pieces (the number of the largest anthologies), but needed to know dozens of pieces. At the height of its popularity, kōwaka had such flexibility. However, from the late sixteenth century when the pieces started to be printed, kōwaka gradually became fixed. Around 1600, its popularity had already begun to decline, and there was less demand for performance, which affected the artistry. Pieces in the memorized repertoire started to be forgotten, and the ability to memorize long pieces started to fail. The creativity essential to art is the first thing to be lost in such a situation. This was when texts with detailed musical indications were created. The texts functioned firstly as memory aids to performers, then were used in teaching the next generation of performers, and finally for teaching amateurs. At its peak, kōwaka would have been characterized by the typical repetition and redundancy of performed narrative, which has its own charm, but this becomes reduced in texts intended for reading (Muroki 1982: 115–17).

Nō has often been regarded as a text-centred performing art, with over 2,500 play texts known, of which 240 can still be performed. Nishino shows the flexibility of the early plays, making a case for their loose structure and non-literary character (Nishino 1987: 145–7). His discussion of the sources for Kannami's plays shows that they were not text-based, but drew from various setsuwa and religious stories that Kannami adapted and performed himself. They lacked the clear structure and the lyric nature that Zeami gave them. This suggests the improvisatory and flexible nature of performance in Kannami's time, who had a large repertoire, though only a handful were artistically moulded and written down by Zeami.

Orality and Literacy

Could Kannami write? Was it necessary for him to write? Kannami's plays that have come down to us are all in Zeami's hand. The plays *Eguchi* and *Matsukaze* have always been attributed to Kannami, but now it is thought likely that Zeami wrote them (Uchiyama 1997: 204). The plots of plays originating in Kannami's time, such as *Sotoba Komachi, Jinen Koji, Kayoi Komachi*, are all loose and rambling. According to Uchiyama, any dramatic merit they have is due to Zeami's hand (ibid.). Most known nō plays, whether in the current repertoire or not, have an ascribed author. However, it is significant that no kōwaka pieces are ascribed an author. Authorship is not an issue; they are 'traditional' art. The texts of nō, while having some oral features in their structure, are imbued with the principles of classical court poetry, whereas even a cursory look at the kōwaka texts reveals all the hallmarks of oral narrative.

The endings of the eight extant kōwaka pieces illustrate the formulaic nature of the kōwaka diction.

> *Nihongi*: 'Jumyō ni te nagaku sakauru medetasa yo'.
> *Hamaide*: 'Onmae no hitobito, onshoryō tamawari, shochi iri to koso kikoekere'.
> *Nasu no Yoichi* (*Ōgi no mato*): 'Ichimon nokorazu hikitsure, shochi iri to koso kikoekere'.
> *Togashi*: 'Musashibō ga arisama, ningen no waza de nakarikeri'.
> *Izumi ga jō*: 'Kisen jōge oshinabe kanzenu hito wa nakarikeri'.
> *Yashima*: 'Kisen jōge oshinabe, kanzenu hito wa nakarikeri'.
> *Takadachi*: 'Kisen jōge oshinabete, nikumanu mono wa nakarikeri'.
> *Youchi Soga*: 'Kisen jōge oshinabe, nikumanu mono wa nakarikeri'.

The typical opening phrases of pieces and of some sections of a piece such as 'saru aida' are also obvious examples of the (verbal) formula, and the way the change of narrative focus is achieved with naming the character. Examples abound in the text of *Togashi*: 'Togashi kiite …'; 'Musashi kiite' and so on. Further clear signs of oral narrative are the michiyuki passages that describe the stages of a journey, and the monozukushi passages which catalogue related objects; the descriptions of a castle, a warrior, and a mansion are all themes in the Parry-Lord sense.

Both nō and kōwaka have strong elements of oral expression, because they both derive directly from the deep stream of oral narrative at the heart of medieval Japanese culture. Despite their textualization, orality is still a core feature. However, under Zeami's hand nō received the imprimatur of courtly literary culture and became part of the literary canon.

Generic Analysis of kōwaka

The musical and narrative structure of kōshiki, heike and kōwaka are highly congruent, as has been demonstrated by Gamō (1989). Table 4.2 shows that kōwaka can be analysed in the same structural framework as the earlier genres.

Table 4.2   The structure of kōwaka

Context	Programme of five pieces, performed as 'offering' (hōnō) at shrine in Ōe Village once a year, 20 January.
(Larger Work)	Most plays are extracts / episodes from larger narrative cycles: heike, Soga, Yoshitsune, sekkyō, auspicious.
Piece	The largest discrete performance unit in this genre (kyoku, kōwaka).
Sections and Sub-sections Substyles	Section starts with spoken delivery (kotoba), finishes with fushi and/or tsume. Sub-sections are coterminous with substyles, delineated by the change from one style of delivery to another Three basic substyles: kotoba, fushi, tsume.
Phrase	Lines of 12 (7 + 5) syllables are the basic textual unit for which melody is delivered.
Motives; Ornamentation	The oshi ornament in the sashi melody type. Drum calls which punctuate the lines in tsume melody type.

The kōwaka performance is transmitted to the present day in the annual performance on 20 January at the Tenmangū shrine in Ōe village, in the form of an offering to the gods (hōnō). Customarily a programme of five pieces is presented by a number of different combinations of performers, and the repertoire is chosen so that all pieces are performed regularly to prevent further attrition of the repertoire.

The Pieces

Most pieces are episodes deriving from larger narrative cycles: *Nasu no Yoichi* from *The Tale of the Heike*; *Takadachi* and *Youchi Soga* from *The Tale of the Soga Brothers*; and *Ataka* (*Togashi*), *Izumi ga jō* and *Yashima* from the same narrative cluster as the *Chronicle of Yoshitsune* (*Gikeiki*). The auspicious *Hamaide* and *Nihongi* are originally from *The Tale of the Heike* and the *Nihongi* chronicle respectively, but like the other pieces were also independent narratives from the world of circulating oral tales (setsuwa).

As already mentioned, of more than 50 pieces extant in textual form, eight are transmitted in the current performance repertoire, of which only *Nihongi*, *Hamaide* and *Ōgi no mato* are performed in full; for *Ataka*, *Izumi ga jō*, *Youchi Soga*, *Takadachi* and *Yashima* only the first half is performed. A Ministry of Culture (Bunka-chō) survey was carried out in 1961 when *Izumi ga jō* was still performed in full, so it is recorded in its entirety, and has been structurally analysed (Gamō and Kumada 1990: 18–19).

Sections and Styles of Delivery

Kōwaka narrative is made up of named sections and sub-sections. The sections are clearly delineated by the progression of units in a certain style of delivery in a predictable sequence. In this patterned sequentiality, a section commences with a lengthy sub-section in kotoba delivery (close to speech), and finishes with either fushi or tsume, or a sequence of fushi-tsume. Before that there are transitional sub-sections of subsidiary melodic units. The sections are not divided by an instrumental interlude, as the only accompanying instrument is the tsuzumi (hourglass drum), played only in tsume sub-sections. This contrasts with the role of the biwa in heike and of the shamisen in jōruri.

Fujita (2009: 22–4) gives the most succinct account of the structure of kōwaka narrative (Table 4.3). Each piece consists of sections (dan) and each section is made up of substyles arranged in a fixed order.

Table 4.3 The substyles of kōwaka narrative and their sequencing

Kotoba → kakari → iro (or sashi or kudoki)
→ iro (or sashi or kudoki) → fushi
→ tsume
→ fushi → tsume

These three styles of delivery – kotoba, fushi, tsume – are performed in this order; occasionally there are two consecutive kotoba sections, each finished with melodic phrases (such as kakari, sashi, fushi). Each time a cycle of these three units finishes, we can see a narrative division in the text.

In contrast to kōshiki and heike narrative, where the structural sub-section is congruent with a single style of delivery, or narrative substyle, a kōwaka section comprises more than one substyle. The narrative section is built up from the accumulation of phrases or lines, which tend to take the classical prosody of a phrase of seven syllables followed by five syllables.

The next level is the substyle, or style of vocal delivery, 'the basic unit of kōwaka musical structure' (Gamō and Kumada 1990: 19). This accumulation of substyles then forms the larger section.

There are three basic substyles: kotoba, fushi, tsume, with some subsidiary melodic units. Kotoba, literally 'speech', is almost a musical delivery that can be written as music (see Examples 4.1 and 4.2). It is the 'basic' neutral narrative style of kōwaka. Fushi, literally 'melody', is soft narrative, like nō yowagin utai. It is rhythmic but melody is more important than rhythm. Tsume, literally 'final', is the highly rhythmic sung narrative at the end of a section with drum accompaniment and dance movement. It is hard narrative. Araki enumerates additional fushi types: kakari, iro, kudoki, tsuke (Araki 1964: 97–8). Gamō, like Araki, identifies two fushi types. She alone posits two tsume types, whereas Araki lists tsuke and tsume. The names of transitional patterns very more between different text-scores (shōhon) and lineage traditions.

On the whole, the narrative is structured from lines tending towards 12 syllables, patterned in the conventional grouping of 7 + 5. For the great bulk of the narrative, these lines are also congruent with the musical phrasing, but some enjambement occurs. There are no sections or substyles which have a fixed number of lines, unlike many nō sections.

Different writers analyse these musical units in confusingly different ways, which arises mainly because of the variation in terminology in different texts. Sixteen named musical patterns are noted in the *Ongaku Daijiten* (ODJ: Kōwaka-mai) based on the varied names of melodies in the mai no hon, but these can be reduced to the three main styles of delivery: kotoba, fushi and tsume.

In different versions of the texts as transmitted in Kyūshū (collectively called 'Ōe-bon'), about 20 names of melodies (fushi or kyokusetsu) appear.[7]

Gamō and Kumada's analysis of *Izumi ga jō* shows in detail the sections (dan) and substyle (kyokusetsukei) structure of the recording kept at the Tokyo National Institute for Cultural Properties, comparing the names given in four variant texts, the Matahei, Ōe, Sugihara and the Kansai University texts. This listing of the pattern names in four sources, as well as their own rationalized names based on analysis, illustrates how the names of patterns are highly variable. It is probably

---

[7] There are several versions of 'Ōe-bon', among which some handwritten books, such as *Matahei-bon*, date from the Meiji period, and show very detailed musical markings. About 20 kyokusetsukei are named in the *Matahei-bon*. The basic ones – kotoba, fushi, tsume – correspond with other known texts. Some names, mostly of transitional or cadential phrases, do not appear elsewhere. There are many discrepancies between the various notations in written texts and actual performance.

true to say that there is more variability in the names than in the musical content (Gamō and Kumada 1990: 22–4).

Although the English terms Araki applied are less than helpful, his transcriptions of the melody types and his musical analysis is thorough and accurate (Araki 1978 [1964]: 97–108). The three basic styles of delivery are there. Kotoba (recitative sections or 'narrative' in Araki's terminology) occupy one third to one half of the text (Araki 1978 [1964]: 98). He identifies five solo melodic patterns which are transitional melodies. Within fushi he identifies two melodies for 'unisono-chorus' (when the three performers sing together in unison), and within tsume an additional melody is identified, tsuke (Table 4.4).

Table 4.4   Araki's analysis of kōwaka melodies

	Japanese names*	Araki's English equivalents
Speech:	**kotoba**	narrative
Solo melodies:	kakari	prefatory
	iro-kakari (type I)	solo pastorale
	iro	solo pomposo
	iro-kakari (type II)	solo recitativo
	kudoki	solo delicate
Melodies for unisono-chorus:	**fushi** (type I)	coro melos pastorale
	fushi (type II)	coro melos pastorale
	tsuke	coro pastorale
	tsume	coro risoluto

* Bold type indicates the main substyles.

Kōwaka, *Togashi* (CD Track 6)

Table 4.5   Outline of kōwaka *Togashi*

Sections	Text	FMM*
(1) Yoshitsune, Benkei and the party of warriors disguised as yamabushi arrive at Ataka no matsu. Yoshitsune asks Benkei to enquire about the name of the pine tree. Benkei asks the local children playing there, and is told it was named Ataka no matsu, and also neagari no matsu, by the poet Saigyō when he was in love.	Saru aida, Hōgan dono	**kotoba**
	Saigyō to kare wa nanoru	kakari
	Kano Saigyō no uta ni mo	sashi
	Neagari no matsu to yomaretari. Nō yamabushi to mōshikeri.	**fushi** (unison + drum)
(2) Yoshitsune praises the children for their knowledge and tells Benkei to reward them, and to ask them the best way to get to Hiraizumi. He is answered in riddles from a knowing, even cunning child. There are three possible ways, each with its own hardship or impossibility: the lower road, the upper road and the middle road. (This is like a lyrical michiyuki passage, though not an actual journey.) While the middle road might seem the easiest, this is where Togashi's men lie in wait for travelling yamabushi to behead them. The children take Benkei to see the heads of the unfortunate monks already slain. This passage in tsume delivery with drum and movement on stage is a dramatic highlight.	Hōgan dono, kikoshimesarete (Waki I) Benkei uketamatte (Waki II) Sono naka ni (solo – waki I) Benkei ga oi yori mo (solo – tayū) Waranbe kiite	**kotoba** (solo – tayū)
	Nisan no hazama, Mogamigawa	kakari – starts to be melodic
	Aneha no matsu Kamewarizaka to mōshizutsu	kakari/iro
	Shijūni tokoro no meiyo no … kayou beki yō wa sara ni nashi	**fushi** – drum comes in, three singers in unison, goes up to high pitch
	Nakamichi to mōsu wa … nō kyakusō, to mōshikeru	tsume
(3) Yoshitsune expresses chagrin that those innocent priests were slain because of him, and goes to mourn them. The group perform rites for the dead. Benkei turns and glares at the children; he rants angrily that Togashi has performed a meaningless act. The children reply hotly, 'there is a reason', and tell of Yoritomo's warrant to capture and kill Yoshitsune. Benkei claims their holy status as priests, and the children laugh and clap their hands, pointing to the pictures of	Hōgan kikoshimesarete (Waki I) Jūichi nin (Waki II) Waranbe kiite	**kotoba**
	Shushu no hoi o mi matoi	han gakari
	Hōkai dōgyō ni shite	kakari chū (naka)

continued

Table 4.5   continued

Sections	Text	FMM*
Benkei and Yoshitsune above the heads, and describe them in unflattering terms, matching them to the actual people before them. Benkei listens and his knees tremble.	Umare o nasouzu hōshi no kubi ... hiza furuute tattari keri.	**tsume**
(4) Benkei ruminates to himself about what to do, and decides to first go alone to Togashi's castle. He then reports his decision to Yoshitsune. Yoshitsune demurs, saying, 'You survived all the troubles in Kyoto, only to perish in this northern clime: what a cruel fate.' Benkei replies, 'It is better for just one to be executed than thirteen. I'll survey the situation. If I am safe, I'll blow the conch shell two or three times, but if I know I am to meet my end, I'll blow it just once. If you hear just one sound, you must all kill yourselves: farewell.' Then, realizing this could be their final farewell in this world, he feels pangs of separation, calls their names and again urges them where, when and how to die.	Musashi kokoro ni omou yō	**kotoba**
	Mata mi sonzuru mono naraba	**kakari**
	Kaibashi hitotsu	**fushi**
(5) Benkei goes to Togashi's castle, praying a nenbutsu to steady his nerves. The narrative describes the external appearance of the mansion, huge and imposing, intimidating, then the inside is described, where the young men and the old men are playing gambling games while having a kind of banquet. Benkei realizes Togashi's wealth and power. He says to himself, 'Oh my god (kuchioshiya!), I am being punished for all my misdeeds.' However, out loud, he announces himself as a yamabushi priest from Kumano, who needs to pass the barrier. When Togashi sees him, he throws his fan to the floor and cries in glee, 'he's walked straight into our hands like a moth to a flame. Take him!' Benkei pretends not to hear, and stands there calmly as if watching the scenery.	Saitō no Musashi Tanda hitosuji ni omoikiri	**kotoba**
	Jogon shite Itarikeru wa	**kakari**
	Kore zo kono kuni no ō Togashi no suke to ōete ari	**tsume**
	Togashi no oidetaru tokoro ni Nanigashi kitaru wa	**hirou**
	Togashi goranjite Mottaru ōgi ni te	**katakiri**

Dance and Narrative: Kōwaka and Nō 109

Sections	Text	FMM*
(6) Togashi's men surround Benkei. Togashi challenges and says it is Benkei, the renowned servant of Yoshitsune. The following verbal exchange between Benkei and Togashi is a test of wits, a battle in words: T: 'You are like Benkei in your eloquence and cleverness with words.' B: 'Well you also are eloquent and clever with words, so perhaps you are Benkei!' B: 'Do I have Benkei written on my forehead?' T. 'No, but here is your portrait, your warrant of arrest!' The likeness is truly remarkable.	Tokikomo utsusazu Togashi ga wakamono hyakunin bakari Musashi kite, Hee, yomo tanjō ha araji ... Ara, muzanya, Benkei ga ...	**kotoba** (CD from here)
	Musashi ga mae ni satto tate	kakari
	Ezu mo roku shaku nibun nari Iro kuroku Take takaku	**fushi**
(7) Benkei decides to change his spiel given the gravity of the situation. He weighs up in his mind which is better, to say he has a list or that he doesn't. He decides to take the risk of saying he has it, and then rebukes Togashi for doubting him. He soliloquizes, 'If only I had a kanjinchō!' (Kanjinchō ga araba koso.) He then 'searches' for it in his pack, praying to all the possible gods for help (fushi section). Indeed, the gods come to his aid, as he finds a blank letter scroll which he takes out and triumphantly claims, 'Here is the subscription list!'	Musashi kokoro ni omou yō Ima wa mata kotoba o kae ... ... tattō hijiri ... Miyako ni te iretaru koto no sōrawaneba	**kotoba** (CD to here)
	Oi ni wa sara ni nakarikeri	kakari
	Namu ya Hachiman Daibosatsu	**fushi**
(8) Togashi looks, and says 'I want to see it and pay my respects to the list.' Benkei panics and thinks, 'How can I let him see it?!' However, he says, 'You fool, Togashi, how can you cast your eyes on this sacred document when even emperors bow before it? Heaven would punish you.' Togashi replies, all right, just read it then. Benkei again says to himself: 'If I read it, who knows what will happen? If I don't read it, the outcome is certain. Anyway, I am damned if I will let this fellow take me alive. I'll jump on that fast-looking roan horse and go the Mimandō temple and join the others. First I must kill Yoshitsune, then myself. The others can also only serve him now by dying. What I wish we could do is go to Kamakura and	Togashi goranjite Konata e tabe ogaman to kowaru ... Ika ni kakeashi no hayakaruran ni ...	**kotoba** (CD resumes from here)
	Shinde kō o nasubeki nari	kakari (Example 4.2 from here)
	Higoro waga kimi shichi shō made to Chigiri o tamaitaru	kakari shidai
	Yamayama no Shō Tengu Tennō Yashin	tsuke / katakiri **tsume** / katakitsuke

continued

Table 4.5   *concluded*

Sections	Text	FMM*
get that Kajiwara, and torture him with a slow death.' While thinking all this, he looked totally unmoved.	Igyō irui no onidomo o … chittomo sawagu keshiki wa nashi.	**tsume** (CD track ends here)
(9) Benkei 'reads' the subscription list. When finished, he rolled up the scroll and threw it into his pack; his appearance and mien were anything but human. (No longer performed)	Musashi kono kanjinchō o takaku motte yomu naraba Sotto hiroide sōgan ni ōshiate ōshiate, Nani to wa shiranedomo Uyamatte mousu to, agetarikeru. 'Uyamatte … Kanjin no shōmon kou … Namu kimyōkei' to yomiagete, kurukuru to hinmaite, hon no oi e nageiretaru, Benkeibō ga arisama, ningen no waza de nakarikeru.	**kotoba** kakari yomimono **tsume** Ōe-bon

*   Bold type indicates the main substyles.

Text 4.1   Kōwaka, *Togashi* (1)
(from part-way through section 6 to first part of section 7. CD Track 6)

コトバ   **kotoba**
… 武蔵聞て、ヘエーよもたん上はあらじ、たばかり事に云よと思ひ、ししやう（支証）のあらば見んとかうた。
Surely there is no 'Wanted' poster. He thinks they are just trying to trick him. 'If you have the evidence let me see it', he asked.

(CD Track 6 starts here)
1. 富樫聞て、あらむざんや弁慶が   Togashi heard and thought, 'Poor Benkei!
Togashi kiite, Ara muzanya, Benkei ga
2. いつ迄いのちながらゑんと   How much longer does he think he can live?
Itsu made inochi nagaraen to
3. たん上かうつるやさしさよ   I admire him for asking to see the poster.'
Tanjō kōtsuru yasashisayo
4. それそれ見せよと仰せければ   He orders, 'Hey, show him'.
Sore sore mise yo to ōsekereba
5. 承ると申して   'Yes sir', they say.
Uketamawaru to mōshite

Dance and Narrative: Kōwaka and Nō

6. 富樫が若等四五人
Togashi ga wakatō shigonin
7. 座敷をはらりと立て
Zashiki o harari to tate
8. 八尺屏風を取出し
Hasshaku byōbu o toriidashi

Four or five of Togashi's young men

hurriedly get up and

bring back the eight-foot-high screen

カカリ
9. 武蔵が前にさつと立
Musashi ga mae ni satto tate
10. ゑづをざらりとなげかけ
Ezu o zarari to nagekake
11. 弁慶に見する
Benkei ni misuru
12. うつしもうついたり
Utsushi mo utsuitari
13. 書もかいたる絵師かな
Kaki mo kaitaru eshi ka na
14. 武蔵がたけは
Musashi ga take wa
15 六尺弐分
Roku shaku ni bu

kakari

They set it up right in front of Musashi,

hung the picture up on the screen

and showed it to Benkei.

What a striking likeness!

What an artist to be able to draw like this!

Musashi's height is

six feet two inches.

フシ
16. 絵づも六尺、二分也
Ezu mo roku shaku ni bu nari
17. 色黒く、たけたかく
Iro kuroku, take takaku
18. まなこの、にくぢをうついてあり
Manako no nikuji o utsuite ari
19. あまつさへは、武蔵めが
Amassa e wa, Musashi me ga
20. 左りのまな先に
Hidari no manasaki ni
21. あざの有るまで
Aza no aru made
22. うついたはのがれ
Utsuita wa nogare
23. つびふは更になし
Tsubyō wa sara ni nashi

fushi

The picture is also six feet and two inches.

Black in complexion, towering in height,

the eyes depicted large and forbidding.

What's more, the fellow Musashi

has at the edge of his left eye

a birthmark, and even this

is drawn, so

there is no way of escape.

(Example 4.1 finishes here)

Example 4.1 Kōwaka, *Togashi* (1)[8]

[8] Note on transcriptions of CD extracts: I have transcribed the entire sections in the extracts on the CD, rather than a representative example of each substyle type, in order to show the nature of the fluidity of each substyle in context. I have not, however, included the drum beats and the vocal interjections in the fushi and tsume sections.

Example 4.1   *concluded*

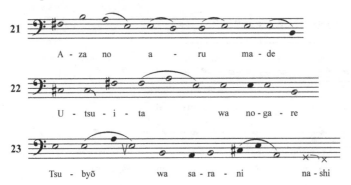

Text 4.1   *continued*

コトバ **kotoba (Section 7)**
武蔵心に思ふよふよ、今は又言葉をかゑ、ちんぜばやと思ひ、いかにのふ富樫殿、以前に此法師、熊野山伏とは、御身の心そつと引み申さんがため也、是社なんと東大寺の、勧進ひじりぞうよ、富樫聞て、たつたうぞふおひじり、
Musashi thinks in his heart this way, 'Now I had better change my spiel, so I can talk my way out of this situation.' 'Well now, My Lord Togashi, before I said that this humble priest was a Kumano yamabushi, in order to attract your sympathy. Actually, I am a subscription collecting ascetic from Nara Todaiji.' Togashi listens and says, 'So you are a holy priest...'

(CD break here)

Much research on kōwaka is text-based, centring on pieces outside the Kyūshū repertoire of eight. *Atsumori*, for example, has been written about by many.[9]

The kōwaka chosen for this study is the same basic story as the nō play, *Ataka*, and the kabuki piece *Kanjinchō* set to nagauta-ōzatsuma music (Chapter 7). The piece enables a comparison between the music of the three genres, and how narrative material is realized differently in different genres.

The kōwaka version of the story is closely related to Chapter 7 of the *Gikeiki*, which recounts Yoshitsune's journey to take refuge in Ōshu. Yoshitsune, wanted by his brother Yoritomo, is in flight with his band of followers, led by the monk Musashi-bō Benkei. They are all disguised as mountain ascetic priests (yamabushi). As all barrier guards have been instructed to arrest and kill any groups of yamabushi, Yoshitsune is disguised as a porter. When they approach the Ataka barrier, local children tell them how previous parties of travelling priests have been killed and point to their heads on display.

---

[9] Saya's (2002) comparison with nō and setsuwa versions; Tokita (2003). *Manjū* was written about by Squires, Anzako and Kobayashi showing kōwaka's ritual function, and its connection with sekkyō and setsuwa, not just with gunkimono.

Dance and Narrative: Kōwaka and Nō

Benkei visits Togashi's mansion and brashly asks for a contribution to his Tōdaiji fund. The kōwaka piece elaborates this episode and adds an episode that is not in the *Gikeiki*, the dramatic reading of the subscription list with similarities to the monk Mongaku's in *The Tale of the Heike*, Book 5, Chapter 7 (Parker 2006: 101–33). It also incorporates other story elements which form separate incidents in *Gikeiki*. In *Gikeiki*, the next morning the fugitives are questioned by a ferryman, and Benkei beats Yoshitsune to allay his suspicion. Soon after, Benkei outwits a hostile warrior who searches their luggage. The kōwaka piece *Oisagashi* combines the master-beating element and the luggage search.

Text 4.2   Kōwaka, *Togashi* (2)
(from part-way through to the end of section 8. CD track 6 resumes here)

コトバ **kotoba**
…　いつかにかけ足のはやかるらんに、ひんぼうで打乗、みまんどへまいり、一のかたなにて、ごんぜんがいし奉り、武蔵め腹を切らず、君御腹を召れなば、拾壱人の人ゝも、皆ゝ腹を切ず、いきてはかうをなさず共

'…grab and get on the fastest possible horse, go to Mimando, then I will report to Yoshitsune. The first blow will be to slay Yoshitsune; then I will cut my belly. When Yoshitsune has committed seppuku, the eleven of us will all follow suit. Alive, even if we cannot be of service to him…

カカリ	**kakari**
1. しんではかうをなすべき也	by dying we can serve him.
Shinde wa kou o nasu beki nari	
2. 日ごろ我君七生迄と	We have always taken an oath
Higoro waga kimi shichi shō made to	
3. ちぎりをかせ玉ひたる	to serve our lord for seven rebirths.
Chigiri o kase tamaitaru	
4. あたごの山の太郎坊	Atago no Yama no Tarōbō and
Atago no Yama no Tarōbō	
5. 平の山の次郎坊	Hiranoyama no Jirōbō
Hiranoyama no Jirōbō	(will bring to our aid the following gods)

ツメ	**tsume**
6. 山ゝの小うてんぐ	Yamayama no shō tengu
Yamayama no shō tengu	
7. 天王やじん八しやう人	Tennō yajin Hashōjin
Tennō yajin Hashōjin	
8. こづめんづあぼらせつ	Gozu menzu abora setsu.
Gozu menzu aboora setsu	
9. い行いるいのをに共に引ぐし候らいて	We'll take misshapen demons with us.
Igyō irui no onidomo o hikigushi sōraite	

10. 本もうならば関東へ Honnō naraba Kantō e	What we really want to do though
11. せつながあいだにみだれ入て Setsuna ga aida ni midare itte	is immediately rush to the East;
12. 箱根山の峠より Hakone no yama no tōge yori	from Hakoneyama Pass
13. こくうんの棚引 Kokuun no tanabiki	to make black clouds form
14. でん光をとばせ Denkō o tobase	and lightning strike.
15. 玉をみがく鎌倉に Tama o migaku Kamakura ni	On Kamakura, shining like a jewel,
16. しやぢくの雨をふらせ Shajiku no ame o furase	to make torrential rain fall
17. 八ツ七合をあらひ流し Yatsu shichi gō o arainagashi	and wash away their villages.
18. にくかりし梶原を Nikukarishi Kajiwara o	As for detestable Kajiwara,
19. そうなくもころさずして So naku mo korosazu shite	to kill him not quickly, but
20. 百きじんにおおせ付 Hyakkijin ni ōsetsuke	to summon 100 demons
21. ねつてつのゆをわかし Nettetsu no yu o wakashi	and boil water like hot iron melted iron
22. 口の内に流し入 Kuchi no uchi ni nagashi ire	and pour it down his throat,
23. 六ぷ五ぞふを、焼きはらい Roppu gozō o yakiharai	burn out his entire innards.
24. 七代子孫の取ころして Shichidai shison no torikoroshite	We'll curse and kill his descendents for seven generations.
25. 本もをとぐるならば Honmo o toguru naraba	This way our original wish will be fulfilled.
26. かんしやうじやうにてあらずとも Kanshōjō ni te arazu to mo	I am not Michizane
27. あら人がみと武蔵めが Arahitogami to Musashime ga	but I am sure I will be worshipped as
28. あをがれんずる事共を Aogarenzuru kotodomo o	a living god like him.'
29. あんの内と思ひければ An no uchi to omoikereba	Benkei thought all this to himself,
30. ちつ共さはぐけしきはなし Chittomo sawagu keshiki wa nashi.	and didn't show any sign of disturbance.

(Text from Fujita 2009).

Example 4.2 Kōwaka, *Togashi* (2)

continued

Example 4.2 *continued*

Benkei asks Togashi for safe passage. He says he and his band are soliciting donations to rebuild Tōdaiji temple. Togashi pulls his bluff and asks to see the subscription list (kanjinchō). Benkei does not have one, but scrambles through his pack and finds an empty scroll which he pretends to read out.

The extant kōwaka texts of Togashi unaccountably finish with the reading of the subscription list. Presumably there was once a sequel piece, or perhaps the piece was originally longer. As it stands, the piece has nine sections. The two extracts on the CD (Track 6) are from sections six and eight.

The Kyūshū transmission actually ends at the end of the eighth section, omitting the reading of the kanjinchō which can be thought of as the narrative and dramatic highlight, occupying the lengthy section nine. From the length of the text, this must have been a very long section all in the one style of delivery, replete with abstruse Buddhist content, so possibly of minimal interest to singers and deemed to be similarly so for the audience. The short narrative at the end of the reading of the kanjinchō (section 9) has a strong impact, however, underlining Benkei's superhero status: '... to, yomiage, kurukuru to hinmahite, moto no oi e nageiretaru, Musashibō ga arisama, ningen no waza de nakarikerku': Benkei's feat is that of no ordinary mortal (Araki 1964: 130). This abrupt ending is very different from the final lines of other pieces, and confirms the suspicion that it may not always have been the end of the narrative, but just of one scene. These days, only one half of these eight sections are performed at a time. The Kyoto University of the Arts public seminar performance in February 2009 did sections 5 to 8.

Thus, the story of the band after Benkei's reading of the subscription list and their passing the barrier is no longer performed in kōwaka, whereas this part is highly developed in both the nō *Ataka* and its kabuki adaptation, the nagauta-ōzatsuma *Kanjinchō*. On the other hand, in kōwaka the early part of the story before the barrier is approached is richly embroidered with sections and episodes not found in nō and ōzatsuma. Some appear in the kyōgen interlude narrative in nō *Ataka*, and the encounter with the children is alluded to in the nagauta piece, *Ataka no matsu*.

Though not marked by a change in musical style, the kōwaka narrative is remarkable for the internal monologues of Benkei and Togashi that occur when they are engaged in a battle of wits. Togashi 'thinks': 'Poor Benkei, how long does he think he is going to survive?!' Benkei 'thinks': 'Surely there is no "Wanted" poster!' And again when he is thinking very fast trying to decide what strategy to take with Togashi: 'If only I had a kanjinchō ...' and so on (see translation).

Each section of the narrative begins with spoken (kotoba) delivery; all sections but the fifth end with fushi or tsume or fushi-tsume (Table 4.5). In between kotoba and fushi and/or tsume, there are transitional patterns: kakari and/or sashi/shidai/iro. Examples of verbal formulaic expression include 'araba koso' and 'sara ni nashi'.

The tsume part of section 8, with which the piece as currently transmitted finishes, is a powerful expression of Benkei's fierce loyalty to Yoshitsune, indeed the warrior ethic of loyalty and revenge. The kanjinchō reading might have been an anti-climax after this.

Generic Analysis of nō

The formal structure of nō music, text and dance is similar to that of other performed narrative traditions (see Hoff and Flindt 1976–7; Bethe and Brazell 1982; and Fujita 2008). Yokomichi's seminal analysis of the structure of nō influenced a great deal of research on other types of katarimono (Table 4.6).

The influence of the dramatic context gives rise to a much tighter structure than is seen in heike or kōwaka. The musical structure of nō has a more clearly specific function than that of heike. There is more specialization of melodic types or substyles, such as those used for opening or closing sections. This would seem to be the influence of the dramatic context of theatre, a feature which will be observable with the entrance of jōruri into the context of the puppet theatre (gidayū-bushi) and the context of kabuki dance (itchū-bushi, tokiwazu-bushi and so on). The complexity of the theatrical performance context also severely reduced the possibility of improvisation by performers.

The instrumental ensemble of nō developed from the flute and drums of the gagaku ensemble, and also from shrine music. It has no stringed instrument; furthermore, the nō flute does not really function as a melodic instrument, but as a coloristic device, because its pitch does not agree with the pitch of the singing-narrating voice (utai).

Table 4.6   Structural levels of nō

Context	Nō theatre: programme of five plays + *Okina*
Larger work	Not part of nō performance, but many plays are episodes from larger narratives
Piece	This is the nō *play*; the largest discrete performance unit in this genre Categories of play: five by content, two by narrative structure: mugen nō and genzai nō
Sections: with song	Ba: most plays have two distinct halves: maeba and nochiba Dan Sections: most are named Sub-sections: setsu
Sections: hayashi ensemble only	Hayashi instrumental interludes for dance without song-narrative
Phrase	One line of 12 (7 + 5) syllables

The Piece/Play

Unlike the purely narrative genres of heike and kōwaka, the concept of the piece or play as the self-contained item of performance is watertight in nō, because of the clearly defined dramatic structure in which beginnings, middles and endings are clearly articulated, related to the progression of jo-ha-kyū (beginning, development, denouement).

The wide range of sources of nō drama gave rise to five categories of play based on content:

1. kami nō / waki nō (plays about gods)
2. shura nō (plays about warriors)
3. onna nō / katsura mono (plays about women)
4. miscellaneous
5. kiri nō (plays about non-human creatures)

Folk religious ritual, where the main character is a god, informed the first category. Heike and Soga narratives are the main sources of the second category. Classical court literature by women is the principal source of the third category. Kusemai was a source for the mad woman plays which are mostly placed in the fourth category. Folk tales, tales about the origins of shrines and temples (engi) and about demons can appear in both the fourth and fifth categories. *Dōjōji*, for example, is from a setsuwa-folk tale connected to the Dōjōji Temple and is in the fifth category.

A full day's programme should consist of the auspicious piece, *Okina*, followed by one play from each of these five categories, with a kyōgen farce included in between each of the five.

There are also two categories of piece / play based on structure: normal dramas that relate a story that unfolds in real time (genzai nō), and the dream (mugen) nō, which recalls events of the past, and re-enacts them as memory, or as the dead coming back to this world to tell the story to the living. The latter were largely Zeami's invention, and are artistic realizations of the religious ritual of calling on dead spirits and exorcism.

The nō play normally has two acts or scenes. The two parts are frequently separated by a kyōgen interlude, which comments on or amplifies the situation, in a directly narrative style, including a question-answer dialogue between two characters. The details of this are not written in full in the utai text. In *Ataka*, the kyōgen role is used to amplify the play with additional small scenes, such as reporting on the ghastly sight of the severed heads, but this is not written in full in the play books (utaibon).

Sections and Narrative Substyles

In nō, we can distinguish (1) the spoken parts, from (2) those where the voice is melodically delivered in free rhythm (hyōshi awazu), and then (3) those parts which are sung with definite melodic movement, and with a rhythmic complexity supported rhythmically by the instrumental ensemble (hyōshi au). Yokomichi created the term gingata for chant style: yowagin (soft chant) and tsuyogin (hard chant). This much the same as Hirano's concepts of ginshō, rōshō and eishō, and Tokita's narrative substyles. The rhythmic forms (Yokomichi calls these norigata) are hiranori, chūnori and ōnori.

Yokomichi's influential analysis, first published in the 1960s, showed the complex but formulaic structure of the nō drama as a whole, including the music. He put forward a model of layered structure:

play
ba (scene)
dan (section)
shōdan (small section)
setsu (set of lines)
line
phrase

and proposed that the most important structural unit is the small section.

There are several types of section, most with traditional names, which have a formulaic character and style, and which combine to create a sense of a highly organized composition. There are sections in which utai is central (usually with hayashi accompaniment), and sections for hayashi only. Yokomichi says that, broadly speaking, there are about 50 types of utai section and 50 types of hayashi section.

The main utai sections are: shidai, sageuta, ageuta, kurui, kuse, noriji, chūnoriji, issei, waka, kuri, sashi, kudoki, nanori, mondō, rongi, kiri. Of these, kuse and kudoki are unequivocally narrative. The main hayashi sections, as listed in the *Nō kyōgen jiten* (Dictionary of nō and kyōgen) are: jo no mai, chū no mai, hayamai, otoko mai, kami mai, kagura, gaku, kako, iroe, kakeri, hayabue, ōbeshi, sagariha, issei, deha, shidai.

Nō: *Ataka*

Like all nō plays, *Ataka* is a rich combination of song, narrative, dialogue and dance. The main actor (shite) is Benkei; the supporting actor (waki) is Togashi, and Yoshitsune is a child actor (kokata). This is a so-called 'present time' (genzai) nō with a lot of action that unfolds in a conventionally chronological way, unlike 'dream' (mugen) nō, where past deeds and states are elicited by the questioning by the supporting character (waki) of the main character (shite).

Table 4.7   Outline of nō *Ataka*

Sections	Text	FMM*
(1) Togashi (waki) introduces himself, explains the situation. Dialogue between Togashi and a guard (kyōgen actor).	Kayou ni sōrō mono wa ...	**nanori** **mondō**
(2) Yoshitsune (kokata), Benkei (shite) and ten followers (shitezure) enter. (Michiyuki) Arrival words	Tabi no koromo wa, suzukake no ... Kōmon tateyabure Toki shimo koro wa kisaragi no ... Kore ya kono ... Namiji haruka ni ... Kehi no umi ... Ika ni mōshiage sōrō ...	**shidai** **sashi** **ageuta** High song **ageuta** **sageuta** Low song **ageuta** **tsukizerifu**
(3) Discussion between Yoshitsune and Benkei Benkei addresses footman (kyōgen), tells him to go and scout.	Ika ni Benkei ...	**mondō** **mondō**
(4) Reconnaissance of footman (kyōgen): he goes to the Barrier, sees severed heads and rushes back.	(Not in nō text)	(Kyōgen)
(5) Benkei and footman: the footman reports the previous scene to the party.	(Not in nō text)	**mondō**
(6) Yoshitsune dons a porter's garb as his disguise; they approach the barrier. Yoshitsune is noble but weak, not used to hardship.	Ge ni ya kurenai wa sono fu ni uete mo kakurenashi ... Yoroyoro to shite ayumitamō on arisama zo itawashiki. ... mina, ontōri sōrae.	**kakeai** **uta** (yowagin) **mondō**
(7) Benkei and party arrive at the barrier. Togashi's man (kyōgen) reports the appearance of Benkei and party. Togashi and Benkei's repartee; Benkei says they are collecting for Tōdaiji. Togashi says they will be executed. Benkei: we will perform last rites.	 Mina mina, uketamawari sōrō.	**mondō**: kyōgen and Togashi **mondō**: Togashi and Benkei

Dance and Narrative: Kōwaka and Nō 125

Sections	Text	FMM*
(8) Last rites. Mantra	Ide ide saigo no tsutome o hajimen Sore yamabushi to ippa ... On-abira-un-ken to juzu sarasara to oshimomeba	**notto** Prayer **uta** Song
(9) Togashi hesitates, maybe it is a mistake; show me the kanjinchō. After finding an empty scroll in his pack, Benkei 'reads' the kanjinchō. The people at the barrier are in awe. Togashi tells them to pass on quickly.	 Moto yori Kanjinchō wa araba koso, oi no naka yori ōrai no makimono ichikan ... Takaraka ni yomiagekere. Seki no hitobito kimo o keshi ... tōshikere. Isoide ontōri sōrae. Uketamawari sōrō.	**mondō**: waki and shite (**unnamed**): shite – kakaru **yomimono** **uta**: tsuyogin. **mondō**: waki – shite
(10) Togashi is again suspicious, and stops the 'porter' (Yoshitsune) (Our Lord is in danger). Benkei beats Yoshitsune. Both sides line up menacingly. Togashi: Must be a mistake; you may pass. Kyōgen: they are genuine.	Ika ni mōshi sōrō, Hōgan dono no ontōri sōrō. Suwa waga kimi o ... to tachikaeru. Katagata wa nani yue ni ... osoretsubyō zo mietaru. Chikagoro ayamarite sōrō ... Makoto no yamabushi ja.	**mondō** **uta** **uta** **mondō**
(11) Past the barrier, they rest. Distress of Benkei: he apologizes. Yoshitsune thanks him for his quick-wittedness, a gift from the God of War.	Saki no seki o ba ... Seki no monodomo ... Hachiman no O-takusen ka to omoeba ...	**mondō** **kakaru** **sageuta**
(12) Distress of Yoshitsune: a lyrical evocation of the hardships of the warrior.	Sore yo wa massei ni oyobu to iedomo ... Ge ni ya genzai no ka o mite ... Shikaru ni Yoshitsune yumi-ba no ie ni umarekite ... Ge ni omou koto, kanawaneba koso, ukiyo nare to shiredomo sasugo ... ukiyo ya.	**kuri** **sashi** **kuse**
(13) Togashi brings a gift of sake to Benkei.	Ika ni tare ka aru.	**mondō**: Togashi, kyōgen; Benkei, kyōgen
(14) Benkei drinks, thinking 'I don't trust him'.	Omoshiroya ... Ayashimeraru wa men men to ... Omoshiroya yama mizu ni Moto yori Benkei wa Santō no ...	(**unnamed**) kakaru **dan uta**

continued

Table 4.7   *concluded*

Sections	Text	FMM*
(15) Benkei offers sake to Togashi, who asks him to dance. Benkei dances.	Naru wa taki no mizu … Naru wa taki no mizu … Naru wa taki no mizu …	**waka** Poem **mondō** **waka** Poem **otoko mai**
(16) Finale The party travel on to the province of Mutsu.	Hi wa teru to mo taezu toutari … Mutsu no kuni e zo, kudarikeru.	**noriji** Ōnori rhythm

* Bold type indicates the main substyles.
Based on cassette *Kanze-ryū Yōkyoku Hyakuban-shū*, no. 87. King CNT-815.

Text 4.3   Nō: *Ataka* (CD Track 7)
(From Sections 11 and 12)

下歌
1. 御託宣かと思えば、忝くぞ覚ゆる
O-takusen ka to omoeba, katajikenaku zo oboyuru

sageuta
A revelation from the God of War! When I think of this I feel deep gratitude

(Section 12)
クリ
2. それ世は末世に及ぶといへども、
Sore yo wa masse ni oyobu to iedomo
3. 日月は未だ地に落ち給はず
Nichigatu wa imada chi ni ochitamawazu
4. たとひいかなる方便なりとも
Tatoi ikanaru hōben nari to mo
5. まさしき主君を打つ杖の
Masashiki shukun o utsu tsue no
6. 天罰に当たらぬ事や有るべき。
Tenbatsu ni ataranu koto ya arubeki

kuri
Even if this world of ours has now entered the later stage of time
Still the sun and moon on high have not yet fallen off this earth
Whatever can be said for my improvisation
Still with a staff I struck the Lord, our rightful master.
Is it not then true that the judgement of Heaven must fall on me?

サシ
7. 実にや現在の果を見て過去未来を知るといふ事
Ge ni ya genzai no ka o mite, kako mirai o shiru to iu koto
8. 今に知られて身の上に、憂き年月の如月や
Ima ni shirarete mi no ue ni, uki toshitsuki no kisaragi ya

sashi
Truly it is said that the present comes deep from the past and shapes the future, had we but known it,

As I do now, from sorrows suffered in my flesh from months and years of hardship

9. 下の十日の今日の難を、遁れつるこそ不思議なれ Shimo no tōka no kyō no nan o nogaretsuru koso fushigi nare	To this frosty close at the end of February we have come, surviving the dread dangers of this day miraculously
10. たださながらに十余人 Tada sanagara ni jūyonin	Overwhelmed, the chosen band of ten and more men
11. 夢の覚めたる心地して、互ひに面を合はせつつ、 Yume no sametaru kokochi shite, tagai ni omote o awasetsutsu	Are held by the sensation of dreamers roused, and not yet wakened from their dreams, staring numb and blank from one face to another,
12. 泣く計なる有り様かな。 Naku bakari naru arisama ka na.	They cry and weep aloud

クセ	**kuse**
13. 然るに義経、弓馬の家に生れ来て、 Shikaru ni Yoshitsune, kyūba no ie ni umarekite	Even noble Yoshitsune, scion of a warrior's house of bows and horses
14. 命を頼朝に奉り、屍を西海の浪に沈め、山野海岸に、起き臥し明かす武士の、 Mei o Yoritomo ni tatematsuri, kabane o saikai no nami ni shizume, sanya kaigan ni, okibushi akasu mononofu no	Who offered to Yoritomo his life, or his corpse, plunging all his foes beneath the waves, down to the western deeps of Dannoura. In hills and fields and by the shore, he rose and lay and rose once more, through long nights to dawn, with no moment to pillow his head on his
15. 鎧の袖枕、片敷く隙も波の上、 Yoroi no sodemakura, katashiku hima mo nami no ue...	armor sleeves, half-spread by the lapping waves...

Translation based on Yasuda 1972: 391–3.

The first part is dominated by 'strong chant' (tsuyogin), a hard style of delivery, reflecting the warrior ethos of the characters (see Fujita 2012 on tsuyogin and the expression of masculinity). Even the ageuta song and related sections are in tsuyogin delivery. This contrasts with the strongly lyrical nature of the text, depicting the journey, but reflects musically the masculine nature of the warrior band and their grim mission. Whereas in the kōwaka, the scenes of the journey and arrival at Ataka by Benkei and the band of fugitives are the focus of the opening sections of the narrative, in the nō *Ataka* Togashi enters first and explains the situation at the barrier, because the form of nō requires that the waki always enters first and elicits the story from the shite.

When challenged to show the subscription list, as in the kōwaka Benkei has some internal monologue (not intended for the 'ears' of other characters on stage):

'Motoyori kanjinchō wa araba koso ...'. This is a condensed or telescoped version of the kōwaka lines.[10]

The reading of the subscription list is in a style called yomimono, essentially close to speech. The party of monks are permitted to pass, but one of Togashi's guards recognizes the porter as Yoshitsune, and they are held back again. The episode of Benkei beating Yoshitsune is full of tension. The intense confrontation between the band of false yamabushi and Togashi and his men is very powerful on stage, and the chant is here tsuyogin (section 10, 'Katagata wa nani yue ni ...'). The section ends with a brief dialogue (mondō) with Togashi who grudgingly acknowledges their authentic status and urges them to go on quickly.

After the dramatic climax of getting past the barrier, the mood mellows and relaxes, and the dominant musical mode changes to yowagin. (CD track 7: sageuta – kuri – sashi – kuse.) Section 11 begins with a mondō between Benkei and Yoshitsune, reflecting on what has just happened; Benkei begs his master's forgiveness and Yoshitsune praises him for his quick-wittedness that saved them. The kuse is a narrative about Yoshitsune's unfortunate lot in life. Its pathos seems to foreshadow the jōruri kudoki.

The piece reverts to tsuyogin for Benkei's auspicious, celebratory dance sections with which the play finishes. Tsuyogin is used for both military 'strong' narrative, and for auspicious narrative with a kami – Shintō focus.

As a form of mai accompanied by drum, kōwaka is closer to nō than to heike and jōruri with their lute accompaniment. When contrasting kōwaka with nō, the most obvious difference is kōwaka's complete lack of dramatic mimicry. Related to this is the formalistic sequencing of the substyles from kotoba to fushi to tsume with little relation to the narrative content. Also striking is the extremely loose episodic structure of kōwaka narrative. There is no section with a fixed number of lines or phrases like the ageuta or the kuse in nō; in this kōwaka shows the same narrative form as kōshiki and heike.

Both have a neutral, a soft and a hard style of delivery. In nō the neutral is the hyōshi awazu style; basic and soft is yowagin, and hard is tsuyogin. In kōwaka, kotoba is neutral, fushi is soft and tsume is hard. These distinctions are related to dance and accompanying drum rhythm as well as melody.

Kōwaka remains intrinsically a narrative, albeit with mai movement, with none of the dramatic elements of nō.

---

[10] The English translation is based on Kenneth Yasuda's translation (in Yasuda 1972: 391–3). Yasuda has: 'As if there were ever such a subscription book!' Website the-noh.com gives: 'We have no such kanjinchō. However, I remove an ordinary scroll from my oi and start to read it loudly, pretending that I am reading the kanjinchō'. I feel it means: 'If only there were a kanjinchō!'

The Legacy of kōwaka

Kōwaka flourished at a turning point in the history of the performing arts, between medieval and kinsei. Looking at its fellow medieval arts, heike and nō, we have seen that kōwaka's key characteristics lie in the reciting and dancing of verbal narrative without dramatic mimicry. Its strong bias towards hard narrative military content is common with heike, and the warrior (shura) category of nō plays, while a few pieces still link it with the soft narrative of religious tales and myth. The analysis has shown that formal elements of narrative musical performance, that is, named formulaic materials at the levels of section and phrase, are congruent with the structural and musical form of all medieval vocal music. This performative element links the narrative kōwaka and nō drama, and other medieval performing arts.

Looking forward, there are also easily identifiable continuities between kōwaka and the early Edo period arts that supplanted it, kabuki and jōruri. Kōwaka is linked with jōruri through its formal elements of sung narrative musical performance, the named formulaic musical materials at the levels of section and phrase, as the following chapters will demonstrate. Kōwaka texts and content were appropriated by jōruri, and subsequently kabuki (Dunn 1966: 43–4). The chigo mai aesthetic which was part of kōwaka, as in the piece *Manjū*, found a place in wakashū kabuki (see below). Early jōruri borrowed from kōwaka texts much more than from nō, because mai was not as refined as nō, but had its own tradition as katarimono, and appealed to ordinary people (Muroki 1998: 80).

The conundrum of kōwaka mai is that it rose to such great heights of popularity during the Sengoku period (mid-fifteenth century to the end of the sixteenth century), and yet by the middle of the seventeenth century it had all but dropped from view.[11] This is surprising, since their widespread performances are well-documented, their texts were written and printed, the head performers were given stipends and fiefs 'in perpetuity', and kōwaka became one of the ceremonial musics of the Tokugawa bakufu.

How can we account for its popularity and its virtual disappearance from the urban performance landscape? Is it just a withered appendix to the medieval performing arts, which failed to attract sufficient patronage to keep it on life support? Or did it respond to the catalyst of kabuki and transform into wakashū kabuki?

Muroki tells us that from the early fifteenth century to the late sixteenth century, kōwaka was a popular plebeian art, active mainly in Kyoto. However, its popularity was already declining by the time that Nobunaga embraced the art and raised its status from that of outcaste to one that garnered the patronage of military leaders, which lasted till the end of the Edo period. The military patronage

---

[11] The Sengoku period or Warring States period is generally held to have begun with the Ōnin no ran (1467–1477). It ended with the Azuchi-Momoyama period (1573–1600) and the victory of Tokugawa Ieyasu in the Battle of Sekigahara in 1600.

which began in the Sengoku era was, according to Muroki (1992: 89), also the cause of its decline. The Tokugawa shoguns also continued for a while to solicit kōwaka performance, and to pay stipends to the troupe leaders. Hattori believes that kōwaka lost its raison d'être and that its energy was sapped because it became a ceremonial music (like nō and heike) supported by bakufu (1968: 107). Perhaps most importantly, this is the time that print culture developed, when kōwaka scripts (mai no hon) were printed in great number.[12]

In the unification period, a time of incipient social stability, kabuki became part of a newly emerging urban culture. Nō and heike survived, albeit in an artificially protected environment, whereas kōwaka withered. The medieval oral narrative of jōruri thrived by feeding on the narratives of kōwaka, and by being adopted into the theatrical forms of puppet drama and later kabuki theatre, supported by a new commercial theatre system, largely replacing the medieval patronage system. The urban classes (chōnin) had disposable income to support and sustain a new urban culture, including pre-eminently these forms of entertainment.

Part of the contribution of (women's) maimai and the male kōwaka mai to kabuki was the emphasis on the privileged (though discriminated against) attractive actor's body, which continued even after the demise of women's and wakashū kabuki. Women's performance was certainly not a new phenomenon, but Okuni's kabuki created the shock of the new. First, she had new content: skits about prostitute and customer in the licensed districts, which were incipient contemporary plays (sewamono). Second, was her use of furyū group dance, the first time that odori (as distinct from mai) became a stage art rather than a communal practice. Her lively, dynamic and rhythmic dance attracted the epithets of off-beat, non-mainstream, trendy (kabuki mono). The music for Okuni kabuki's dance was kouta song accompanied by nō hayashi and tsurigane gong. The shamisen became a fixture somewhat later. Third, was the element of cross-dressing, again, not a new phenomenon whether by women or men performers, but titillating in this new context. Her costumes were complemented by exotic props such as a crucifix (brought in by Jesuit missionaries), and other European artefacts. Fourth, were the increasingly affluent new urban audiences, rather than the daimyō.

Women's kabuki caused such a stir that it was banned in 1629, and kabuki developed instead as an all-male art, first by young men (wakashū), where we might look for continuities with the male art of kōwaka mai, and from 1652 by mature men (yarō).

The dominance of beautiful male performers, who like women's kabuki paraded their physical beauty in dance as a preliminary to selling favours, should have given kōwaka an advantage after the banning of women's kabuki (Takei 1997: 38, 41–2). Perhaps we can trace a certain degree of continuity between kōwaka and

---

[12] The first kyōgen prompt book was printed in 1580; jōruri plays appeared in print from the 1650s; kabuki readers somewhat later. Print enshrines an art which no longer is composed in performance. Kōwaka by the 1620s was becoming fossilized, whereas earlier it had been improvised in performance, and did not need scripts (Muroki 1982: 115–16).

wakashū kabuki. If so, in addition to the formal and thematic continuities between kōwaka and subsequent performing arts, we can include also the aspect of male-male eroticism and sexuality, which was raging in Japanese urban culture in the seventeenth century (Saeki 1992).

We can posit a continuity of soft narrative content and expression from women's mai combined with furyū odori which was the basic ingredient of kabuki dance (both women's and wakashū) (Hattori 1968: 102–16) on the one hand, and from gunki to ningyō jōruri to yarō kabuki's aragoto on the other. Kōwaka combined both aspects, the soft physical appeal of male dance and some setsuwa soft narrative with hard, adult male gunki pieces.

Chapter 5
Jōruri and the Puppet Theatre

Introduction

With this chapter we move from medieval to the 'early modern' Edo (or Tokugawa) era (1603–1867), also called the Closed Country era, during which the katarimono scene was dominated by jōruri, musical narrative accompanied by the shamisen.

Jōruri as a cluster of genres of musical narrative has its origins in late medieval Japan as part of the same maelstrom of performed narratives such as heike, sekkyō and kōwaka mai, with which it is linked thematically and musically. It was transformed towards the end of the sixteenth century, when its reciters took up the shamisen (three-stringed lute) as accompanying instrument, and collaborated with puppeteers, in effect creating a new art form.

Jōruri can be seen broadly as one unified entity, but with several constituent narrative genres, all accompanied by the shamisen. This chapter is devoted to that variety of jōruri called gidayū-bushi, the narrative music of the puppet theatre (ningyō jōruri, or bunraku). In Chapter 6, we study a parallel stream of jōruri whose branches developed centrally in the context of kabuki dance, known as the bungo-kei jōruri group (itchū, tokiwazu, tomimoto, shinnai, kiyomoto and others). Then in Chapter 7, we turn our focus to nagauta, kabuki theatre music which has close affinities with jōruri, and its incorporation of ōzatsuma-bushi.

After an extended period of civil war and general social unrest (1467–1573; Sengoku jidai, or period of Warring States) followed a time of cultural renewal, efflorescence and innovation starting in the closing decades of the sixteenth century. Over these decades something of a change of episteme occurred, a turning point in Japanese cultural history. There was a clear break between medieval and 'early modern' culture and society. A process of political unification and the restoration of central control culminated in the seizing of power by Tokugawa Ieyasu in 1600, ushering in the Tokugawa or Edo period. These transitional decades were a time of cosmopolitan openness, during which Jesuit missionaries were active in Japan; Okuni wore a crucifix as she performed kabuki dance; and Jesuit missionaries from Spain, and traders from Holland, England and elsewhere were frequent visitors, until the final ban on Christianity and the edicts enforcing the Closed Country policy in 1636, when all foreigners but Dutch, Chinese and Koreans were banned.

Socially, economically and culturally dynamic, the Edo period saw the development of the kabuki theatre and of the puppet theatre now known as bunraku.[1] By the Genroku era (1688–1703), both of these commercial theatres

---

[1] This name did not attach to the puppet theatre until 1805 but it is now the customary name for the puppet theatre accompanied by gidayū-bushi.

were firmly established as important loci of urban culture in the major centres of Osaka, Kyoto, Nagoya and Edo. The principal patrons of these commercial ventures were the townspeople: merchants and artisans whose tastes were the prime drivers of the content, and of the aesthetic and the forms of the dramas.

Jōruri sung narrative accompanied by shamisen was at the core of the musical expression of both bunraku and kabuki. In the Edo period, what had with heike, kōwaka and old (primitive or proto) jōruri been straightforward musical narrative performed by one singer-instrumentalist became music-drama on the stage for the theatre of puppets and of live actors.

Jōruri narrative was the product of a number of confluences. Among its medieval predecessors were heike, nō, mai and kōwaka, as seen in previous chapters. Also formative were the popular quasi-religious sermon-storytelling of sekkyō (sekkyō-bushi) (Matisoff 2001; Ishii 1989) and the many entertainers who told moral tales, such as those anthologized in the collection known as otogi zōshi (Ruch 1971; Mulhern 1974; Araki 1981; Okuhara 2000). Most important among the latter were the tales about the (eponymous) Lady Jōruri, whose name became that of a whole new genre of musical narrative in the Edo period.

Jōruri was transformed from a medieval to a proto-modern (kinsei) performing art by two factors: the shamisen and puppets. In the two or three decades around 1600 musical storytelling changed from being a simple narrative performance situation with one narrator and an accompanying lute (biwa was replaced by shamisen), to being associated with puppet performance. Around the same time, the narrator and shamisen player became separate roles. The context of jōruri changed further from around Genroku when kabuki was taking on more dramatic features, and started to use jōruri narratives to accompany kabuki dance. The changes included the increase of dramatic dialogue in spoken delivery (serifu), delivered increasingly dramatically and realistically. The growth of the theatrical dimension of the puppets, followed by that of the dance dimension of kabuki performance, radically changed the nature of narrative music.

However, even in these new theatrical contexts, the narrative nature of jōruri as musical narrative (katarimono) was never fully submerged. Japanese culture has the tendency to embrace the new without fully rejecting the old. Alongside the development of literate culture, the oral narrative arts continued to thrive up until the modern era. In the puppet theatre, the narrator and his accompanist are in full view of the audience, foregrounded as narrative voice and music: as the puppets act out the story, they deliver the third person narrative and dialogue of the puppets. The narrative was retained, even though it is superfluous, and could have been dispensed with. The act of narration with the narrator in full view of the audience attests to the enduring importance attached to storytelling in musicalized form. Even in the live theatre of kabuki, many of whose plays are adaptations from jōruri, the narrators and musicians are seated on the stage in view of the audience. The actors deliver the dramatic dialogue, but the third person musicalized narrative is delivered by the singers. Narrative was not eliminated from the theatre.

The seventeenth century saw the development of a new print culture in which jōruri thrived as reading matter as well as performance with the publication and commercial distribution of jōruri texts (see Kimbrough and Shimazaki 2011). The performer's own texts (yukahon) were (and still are) handwritten, as are the lesson books (keikobon) and the complete plays (maruhon) which were adapted for kabuki (see Takeuchi 2008).

This chapter provides a historical overview of early jōruri and the development of gidayū-bushi. It then discusses issues of orality and printing (textuality), and finally proceeds to musical analysis.

Early jōruri

Jōruri narrative before teaming up with shamisen and puppets is known to us mainly through a few diary entries, and through texts which tell the romantic tale of the Lady Jōruri.[2] Many versions of the jōruri tale have been transmitted in written form, with a variety of titles and formats (see Dunn 1966: 30–31; McCullough 1966: 47–50). The Lady Jōruri is posited as the childhood sweetheart of Yoshitsune, so her tale is a late off-shoot of the heike narrative. That the jōruri story seems to have originated with the oral storytelling of itinerant women entertainers is argued by Muroki (1998: 7), Hyōdo (1985/2002), Wakita (2001) and Goodwin (2007).[3] It emerged in the fifteenth century. In an expanded textual version of *Jōruri gozen monogatari* there are parts that resemble another old jōruri text, *Yamanaka tokiwa*, and the kōwaka *Hidehira iri*. That is, it incorporated bits from other genres and stories. In this, the jōruri tale is similar to the tale of *Yokobue* in the heike narrative, and other tales of setsuwa provenance that combine romance and salvation by means of women's agency.

The jōruri story derives directly from a number of disparate oral tales, particularly from the Mikawa region around present-day Nagoya. According to Muroki (1998: 3–4), of a number of extant texts, the earliest was known as *Yahagi monogatari*, whose carriers were itinerant groups of women entertainers (yūjo no me), based at the Yahagi River bank. A sequel called *Fukiage monogatari* was contributed by women entertainers from Kanbara, who had exchanges with the Yahagi women: a tale of resurrection – with her tears, Jōruri-hime revived Yoshitsune, who had been abandoned and buried by robbers (Muroki 1992: 10–12).

---

[2] Jōruri gozen; also Jōruri hime or 'Princess' Jōruri, where hime is a nice word for young woman.

[3] The connection between women and narrative arts was lost with the separation of performance and sexual favours in the seventeenth century, when officially controlled licensed quarters were established, and women were banned from performing in public. Interestingly, women's performance of jōruri (onna gidayū) became important again in the Meiji period.

Such formative tales were eventually collated as an extended narrative about the Lady Jōruri.

It is believed that the jōruri story had spread to the capital by the late fifteenth century (Yamaji 1998: 39). It is documented as having been performed by the same blind biwa priests who performed heike, bringing the heike musical form to jōruri. The lower rank heike performers (zatō) in the Tōdō-za were enthusiastic in taking up jōruri and other popular performing arts. The earliest known record is in the diary of the poet Sōchō, who records that on the 15th day of the 8th month, 1531, a zatō was asked to sing jōruri (Muroki 1998: 16–17).

Eventually the tales were worked together into a continuous narrative cycle, and written down as a text called *Jōruri jūnidan sōshi* (*The Tale of Princess Jōruri in Twelve Parts*), or *Jōruri-hime monogatari*, or *Jōruri gozen monogatari*.[4]

These early jōruri texts, having emerged from oral narrative, had strong oral features, including catalogues of related objects (monozukushi; see Muroki 1998: 4–6) and poetic journeys (michiyuki), and other descriptive verbiage, all indicators of oral provenance.

Similarities and Differences between heike and jōruri

This process of formation of a narrative cycle from many oral and perhaps also written sources is similar to the formation of *The Tale of the Heike*, *The Tale of the Soga Brothers* and *The Chronicle of Yoshitsune* (*Gikeiki*). All gathered up sometimes only tenuously connected apocryphal episodes to form a long narrative cycle.

Whereas the heike cycle was based on historical events with political and religious significance, jōruri is not epic, but romance, and is nowhere near as long as heike. Jōruri is loosely connected with the heike story in that it involves Yoshitsune when he was a youth, still called by his childhood name Ushiwaka. It uses the literary trope of the exiled noble who forms a brief liaison with a local girl (like Genji in Suma).

Both cycles derive their generic names from the eponymous central character; the jōruri tale developed such popularity that it gave its name to a whole genre. By the late sixteenth century there were already stories apart from the jōruri narrative which took the generic name of jōruri; for example *Amida no munewari* (Dunn 1966: 42). Eventually the Jōruri story gradually dropped out of the repertoire of most jōruri genres, though there are some kabuki plays on this theme, including itchū (see Shimazu 1935: 99, 100, 103, 117). Jōruri almost entirely left its original content behind, as it developed beyond the original tale into a new narrative genre incorporating military themes into its romantic-religious world. But while new subject matter emerged, there was continuity of form.

---

[4] It is summarized or rather paraphrased in Dunn (1966). Sieffert (1994) is a French translation and Ryūjin (1980) is based on the first printed version. Dunn (1966: 31–6) gives a detailed outline of the story.

Whereas heike narration was a monopoly of blind minstrels who wore priestly garb and had a system of ranks based on Buddhist clerical ranks, the performers of jōruri came to wear the formal samurai attire of kamishimo and hakama, indicating that it had the tacit approval, if not the patronage of the bushi ruling class. It was actually patronized in commercial theatres by the townsmen class. Such secularization and commercialization can be considered an aspect of modernization.

Jōruri as Meta-genre

The various branches of jōruri share many fundamental features, which enables them to be seen as one large meta-genre. Jōruri came to be performed, not by a blind person but by a sighted male, although the instrumental accompanist often was blind. Texts became central: jōruri is sung and narrated directly from a pre-written text, but its musical notations are neither precise nor prescriptive. All the jōruri genres share much thematic content, with a common stock of narrative plots. Furthermore, they share musical structure and formulaic musical materials. These similarities relate them to medieval narrative genres, showing significant formal continuity with medieval narrative. Jōruri has the same kind of 'vertical', layered structure of dan and shōdan as kōshiki, heike and kōwaka, as discussed in previous chapters; they use multiple melodies and delivery styles; they feature named musical formulaic material that functions like an oral notation, with progression through different pitch registers.

The musically delivered parts of jōruri texts are in 7-5 poetic metre, like nō and sekkyō, whereas kōshiki and heike texts are largely non-metrical. The puppet theatrical context encouraged the development of dramatic, realistic elements, especially through the inclusion of dramatic speech. It also has greater melodic variety and it makes frequent use of quotations from other performance genres, especially songs. Jōruri focuses more on the formulaic phrase than on the section with a unified style of musical delivery; it has a strong sense of phrase-length musical patterns (senritsukei) in either the seven-syllable or five-syllable parts of a line; the latter are generally cadential in nature.

Shamisen

Zatō, the lowest-ranking biwa hōshi, first performed jōruri with biwa, but when the shamisen was introduced from Okinawa to Japan in the late sixteenth century, the biwa hōshi were the first to adopt it, using it to accompany jōruri.[5] Many of them stopped performing heike and jōruri narrative altogether, and turned instead to the more popular jiuta, songs combined with koto and shamisen. The practice of

---

[5] In 1592 a zatō called Fukujin performed heike, jabisen, jōruri, kouta, hayamonogatari (Muroki 1998: 17).

the blind performing shamisen and koto with heike as an optional extra continued through to the modern period.[6]

Although both shamisen and biwa are plucked lutes, the shamisen differs from the biwa in significant structural ways. With only three strings, the long neck with its unfretted fingerboard gave more tonal flexibility. The body is covered front and back with cat or dog skin. It had easier portability, more melodic flexibility, and a brighter tone than the biwa. Furthermore, the separation of narrator and instrumental performer meant the shamisen part could be more active and support the narrative more fully. The sawari buzzing effect was probably developed for the shamisen in Japan, and then transferred to the biwa (Komoda 2008).

The organology and other aspects of the shamisen are dealt with in de Ferranti (2000), Tokita 1999 (67–91), Johnson (2010) and other sources. The shamisen of each jōruri genre has structural differences in the thickness of the neck, the size of the body, the size and shape of the bachi, the thickness of the strings, and the weight and height of the bridge. However, in all the length of the neck (the fingerboard) is the same, the basic fingering techniques are the same, and all feature the sawari device. The nagashi pattern, a playing technique distinct from biwa style, is used by all shamisen genres. The honchōshi tuning is the standard tuning used in jōruri genres, except in some quotation song sections, when niagari and sansagari are often used. In nagauta, on the other hand, tunings are less predictable.

Old jōruri effectively survived only in Kyūshū as zatō biwa and in the Tōhoku region of north-east Japan as oku jōruri accompanied by shamisen (Hyōdō 2000: 192–4).

Blind shamisen players persisted, but it was sighted narrators who performed with them, using texts, and developed the new form (Sakaguchi 2008: 296), probably due to the new visual element of puppets.[7] Shamisen was used with jōruri and puppets much earlier than it first appeared in kabuki.

---

[6] Rather than playing shamisen as an accompaniment to puppet drama, the blind retained more artistic freedom by playing jiuta with shamisen and koto (Katō 1974 [1984]: 105). Kengyō-rank blind secured the patronage of daimyō and received regular stipends. They would perform heike, koto, kouta and shamisen in zashiki private residences, according to records from the Genroku era. In Edo there were about 60 kengyō and kōtō rank blind musicians. About half were employed by daimyō. The situation was similar in regional domains (ibid.: 107–10).

[7] Takemoto Gidayū's first shamisen player was the blind Takezawa Gon'eimon (Katō 1974 [1984]: 104). The latter's disciples also played with Gidayū, notably Tsurusawa Sanji (Yūjirō from 1720) and Tsurusawa Ichitarō. All the main groups of shamisen players, Takezawa, Tsurusawa and Nozawa, were blind. Furthermore, Miyakodayū Itchū was accompanied by former kōtō rank player Miyako Rizō, Yadayū (bun'ya-bushi) by Bungo, and Miyakoji Nakadayū by Tsumaichi. In 1674, blind musicians other than members of the Tōdō-za were forbidden to play heike, shamisen and koto (Kojima 2008: 489).

Puppets

The other big change was the combination of jōruri and puppet performance. Concerning the antecedents of puppet jōruri, sarugaku (nō) was performed with puppets (tekugutsu) in 1416, and in 1469 similarly puppets performed kusemai (Yamaji 1998: 30–31). In 1555, puppets (or puppeteers) called ebisukaki performed nō. As the new shamisen-accompanied jōruri narrative developed, other stories taken from kōwaka and sekkyō-bushi were added to the repertoire. The first documentary evidence of puppet jōruri is an entry in Tokiyoshi Kyōki's diary dated 21 September 1614, which records that 'Amida no munekiri [sic for munewari]' was performed by ebisukaki for the retired Emperor Yōzei (Yamaji 1998: 41–4). Other pieces performed on the same occasion were the nō plays 'Kamo', 'Daibutsu kuyō' and 'Takasago' (ibid.: 41–4). Other evidence confirms that the earliest puppet jōruri plays were largely religious in nature, such as *Amida no munewari*. Even the jōruri story itself is strongly Buddhist.

Puppet jōruri rapidly gained popularity from the 1620s. By co-opting (or being co-opted by) puppets, the jōruri narrators took the first step towards making jōruri a dramatic art form, and in a completely different way from kōwaka or even nō. The puppets provided a visual dimension to the narrated story, a kinetic illustration.

Clearly, the simple puppets in the early stages of collaboration were ancillary to the jōruri performance. However, as jōruri narrative developed in the context first of the puppet theatre and later kabuki, it was sidelined (though never eliminated) by the increasing emphasis on visual representation of the story.

As noted above, blind shamisen players tended to go into jiuta; however, many jōruri shamisen players were blind, but the narrators were sighted males, a separation of roles which opened the way for the elaboration of the musical aspect of the narrative, especially in the instrumental accompaniment. It also led to the practice of written texts being used by the narrators in performance. This paradoxically links the new jōruri with kōshiki, whereas texts for heike and nō were not used in performance. Furthermore authorship, as distinct from oral transmission, became a separate role from the narrator (tayū) and plays were written down as a script to perform from. In what can be called the Chikamatsu factor, the auteur sakusha became important. Most kōshiki also have known authors.

Development of jōruri and the Puppet Theatre in the Seventeenth Century

Probably all or most jōruri from at least 1614 to the 1680s was performed with puppets, as far as this history is known – it has been written about in English by Dunn (1966) and Gerstle, Inobe and Malm (1990), among others.

Early shamisen jōruri with puppet drama displayed the influence of heike, sekkyō, kōwaka and later nō (Dunn 1966). The notable exception to the appropriating nature of early jōruri was kinpira-bushi, which flourished in Edo in the 1650s and 1660s, the first jōruri genre to create original narratives, and the first to have a text writer separate from the narrator (Kanemitsu 2011).

Much writing about jōruri is strongly gidayū-centric, but, as the next two chapters will make clear, gidayū did not sweep all other rival jōruri genres aside; contemporary with gidayū were genres such as itchū-bushi, bun'ya-bushi, tosa-bushi, bungo-bushi and satsuma-bushi (which became ōzatsuma-bushi, and eventually survived as part of nagauta). Looking back from the vantage point of the present, the major lineage apart from gidayū was bun'ya – itchū – bungo – tokiwazu (and other off-shoots). Most Japanese researchers use the term 'old jōruri' (ko-jōruri) to refer to any jōruri which existed before the emergence of gidayū-bushi in 1684, whereas they refer to the latter as tōryū (contemporary or modern) jōruri. However, this ignores the fact that many other jōruri styles (named after their reciters: bun'ya-bushi and so on) were active including in the puppet theatre. It is more appropriate to use the term 'old jōruri' for what preceded the combination of jōruri narrative, shamisen and puppets around 1600.

In the burgeoning urban culture, a proliferation of jōruri performers paraded their individual styles whose differentiation eventually led to new genres, each named (name)-bushi (so-and-so's melody). In this formative stage, clearly there was not one entity called jōruri, but the performances of a number of individual reciters. The art was extremely eclectic, open to all sorts of influences, building on the basic traditional ingredients of musical storytelling with its core of musical and formal resources, with the new elements of shamisen and puppets.

Many jōruri singers were given honorary or nominal titles such as Governor of Bungo Province (Bungo no jō) by the imperial court in recognition of their status as artists. Such a title was helpful in acquiring performing rights and was an important factor in the foundation of the new puppet theatre in Osaka and Kyoto (Yasuda 1998: 97–100). The oldest record of a jōruri singer receiving such a title is in 1613, when a certain Kenmotsu was made Kawachi no kami (Governor of Kawachi Province); later, in 1642, a Yamashiro Sanai was given the title Wakasa no kami.

Uji Kaga no jō (1635–1711) actively incorporated elements of nō into his jōruri, both the plays and his concepts of art (Hayashi 1998: 157–61; Dunn 1966: 97–107). He wrote about his jōruri in the preface to collections of his popular plays, or danmono-shū, mostly michiyuki scenes, with some musical notation included, specifically the terms ji, iro, kotoba. His preface to the 1678 *Takenoko-shū* and also Takemoto Gidayū's preface to the 1687 *Gidayū Danmono-shū* have been translated by Gerstle (Gerstle 1986: 183–96). Further, Kaga's jōruri absorbed content and formal elements from kōwaka, heike, sekkyō, saimon, popular songs (hayariuta), dance songs (odoriuta) and other elements (Hayashi 1998: 164). The textual and musical features of his jōruri thus retain medieval oral narrative characteristics such the invocation of a god (kamioroshi), lists of related objects (monozukushi) and lists of famous places (meisho-zukushi). In keigoto dance pieces and michiyuki, melodic setting was developed actively. All scenes in his jōruri came to include a musical highlight (kikase-dokoro). In his compositions dating from the 1670s, a meisho-zukushi and/or michiyuki occurred usually in the third act.

Another significant figure, about whom less is known, was Gidayū's mentor, Inoue Harima no jō (1632?–1685; Dunn 1966: 97–9). He wrote and published as shōhon a number of Soga themed plays, and was the first chanter to publish a collection of danmono in 1674 (Kominz 1995: 87; 93, n. 174).

Yamamoto Kakudayū, a contemporary of Kaga and Inoue, specialized in soft jōruri with a religious theme and lots of pathos, such as *Yokobue Takiguchi koi no dōshin* (based on the Yokobue and Takiguchi legend) and *Nanatsu Komachi* (based on the legend of Heian period poetess Komachi). He effectively used combinations of the melody patterns ureibushi, haru and kan in the highlight passionate scenes. He also depicted strong and attractive female characters (Wada 1998: 184–8).

Other jōruri narrators of this time will be introduced in Chapter 6 (Okamoto Bun'ya, Miyakodayū Itchū) and Chapter 7 (Satsuma Jōun I; Dunn 1966: 78–81, Satsuma Jōun II; Dunn 1966: 85–7).

Jōruri and the Puppet Theatre after 1684

The narrator Takemoto Gidayū (1651–1714), a contemporary of the three figures just mentioned, built on the work of Kaga, Inoue and Yamamoto to establish gidayū-bushi as a separate genre of jōruri in 1684 through his collaboration with Chikamatsu Monzaemon (1653–1724). This partnership with the prolific playwright who had been writing for kabuki was significant for the further development of jōruri. At first their plays were 'historical' dramas with stories about samurai and superheroes. From 1703, they created their first contemporary play about the love suicide of a prostitute and a clerk (*Sonezaki shinjū*), the so-called sewamono genre. After Gidayū's death, Chikamatsu and his younger contemporary playwright Ki no Kaion (1663–1742) continued to write jōruri texts prolifically for the puppet theatre.

After Chikamatsu's time, the puppet theatre developed further in the direction of dramatic art. By the 1740s, each principal puppet was manipulated by three men, and puppets were technically developed to be highly realistic in actions and even facial expression. In this process, the focus of the performance shifted more and more to the puppets and the proportion of dramatic dialogue increased. In this sense, the third-person narrative of the gidayū-bushi performer became decentred and marginalized, but the narrator was still the voice of the puppets; as the voice actor, his dramatic expression and realistic imitation of different characters gave life to the puppets and was crucial to the popularity of the plays.

It is important to realize that bunraku was the commercialized popular culture in its time. The puppet theatre was highly expressive, given to exaggerated emotional portrayal, and, in contrast with heike and even nō, strove for realism in differentiating the different characters (see Chikamatsu's comments on realism[8]). This was achieved to a large extent by the formulaic character types as

---

[8] 'This is what I mean by the slender margin between the real and the unreal. It is unreal, and yet it is not unreal; it is real and yet it is not real. Entertainment lies between the two'

represented in the puppet heads, narrative tropes or formulaic sections, roughly equivalent to the bunraku term shukō, formulaic verbal expression and formulaic musical expression.

There is a prominent crossover with the kabuki theatre repertoire, as so many puppet plays were transposed to kabuki, in which it is called takemoto, not gidayū. About half of the kabuki repertoire derives from jōruri, and it retains the formality of using third-person sung narrative.

Edo period performing arts are said to have developed in response to chōnin tastes and values; human affection of the common people is depicted vividly, including between parents and children, lovers and married couples. However, they also show the pervasive social control of bushi values. At the same time, they contain countercultural values within an overall framework of social order and control. It is true, however, that giri, or social obligation, always wins over personal feelings. The giri-ninjō conflict and its musical and literary manifestations will be discussed below.

Jōruri and Print Culture

One of the prominent features of all jōruri narratives is that the narrator performs with a hand-written text prominently placed before him on a lectern. He actually reverences the text before commencing the performance, suggesting more than a practical, but also a symbolic function. The shift from blind to sighted narrators does not fully explain this feature of jōruri. Why does the jōruri narrator need a written text in performance? Is this just recitation? We should consider this in relation to the emergence of an urban print culture in seventeenth-century Japan, in which printing used jōruri, and jōruri benefited from printing: the use of texts in jōruri performance would seem to be a gesture towards a new medium, and respect and admiration for the written word, for textuality itself (Takeuchi 2008: 2–11).

The seventeenth century saw the rapid growth of print culture in Japan (Chibbett 1977; Kornicki 1998). This new urban print culture indicates the expansion of literacy to the bourgeois classes, not just the elite (Rubinger 2007).

Following on from Barbara Ruch's argument for oral narratives in the medieval era forming a 'national literature' (Ruch 1977), these widely circulated and familiar medieval narratives were appropriated by the commercial publishing houses preceding the development of popular literature such as the 'fiction of the floating world' (ukiyo-zōshi).[9] The early publishers printed Muromachi era monogatari or otogi zōshi and the lavishly illustrated nara e-hon; the texts of performed

---

(*Naniwa miyage*, http://www.beholdmyswarthyface.com/2008/03/chikamatsu-on-art-of-puppet-stage-from.html, accessed 8 September 2014).

[9] Ever since Ihara Saikaku's *Kōshoku ichidai otoko* in 1682, many realistic novels set in the entertainment quarters were published. However, around 1600, kanagaki shōsetsu and kanazōshi were being published.

narratives, such as mai no hon and utai; and classical literary works such as Genji and Heike and Soga monogatari. The era of moveable type (kokatsuji) gave way to woodblock printing by the middle of the seventeenth century (Kornicki 1998: 136). An important source of material for the printing industry was jōruri.

A tie-up developed between jōruri performers and publishers. For their own use, narrators created their own hand-written texts with their personal annotations, but their texts were commercially printed for mass circulation and sold as reading material for enjoyment. The texts were also used for learners, both professional and amateur (Yamane 1998: 19). Jōruri was popular with Osaka townsmen (Nagatomo 1998: 257).

Jōruri became popular as reading matter at the end of the seventeenth century. Chikamatsu's plays were widely read. Lending libraries (kashi-hon'ya) catered not only to readers in the urban centres, but to those in rural regions too. The jōruri of this time started to reflect contemporary society, and were informative for readers (Nagatomo 1998: 262–6).

The printed texts developed into illustrated storybooks and illustrated puppet plays were sold, circulated and read independently of their stage performance. The authorized versions of the performed text – shōhon – were also sold and circulated. However, the lesson books – keikobon – used by amateurs who wished to learn or imitate the musical performances, were handwritten by a student from the teacher's model: the student would notate enough mnemonic symbols into the text to enable effective learning. The keikobon had an eight-line per page layout. Also popular were collections of favourite scenes (danmono-shū) containing the names of the prominent melodies used (Yamane 1998: 22–3).

Uji Kaga no jō's keikobon were published in 1685, according to an index of titles (*Gedai nenkan*) published in Hōreki (1751–63). An older still extant keikobon *Ushiwaka senningiri* was published in 1679 (Yamane 1998: 21–2).

Other printed material related to theatre included the play bills or rankings (banzuke) – used to advertise performances and serving as a type of programme with names of pieces and of performers – and the compendia of critiques (hyōbanki).

Jōruri, Orality and Textuality

Early jōruri narrators created their own texts or adapted them from other genres or performers' published texts. They narrated them musically with their own individual style, supported by shamisen (like naniwa-bushi today). The narrators 'owned' the narrative. This started to change with the kinpira plays that were written by Oka Seibei. Then Chikamatsu emerged and changed the pattern completely to authorship by a playwright.

As performed narrative, gidayū-bushi is clearly not oral in the usual sense of the word: the sighted performer uses texts, and the verbal aspect of the narrative is fixed from the time of the first performance – there is almost no textual variation, except for editing or cutting in response to theatrical considerations. Although jōruri texts seem to be central to the genre, they have vestiges of oral narrative features.

As for the musical aspect, musical notation, which is musical literacy, consisted firstly in noting the names of some melodic features and the commencing pitch for some sections in many of the published texts. A more precise tablature notation for gidayū-bushi shamisen was developed in the late eighteenth century by Matsuya Seishichi, but was not commercially printed (Yamada in Kojima 2008: 311). Although a notation system does exist, the shamisen player does not use this notation in performance, or even in lessons. The notation is not prescriptive, nor is it comprehensive, it is a kind of mnemonic. It can be found in the texts of the singer too, to indicate the shamisen interludes.

No-one attributes a composer to the music of heike narrative, and neither can the text be attributed to one specific author. The style of gidayū-bushi stands intermediate between this traditional narrative, and a modern style of composition which is the product of an individual artist, realized by professional interpreters, as in Western music. However, in gidayū-bushi, the author of the text *is* identified; there exists a 'playwright' and perhaps also a 'composer' for each work in the repertoire, but the performer can recreate the musical narrative in each performance. The formulaic nature of the music and the text suggests that the concept of composition should be used with care, as the individual freedom of the *creator* is limited by the force of tradition. The concepts of composition and playwright are not really appropriate for this tradition, since the role of the performer is so big (acknowledged in the concept of fū, or individual style). The playwright and the musician-composers must work within fixed conventions, and can be innovative only within strict limitations; however, the narrator has a much more creative role to play than in the Western model of dramatic and musical performance.

In both bunraku and kabuki, a new play was created within the framework of a narrative world (sekai) and innovation (shukō). For example, kabuki plays in the first month always use the 'world' of the Soga brothers, a given world of narrative. But each time something new must be included: the shukō is the innovation, the new twist to make viewers interested in an old story.

Generic Analysis of gidayū-bushi

The music of gidayū-bushi has seemed to resist musical analysis because of the fluidity of the relationship between fixed formulaic musical material and non-fixed material, which makes the music difficult to pin down and transcribe as well as to analyse.

The narrative of gidayū-bushi is distinguished from most other styles of jōruri in its masculine character: it features a deep voice, even among female performers; the gidayū shamisen is the low-pitched 'thick neck' variety (futozao). As a genre, its predominant musical styles designate it as hard narrative. But it also developed elements of soft feminine narrative with the capacity to express pathos.

Table 5.1   Vertical structure of gidayū-bushi

Context	Bunraku puppet theatre Kabuki theatre
Larger Work	A play with several acts and scenes Jidaimono, sewamono
Piece (dan)	One scene or act of a play Michiyuki Keigoto Can be performed independently in dance or concert recitals
Sections	A number of clearly identifiable sections are delineated by a cadential formula and an instrumental interlude Sections with musically defined character: makura, kudoki, monogatari
Narrative substyles	Each section, narrative or kabuki dance is marked by a unified substyle: 1 basic / neutral; soft; includes oki, kudoki 2 urgent; hard; includes chirashi, narrative coda 3 declamatory old-style narrative; rōshō phrases Quotation song / dance
Phrases	Formulaic phrases (senritsukei), some with widely-known names: sanjū, otoshi ... Unnamed patterns No particular pattern
Motives; Ornamentation	Shamisen backing for dramatic action: meriyasu Role of shamisen interludes

Gidayū-bushi has large amounts of dialogue (serifu), most of which is delivered in realistic dramatic style by a single narrator conveying the dramatic characters in the play. Because of this dramatic nature and the high degree of realism, puppet plays could be transferred easily to the kabuki stage, where the puppets were replaced by live actors. In this process, however, the third person narrative was not removed, as happens in the transposition of a novel to cinema; instead the narrative duo of tayū and shamisen player are seated at stage left, and deliver the third-person, musical narrative as in bunraku, while dialogue is delivered by the actors. Not only was the narrative content or plot transposed to another medium (as analysed in Parker 2006), but the form itself was transposed.

The following analysis will look at the larger work of the whole play, the nature of the constituent acts and the smaller scene units, narrative and musical sections, and phrases (Table 5.1).[10]

---

[10]   Much of the following discussion is indebted to Yamada (2003).

Larger Work

A bunraku play or gidayū-bushi work is a long drama consisting of several acts. In the Edo period, two complete plays, one historical and one contemporary, were presented in a day's programme. From the modern period, it became customary to present famous popular scenes or highlights from a number of plays in one day's programme rather than a single complete play.

Historical plays (jidaimono) were set in an era before the Edo period. They followed conventions of a particular 'world' (sekai), and some 'innovation' (shukō) to bring it up to date. They typically had five acts. For a comprehensive analysis of the structure of one act of a historical puppet play ('Yama no dan', in *Onna teikin*), including dramatic and musical elements, see Gerstle et al. (1990).

Plays on 'contemporary' or 'domestic' themes (sewamono) related to the contemporary world of the Edo townsmen of the eighteenth and nineteenth centuries, particularly the licensed entertainment districts (kuruwa). They could even be called gossip or scandal plays. These plays had three acts (called maki).

Act and Scene

Each act (dan or maki) has a typical character according to its sequence in the whole work: the third is the most important dramatically; the fourth is in a lighter mood. The dan has the completeness of form of a nō play or a kōwaka piece, and can be performed as an independent unit. Musically speaking, this can be called a 'piece'.

The act can be very long, and is further divided into two, or perhaps three scenes (ba), performance units that are sometimes seen as independent items, and are called, for example, 'Sushiya no dan', 'Mamataki no dan'; that is, the term dan is used for the ba unit within a dan. At this point there may be a change of performers (the narrator and shamisen duo). However, wherever a dan is divided into smaller units, narrative and dramatic continuity between dan and ba is achieved by the structural musical patterns okuri and sanjū. Each has two forms, one for the end of the act or scene, and a corresponding pattern for the opening of the next act or scene; the text is apportioned between two dan: for example '... oku no ma ni ... hairiyuku'. In this situation, the textual break and the musical break do not synchronize at all.

One type of act or scene is the michiyuki, a lyrical depiction of a journey interpolated as a whole narrative scene in a long play. It functions as a light interlude in a historical play (typically the first scene of act four, following the climactic kiri or finale of the third act); whereas, in a contemporary love suicide play it depicts the lovers' final journey to death (the second scene of the third maki or act).

Single-scene, stand-alone pieces, called keigoto, also exist. Whereas most of the time, gidayū-bushi is performed by one narrator (tayū) and one shamisen player, in keigoto pieces, which focus on musical interest more than narrative and dialogue, at least three narrator-singers and three shamisen players perform. The keigoto is an independent dance-like piece, musically similar to the michiyuki scene. They are congruent with kabuki dance, and many were created in the nineteenth century, under the influence of kabuki shosagoto dance pieces. They provide a bridge between gidayū as puppet theatre music and the jōruri of kabuki. The michiyuki scenes of puppet plays when transposed to kabuki were allocated not to the gidayū (takemoto) pair, but to bungo-kei jōruri, such as tokiwazu and kiyomoto. Many keigoto are ceremonial pieces (shūgi mono) – for example *Sanbasō* and *Shichifukujin* – and are performed in the New Year's programme. The bunraku version of *Kanjinchō* (1895) is a keigoto.

Narrative Segments and Musical Sections (Shōdan)

Within the scenes are clear narrative segments, or scenelets, dramatic units. As narrative they are often congruous with formulaic scenes, such as 'sacrifice for loyalty' (migawari), 'murder' (koroshi), 'severing ties' (enkiri) and 'hair-combing' (kamisuki).[11] While these narrative segments are not particularly marked musically, verbally they always finish with a final form of the verb.[12]

Commonly used transitional phrases mark a change of scenelet, particularly with an added or reduced number of characters on stage. Yamada states that these examples of formulaic phrases function as verbal transitions opening a new narrative segment, and also have a degree of musical consistency:

- ato miokurite dare dare ga (afterward, watching [someone] leave ...);
- atosaki mimawashi, ... (looking around ...);
- ato ni wa futari ... (later the two of them ...).

(Yamada 2003: 142–7)

---

[11] Inobe (in Gerstle et al. 1990: 35) lists the themes or theme-types of aisō-zukashi, migawari, enkiri, renbo, seppuku, kaishin, koroshi, miarawashi, chushin, kando, iken, kyoran, seme, sengi, kudoki, monogatari, chari, shura, jikken, fushigoto. Kudoki is elaborated on p. 36. These are usually called shukō in Japanese, which is confusing. Shukō as a broader concept in Japanese culture means innovation, a novel twist to an established world (sekai), a codified image or familiar story. However, in jōruri and kabuki the original twists became in turn codified and stereotyped scene types. They therefore correspond to the Parry-Lord theme.

[12] In Kanpei seppuku no dan, these verb forms are mienikeru (actually a rentaikei), isogiyuku, tachikaeru, ori koso are (mizen-kei), odoroku bakari nari, and hakanaki. The jōruri texts in general, not just gidayū-bushi, use final verb forms rather infrequently. If one considers the third person narrative sections which are mostly in lines of 7 + 5 syllables, the most frequent ending is a noun; next frequent is a continuous or interrupted form of the verb; for example iitsutsu haireba, oshikomi, shirazu; also the verb final form followed by various particles, that is, nominalized: to iu ni, naku yori, hikidasu wa, nezu ni; also namida nagara.

An example can be seen in the transcription, Example 5.4, line 11: 'Haha wa ato o, miokuri miokuri ...'. These verbal devices indicate narrative and dramatic structure. The transitional narrative phrase 'saru hodo ni', so common in heike and kōwaka, rarely appears in gidayū-bushi. It is outmoded by this time.

Musically, the shōdan ('small dan') is the most important structural unit for analysis. It is a musical paragraph, and provides the basic building block for the narrative as a whole. Distinct from the content segments just discussed, these smaller musical sections need not correspond to a textual paragraph and are not always clearly marked with verbal finals (see Example 5.4, for example). Here is another case where the textual structure and the musical structure do not coincide, indicating that the musical structure has a logic of its own. These musical sections are marked with a cadential musical formula such as fushiochi (the most common), and the more limited suete and mitsuyuri. Regardless of the cadential pattern, it is marked in the text only as 'fushi' (in the meaning of joint, node, a point of change, not melody). The length of the sections of narrative between these cadences can vary from a couple of lines or phrases, to several minutes.

As already noted, only a small number of gidayū-bushi musical sections have a specific formulaic musical character. These are the opening section of an act (makura), the plaint (kudoki) and 'story, monologue' (monogatari) (Yamada 2003). After the initial makura section, the narrative progresses through an indeterminate number of musical sections of uneven length. Some acts begin with a quotation song instead of the narrative makura section (see analysis of 'Kanpei seppuku no dan'). The kudoki section was not a feature of early gidayū-bushi, and did not become clearly defined until the 1730s (Inobe 1991), which suggests the influence of bungo-bushi, one of whose forebears was bun'ya-bushi, also dubbed nakibushi ('sobbing music').

A musical section is not congruent with a single substyle. In this it is more like kōwaka than kōshiki or heike. As can be seen in the transcriptions (Examples 5.1–5.4), a typical section consists of the alternation of long dialogue passages and narrative sub-sections with varied styles of musical delivery or substyles that flow into each other. The section finishes with sung narrative and a clear cadential pattern such as fushiochi.

Within the musical section, sub-sections are formed and marked by less definite semi-cadential formulas. Most important is the semi-cadential phrase that introduces dialogue, the pattern called irodome (because of the use of Sprechstimme or irokotoba or ji-iro in the voice part). This small motive is the musical equivalent of a colon: it announces and leads into speech or dialogue (Example 5.1). Malm (1982: 81–2) calls it a 'trailing cadence'.

Phrase-length Melody Patterns (senritsukei)

Named phrase-length patterns in gidayū-bushi and indeed in shamisen music as a whole have been discussed and categorized by many. In the Edo period, compendia of named melodic patterns called fushi-zukushi were drawn up (Tanaka 2001).

This is related to the literary trope of monozukushi, and the propensity of oral culture to enumerate lists of related objects. At the same time, they functioned as a learning device, and served to systematize the prominent patterns. (We will come across this again with ōzatsuma-bushi in Chapter 7.) In the twentieth century, senritsukei analysis became a research tool (see for example Koyama 1962: 151–534) and the focus of commercially released record sets, the most thorough one being *Gidayū-bushi no kyokusetsu* (Victor 1967), itself a self-confessed fushi-zukushi.

Machida Kashō's (1955 [1982]) analysis of senritsukei in many genres of shamisen music was also important in drawing attention to the existence of this phenomenon in shamisen music. This compendium presents 566 examples of patterns in staff notation; the examples are categorized by genre and type, mostly using traditional names found in text-scores (shōhon), sometimes assigned names by Machida. About 200 of the patterns are from gidayū-bushi. The collection serves to highlight the shared nature of musical patterning across a number of shamisen genres and within particular genres (see Yamada and Ōkubo 2015).

The pattern names can, however, be a distraction in understanding the nature of the music. For example, the term fushi in gidayū-bushi is ambiguous, and has been interpreted variously as sung narrative (melody, as distinct from spoken dialogue), as borrowed or quoted melody, and as cadential formula (as in fushiochi) (Tanaka 2001).

Gidayū-bushi has a lot of unnamed formulaic material, far more than the prominent named patterns. Both Yamada and Tanaka stress the importance of analysing the fluid unnamed parts of the narrative. When we consider the musically delivered gidayū narrative, we are struck by its variety of styles and expression. Once familiar with a large number of pieces (plays), the patterned nature of the music becomes apparent. Yamada Chieko has shown that the definitely identifiable musical patterns (senritsukei) account for only about 10 per cent of the narrative, including dialogue (or 20 per cent of the musical narrative); the remainder is fluid and hard to capture and characterize; furthermore it is unnamed. In contrast, heike narrative can all be accounted for in terms of formulaic melodic material.

Yamada (2008) classifies named formulaic musical phrases as follows:

- for opening and closing an act or scene: okuri, sanjū, sonae, dangiri;
- for closing a section: fushiochi, suete, mitsuyuri, otoshi, oroshi;
- for partial closure: irodome (sung narrative is ji-iro style), followed by speech;
- borrowed or quotation phrases: utai, heike, reizei, hyōgu and so on.

Unnamed formulaic phrases with a looser formulaic character she calls 'rōshō phrases', as they are declamatory, in free rhythm and largely unaccompanied (Yamada 2008).

Yamada (2003) makes the important point that while the named patterns have been the focus of research, the unnamed ones are the most important. She coined the term 'normal narrative' (tsune no ji) for this. Some named phrase types, however, are also 'normal narrative'.

Tanaka (2001) advocates abandoning all conventional and traditional names of formulaic music material and conducts her analysis using numero-alphabetical categories. Her broad division is simply:

- structural patterns (opening and cadential phrases; for a piece or dan, and for a section or shōdan);
- quotation patterns;
- basic narrative patterns.

The last category is broader than Yamada's 'normal narrative' because it includes named and unnamed patterns. Both agree that the unnamed basic narrative patterns are the most important, and also the most elusive to systematize.

Tanaka stresses that gidayū absorbed many different melody patterns from earlier jōruri (ko-jōruri), since the names of most of the prominent patterns can already be found in published ko-jōruri texts (Tanaka 2001: 43). Gidayū-bushi continued to absorb materials from other genres – the kudoki, for example, postdates the time of Gidayū and Chikamatsu. The borrowed or quotation phrases are all integrated into the musical narrative flow, and have become naturalized, so could be seen as part of the basic narrative.

Narrative Substyles

Speech (kotoba)
The basic, broad structure of gidayū narrative is the rapid and frequent alternation of sections of sung musical narrative (ji) and sections of dramatic dialogue (kotoba) in spoken delivery. Dramatic dialogue is not sung but is delivered as speech, and is only occasionally joined by shamisen. The extensive spoken sections are all the speech of the characters, unlike in heike and kōwaka, where it is in effect another narrative substyle. The one narrator dramatically differentiates the characters in terms of gender, age, status and personality, using conventionalized styles of delivery for each character type (coinciding with the typical character puppet 'head'). He also exaggeratedly expresses a wide range of emotions in the delivery of dialogue. Tears and laughter are portrayed with gusto. A section of speech always concludes with the grammatical particle 'to', which functions like quotation marks. This kind of narrative is therefore called togaki-teki. Yamada identifies a loosely formulaic musical substyle of the phrases following speech and the particle to (see below).

Sung narrative (ji or jiai)
The term ji (literally 'ground') is used for musical narrative in all jōruri genres, and is applied in gidayū-bushi to the basic sung narrative in various compounds: ji-haru, ji-u, ji-naka, nakaji, ji-kami and so on, usually indicating a pitch area. However, I am trying to avoid focusing on pattern names so will not spend time explaining these terms. These are related to what Yamada calls tsune no ji 'normal ji', in distinction to senritsukei or fixed named patterns.

The musical narrative (ji) is mostly the third person narratorial voice, but at times can also be a quasi-first-person internal monologue. Dramatic characterization is achieved through varied vocal register and musical styles. This variety of musical expression and delivery styles creates dynamism and variety, and in addition it has the narrative function of focalization; that is, the shift of point of view from one character to another, or from the narrator to the perspective of a dramatic character. The verbal shift is vividly supported by a shift in musical style. The sung narrative is supported effectively by the shamisen in a variety of ways.

In her analysis of 'normal narrative' (or what we can term 'basic narrative', the equivalent of Tanaka's kihon ji), Yamada identifies the following formulaic themes or sections, and formulaic phrases, in which textual and musical content match each other (Yamada 2003: 137–47):

- makura ji: the opening section of an act; starts with the patterns sanjū or okuri; then harufushi; ends with fushiochi; it never contains speech or dialogue.
- togaki ji (after dramatic dialogue): text tends to be … (to), naninani ga. Shamisen on open string to open the phrase. Straight narrative. See examples in Example 5.2 and Example 5.4, lines 6–8.
- seppaku ji: surprise and shock. For an example, see Example 5.1, lines 1–10.
- noriji (or kotoba nori): for fast action or surprise. The shamisen is active and rhythmic, while the voice part is in rhythmic spoken delivery.
- shūtan ji: expresses emotion, suffering (such as in but not limited to the kudoki). See Example 5.4, lines 2–5.

Sections or sub-sections are created by shifts between such formulaic styles, marked by semi-cadential formulas. However, sometimes the shift is no more than a change of vocal timbre or expression, in response to a change in character focalization, and a formal musical cadence is not evident. This is the reality of the elusive character of gidayū narrative that is in constant flux in response to shifts in the verbal text.

Kanadehon Chūshingura: 'Kanpei seppuku no dan'[13]

Table 5.2　Outline of the play *Kanadehon Chūshingura*

I	Daijo: Tsurugaoka kabuto aratame	Prelude: Japan is 'a country at peace'; aftermath of rebellion quashed, Hachiman Shrine.
II	Momonoi yakata no dan Scene for the deed is set.	Moronao (Kira) ogles at, tries to seduce Okayo, Enya Hangan's wife = the cause of the drama.
III	Matsu no ma no dan	Hangan is provoked and strikes Moronao.
IV	Hangan seppuku no dan	Hangan commits seppuku. Kanpei is disgraced by his absence due to a tryst with Okaru. Ōboshi arrives late, is distraught.
V	Yamazaki kaidō	Kanpei and Okaru have fled to her home in the country; Kanpei is hunting boar; he unintentionally kills a man, and finds the large sum of 50 ryō on the body.
VI	Kanpei seppuku no dan	Okaru is sold to the Ichiriki-jaya brothel to raise money for Kanpei; Kanpei commits suicide believing he has killed his father-in-law. Expiring, he is finally received into the brotherhood of the rōnin.
VII	Ichiriki-jaya no dan	Ōboshi is carousing with Okaru, pretending to be unconcerned about revenge.
VIII	Hachidanme: Michiyuki tabiji no yomeiri (bridal journey)	Tonase (daughter of Honzō) travels with her mother to Kyoto hoping to be married to Ōboshi's son Rikiya.
IX	Yamashina kankyo no dan	Tragic encounter at the residence of Ōboshi's wife.
X	Amakawa no dan	At the port of Sakai, a merchant is providing armour for the rōnin attack.
XI	Uchiiri no dan Climax, denouement	The revenge scene when the rōnin attack Kira's house in Edo and kill him.

The play chosen for analysis is *Kanadehon Chūshingura*, first performed in 1748. It is among the longest plays in the puppet play repertoire with 11 acts, instead of the usual five. Discussion here follows the characters and story in the 1748 puppet play not its kabuki adaptation. The analysis focuses on the sixth act, 'Kanpei seppuku no dan'.[14] In January 2004, to mark the 300th anniversary of the events, the entire play was revived at the National Bunraku Theatre in Osaka,

---

[13] Translated by Keene, in Takeda et al. (1971), as *Chūshingura: The Treasury of Loyal Retainers*.

[14] This is the equivalent of sandan no kiri, the climactic last scene of the third act of a historical play. According to Yamada Chieko (personal communication, January 2004) such scenes are the most appropriate part for musical analysis, as they include the widest range of narrative musical expression and styles. The whole play is rarely performed in its entirety, but in 2004, it was staged at the National Bunraku Theatre covering the whole day, to mark the 300th anniversary of the events on which the play is based.

presenting it in the matinee and evening performances, about eight hours. The discussion and analysis is based on the recording of *Kanadehon Chūshingura* by Takemoto Tsunatayū VIII (1904–1969) (King Records KICH 2148–54, 1994, 7 CDs). This recording omits the fifth, tenth and eleventh dan, the least seldom performed parts of the play.

The authors of the play were Takeda Izumo II, Miyoshi Shōraku and Namiki Shōzō (Sōsuke), the same team responsible for two other great jōruri plays, *Sugawara denju tenarai kagami* (1746) and *Yoshitsune senbonzakura* (1747).

The historical events behind the play took place between 1701 and 1703. These and an overview of the plays written about the events between 1703 and 1748 can be found in Takeda et al. (1971). The essay by historian Henry D. Smith (1990) outlines the historical incidents that were the source of the play. Smith says that the motive of the revenge is unclear: normally one took revenge for the murder of one's lord, or one's father. Neither applies, because Asano was not killed by Kira, but was the aggressor, and was made to commit seppuku as punishment. His retainers who thus became masterless samurai (rōnin) maintained a pretence of inaction, but eventually attacked Kira's mansion and killed him nearly two years later. Maruya Saiichi (1984) argues that the Soga tale was a model for the development of the Chūshingura subject matter.

The play has a pseudo-historical setting in the fourteenth century (the world of *Taiheiki*). Although it was based on relatively recent events (1701–1703), it was transposed to a safer, more distant period, because of the sensitive nature of the story to the government of the day (Shively 1982). Edo-period culture is included in scenes such as the selling of Okaru to a Kyoto brothel and the Ichiriki-jaya act. This kind of anachronism is typical of kabuki jidaimono plays (cf. *Seki no to*, Chapter 6).

The events which took place over 21 months were in the play expanded to fill nine acts compared with the conventional five. *Chūshingura* is one of the core plays of the bunraku repertoire; it enjoys a status of enduring popularity in the repertoire of both the bunraku puppet theatre and kabuki. When adapted for performance in the live kabuki theatre the michiyuki scenes are performed by kiyomoto or other bungo-kei jōruri. (The kiyomoto piece, *Ochiudo*, is an example.)

Table 5.3 Outline of Act VI 'Kanpei seppuku no dan'

Sections	Text	FMM
(1) Okaru and Mother waiting for Yojibei to return. Instead of a makura narrative section, the act starts with a barley-mowing song, evoking the rural setting, and referring to an old couple dancing with the young people. Okaru and her mother are waiting at home sharing mother and daughter intimacy similar to the kamisuki shukō. They are worried because Yojibei, the old man, has not returned from his trip to Kyoto.	(Sansagari barley mowing song) 'Misaki odori ga shundaru hodo ni Oyaji dete miya, babantsu babantsurete Oyaji dete miya, babantsu' Mugi utsu oto no zaigou uta	
	(Kamisuki) Tokoro mo na ni ou, Yamazaki no … Zaisho ni oshiki sugata nari. (fushi) Haha no yowai mo tsuetsuki no … Ki mo wasa wasa to mienikeru (fushi)	
(2) Okaru is sold to Ichimonjiya brothel. The agent of the brothel, Ichimonjiya, comes to take Okaru, saying he has paid 50 ryō to Yojibei last night, and can't wait for him to get back.	Nanbo sono you ni, omoshiro o kashiu iyatte mo … Oyako hanashi no nakamichi zutai	harufushi
	Kago o kakasete, isogikuru wa … Kadoguchi kara	
	Yoichibei dono uchi ni ka to … Tsuchi de o-ie o, hakujinya no teishu	Irodome
Kanpei returns from hunting, and Mother asks him whether they should let Okaru go or wait for Yojibei to return. Monji convinces them that he gave the money to Yojibei, in a makeshift purse from his kimono, same stripes. This strikes terror in Kanpei's heart, as it is the same material as that in which he took the 50 ryō from the body of the man he killed. He concludes he must have killed his father-in-law. He agrees that Monji should take Okaru. There is a moving parting scene, with Mother and Okaru crying, Kanpei is apparently unmoved and stony-hearted but inwardly he is in agony, wondering if he should confess.	Sate yūbe wa kore no oyajidono mo ikai taigi… Katsugiaguru kado no kuchi	kotoba fushi
	Teppō ni minogasa uchikake … Dou shiyou zo, Kanpei dono? Kiku yori hatto Kanpei ga … to wa shirazu shite nyoubou Kore kochi no hito Sore nara sou to … to Monji mo zu ni note Sore miyashare	kotoba kotoba
	… kudasanse to Oya no shinime o tsuyu shirazu Kokoro o itame, kotaeiru.	fushi (1st string)

Sections	Text	FMM
The palanquin bearers take the young woman away callously unconcerned.	O, Muko dono, meoto no wakare ... Kago ni noru made kokoro o tsuke Nan no inga de hitonami no musume omochi ... nakikereba Musume wa kago ni Koe o mo tatezu, musekaeru	kotoba shūtan ji mitsuyuri fushi
	Nasake naku mo, kago kakiage Michi o hayamete, isogiyuku.	fushi
(3) Yojibei's body is brought in by hunters.	Haha wa ato o, miokuri miokuri ... O, kono hito wai na ... Tanegashima no Roku, tanuki no Kakubei	fushi
	Tokoro no karyuudo sannin zure oyaji no shigai ni Hoka no koto zo naki	fushi
	Karyuudo domo kuchiguchi ni Minamina wagaya e, tachikaeru.	irodome ... fushi
(4) Yojibei's wife's anger (uramigoto).	Haha wa namida no, hima yori mo Kappa to fushite, nakiitaru.	fushi
	Mi no ayamari ni Kanpei mo ... Omoi shittaru ori koso are.	fushi
(5) Goemon and others arrive; Kanpei commits suppuku. It is discovered that the way Yojibei was killed could not have been Kanpei's bullet, but instead he was killed by the highwayman, the one Kanpei killed.	Fuka-amigasa no samurai ninin ... Zutto toori za ni tsukeba	fushi
	Ninin ga mae ni ryou te o tsuki Mi o herikudari nobekereba	irodome ...
	Goemon toriaezu Mazu motte sono hou ... Mi o nage fushite nakiitaru.	fushi irodome fushi
	Kiku ni odoroki ryounin katana ottori ... Iu ni, teoi mo mite bikkuri, haha mo odoroku bakari nari.	fushi

continued

Table 5.3   concluded

Sections	Text	FMM
(6) Kanpei is forgiven and signs his allegiance to the league of rōnin with his blood. He is permitted to join the revenge alliance, and then expires.	Goemon kokorozuki, Iya, kore, Senzaki dono ... Ninin ga mae ni sashiidashi	kotoba fushi
	Kanpei dono no tamashii no itta kono saifu, (shamisen) mukodono ja to omoute, katakiuchi no otomo ni surete gozatte kudasarimase ... Me mo aterarenu, shidai nari.	kotoba fushi
	Goemon tsuttachi agari, Yaa, kore kore, roubo ... Miokuru namida, mikaeru namida Namida no nami no, tachikaeru hito mo Hakanaki.	kotoba nori ōsanjū

Text 5.1 (CD Track 8)
(Translation adapted from Takeda, Keene et al 1971: 91–4)

(Speech)
どうせうぞ勘平殿。是は是は先づ以て舅殿の心遣ひ忝い。したがこちにもちつとよい事が有れども夫れは追つて、イヤコレ親父殿も戻られぬに、女房共は渡されまい。とは又何故。ハテ謂はゝ親なり判がゝり、尤もゆふべ半金の五拾両渡されたでも有らうけれど。イヤこれ、京大阪を股にかけ、女護島程奉公人を抱える一文字屋、渡さぬ金を渡したと言ふて済むものかいの。これ済むかいの。まだまだ其上に慥かな事があるてや、是の親父が彼の五拾両と言ふ金を手拭にぐるぐると巻いて懐に入れらるゝ、そりや危ないそりや危ないと、是に入れて首にかけさつしやれと、おれが着て居る此の単衣物の縞の裂布で拵へた金財布貸したれば、やんがて首にかけて戻られう。ヤア何と此方が着て居る此の縞の裂布の金財布か。ヲゝてや。此の縞ぢや。何と慥かな証拠で有らうがな。

Mother: What shall we do, Kanpei?
Kanpei: To begin with, I must tell you how grateful I am for Father's solicitude. But I have had rather a piece of luck myself, which I'll tell you about in a moment, and I'm not turning over my wife until my father gets back.
Ichimonjiya: Why not?
Kanpei: Well, he's her father and the man who signed the bond. You claim you paid him half the money, fifty ryō in gold, last night. No doubt that's true, but ...
Ichimonjiya: Do you realize who I am? I'm Ichimonjiya. I cover the whole Kyoto-Osaka area, and I've enough women in my employ to populate the Island of Dames. Would I say I'd paid him the money if I hadn't? But I have even more positive proof. When I saw your old man wrap up the fifty ryō in his little towel and tuck it into his

kimono, I said, 'That's dangerous. Put it in this and carry it around your neck.'
I lent him a wallet made out of striped cloth, the same material as this kimono I'm wearing. He's sure to be coming back soon with the wallet round his neck.
Kanpei: What did you say? Did you say the wallet was made from the same striped material as your kimono?
Ichimonjiya: That's right.
Kanpei: The exact same striped material?
Ichimonjiya: What more positive proof could there be?

Noriji / urgent narrative

1. 聞くよりはつと勘平が、	As soon as he heard this,
Kiku yori hatto Kanpei ga	
2. 肝先にひしとこたへ、	Kanpei is stunned.
Kimosaki ni hishito kotae	
3. 傍四辺に目を配り、	He glances cautiously around him,
Soba atari ni, me o kubari	
4. 袂の財布見合はせば、	then takes the wallet from his sleeve and
Tamoto no saifu, miawaseba	compares it with the kimono.
5. 寸分違はぬ糸入縞、	Both are of a mixed cotton and silk striped
Sunbun chigawanu, itoirijima	cloth, absolutely identical in pattern.
6. 南無三宝。扨は	'Good heavens!
Namu sanbō, sate wa	
7. ゆふべ鉄砲で打ち殺したは、	Was the man I shot last night
Yūbe teppō de uchikoroshita wa	
8. 舅であつたか、	my father-in-law?'
shūto de atta ka.	
9. ハアはつと我が胸板を二ツ玉で、	Aah! As if his own breast has been
Haa, hatto waga munaita o futatsudama de	pierced by the two bullets
10. 打抜かるゝより切なき思ひ。	There shoots through him an even more
Uchinukaruru yori setsunaki omoi	severe pain.
11. とは知らずして女房。	His wife, knowing nothing of his anguish,
To wa shirazu shite, nyōbō	asks:

Example 5.1 Gidayū, 'Kanpei seppuku no dan' (1)

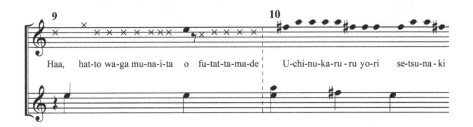

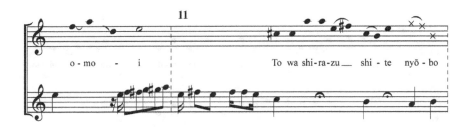

Text 5.2

(Speech)
コレこちの人、そはそはせずと、遣るものか遣らぬものか、分別して下さんせ。ヲゝ成程、ハテもうあの様に慥に言はるゝからは、往きやらずばなるまいか。アノ父様に逢はいでもかエ。イヤイヤ親父殿にもけさ一寸逢ふたが、戻りは知れまい。フウそんなりや親父様に逢ふてかエ、

Okaru: Kanpei, please don't hesitate so, but make up your mind whether you're going to send me away or not.
Kanpei: Oh, yes. He's given such convincing proof I don't suppose we have any choice but to let you go, have we?
Okaru: Without seeing Father?
Kanpei: I ran into your father briefly this morning. There's no telling when he'll get back.
Okaru: Then you saw Father?

Ordinary narrative (tsune no ji)

1. 夫れならさうと言ひもせで、 Then why didn't you say so,
Sore nara sou to iimose de

2. 母様にもわしにも、 instead of making Mother and me
Kaka san ni mo washi ni mo worry (so much)?

3. 案じさしてばつかりと、言ふに
anji sashite bakkari to iu ni

4. 文字も図に乗つて。 Ichimonjiya takes advantage of the
Monji mo zu ni notte situation.

Example 5.2 Gidayū, 'Kanpei seppuku no dan' (2)

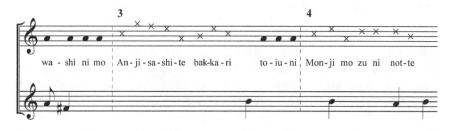

Text 5.3

(Speech)
それ見やしやれの、七度尋ねて人疑へぢや。親父の有所の知れたので、そつちもこつちも心が宜い。また此の上に四の五の有れば、否ともにでんど沙汰、マアマアさらりと済んで目出度目出度、ハゝゝ、イヤコレお袋も御亭も六条参りして一寸寄らつしやれ。サアサア　お娘駕篭に乗りや、早う駕篭に乗りや。アイアイコレ勘平殿もう今彼方へ行くぞエ、年寄つた二人の親達、どうでこな様の皆世話、取分けて父様は強い持病、気を付けて下さんせと、

Ichimonjiya: Ask seven times before you suspect a man, they say. Now that we know where the old man is, it's a big load off your minds and mine too. If you still have any complaints to make, whatever they may be, we'll leave them for a court to decide. Anyway, I'm glad everything has been settled. I hope the old folks will pay me a little visit when you worship at Rokujō. Come now, into the palanquin with you.
Okaru: Yes, yes. Kanpei – I'm going now. From now on it's up to you to look after my old parents, especially Father – he's got such a bad complaint. Please take good care of him.

Urei

1. 親の死目を露知らず、 Oya no shinime o, tsuyu shirazu	Having no idea her father is dead,
2. 頼む不愍さいぢらしさ。 Tanomu fubinsa, ijirashisa	she asks him, so pathetic, so touching
3. いつそ打明け有りの儘、 Isso uchiake, ari no mama	that Kanpei wonders if he shouldn't confess and tell her the truth.
4. 話さんにも他人有りと、 Hanasan ni mo, tanin ari to	But others are present;
5. 心を痛め堪へ居る。 Kokoro o itame, kotaeiru.	so he bears in silence the agony in his heart.

Example 5.3   Gidayū, 'Kanpei seppuku no dan' (3)

Text 5.4

(Speech)
ヲゝ賢殿、夫婦の別れ、暇乞ひがしたからうけれど、そなたに未練な気も出よかと、思ふての事であろ。イエイエ何ぼ別れても、主の為に身を売れば、悲しうも何ともない、わしや勇んで行く母様、したが父様に逢はず行くのが。ヲゝそれも戻らしやたら、つひ逢ひに行かしやろぞいの、病はぬやうに灸すゑて、息災な顔見せに来てたも。アイ鼻紙扇もなけりや不自由な、何もよいかと、とばついて怪我しやんなと、

Mother: I'm sure Kanpei would like to take a proper leave of you and say good-bye like a husband to his wife. He must be afraid you'll break down.
Okaru: There's no danger of that. I'm leaving my husband, it's true, but I'm selling myself for our master's sake, so I don't feel sad or anything like that. I go in good spirits, Mother. I am only sorry I'm leaving without seeing Father.
Mother: I'm sure he'll go and visit you as soon as he gets back.
Okaru: Take moxa treatment so you don't get sick, and please come and see me, so I'll know you're all right.
Mother: Oh, if you haven't handkerchiefs or a fan you'll need them. Have you everything else? Don't rush about too much and hurt yourself.

Kudoki and urgent narrative

1. 駕篭に乗るまで心を付け。 Kago ni noru made, kokoro o tsuke	She fusses over Okaru until the girl is actually inside the palanquin.
2. さらばやさらば、何の因果で Saraba ya, saraba! Nan no inga de	As they bid other each good-bye,
3. 人並みな娘を持ち、 Hitonami na musume o mochi,	she wonders
4. 此の悲しい目を見る事ぢやと、 Kono kanashii me o miru koto ja to	what ill fate has decreed that a daughter as attractive as the next girl should have to experience such sadness.
5. 歯を食ひしばり泣きければ、 Ha o kuishibari, nakikereba	She clenches her teeth and weeps,
6. 娘は駕篭にしがみ付き、 Musume wa kago ni, shigamitsuki	Her daughter, clinging to the sides of the palanquin,
7. 泣くを知らさじ聞かさじと、 Naku o shirasaji, kikasaji to	tries so hard not to let her sobs be heard
8. 声をも立てず咽せかへる。 Koe o mo tatezu, musekaeru. (fushi)	and not to make a sound that she chokes.
9. 情けなくも駕篭舁上げ、 Nasake naku mo, kago kakiage	The bearers, indifferent to their grief, lift the chair
10. 道を早めて急ぎ行く。 Michi o hayamete, isogiyuku. (fushi)	and hurry down the road.
11. 母は後を見送り見送り。 Haha wa ato o, miokuri miokuri	The mother gazes after them.

12. アヽ由ない事言ふて娘もさぞ悲しかろ、
Aa, yoshi nai koto iute, musume mo sazo kanashikaro (irodome)

Mother: I'm sure I upset Okaru by saying such foolish things.

(Speech)
ヲヽこな人わいの、親の身でさへ思切りがよいに、女房の事ぐづぐづ思ふて、煩ふて下さんなや、

Kanpei, I hope you won't keep fretting over your wife. You'll only make yourself sick. I'm her mother, but you saw how bravely I've resigned myself...

Act VI, 'Kanpei seppuku no dan', is not a central part of the historical events, but it forms one of the key dramatic highlights of the play, as part of the lore (gaiden) which accrued about individual retainers in the nearly two years between Asano no kami's attack on Kira in the palace and the revenge taken by the 47 rōnin. Such material generated legends with little or no historical basis. The equivalent of sandan no kiri, the last part of the third act, its dramatic intensity and many plot twists result in a variety of musical substyles. It combines the most harrowing and intense scenes of both the sewamono type and of the jidaimono type. The bridal journey michiyuki in Act VIII that follows gives the customary light relief to the solemn narrative (usually such a scene occurs at the beginning of Act IV).

Let us provide a more detailed outline of this act and its composite scenelets.

Instead of the usual makura, the act starts with a barley-mowing song, evoking the rural setting and an old couple dancing among the young people, referring obliquely to Okaru's parents. Okaru and her mother are waiting at home sharing an intimacy similar to the kamisuki (hair combing) scene type. They are worried because Yojibei, the old man, has not returned from his trip to Kyoto.

The agent of the brothel, Ichimonjiya, comes to take Okaru, saying he has paid 50 ryō to Yojibei the previous night, and can't wait for him to get back.

Kanpei returns from hunting, and Mother asks him whether they should let Okaru go or wait for Yojibei to return. Monji convinces them that he gave the money to Yojibei, in a makeshift purse made from his kimono, with the same stripes. This strikes terror in Kanpei's heart, as it is the same material as that in which he took the 50 ryō from the body of the man he killed. He concludes he must have killed his father-in-law. He agrees that Monji should take Okaru.

There is an emotional parting scene between Okaru and her mother, but Kanpei is apparently unmoved and stony-hearted. However, his soliloquy indicates that inwardly he is in agony, wondering if he should confess. The palanquin bearers take the young woman away callously unconcerned.

Left alone, Mother accuses Kanpei of hiding something. She has noticed him glancing at the striped purse in his sleeve. (The CD track finishes here.)

Example 5.4 Gidayū, 'Kanpei seppuku no dan' (4)

166 *Japanese Singers of Tales: Ten Centuries of Performed Narrative*

Example 5.4 *continued*

Then Yojibei's body is brought in by hunters. Kanpei commits seppuku. It is then discovered that the way Yojibei was killed could not have been Kanpei's bullet, but instead he was killed by the highwayman, the one Kanpei killed. He is forgiven and signs his allegiance to the league of rōnin with his blood.

Musical Analysis of CD Extract and Examples 5.1 to 5.4

The excerpt on CD Track 8 is just over 10 minutes of the whole act which takes nearly an hour to perform. Gidayū-bushi sectional structure normally follows a sequence of [ji – irodome – kotoba (repeated any number of times)] – ji – fushiochi. In this extract, the first shōdan section is very long, finishing at line 5 in Example 5.3 with the cadential pattern suete. The first fushiochi cadence is musekaeru (Example 5.4, line 8). Other less definite semi-cadential patterns occur (Example 5.4, line 5), notably the use of irodome before most sections of speech (Example 5.1, line 11; Example 5.2, line 4; Example 5.4, line 12). The actual sequence in the examples is:

Example 5.1: ji (11 lines) – irodome – kotoba;
Example 5.2: ji (4 lines) – suete (kotaeiru) – kotoba;
Example 5.3: ji (5 lines) – irodome – kotoba;
Example 5.4: ji (lines 1–5) – semi-cadence (nakikereba);
– ji (lines 6–8) – fushiochi (musekaeru);
– ji (lines 9–10) – fushiochi (isogiyuku);
– ji (lines 11–12) – irodome (kanashikaro) – kotoba.

The following discussion points out the shift in substyles with **bold**.

Example 5.1
Lines 1 to 10: The narrative takes Kanpei's perspective, expressing his emotions. This **urgent hard rhythmic narrative (seppaku ji)** has distorted tonality, but a fast, driving rhythm; the voice part is mostly Sprechstimme (irokotoba), syllabic and intensely clipped, expressing the agony of Kanpei's realization of what he must have done, especially his internal monologue in lines 8 and 9. It is somewhat like the noriji pattern, because of the shamisen motive which pushes the music along; it ends with the shamisen's rapid chromatic rise (end of 10).
11: An abrupt change to **softer style**, which focalizes Okaru's perspective on the situation. This tactic is common: the phrase immediately preceding a section of dialogue introduces another character: it is not just the end of the sung narrative section, but it leads into the next passage of spoken dialogue with the 'trailing cadence' of irodome, functioning like a colon.
Speech (kotoba): In this section, the shamisen occasionally chimes in to underline the pathos of the speech.

Example 5.2
> Lines 1 to 3: **Soft feminine narrative** as Okaru gently reproaches Kanpei; this is plain unadorned narrative, almost unaccompanied, with some Sprechstimme: the shamisen just punctuates, supporting the voice in a desultory way. This is similar to internal monologue, a rather intimate exchange between the two of them.
> 4: Abrupt change to third person narrative, **masculine rough style** of Monji, announcing his speech with irodome, then the spoken dialogue.
> Speech: Again, in this dialogue, the shamisen chimes in to heighten the pathos of the farewell.

Example 5.3
> Line 1: **Plain narrative**, minimal musical movement, speech rhythm, almost unaccompanied; soft, Okaru's perspective.
> 2 to 4:
> 2: **Pathos (urei, shūtan ji)**, use of tone F (non-nuclear), resolves on E.
> Kanpei's internal monologue. Although apparently cold and gruff, he responds inwardly to Okaru's appeal.
> 3: He wants to confess, but can't because of the situation. Almost unaccompanied.
> 4: **Pathos**, like phrase 2.
> 5: Pathos builds, leads to strong cadence. Return to narrative voice; **passionate narrative**, male emotions suppressed, descends to first string, resolves on the second string, with the cadential pattern suete, always associated with weeping.
> Speech

Example 5.4
This figure shows four narrative sections in a continuous consecutive sequence, but with contrasting musical styles, each delineated with a definite musical cadence or semi-cadence.
> Lines 1–5: **Quasi kudoki**; Mother's internal monologue. Starts with rōshō phrase then goes into urei in high pitch register. Cadence: rising two-step nagashi, leading into a rhythmic passionate narrative section.
> 6–8: **Passionate narrative**; Okaru's perspective. Fushiochi variation.
> 9–10: **Urgent**; palanquin bearers' perspective. Cold, unconcerned; contrasts and therefore underlines the pain of the main characters. Isogiyuku, conventional fushiochi cadence.
> 11–12: Mother's focus; plain, unaccompanied **rōshō phrases**; ends in irodome, leading in to her next speech.
> Speech

This short extract shows the characteristics of gidayū narrative: the alternation of (1) sung narrative, third person but occasionally internal monologue or soliloquy, and (2) extensive sections of dramatic dialogue. The sung narrative is characterized by a variety of musical delivery styles, articulated in a series of short sections by the use of cadential and semi-cadential patterns. The shamisen has different roles in the different styles of delivery, from offering an open pitch then being silent, to driving the sung rhythm forward with an insistent pulse. It also chimes in at certain points of the dialogue to accentuate moments of emotion. The emotions of the characters and their psychological drama are thus told not only through words but also through musical means.

Conclusion

This chapter has shown that jōruri is the major type of musical narrative of the Edo period; having emerged as a genre from the late fifteenth to late sixteenth century as one of many streams of medieval narratives it coalesced into a new type of musical narrative with shamisen and puppets.

Jōruri is an over-arching genre, within which a number of sub-genres stabilized, of which gidayū-bushi, the narrative of the bunraku puppet theatre that has been examined in this chapter, is only one. Jōruri narrative as a meta-genre had a central place in Edo-period theatre, both live kabuki theatre and the puppet theatre, as well as in private entertainment in salons. In the theatrical context it increasingly took on strongly dramatic features, such as highly realistic dialogue, a key feature of mature gidayū narrative of the mid-eighteenth century.

Just as heike narrative is the most important, representative narrative art of the medieval period, jōruri is the kinsei-period equivalent, and within jōruri, gidayū-bushi is the pinnacle of narrative art. Gidayū-bushi is the narration of the bunraku puppet theatre, which in 2003 was recognized by UNESCO as a world heritage of oral tradition, giving it world significance. Within Japan, it ranks with nō and kabuki among the most loved and enduringly popular of the traditional performance genres, mainly for its exquisite puppetry. The narration of this puppet theatre is the most prominent of the musical narratives of Japan, and understanding it can throw light on many other related genres.

A large part of the kabuki repertoire is straight drama, with no narrative, and supported only by 'background music' and sound effects from offstage musicians. However, the plays transposed from the puppet theatre retained the gidayū pair of narrator and shamisen and their musicalized third-person narrative. In addition, michiyuki journey scenes of such plays were fully musicalized narrative with only small amounts of dramatic dialogue. Puppet jōruri was largely responsible for the full dramatic development of kabuki.

The following chapter looks at another stream of jōruri which developed in the context of kabuki dance.

Chapter 6
Sung Narratives and Kabuki Dance: Bungo-kei Jōruri

Introduction

This chapter tells the story of how jōruri musical narrative found a place in kabuki and was transformed into kabuki dance music. This is analogous to the blend of narrative, drama and dance in nō: in both the actor-dancer kinetically narrates (or mimetically dances) while a chorus of on-stage musicians take the musical narrative. There are of course differences: in nō the dancer also sings, unlike the kabuki dancer; kabuki has dramatic dialogue; it has a melodic instrument, the shamisen, and its main dance style is the mimetic furi, not mai.

The story starts with itchū-bushi, roughly contemporary with gidayū-bushi. Gidayū and itchū took jōruri in two different directions, gidayū in the puppet theatre, and itchū in salon (zashiki) performance and kabuki. Particularly important was the activity of Miyakodayū Itchū's follower Miyakoji Bungo no jō, whose music was banned in the late 1730s, but from whom emerged a number of genres collectively called bungo-kei jōruri. At the same time, many other jōruri genres continued to be active in Edo, such as katō-bushi (from Tango no jō) and ōzatsuma-bushi (from Satsuma Jōun; see Chapter 7).

Jōruri started to be used in kabuki to accompany shosagoto from the Genroku period (1688–1704), and its narrative style had an impact on the development of nagauta. The spectacular success of the puppet theatre inspired the kabuki theatres to adopt and adapt jōruri puppet plays for the theatre of live actors.

The popular culture of the Edo period flowered in and around the live kabuki theatre, the puppet theatre now known as bunraku, and in the licensed entertainment quarters, particularly the Yoshiwara quarter of the city of Edo; there were also many performers and listeners in a variety of smaller theatres, in private settings, and in the street. In all these spaces, music played a central role and experienced exponential development. The speed with which new styles of jōruri accompanied by shamisen emerged in the seventeenth and eighteenth centuries was dizzying, testifying to the creative energy and productivity of the culture of the time. This development stabilized by around 1800, the latest genre in this line of jōruri being kiyomoto (1814).

No styles of jōruri from before the 1680s survive to the present. From Genroku, genre consolidation and continuity became evident. Takemoto Gidayū's (1651–1714) gidayū-bushi was established in 1684 (*Ongaku Daijiten* 1983: 668); Miyakodayū Itchū's (1650–1724) itchū-bushi appeared at about the same time (*Ongaku Daijiten* 1983: 96). Nagauta became a clear identity in the early eighteenth century (*Ongaku Daijiten* 1983: 1681–2).

This chapter outlines the development of kabuki dance music and explains the impact of jōruri on its development. It argues that mature kabuki dance form emerged as a blend of lyric song and narrative music as the accompaniment of kabuki dance whose essence is mimetic furi. It then discusses the musical features of kabuki dance, followed by analyses of individual pieces.

Kabuki Dance Music: nagauta and bungo-kei jōruri

Kabuki developed in the early seventeenth century as 'women's kabuki', roughly at the same time as puppet jōruri. The first music used in kabuki was the nō hayashi ensemble of three drums and flute, with the addition of tsurigane gong and the folk bamboo flute. This expanded hayashi continued to be basic to all kabuki music, onstage for nagauta, and in the wings for other genres. The shamisen seems to have been included from the 1650s. The earliest kabuki dance was communal folk dance: nenbutsu odori, furyū odori, kouta odori. This was lively and appealed immediately to the senses. In the earliest sources there are also references to skits called jōruri modoki.

The banning of women from public performance in 1629 changed the nature of kabuki performance somewhat, but the emphasis was still on the appeal of beautiful dancers, though young males now. With the banning of young men's (wakashū) kabuki in 1652, kabuki dance as performed by mature male actors took on more mimetic qualities, and by the Genroku period (1688–1704), the mimetic dance form of shosagoto told a story through the portrayal of a character. From this time, jōruri narrators started to be hired to accompany kabuki dance, which was developing a mimetic style called furi (gesture). Their presence in kabuki dance stimulated the kabuki theatre musicians to develop a longer musical structure using some jōruri features. Up to now kabuki music had consisted of song suites (kumiuta) as dance music, lyrical songs rather than narrative music. Now the song suite structure started to incorporate jōruri-like sections, and came to resemble jōruri. The name nagauta is first noted on a banzuke playbill in 1704, and in 1727 it first appears without the prefix Edo (Tokita 1999: 56; Machida and Ueda 1967: 33).

Nagauta is indeed the 'heart of kabuki music' (Malm 1963). The off-stage music (geza or kage bayashi, supplementary instrumental accompaniment) is in principle also nagauta. The musicians are hidden from the view of the audience behind the kuromisu screen at stage right and play a variety of percussion, flutes and shamisen as well as songs to underscore the atmosphere of the drama, and to enhance the musical texture of the onstage musicians. The onstage nagauta musicians consist of singers, shamisen players and an ensemble of drums and flutes (called the debayashi). The offstage nagauta musicians also support jōruri performances when required. In addition to structural similarity, nagauta has a lot of formulaic musical material in common with jōruri, but it can be distinguished by much of its musical material and by its aesthetic (Tokita 2008).

The root stock of nagauta is the lyric music used in the early kabuki theatre. It is related to various genres with the name uta, especially kouta, and even the utai of nō theatre. However, over the eighteenth century, this lyric music became narrativized; onto the root stock was grafted in several stages aspects of narrative music, through the influence of jōruri.

Kabuki dance is intrinsically narrative; its mode of dance is called furi (gesture); as a genre it is called shosagoto, or mimetic dance. It became a repository of legend and lore, ancient and contemporary. Kominz's (1995) study of the Soga story demonstrates how a medieval narrative of revenge became the stuff of kabuki dance.

By the 1720s, jōruri genres were being called on for poetic journey (michiyuki) scenes in Chikamatsu's love suicide plays, and many other puppet plays were adapted for kabuki. Bungo-bushi flourished in this way in the 1730s. This continued as journey scenes came to be included in historical dramas such as *Yoshitsune senbonzakura*. Such dance-like scenes were called shosagoto, or mimetic pieces, because they consisted of mimetic movement (furi), not the formalized movement of earlier dance (mai and odori). Dance complemented the dramas by providing visually and musically attractive interludes, which were an intrinsic part of the unfolding plot of the dramas.

Over the eighteenth century, kabuki dance scenes came to incorporate more formal dance sections, especially the musically and rhythmically lively odoriji section. In the later eighteenth century, it became customary to finish plays with a spectacular dance scene (for example *Seki no to*). Later, dance scenes were threaded together to make dance suites called 'quick change dances' (henge buyō); these suites picked up, or created anew, shorter pieces drawn from a variety of narrative worlds or longer plays, making a variety show like a medley performed by one dancer, who changed character and costume for each dance. The dances were linked by a poetic, rather than a narrative theme, such as the four seasons. In the nineteenth century, playwright Kawatake Mokuami (1816–1893) included musical shosagoto scenes in many of his plays, for example *Izayoi-Seishin* and *Michitose*.

The bungo-kei jōruri styles developed in the context of kabuki theatre. Extant genres are only the tip of the iceberg compared with all the jōruri styles which came and went in the Edo period. Those that have survived to the present made effective use of musico-social structures, mainly the iemoto system from the mid-Edo period: an artist needed to establish a new name and artistic identity within a musico-social structure relying on teaching to amateurs as well as performance in order to be economically viable (Nishiyama 1980: 152–4).[1] If an artist could

---

[1] From the mid-Edo period, this system emerged in the arts of music, tea, calligraphy, martial arts as a social system for accreditation and licensing of teaching and transmission. It enabled members of the townsmen class (chōnin) to cross status boundaries by taking lessons and acquiring teaching and performance rights and thus a position in the world

announce his new artistic identity, attract some supporters and gain public support in the form of professional engagements, he could establish a new artistic domain. He might even be able to acquire an honour in the form of a title from the Imperial Household, such as Miyakoji Bungo no jō ('Governor of Bungo Province'), a practice going back to ko-jōruri (as noted in Chapter 5).

The bungo-kei genres – tokiwazu, tomimoto, shinnai, kiyomoto, miyazono and shigetayū – are the offshoots of the defunct bungo-bushi. Tokiwazu, tomimoto and kiyomoto in particular were in demand for kabuki dance scenes. Unlike gidayū-bushi, they are not used for a whole multi-act drama, but for a particular scene in a multi-act kabuki play. Itchū-bushi, the predecessor of bungo-bushi, is included in this group, though it is less influenced by kabuki dance, and its earliest repertoire is closer to what is often called 'old jōruri' (ko-jōruri), being more formulaic than the other genres (Tanaka 2002). In recent years, it has been included in a group of genres called 'old music' (kokyoku), with ogie-bushi, katō-bushi, tomimoto-bushi and miyazono-bushi.[2] This categorization can be seen in many commercially produced record sets, for example *Hōgaku Taikei*, *Nihon Koten Ongaku Taikei*. Other bungo-kei genres no longer have an independent existence: shigetayū-bushi was absorbed into jiuta (Iwasa 1968: 65), and handayū-bushi was absorbed into katō-bushi (Iwasa 1968: 613). Separate again from bungo-kei, the hard genre called ōzatsuma-bushi was absorbed into nagauta (see Chapter 7).

While nagauta musicians were regular employees belonging to a particular theatre, jōruri musicians were not as integral to kabuki (they were outsiders), and were hired for specific plays and pieces in a kabuki programme.

Itchū's notorious disciple Miyakoji Bungo no jō (?–1740) achieved great popularity in puppet and kabuki theatres due to his exquisite singing of love suicide narratives; he was also reputed to have been a fashion leader. Bungo-bushi was banned by the Edo authorities three times on the grounds that his performances were lascivious and incited young people to commit love suicides (Kasaya 2006: 94–8). From 1731, Bungo no jō was forbidden to give lessons from his home, and to perform in private homes. Performance of bungo-bushi was then banned in large theatres from 1736, with the most severe prohibition of being banned from the stages of the largest theatres coming in 1739. His music is known only from the published collections of his texts. From among his disciples emerged a group of related styles of jōruri collectively known as bungo-kei jōruri; the surviving

---

of performing arts. It was significant in enabling the continuity of performing arts into the modern period. In comparison, the Tōdō guild for blind musicians was abolished in 1871 following the Meiji Restoration of 1868; social support for heike and jiuta was thus removed, and new organizational structures had to be formed in various urban centres.

[2] Machida Kashō and others formed the Association to Preserve Old Shamisen Music (Kokyoku Honzonkai) in 1922; the member genres changed in 1955; it was reconstituted in 1962 with a new name, Kokyoku-kai, and is still active, headed by Takeuchi Dōkei (Kishibe Shigeo Hakushi Koki Kinen shuppan iinkai 1987: 67, 467).

genres are: tokiwazu (1747), tomimoto (1748), shinnai (1750s), miyazono and kiyomoto (1814).

The plethora of jōruri genres each named after its first exponent in the seventeenth century reduced to a much smaller number after the emergence of gidayū-bushi as the pre-eminent narrative for the puppet theatre, but the older styles still appeared in small theatres in the eighteenth century. Takenouchi makes it clear that the dominant genres up to 1740 were gidayū-bushi and 'miyakoji-bushi' (this would include bungo-bushi). Takenouchi argues that the supremacy of gidayū-bushi put other jōruri styles on the defensive, relegating them to less prominent performance venues, such as salons in the entertainment quarters, small theatres and temporary venues in shrine and temple compounds, and street performance. The one style which was able to compete successfully with gidayū was bungo-bushi. Miyakoji Bungo no jō performed in a variety of venues, and although gidayū undoubtedly dominated in Osaka, with its two major puppet theatres as well as many smaller ones, in other contexts bungo-bushi held its own against gidayū (Takenouchi 2002: 270–80).[3] The most prominent venue was of course the kabuki theatre, where it was under the vigilant eye of the Tokugawa authorities.

If the 1680s was a turning-point in the development of jōruri, with the emergence of gidayū-bushi as the premier narrative for the puppet theatre, out-shining its many rivals, another turning point followed the popularity of bungo-bushi in the 1730s.

After the final ban on bungo-bushi in 1739, it continued in the form of tokiwazu, tomimoto and shinnai, each carrying on the soft narrative tradition of bungo. In particular, tokiwazu, tomimoto and later kiyomoto came to regularly incorporate a dance section (odoriji) as an integral component of most pieces. By the 1780s, nagauta and bungo-kei genres came to work very closely with each other in the kakeai repertoire, pieces in which two genres performed antiphonally, and also in the new dance-dramas (buyō geki; see Tokita 1999). A lot of pieces from this time are still in the extant repertoire. From the 1790s to the early 1800s, the fashion for 'quick change' (henge) dance suites brought nagauta together with narrative genres. Suites consisted of three, four, five, six, even twelve pieces; the first piece might be nagauta, the second kiyomoto, the third tokiwazu, the fourth nagauta and so on. This meant that one genre drew close enough to another to blend with it. This flexibility in narrative expression made possible a convergence with nagauta. The tokiwazu piece *Matsu no hagoromo* (1898), for example, was originally a kakeai with nagauta, and is very similar in style to nagauta. Incidentally, this piece belongs to the world of *Ataka*, *Togashi* and *Kanjinchō*.

The competitive nature of kabuki dance music meant that nagauta and bungo-kei jōruri had a lot of direct contact and over the eighteenth century grew to be more like each other in structure, thematic content and their categories of piece. Nagauta and bungo-kei genres came to share not only the kabuki dance form,

---

[3] Groemer's article on theatres in Osaka in the Edo to Meiji periods confirms Takenouchi, as he outlines how theatres made contracts with performers (Groemer 2013).

but also a lot of thematic material, such as the *Dōjōji, Echigo-jishi* themes. Despite musical differences, there is little significant difference in dance style between pieces using different accompanying genres, and audiences are not generally aware of the musical differences. They are also served by the same repertoire of off-stage music (kage bayashi or geza ongaku), and share a body of shamisen interludes and atmospheric melodies which back spoken dialogue.

In 1743, one of Bungo's disciples, Miyakoji Mojitayū, appeared in the Naka-za theatre in Edo (Iwasa 1968: 81). He was acclaimed for the same michiyuki pieces his master Bungo no jō had performed; he successfully incorporated this style of narrative into the kudoki section of the emerging kabuki dance form.

When Mojitayū changed his name from Miyakoji to Tokiwazu in 1747, tokiwazu-bushi was born as a new musical entity. At first it would have been virtually the same as bungo-bushi, characterized by michiyuki-mono and erotic (iroppoi) narrative, with a kudoki as the highlight of every piece. With its new identity as tokiwazu-bushi, it gradually took on new characteristics in the context of kabuki dance. The newly formed genre had plenty of work accompanying kabuki dance, and it embraced this new form. Not abandoning the poignant singing associated with suicide narratives, Tokiwazu Mojitayū, however, drew on a much broader palette of musical resources than his predecessor, specifically the inclusion of hard narrative for which gidayū and ōzatsuma could have provided models, especially in historical narratives, or jidaimono.

Although it is not possible to compare tokiwazu with its direct predecessor, the no longer extant bungo music, it is instructive to compare tokiwazu with early itchū pieces. The early itchū pieces represent the early stage of development which went via bungo-bushi to tokiwazu, the internally inherited essence of the narrative tradition. Tanaka's (2002) analysis of itchū-bushi is based on five extant pieces which are thought to be early itchū, well before the establishment of the kabuki dance form. Some of them were possibly created by Miyakoji Bungo no jō (when still under the Itchū umbrella as Miyako Hanchū) (*Ongaku Daijiten* 1983: 97–9).

Tokiwazu broadened the expressive capabilities of jōruri musical narrative. A conspicuous difference between the two genres is the increased use of hard narrative elements in tokiwazu; and through the influence of kabuki its addition of dance elements, especially the odoriji section, and the accompaniment of dance sections by the offstage hayashi instrumental ensemble.

Kabuki jōruri in Contrast to Puppet jōruri

Compared with gidayū (Chapter 5), overall the bungo-kei group of jōruri genres can be called soft jōruri, because they are predominantly romantic and lyrical. Much of their central repertoire originated from michiyuki scenes of puppet plays transposed to the kabuki theatre.

All the bungo-kei jōruri genres are or have been kabuki dance music, and they are hence structurally very similar, sharing a lot of *formulaic musical materials*.

There is also a lot of overlapping *repertoire*. However, even if they present the same narrative, their 'personality' or prevailing mood or atmosphere is different; they are differentiated by stylistic characteristics, such as the details of how a pattern is rendered, ornamentation, shamisen and vocal timbre. Overall, though, they are all closer to each other than they are to gidayū on the one hand or to nagauta on the other.

The fundamental contextual difference between tokiwazu and its musical ancestor, itchū, is the factor of kabuki dance, in which context tokiwazu re-emerged and developed after the banning of bungo-bushi in 1736. Tokiwazu had to dissociate itself from Bungo's soft erotic style, and develop a more masculine and vigorous style, inspired by other models, such as ōzatsuma-bushi and gidayū-bushi.

There are relatively few records of Miyakodayū Itchū appearing in kabuki (Takeuchi 1988: 129–33). He did create music for michiyuki scenes, but they were few compared with his activity for private patrons in zashiki entertainment situations and private residences (Iwasa 1968: 635). It seems he rarely performed for puppet theatre (Iwasa [1968: 634] mentions one record of him in a puppet theatre in Osaka, whereas his appearances in kabuki are more frequent [ibid.: 635]). In contrast, tokiwazu was in demand for theatres large and small, especially for kabuki dance. The change in performance context from zashiki to kabuki must have been decisive, and the primary influence on kabuki dance: this was the time at which the kabuki dance form – a hybrid form which shows elements of the song suite form of nagauta and the use of hayashi instrumental support – developed. This added to the types of pieces created, and added also to the variety of substyles and sections in the pieces.

Contemporary Performance Contexts

Today tokiwazu and kiyomoto are still regularly performed in kabuki, alongside nagauta, but with a shrinking repertoire. They are also active in recitals of classical Japanese dance (nihon buyō), with a much broader repertoire than in kabuki, along with other genres. In this context, they appear together with nagauta, and many others, including from time to time gidayū, tomimoto, shinnai, jiuta and some modern offshoots such as tōmeiryū. Many of these genres have been able to retain considerable musical and narrative appeal in contemporary Japanese musical culture as amateur hobbies. The enduring popularity of Japanese dance has supported the viability of the musical genres, providing the most secure source of income for musicians. Recordings also appear commercially in order that dancers can practise. I have, however, never seen a nihon buyō recital to recorded music, except outside Japan. The bungo-kei genres are still actively performed by both professionals and amateurs, due to the natori system and okeikogoto tashinami culture. This is similar to nō, and gidayū in the past, but not heike and kōwaka.

The Formulaic Musical Material of bungo-kei jōruri: Generic Analysis

The next part of this chapter provides a generic musical analysis of the shared features of the bungo-kei jōruri genres, excluding tomimoto and miyazono, but including itchū-bushi. It proceeds to a comparative analysis of four pieces, one itchū and one each of tokiwazu and its cousin genres, shinnai and kiyomoto, which, while retaining similar features to tokiwazu, went through various changes, to develop unique identities with their own musico-social structures.

A comparative analysis of itchū, the predecessor of bungo-bushi, and the successors of bungo-bushi, tokiwazu, shinnai and kiyomoto, will show how these genres developed as a different stream from gidayū-bushi, with a form and structure distinct from gidayū. At the same time a basic core of genetic material of these genres is still fundamentally shared with gidayū.

Listening casually to itchū and tokiwazu, they seem quite different in atmosphere. However, a comparison through musical analysis reveals substantial similarities at the various structural levels. As a group, bungo-kei jōruri genres share the same stock of narrative resources, that is, formulaic musical material and narrative form. They are genetically similar, and the differences are superficial. (We must remember that the itchū-bushi pieces performed today are not identical with their first performance, but will have been influenced by other genres and contexts over the period of largely oral transmission. Similarly for tokiwazu-bushi.)

The differences between bungo-kei jōruri genres have been written about by many. Itchū is dignified and refined. Tokiwazu is said to be boorish (yabo); kiyomoto to be smart, cool (iki); shinnai is licentious; tomimoto is elegant. Tokiwazu has a predominance of masculine and dramatic narrative pieces, such as *Seki no to*, often spiced with humour of a vulgar kind. But there are also refined (jōhin) pieces such as *Matsu no hagoromo*, and light dance pieces such as *Noriaibune*. Kiyomoto is characterized as chic (iki), with many light-hearted pieces, and as erotic narrative, but there are also highly dramatic pieces such as *Kasane*, which feature a wide range of hard narrative substyles. Shinnai is best known for shinjū narratives such as *Ranchō* and *Akegarasu*, but it also has comic pieces like *Hizakurige*, and dramatic pieces like *Senryō nobori*, *Ichi no tani* and *Kuzu no ha*. All the genres have historical (jidai) pieces and dance pieces, and all have ceremonial pieces for solemn and auspicious occasions.

The differences between the genres are not as great as might be thought. At a certain level, all share the same structure and many broad stylistic characteristics. Many of the differences are only elaborations. Others are differences of emphasis. Of course, in many instances new elements are also present. The piece *Yūgiri* exists in all the genres, and has been compared by many to show the differences between the genres. The first *Yūgiri* play was written for kabuki actor Sakata Tōjūrō by Chikamatsu in 1678, not long after her death.[4] It shows

---

[4] The version on *Nihon Geinō Taikei* (video) is a gidayū-kiyomoto kakeai. The *Nihon Koten Ongaku Taikei* offers a comparison of part of the kudoki in five bungo-kei genres.

the commonality in the various jōruri genres, the way bungo-kei were selected when puppet theatre plays were adapted for kabuki, with the most lyrical scenes allocated to bungo-kei.

We tend to think that the different genres are characterized by these emphases. But we find in all these styles a whole spectrum of characteristics. As part of a narrative tradition based on multiple melody patterns, jōruri was extremely eclectic, and developed a much richer stock of resources than previous genres, through the influence of theatricalization, and through the incorporation of elements from other genres. Earlier narratives did not practise quotation in an obvious way, that is, not just by absorbing an influence, but by marking the 'foreign' music as a quotation, in the scores and sometimes even in the sung text.

Contrast of Narrative, Dramatic and Dance Structure

When narrative enters a theatrical context, dramatic structure is brought to bear, creating more complexity and differentiation between sections. Such a process led to the development of patterns such as sanjū and okuri to mark the changeover of scenes and acts, and appears already in texts prior to gidayū-bushi. Nevertheless, as we have seen in previous chapters, musical narrative structure is loose: typically it consists of an accumulation of sections of irregular length, each ending with a musical cadence and also possibly a short instrumental interlude. This loose flexible narrative structure is still the basis of gidayū narrative, like heike and kōwaka. Tokiwazu, tomimoto and kiyomoto retain the looser narrative structure in narrative-dramatic pieces. Shinnai and miyazono retain the narrative structure almost exclusively. In comparison, kabuki dance pieces conform to a neat tight structure, like nō.

In the context of kabuki dance, the formal aesthetic elements of the dance outweigh the story elements, and sections acquire a stronger differentiation and focus, so that each section acquires a highly specific character in the progression of the piece. Thus, kabuki dance pieces are actually more formulaic than gidayū-bushi narrative, which retains considerable fluidity in response to narrative content.

The overall analysis of all the genres in this chapter discusses the performance contexts, the piece, and the structure of pieces in terms of level of section and phrase. Formulaic musical material can be identified at each level (Table 6.1).

Table 6.1   Structural analysis of itchū, tokiwazu, tomimoto, kiyomoto, shinnai

Context	Kabuki theatre; scenes which were dance pieces – shosagoto Private performance (zashiki), concert, dance recitals (nihon buyō).
Larger work	A kabuki play with several acts and scenes; the jōruri musical narrative applies usually only to one act or scene (dan), occasionally a sequence of two. Dance suite of thematically unrelated pieces.
Piece (dan) Sub-genres, each with distinctive musical and structural features: narrative / dramatic; dance; ceremonial	One scene or act of a play if a narrative/dramatic piece; dangire pattern marks end of piece. Three main types of piece, two of which appear in kabuki. One of a suite if henge dance suite. Performed independently in present-day kabuki programmes; can be performed independently in dance or concert recitals.
Sections	A number of clearly identifiable sections are delineated by a cadential formula and an instrumental interlude. Kabuki dance form: oki, hanamichi, kudoki, monogatari, odoriji, chirashi and so on.
Narrative sub-styles	Each section, narrative or kabuki dance, is marked by a unified substyle: 1. basic / neutral; soft; includes oki, kudoki 2. urgent; hard; includes chirashi, narrative coda 3. declamatory old-style narrative; rōshō phrases Quotation song / dance.
Phrases	Formulaic phrases (senritsukei), some with widely known names: sanjū, otoshi ... Less prominent in nagauta, except for ōzatsuma patterns.
Motives; Ornamentation	Differentiate the various genres. Idiosyncratic flourish at end of phrase (fushijiri) helps to distinguish genres. (Role of shamisen and hayashi interludes.)

The context of kabuki dance, and the multi-act kabuki play at the level of the larger work has already been discussed.

The piece is usually a single scene from what might have been a longer multi-act play. This unit in all jōruri genres is traditionally called dan, a major section of the narrative which can stand alone as a performance item. In the puppet theatre, and later the kabuki theatre, it becomes the equivalent of an act or scene. Most musicologists now call this a piece (kyoku).

It is most usual for a bungo-kei piece to form just one act: whether the michiyuki of a transposed gidayū play; one of a suite of quick-change pieces (henge); or an act in a kabuki play by Kawatake Mokuami (1816–1893).

Some bungo-kei jōruri pieces have more than one dan (a relic of the puppet theatre multi-act plays, or danmono). In the tokiwazu repertoire *Seki no to* has two dan, the final scenes of a full-length play, and *Sanzesō* (1857) uniquely has six dan (Nakauchi and Tamura 1929: 213–21; recorded as a set of six CDs by Tokiwazu Ichihadayū VZCJ-8228-33).[5] The latter was revived in 1957 (Leiter 1979: 329). A comparison of the first five dan of *Sanzesō* and its finale, *Sanja matsuri*, shows the juxtaposition of two extremely contrasting types of piece: a kind of resurrection narrative, *Sanzesō* is a purely narrative danmono, with a lot of speech and third person narrative; its finale, *Sanja matsuri*, is a light dance-oriented piece. Thus even within one play, such versatility can be seen. Kiyomoto also has a version of *Sanja matsuri*, first performed in the Edo Nakamura-za in 1832, but it is not part of a longer play (Nakauchi and Tamura 1928: 5–9).

Comparison of the Repertoire of Pieces in Each Genre: Three Types of Piece

As the repertoire of kabuki dance music became extensive and diversified, sub-genres or categories of piece were created within each genre and generated subsequent musical variety. Each category of piece has its own structural and musical features: narrative/dramatic, dance/lyric, ceremonial/auspicious (Table 6.2) (shinnai also features a comic piece).

Table 6.2 Types of piece in four bungo-kei genres: itchū, tokiwazu, kiyomoto, shinnai

	narrative/ dramatic (historical)	narrative/ dramatic (contemporary or poetic journey)	dance/ lyric	comic	ceremonial/ auspicious
itchū		Wankyū michiyuki Onatsu kyōran			
tokiwazu	Seki no to Masakado	Onatsu kyōran	Noriaibune Toshima		Matsu no hagoromo
kiyomoto	Kasane Ochiudo Inaka Genji Kurama jishi Tadanobu Suma Yamanba	Osome Hisamatsu Ohan Umegawa Gonpachi Michitose Izayoi Yūgiri	Tamaya Yasuna Ukare bōzu		Hokushū
shinnai	Ichi no tani	Akegarasu Senryō nobori Ranchō		Hizakurige	Kodakara sanbasō

---

[5] See http://www.heibonnotomo.jp/japaneseworld+index.id+54.htm (accessed 9 September 2014).

Narrative / dramatic

In these pieces, the longest in the repertoire, the dramatic characters are part of the longer kabuki drama. The musical scene is an integral part of the whole play. Typical examples are the michiyuki scenes of plays transposed from the puppet theatre (maruhonmono).

The core kabuki dance sections of oki, kudoki and chirashi are present, but there are many other narrative sections, and extensive sections of dramatic dialogue that are frequently accompanied by atmospheric shamisen melodies (see, for example, Example 6.6). The oki, kudoki and chirashi sections can be long and complex. There may be two or more kudoki, but there is not necessarily an odoriji dance section. The hayashi ensemble is a nagauta fixture, but in kabuki the off-stage hayashi in the geza room came to be applied to jōruri dance pieces in non-narrative sections, such as borrowed song and dance sections, and also in the narrative chirashi which is a dramatic climax or finale. Other sound effects are also added to the jōruri pieces in kabuki.

Dance / lyric

These pieces are shorter, and most typically are character sketches. However, the characters portrayed are not part of a longer drama, but most often appear in a suite of thematically rather than dramatically connected scenes, the 'quick-change' henge dance suites. The oki section in the suite pieces is sometimes omitted, or, if present, much abbreviated in form. The chirashi too is kept short and rushed. The kudoki, similarly, is relatively short, and can be ironic rather than genuinely pathetic. There is always at least one odoriji dance section following the kudoki, and other quotation song sections. Dramatic dialogue occurs in some dance pieces, but never features the shamisen melodic accompaniment of the narrative pieces. The offstage hayashi is silent in the key narrative sections of oki and kudoki, but comes into action for other sections in kabuki performance. (Recital concerts do not usually have hayashi.)

Ceremonial / auspicious

Ceremonial pieces occur in all jōruri genres; they are the most closely related types of pieces across all repertoires, very similar in structure and style. Regardless of the genre, the ceremonial pieces share the same context and function.

Created for performance in private gatherings, not kabuki, to celebrate occasions such as the New Year, the succession to a title and so on, these pieces are highly lyrical in nature and lack dramatic characters altogether. The dancer expresses the poetic content of the text as it unfolds, but there is no unified story. The kabuki dance sections are present but not so formulaically or strictly applied. However, declamatory and other hard narrative musical resources are appropriated to evoke solemnity and create an auspicious atmosphere. We can recall that in nō utai, the hard tsuyogin style was used not only for battle scenes, but also for auspicious situations such as the utai of or concerning a kami (for example Benkei's otoko mai in nō *Ataka* and nagauta *Kanjinchō*).

In itchū narrative, even though there are different types of narrative content, musically there is less variation, making a more uniform overall soft narrative style. In musical terms, there is only one category of piece, whereas in narrative content there are diverse types: a small number of historical/period pieces (jidaimono), contemporary (sewamono) pieces (which are dominant), including poetic journeys (michiyuki), significant numbers of pieces adapted from nō plays, and ceremonial pieces. However, there are no pure dance pieces of the type which characterize mature tokiwazu and other bungo-kei genres, that is, there are no henge dance pieces. The michiyuki (poetic journey) piece is the most similar between itchū and the later genres, both in content and musically. (See *Ongaku Daijiten* [1983: 97–9] entry for itchū-bushi.)

In comparison, tokiwazu and kiyomoto narrative both exhibit striking differences between different categories of piece, as far as overall musical structure and narrative substyles are concerned. Both have three main categories of piece in terms of music: narrative, dance and ceremonial. The major musical distinction is between a narrative-dramatic group of pieces and the dance pieces. The narrative category can be divided into historical and contemporary stories, corresponding to a dominance of hard versus soft narrative style, and includes some adaptations from nō and kyōgen (matsubame mono). The dance pieces feature many song and dance elements, are shorter, and most were originally part of a 'quick-change' (henge) dance suite.

Tokiwazu and kiyomoto pieces closest to itchū are those of the narrative category which have a large amount of soft narrative. These are narrative pieces such as *Onatsu Seijūrō* which exists in both itchū and tokiwazu, *Masakado*, *Yamamba*, and the michiyuki pieces. The hard narrative pieces such as *Seki no to* and *Kasane* have less in common with itchū, because itchū does not have a fully-developed hard substyle. Pieces which are most unlike itchū are the pure dance pieces, often henge buyō, such as *Noriaibune, Toshima, Sanja matsuri, Tamaya, Komori* and so on.

Shinnai narratives are also varied, with pieces in all three categories. The comic piece with several dan, *Hizakurige* (adapted from Jippensha Ikku's picaresque novel, *Tōkaidō Hizakurige* [1802–1822]), uses heavily narrative resources tongue-in-cheek to depict the adventures and scrapes of the two rascals. It seems to be the only example of a fully comic piece, though comic sections are found in plenty in tokiwazu and kiyomoto. Shinnai also has some serious historical pieces. However, it is best known for the sewamono pieces set in the picaresque entertainment world of sumo wrestlers, gamblers and prostitutes. It also developed an elaborate instrumental style, used especially for street performance (busking) (see further below).

Nagauta's main focus is lyric-dance character pieces, portraying a character type, but like jōruri it also has an extensive category of ceremonial pieces, and a group of pieces with strong narrative and dramatic features. In gidayū, the differences are between the different acts of the drama. There is, however, a repertoire of stand-alone dance scenes, the keigoto pieces.

Structure and Form at the Section Level

Jōruri as accompaniment for kabuki dance follows what has come to be known as kabuki dance form. As kabuki dance music, both nagauta and bungo-kei jōruri share the same form, a hybrid of narrative and song suite structure. Kabuki dance form came about as the product of the interaction and convergence between the kouta kumiuta form of early kabuki and the narrative form of jōruri styles used in kabuki to accompany shosagoto dance. As we have seen, nagauta developed in response to the challenge of narrative music as shosagoto accompaniment. By the 1750s, both nagauta and tokiwazu were converging, using virtually the same form, and became even closer in the subsequent decades.

Basically all kabuki dance pieces follow a form consisting of a sequence of section types, each of which has a clearly defined character: oki, entrance, (variable), kudoki, odoriji, chirashi, in that order (Table 6.3).

Table 6.3 Kabuki dance form

oki	setting the scene musically
hanamichi	entrance music
(unspecified number of sections; narrative or song)	
kudoki	plaint, entreaty
odoriji	dance
chirashi	finale

The oki, the kudoki and the chirashi are narrative in nature, the odoriji is lyric, and the hanamichi is variable. In between the hanamichi section – after the actor-dancer reaches the main stage – and the kudoki, there is no fixed requirement: the passage can consist of narrative, speech, song or dance sections, depending on the category of piece.

The hanamichi, the odoriji and the chirashi were new to tokiwazu. These sections all use the hayashi, an influence of kabuki dance music.

Although this is the basic form, certain pieces in each genre emphasize narrative more, while others emphasize song and dance more. A strongly narrative piece (for example *Kasane*) may have no odoriji and two or more kudoki sections, and an extended chirashi in which a conflict or fight occurs. A strongly dance piece may omit the oki, have multiple odoriji sections, and a short perfunctory chirashi. The dance and song sections are brought back to a narrative voice with the narrative coda, a contracted urgent narrative section.

Tanaka has demonstrated that in itchū, patterns used in the first half of a piece are distinct from those used in the second half. This shows a linear progression throughout the piece, and confirms the multi-melody character of jōruri. However, the sections and sub-sections, though marked clearly with cadential formulas, do not show so much contrast or a clearly distinct character as in tokiwazu and kiyomoto which adhere to kabuki dance form. In their more purely narrative pieces, however, such as tokiwazu's *Seki no to*, or kiyomoto's *Kasane*, there are several narrative sections interspersed with speech, which cannot be explained in terms of kabuki dance form.

Narrative Substyles: Styles of Performed Narrative Delivery

As introduced in Chapter 1, Hirano (1990 and 1993) proposed a model for musical narrative delivery, mainly for medieval genres, with three types of musical delivery: ginshō was close to speech and could not be notated with fixed pitches; rōshō used definite pitches and was syllabic; eishō was 'aria-like', melismatic and tending towards a high pitch register.

The prosimetric model offers a broad definition of narrative that features alternating (prosaic) speech and (poetic) musical delivery, in which Hirano's categories would be divided into speech (ginshō) on the one hand, and sung delivery (rōshō and eishō) on the other.

When approaching jōruri, clearly the prosimetric model of alternating speech and melody fits. However, the melodic part requires a much more detailed analytic approach than either Hirano or the prosimetric model, most of whose proponents consider the poetic text rather than its musical delivery, and assume the non-poetic parts are spoken.

Speech as a style of vocal delivery
The use of speech as a dramatic device is something which developed in jōruri with its theatrical development. It differentiates the Edo-period narratives from heike, kōwaka and even the dramatic nō.

There is no real 'speech' as a delivery style in itchū. What is labelled in the text-scores 'kotoba' is melodically declaimed; whereas in bungo-kei narrative pieces, speech in the form of dramatic dialogue is an indispensable part of the narrative structure. Sections of speech are often accompanied by atmospheric shamisen melodies (ashirai or meriyasu): short melodies or a few phrases repeated cyclically as many times as required, as a kind of background music underlining the mood of the dramatic dialogue (Example 6.6). Since this did not develop in gidayū, it would seem to be a result of the kabuki environment, with the off-stage orchestra of instruments that provide background music and dramatic sound effects.

On the other hand, the spoken dialogue in gidayū portrays dramatic characters with a high degree of realism, within the limitations of the one male voice. This style of dialogue is part of bungo-kei narrative-dramatic pieces which feature extensive dialogue between the characters.

Musical narrative (ji) and narrative substyles
There is a wide array of musical delivery types or substyles in bungo-kei jōruri. As already stated, the term substyle refers to the combination of musical stylistic parameters that characterize a section of sung narrative. Phrase-length musical

patterns (senritsukei) can be an important part of these substyles, and will be mentioned in that respect, rather than being discussed separately. Cadences, however, are treated separately.

In the bungo-kei group of jōruri genres, I identify three broad types of basic narrative substyles: the soft basic (kihon), the hard basic (semeji) and declamatory (rōshō). This categorization derives from my analysis of kiyomoto (Tokita 1999) which here I apply to tokiwazu and shinnai. The analysis by Yamada of gidayū and by Tanaka of gidayū and itchū have been helpful.

The three basic substyles are supplemented by a number of special effects narrative substyles (passionate, eerie and comic), which can be identified in embryo in itchū, but are more clearly developed here.

There is a relatively narrow range of distinct substyles in itchū: the most clearly defined substyle can be called basic (kihon). A declamatory style, kotoba, is not really speech but an unaccompanied syllabic delivery, forming an independent section. It is notable that itchū, even in these early pieces, acquires musical interest and variation by the frequent use of 'quotation' styles. This regular use of musical quotations is a salient feature of jōruri.

Basic Soft (kihon)

Sections in basic soft often commence with a phrase or two in declamatory style (rōshō; see below). The shamisen then picks up a fairly stable steady pulse, while the vocal part weaves in and out of that pulse, close to free rhythm. It avoids coinciding with the shamisen pulse, while following the shamisen tonally, though with more melodic movement and ornamentation. This style is called tsukazu-hanarezu: never together, but never far away; the shamisen does not attach itself to the vocal melody, but neither does it stray too far. It is notoriously difficult to transcribe accurately. For an extended example, see Example 6.6: Hanamichi section of *Kasane*.

This is the core of itchū soft narrative (Example 6.1). It was passed on to (remained in) all the bungo-kei genres as the opening of oki style, whereas in itchū it is not restricted to oki, but can occur in several sections in a piece. This is like the DNA of bungo-kei jōruri.

Reiterative patterns

The basic soft style is characterized by the frequent use of patterns focusing on one pitch. (Tokita 1999: 153–8 et passim). This is strikingly similar in itchū and the bungo-kei genres, though the application and distribution differs somewhat. Most common is the reiteration of one tone by the shamisen, but the reiteration of a two-tone unit forms the basis of one important pattern. All these patterns occupy the seven-syllable segment of a 7-5 syllable line; the five-syllable segment may be occupied by a cadential formula, or a non-descript resolution to a lower pitch area.

Reiteration of two tones
The one narrative pattern with the shamisen reiterating two notes (see Example 6.1, line 1) is called jibushi in some sources (Nakamura 1967: 203). A similar pattern called nakaji is found in shinnai (Okamoto 1972: 38). The equivalent in itchū is called chūbushi (nakabushi) in Machida (1982: 297). In itchū, it is one of the most important narrative patterns and is labelled variously in old texts as bunya, jifushi and nakaji (Tanaka 2002: 55). A sedate, slow narrative pattern, it commonly occurs in a serious oki which has a certain length and scope for development. It does not occur in the kudoki, and of course not in the chirashi. It was found in 14 of the sample of 50 pieces in Tokita's study of kiyomoto, that is, just under one third. It also occurs in many tokiwazu (see Example 6.2) and shinnai pieces. The shamisen part is characterized by the very short upbeat before the first statement of the motive to be reiterated, the nuclear tone B, followed by the weaker nuclear tone A. Rhythmic interest is created by stressing the weaker tone. Both notes are played throughout on the stopped second string. Against the simple shamisen pattern the vocal part has more melodic movement, before settling down to a slightly embellished dwelling on B, the main tone in the shamisen part.

Reiteration of one tone
Most of the patterns in this group are at a slow to steady tempo, and belong to the basic soft styles, including oki and kudoki substyles, but never appear in the semeji-urgent-derived chirashi. Machida lists the initial pattern of this kind, in which the shamisen reiterates the tone C, under the label nagaji (Machida 1982: 322). Ji ('ground', accompaniment) is a common term for basic ordinary patterns in many styles of music, including nō and gidayū. Machida adopted this name from the gidayū pattern nagaji, although the latter is a rōshō type phrase, because they both start from the tone C.

This kind of pattern is the jōruri equivalent of, and most likely ultimately derives from, the simpler narrative styles like the heike kudoki and the kōshiki shojū and nijū, whose musical development was minimal. It would therefore link jōruri with the practice in kōshiki and heike of calling a melodic type after the pitch register in which it was located. It recalls the early stage of the development of narrative music, in which simple stichic narrative with repetitive melody moved through different pitch registers in melodic blocks (Chapter 2).

One tone is repeated by the shamisen for almost the entire phrase, in one of three possible rhythmic patterns. Rhythmically, some shamisen reiterations are steady and equidistant, others are gapped, yet others combine both of these. Most begin with two notes in double time before the voice enters. The length of reiterative patterns is flexible, the number of reiterations depending on the length and rhythmic treatment of the vocal part. Some ungapped examples which progress quickly use the left-hand pizzicato (hajiki) on all notes after the first.

The vocal phrase, always a seven-syllable unit, centres on the same pitch reiterated by the shamisen, but with more flexibility for movement. When the reiterated tone is the upper neighbour of a nuclear tone, melodic tension is created over the long phrase until it resolves onto the nuclear tone. The tonal centres on which this pattern type occurs are C, E, F, F♯, A¹ and B¹.

Oki substyle

The basic soft style includes the oki and kudoki substyles. The oki is the opening section of a piece (equivalent to the makura section in gidayū), but it may be preceded by a declamatory pre-oki, a short section sealed off with a cadential motive or pattern, before it establishes itself with basic soft style, often opening with the three characteristic patterns: jibushi (almost exclusive to the oki), reiterative on C and reiterative on E or F. As already mentioned, this is the core of itchū soft narrative and remained in all the bungo-kei genres as the opening of oki style, whereas in itchū it is not restricted to oki, but can occur in several sections in a piece. Other patterns characteristic of the oki are haruji (reiterative on e with hajiki) and a pre-cadence. The full oki usually consists of two sub-sections, the first ending with the semi-cadential pattern kizami-otoshi.

The substyle of the itchū jo and the bungo-kei oki are strikingly similar. The jo often has a quotation section preceding the commencement of true itchū narrative. In *Wankyū michiyuki*, the entire jo is a quotation song (labelled simply uta), and true itchū narrative starts only from the second section.

Whereas the reiterative pattern on A-B (jibushi) is used almost exclusively in the oki, the reiterative patterns B and C can be found in any shōdan which is in neutral narrative style but are usually dominant in the first half of a piece. What in itchū is used freely in the first half of the piece, in bungo-kei is almost entirely restricted to the standard oki. It can be said, therefore, that the bungo-kei oki preserves faithfully the basic narrative style of itchū-bushi. This illustrates the tendency in many jōruri styles to retain fragments of old narrative styles in the early part of a piece, or to consciously quote older styles such as heike or utai at the opening of a piece.

Kudoki substyle

Kudoki is a more clearly shaped sectional substyle and is more likely to be found in tokiwazu, shinnai and kiyomoto than in itchū. It is the legacy of bungo-bushi, and was derived from Okamoto Bun'ya's 'sobbing music' (nakibushi), also called 'sorrowful/melancholy music' (ureibushi). Shinnai exploited this substyle most fully.

It will be remembered that in gidayū-bushi the kudoki is not a feature of every piece (dan, act, scene) – though it does appear in most plays – and indeed was not a clearly defined musical substyle until the 1730s (Inobe 1991: 135–59). In bungo-kei jōruri, there are very few pieces without a kudoki. In nagauta too, though not as formulaic, the kudoki is still a regular part of the kabuki dance form. The lack of development of a clear kudoki section in early itchū pieces suggests that this section developed fully with kabuki dance form; although I maintain that it is definitely a narrative shōdan, I also believe that it acquired a status as regular fixture in every piece in the context of kabuki dance.

Itchū pieces usually contain a section that suggests the nature of the kudoki – this can be called an incipient kudoki. This is seen in the clearly eroticized content, the frequency of patterns centring on high F (urei, meaning sorrow), and reaching up into the high pitch range. The kudoki substyle in tokiwazu, kiyomoto and shinnai, while sharing much with the basic style, is quite distinct in character from the oki or other basic soft narrative sections. It is characterized by, above all, the patterns otoshi and kan (unique to this section), the use of passionate narrative substyle towards the end of the section, and the overall high pitch range.

The kudoki has the most complex substyle. It starts with declamatory style, settles down to basic soft, and finishes with urgent. It is made up of a number of sub-sections, each typically ending with the semi-cadential pattern otoshi, an exclusively kudoki pattern. One sub-section commences with the high kan reiterative pattern. The kudoki of a narrative piece ends with a cadential pattern such as urei otoshi or two-step nagashi; in a dance piece, it is likely to end with the lyric cadence, and be followed by a narrative coda leading into the odoriji.

One special example of reiterative pattern is that on B^1, called kan (meaning high), applied to kan no tsubo, the finger position on the third string to produce the octave above the open string. It brings the male vocal tessitura into the falsetto range. As a melody pattern (senritsukei), this is specific to the kudoki section, always allotted to the youngest singer (sanmaime), though as a pitch indication it occurs elsewhere. Of course, the high pitch is associated with emotional intensity. The pattern kan shows great variety, especially in the vocal part. Usually the shamisen introduces the phrase by playing B^1 three times; then the voice comes in with the motive that eventually resolves onto the same tone. The melody in both parts stays around the B^1 for the seven-syllable segment of the line, then descends during the five-syllable segment through these tones: B G F♯ E or B A F♮ D, or even modulating to the melody G A B♭ A, and then back to C B♮ A F E (a tetrachord containing A B♭ D). Like other reiterative patterns, the shamisen rhythm is variable and basically elastic; the shamisen bides its time, coming in at the appropriate moment between the greatly prolonged melismatic vocal syllables in the long phrase. Kan always commences a new sub-section of the kudoki, so it often follows the otoshi semi-cadence.

A significant variant is the kudoki kan focused on A^1, and although B^1 is eventually reached, the whole phrase is generally lower in pitch, and is somewhat less intense. The considerable variability found in this pattern reflects its origin as a pitch area, rather than a melodic formula or senritsukei.

Basic Hard (semeji)

In this substyle, which includes chirashi and narrative coda, the voice and shamisen move together in a somewhat syncopated fitted rhythm; it is easy to transcribe. The lively and dynamic melody, though simple and repetitive, is not reiterative. The whole effect is jerky and bouncy, suited to narrating action. Example 6.3 provides a truncated example (second half of phrase 1 and phrase 2). Example 6.4 (phrases 3 and 4, and 6 and 7) provides further examples. It often features iro-kotoba or Sprechstimme vocal delivery. It is related to the hard substyles of noriji in gidayū, and to ōzatsuma basic narrative (Chapter 7).

In itchū, a pattern like semeji occurs, but it does not form an independent section sealed off with a cadential formula. It is more like a phrase-length pattern than a substyle. It is, however, the germ of the bungo-kei semeji substyle. Similarly, in itchū, urei is a phrase or phrases, not a substyle. It is the source (germ) of the urei substyle in tokiwazu. Tanaka (2002) identifies a pattern that seems to be related to semeji, both in function (used toward the end of a piece) and in some formal aspects. This evolved into a structured section, and the chirashi in tokiwazu, tomimoto and kiyomoto.

The bungo-kei section of urgent narrative (semeji shōdan) is normally a compact sequence of two or more 7+5 syllable lines of text; in kiyomoto this is always two lines, but often three in tokiwazu, and no fixed number in shinnai. It ends either with a short cadential motive or an unaccompanied phrase in irokotoba. Its phrase-length patterns are made up of strings of jerky motives in a restricted pitch range.

Declamatory (rōshō)

This is arguably the oldest style of narrative music. In bungo-kei genres it does not usually occur as an independent section as in earlier narrative genres, but only as fragments within basic narrative. Therefore it does not have to double as the name of a section (as with basic soft narrative, urgent, oki, kudoki, chirashi); it is only a substyle. It is, however, a very powerful expressive substyle. Rather than a whole section in rōshō style, one or more phrases occur as part of kihon narrative style. So to discuss the declamatory substyle, we start by discussing phrases (Tokita 1999: 160).

Let us note here that many narrative cadences featuring the nagashi motive, notably the two-step nagashi and the four-step sobbing cadence, are similar in character to declamatory style in their non-metric nature and the melismatic vocal style.

'Declamatory or rōshō phrases' (Yamada 2008; 'kakari phrases' in Tokita 1999) start with kakari patterns or motives. Kakari means beginning, and is used commonly in all sorts of shamisen music. Kakari begins with the shamisen reiterating two notes, sometimes doubling with the open second string (pitch E). In some instances the shamisen strikes only one introductory note. The opening shamisen motive sets the pitch for the singer to enter from; the whole phrase tends to focus on that one main pitch, unaccompanied and completely non-metrical, giving the impression of vocal freedom. The vocal melody is thus unaccompanied by the shamisen, except in a punctuating way, using nagashi patterns effectively between vocal phrases. The shamisen seems coincidental; the focus is completely on the vocal part. It provides the initial pitch or tone for the vocal phrase and then is silent.

The vocal part is in free rhythm, and may move melismatically over a wide pitch range, creating a dramatic and emotionally expressive impact. The shamisen joins in after the first part of the phrase, punctuating and articulating the sung phrase. It often dwells on a tone with the nagashi motive, which leads naturally into a cadential phrase such as urei otoshi.

Like the basic soft style's reiterative (nagaji-type) patterns discussed above, declamatory (rōshō, kakari) phrases exist at many different pitches and have many melodic realizations in the vocal line, since they are defined as a pattern by (free) rhythm and pitch rather than by melody. It is commonly found on the pitches B, E (harugakari), F (ugakari), F♯ (gingakari) and C (Tokita 1999: 159).

As a pattern, it occurs at the opening of sections of neutral narrative, including the oki and the kudoki. Many pre-oki sections are in the declamatory style (for example, Example 6.2: *Seki no to*). Parts of the kudoki are in declamatory style, as are some of the special effects narrative substyles (Tokita 1999: 193; see below). The declamatory pre-oki may start not just with one or two notes on the shamisen, but with a conspicuous motive such as heike-gakari which has several variant realizations, evoking the solemnity of heike narrative. Heike-gakari appears in ōzatsuma under the name kotogakari. Utai-gakari sometimes introduces a quotation of utai, or a phrase that evokes utai. A related motive is ukigin. Utai-gakari is introduced with just a couple of shamisen strokes of the tone A, the sung phrase being centred also on A, then rising to B focus with the beginning of oki substyle and the oki proper.

We can note that other types of gakari at the beginning of a piece are not declamatory substyle, for example sekkyō-gakari in niagari tuning and edo-gakari. The pattern edo-gakari appears at the beginning of a number of pieces, but actually it introduces oki substyle directly, and is not a declamatory phrase. It really belongs to basic soft style, almost qualifying as one of the nagaji-type patterns.

It can be hypothesized that this simple non-metric unequivocally narrative substyle is virtually the original form or predecessor of basic narrative, but without the metrical shamisen accompaniment. The advent of the plucked shamisen with its rhythmic, even percussive possibilities, gave rise to the more fitted rhythm of reiterative (nagaji-type) patterns. (See Table 6.6 for examples in transcriptions.) As already mentioned, it is used as an opening phrase for basic soft narrative, but also can appear during narrative sections in response to the demands of the text, as a fragmentary residue of the old narrative style for the purpose of solemnity.

Just as the group of reiterative patterns form the backbone of basic soft narrative, focusing on one pitch region, similarly, the rōshō phrases are also based on one pitch area, in fact, the same pitches of B, C, E, F, F♯, A^1, B^1. We can see that indeed the reiterative phrases all have counterparts in the rōshō phrases, as shown in Table 6.4. In both types of phrase, the vocal part is very similar, in free rhythm and tending towards melismatic treatment, although the declamatory melody is likely to have more movement over a wider pitch range. The big difference between the two groups of phrases is in the shamisen part. They are the same in offering the focal pitch for the sung phrase, but whereas in the basic style it maintains a steady pulse on the reiterated tone supporting the vocal melody, in the declamatory phrase it hangs back letting the voice take flight, only rejoining in between vocal phrases, and towards the end of the phrase hammering out the important tones of the vocal phrase with nagashi motives.

If indeed the declamatory substyle is the relic of the older pre-shamisen narrative singing, we can argue that it is the precursor, even the origin of the basic soft style, which developed after the adoption of the shamisen (and koto influence as well, no doubt), bringing to bear a more stable pulse and rhythmic framework to the sung narrative. The rōshō phrases can be seen as evolving into the reiterative phrases, with the tsukazu-hanarezu style typical of Edo-period art music, including jiuta-sōkyoku. We can easily see the direct correspondence between the phrases of each substyle by pitch centre, as shown in Table 6.4.

This type of pitch-based melodic patterning in which the music (particularly in the oki section) starts with a pattern based on B (open third string), followed by a pattern on C, then one on E or F, then in the kudoki triumphantly climbing to B^1, is highly reminiscent of the way kōshiki moves through the low pitch shojū, to nijū and then the climactic sanjū, and back again. In this way, these later narrative genres are indeed in the same lineage or tradition as a way of generating musical materials for delivering performed narrative.

Table 6.4 Comparison of basic soft reiterative patterns and declamatory rōshō kakari patterns

Reiterative nagaji-type patterns	Traditional pitch names	Declamatory rōshō kakari patterns	Double stops
A-B	chū/naka	B	B/E^1
C	haru-u	C	
E	haru	E	E/E^1
F	urei	F	
F#	gin / chū kan	F#	
A^1	ukigin?	A^1	
B^1	kan	B^1	
C^1		C^1	
edo-gakari		heike-, ukigin, utai-gakari	

Cadences

Dangire, which is the final phrase of the whole piece, is remarkably uniform across all bungo-kei genres. It is often preceded by a spectacular sanjū pattern. However, bungo-kei jōruri also contains a wide variety of sectional cadences, semi-cadences and pre-cadential patterns, reflecting the variety of narrative substyles. The two-stage nagashi narrative cadence is the most common way of ending a basic soft narrative section. The lyric cadence reiterates the open third string (B) in this rhythmic motive with a clear pulse: ♩♩ ᛉ ♩ ᛉ ♩ ᛉ.

It can end a narrative section in a dance piece, and is most important for ending a quotation song or dance section; it functions to bring the music back to the narrative musical voice. Quotation sections mostly end with this lyric cadence. (See Example 6.6, Line 7.)

The elaborate four-stage nagashi sobbing cadence derives from itchū suete, and in bungo-kei is restricted to ending a section of passionate narrative; its text is always connected to weeping in some way.

The urgent narrative semi-cadence (Example 6.3, phrase 1) leads into an urgent narrative (semeji) section. This nameless pattern is not mentioned in the usual sources, but it occurs regularly in urgent narrative substyle in a semi-cadential function. Morphologically it is related to reiterative patterns, both on one and two tones. It is found mostly in the narrative-dramatic pieces to convey a definite sense of urgency. It clearly leads into a sub-section of urgent narrative substyle or into the chirashi, and as such it can function as a semi-cadence in sections of both neutral narrative and urgent narrative. Its sparing use, not more than once or twice in any piece, suggests an important function as a tension builder (Tokita 1999: 150).

The *narrative coda* is a truncated version of a semeji section, and functions as a bridging passage between a quotation song and the next section (Tokita 1999: 190). It is a short sequence of urgent narrative style, usually five or six bars, set to units of either five, or 7 + 5 syllables, serving a cadential or a bridging function. The narrative coda is inserted after the cadence, usually of a non-narrative section or a kudoki, and brings the music back to the narrative voice. It can link the kudoki and the odoriji in a lyric-dance piece.

Special Effects Narrative Substyles

The *syllabic* passionate substyle (urei katarikuchi) has the same structure as semeji in all three genres, whereas the *melismatic* passionate substyle is non-metric, like rōshō declamatory narrative. Both focus on the tones F and A in the high register. They both end mostly with the sobbing cadence (urei otoshi).

Similarly, the eerie substyle has two rhythmic forms: the eerie syllabic (related to semeji) and the eerie melismatic (related to rōshō).

The comic substyle is related to kihon soft, as is the festive narrative substyle.

Table 6.5 Comparison of substyles in itchū and bungo-kei

Itchū	Bungo-kei (tokiwazu, kiyomoto, shinnai)
Basic	Basic soft (kihon): includes oki and kudoki substyles
Double time basic	Basic hard (semeji): includes chirashi and narrative coda
Declamatory	Declamatory (rōshō)
	Special effects narrative: 　Passionate syllabic (urei) (related to semeji) 　Passionate melismatic (urei) (related to rōshō) 　Eerie syllabic (related to semeji) 　Eerie melismatic (related to rōshō)
Quotation songs	Quotation songs
Kotoba	Speech

Table 6.6 Senritsukei across the transcribed examples

Substyle	Pattern	Example and phrase number	Initial text
Basic 1 (kihon) soft	jibushi	6.1 itchū (1) 6.2 tokiwazu (2)	Hosanu namida no Yuki no tsubana no
	reiterative	6.1 itchū (2)	Kuchinaba sode yo
		6.1 itchū (3) 6.2 tokiwazu (3)	Seishi ga nobe no Oto shizuka ni ya
		6.2 tokiwazu (6) 6.6 kiyomoto (4) 6.6 kiyomoto (5) 6.6 kiyomoto (10)	Na o mo ekou o Yume no ukiyo to Otoko no chōdo Hazue no tsuyu ka
	nagashi	6.1 itchū (3) 6.1 itchū (8) 6.2 tokiwazu (1) 6.2 tokiwazu (4) 6.2 tokiwazu (8) 6.3 tokiwazu (3) 6.4 tokiwazu (1) 6.4 tokiwazu (3) 6.4 tokiwazu (8) 6.5 shinnai (1) 6.6 kiyomoto (13)	omoigusa mukashi ni te koyoi mo masa ni sentei kokoro bakari no tamukegusa oku e iru hoshi no kage kashiko no ishi ni tamachiru bakari monosugoki suekakete tsukinikeru
Basic 2 (hard)	semeji -urgent semi-cadence	6.3 tokiwazu (1–3) 6.4 tokiwazu (3–4) 6.6 kiyomoto (8)	Iza sasetamae to … nokoshite Kashiko no ishi ni … togitatsuru Yōyō to

Substyle	Pattern	Example and phrase number	Initial text
Basic 3 (rōshō; declamatory)	rōshō: -gakari	6.1 itchū (4) 6.2 tokiwazu (1) 6.4 tokiwazu (1) 6.4 tokiwazu (3) 6.5 shinnai (1) 6.6 kiyomoto (1) 6.6 kiyomoto (11)	Mugura no ... Koyoi mo ... Hoshi no kage ... Kashiko no ... En de koso ... Onaji omoi ... Moshi otte ka to ...

The following sections of this chapter examine specific pieces from four genres. These case studies focus on the most strongly narrative and dramatic pieces of the repertoire of each genre in order to show their continuity with earlier genres, rather than how they have been de-narrativized by kabuki dance, and in a ceremonial context. The special capacity of bungo-kei genres to tell stories of unrequited or frustrated love is central to the examples; even in the historical piece chosen for tokiwazu the kudoki has a classic example of this stereotypical musical expression.

Itchū *Wankyū michiyuki*

Wankyū michiyuki is an early itchū piece performed and created by Miyakodayū Itchū. Itchū-bushi seems not to have been performed in kabuki frequently, but thrived more as zashiki entertainment. The *Ongaku Daijiten* (1983: 97–9) lists an amazing 168 extant itchū-bushi pieces, considerably more than other jōruri styles, many of them new creations in the twentieth century. Furthermore, three lineages remain active to the present: Uji, Sugano and Miyako. They all are active in the Kokyoku-kai, established in 1962 (*Ongaku Daijiten* 1983: 909).

Wankyū michiyuki is both a kind of michiyuki and a mad scene. It uses the hackneyed love story trope of the effete young playboy and the courtesan. It is a typical Osaka sewamono in which the petulant weak male lead is the spoiled son of a rich merchant. 'Yūgiri and Izaemon' is a famous example.[6]

The madness of the male character draws from the medieval trope seen in many nō plays. It is, however, very different from the mad character plays of nō. The difference between medieval mad characters and these Edo-period ones is that the earlier stories are about a parent, usually a mother, who has lost her child,

---

[6] Yūgiri (1657–1678) was a celebrated courtesan in Osaka's Shinmachi brothel district. After her premature death, kabuki and puppet plays were created about her, notably by Chikamatsu, who wrote an iconic wagoto play for kabuki actor Sakata Tōjūrō in 1679, and two puppet plays in 1686 and 1712 (*Nihon Denki Densetsu Daijiten* 1986: 918–19). The 1712 play, *Yūgiri awa no naruto*, was reworked many times, to become a stable item of the current kabuki repertoire from the 1770s, known as *Kuruwa bunshō* (also *Yoshidaya*), performed in shosagoto style to a kakeai arrangement of tokiwazu, takemoto (gidayū) and kiyomoto (Leiter 1979: 214–15).

whereas the Edo-period stories are typically about the loss of a lover. A number of kabuki dance dramas feature mad characters, such as kiyomoto *Yasuna*, and *Onatsu kyōran* in both itchū and tokiwazu. Mad character stories do not tend to end in suicide, unlike the more common michiyuki trope of Chikamatsu plays.

The story derives from a real scandal about the son of a rich Osaka merchant in the mid-seventeenth century whose son fell in love with a high-ranking courtesan in the Osaka Shinmachi licensed quarters (*Nihon Denki Densetsu Daijiten* 1986: 962–3). When put under house arrest his lovelorn condition caused him to go mad. His story was publicized, and was soon taken up in a popular song, later published in the 1704 song collection, *Ochiba-shū*. It was made into a kabuki play, and in 1685, Ihara Saikaku wrote a novel about Wankyū, *Wankyū issei no monogatari*. In 1706, Ki no Kaion wrote a puppet play, a still performed contemporary drama (sewamono), *Wankyū sue no matsuyama*. The first act, set in the Shinmachi brothel, ends with Wankyū being disinherited by his father. Act Two shows Wankyū's confinement, where he is visited secretly by his lover, and his wife who urges her to abandon him. In the third act, the michiyuki, Wankyū is dressed as a religious beggar of alms. Finally, a pardon from Wankyū's family is negotiated and a happy ending results. This michiyuki scene is comprised of essentially the same content as the itchū piece and other kabuki dance adaptations, but it is not certain which was created first (Takeuchi notes to recording of *Itchū-bushi koten meisakusen* 1982). The 1774 nagauta *Ninin Wankyū* became a nagauta classic, still frequently performed. A kiyomoto piece on this theme, *Maboroshi Wankyū*, was created in 1925.

This piece is an example of the complementary nature of itchū-bushi and bungo-bushi with plays originating in the puppet theatre. These soft jōruri styles were most suitable for narrating the michiyuki scenes of the drama, when transferred to kabuki, with the remaining scenes narrated by gidayū-bushi (takemoto).

Table 6.7   Outline of itchū *Wankyū michiyuki*

Sections	Text*	FMM
(1) niagari uta	... tadoriyuku. Ima wa kokoro mo, midare sourou Sue no Matsuyama, omoi no tane yo Itsu no koro yori, ainaresomete Kayou kokoro o, kawai to omoe Sari to wa sari to wa, shinobo ka no Hate, dou mo sei Kore kore kore, uketa to na Ano ya, Wankyū wa kore sa, kore sa Tsuzumi no kawa ka no, hon'e Shinzo kono mi wa, kore sa kore sa, uchikonda Tokaku koiji *no*, nuregoromo	Verbally okuri (a device to give continuity to narrative that links it with previous dan), but not musically. Dan begins with a song. Nagashi on f♯; then retunes to honchōshi.

Sung Narratives and Kabuki Dance: Bungo-kei Jōruri 197

Sections	Text*	FMM
(2) (CD Track 9, Example 6.1) jo (oki jōruri) basic narrative	Honchōshi 1. *Hosanu namida no,* tsuyu shibori 2. *Kuchinaba sode yo,* ima no mi wa 3. *Seishi ga nobe no,* omoigu*sa*	Basic narrative substyle Reiterative a-b Reiterative on E (with hajiki) Reiterative on F♮ (gapped) Cadence: nagashi on B (3rd open string)
(3) (CD Track 9, cont.) (hanamichi) narrative	4. Mugura no yado ni, tada hitori 5. Toko hanareyuku, akatsuki *no-on-no* 6. Sono kinuginu no, omokage o 7. Toedo kotaezu, shonbori to 8. Kinou wa kyou no, *mukashi ni te*	Kakari F♯ haru gin-gakari (modulation); rōshō phrase Hon tsukiyuri Shamisen changes to double time Cadence: suete (3-step nagashi, on all 3 open strings)
(4) utai	*Hosshi, hosshi wa, ki no hashi to* *Omou wa yabo yo, wake shiranu* *Kokoro no hana no, kaori o ba* *Shirasetai zo ya, aa, hachi, hachi* Kono juttoku mo, sugishi koro Yukari hosshi ga, hitofushi ni.	Kakari: E+E (1st and 2nd strings) (rōshō phrase) Utai; (unaccompanied till ba, down to 1st open string, low B) Last phrase: iro kotoba Return to basic soft Suete
(5) Basic narrative	Chie mo kiryou mo, shindai mo Mina wa awayuki to, kie usete Kawaseshi koto no, kawaru to mo Hanaremai zo ya, kimi kohaku Ware wa chiri ka ya, mi *ni* tsumo*ru*-un-nu Kokoro no akuta, mune ni michi Sore ga koujita, *monogurui*	Reiterative a-b (jibushi) Reiterative e (haruji) Reiterative f (urei) Reiterative f (urei) Kawari tsukiyuri (Machida 1982: 112) Reiterative b Suete
(6) utagakari	(ai) Totemo nuretaru ya, mi naredomo Hito murasame *o, itowaji to-on-non-no* Tachiyoru noki no, kosu no to ni Kimuku himuku no, soradaki no Morete mieshi wa, hakujin ka Iro de marome*shi,* yoru no tsuma (a-an-na)	Kakari: B+E Tsukiyuri; otoshi (like two-step nagashi) Reiterative b Reiterative e Reiterative f Tsukiyuri; cadence on low b (open first string)
(7) Narrative (kudoki)	(tataki) Horie no fumi no, tayori sae Hashi ga nakereba, watararenu Koi no negai mo, Amida-*bashi* Ukina ga hori mo, waza kure (ne) to Nurete kayou ka, itachi-bori (tataki) To o tsusoranaru, Satsuma-bori Koishi yukashiki, waga tsuma no Yukue o toedo, awazabori Zakoba Ajigawa, Fukushima *o-on-no*	Kudoki substyle; hashizukushi and horizukushi and michiyuki; focus on reiterative high F; no tsukiyuri till end (otoshi) Reiterative f + rōshō Reiterative f (urei) Reiterative c, b Tsukiyuri – fushi otoshi *continued*

Table 6.7 *concluded*

Sections	Text*	FMM
(8) shūdan (chirashi)	Mayoi yukedomo, Matsuyama ni Nitaru hito naki, ukiyo zo to Naitsu waroutsu, kyouran no Mi no hate nani to, asamashiya to Shiba o shitone ni, fushikeru wa Me *mo a*terarenu, fuzei nari.	Reiterative b Reiterative e Reiterative f Hayaji (no semeji) Tome mae: nagashi on BII, E, low BI; tome (dangire)

* Italics indicate the extent of the patterns named under FMM.

Text 6.1   *Wankyū michiyuki* (CD Track 9)

椀久道行き   ***Wankyū michiyuki***

Section 2
1. ほさぬなみだの、露しぼり   Tears that never dry, their dewy moisture
Hosanu namida no, tsuyu shibori   must be wrung
2. くちなば袖の、今の身は   from his sleeves – let these sleeves rot! He is
Kuchinaba sode yo, ima no mi wa   now no more than
3. せいしがのべの、思いぐさ   The longing grass (ominaeshi; valeriana) on
Seishi ga nobe no, omoigusa   the desolate moor. (He can do no more than
                                      long for the past love)

Section 3
4. むぐらのやどに、ただ一人   In a hut overgrown with weeds and thorns, all alone
Mugura no yado ni, tada hitori
5. 常葉なれゆく、暁の   He rises from his bed, remembers the dawn
Toko hanareyuku, akatsuki no
6. その絹絹の、面影を   parting of the shared robes,
Sono kinuginu no, omokage o
7. とへど答えず、しょんぼりと   He addresses that image, but there is no
Toedo kotaezu, shonbori to   reply; with a heavy heart
8. 昨日は今日の、昔にて   Yesterday seems so long ago
Kinō wa kyō no, mukashi ni te

Wankyū michiyuki is loosely structured soft narrative, and consists of six sections. It opens with a quotation song section and has other quotation song sections, but has no dance section (odoriji). On the other hand, it has no dramatic dialogue and lacks the dramatic impact of gidayū. Track 9 on the accompanying CD and the transcription in Example 6.1 cover sections 2 and 3. After the introductory song in niagari, the real beginning of the sung narrative is section 2 (jo, or introduction). This section opens with a three-phrase sequence that, as discussed above, is the classic style of basic soft narrative that appears in the oki section of subsequent bungo-kei genres. This three-phrase sequence occurs again in section 5. The reiterative phrases with a steady pulse in the shamisen part are seen also in the kudoki based on top B (kan) and F♯ (chū kan; Machida 1982: 336).

Example 6.1 Itchū, *Wankyū michiyuki*

continued

Example 6.1 *continued*

In *Wankyū* there are several examples of yuri (e.g. hon tsukiyuri, Line 5), but this is not transferred to bungo-kei as a central trait. Some examples are found in tokiwazu and shinnai, but none in kiyomoto. This seems to be an old-fashioned way to articulate and emphasize a partial cadence, that went out of fashion.

Section 1: (Niagari uta) ... tadoriyuku

The opening phrase is grammatically the final phrase of the preceding act, in the manner of multi-act jōruri scenes, and found in most gidayū-bushi pieces with the pattern okuri or sanjū. This should theoretically be okuri, but musically, it is the beginning of a song in niagari tuning. The first section of the piece is in fact a popular song created about Wankyū, and is borrowed or quoted here. That it is distinct from the narrative style is marked by the shamisen being tuned to niagari, whereas jōruri narrative sections always use honchōshi tuning, unlike sekkyō and rōkyoku. Textually, it uses a lot of almost meaningless phrases such as 'sari to wa', 'kore kore kore', 'kore sa', which suggest the playful nature of the song, depicting Wankyū in the amusement quarter in happier times. The shamisen is quite active. The final phrase brings the music back to narrative mode: 'Anyway, the path of love brings a wet cloak', as the shamisen re-tunes to honchōshi.

Section 2: Hosanu namida no, tsuyu shibori

The classic basic itchū narrative style is clearly evident here: the three narrative patterns in succession, centred on the tones B, C then E, and closed with the cadential pattern nagashi on third string. The text brings us to the narrative present with the weeping Wankyū pathetic in his tear-stained robe, never dry, wandering on the grassy field, deep in longing.

Section 3: Mugura no yado ni, tada hitori

This section uses patterns haru gingawari and hon tsukiyuri, and finishes with the extended cadential pattern suete. After the opening rōshō phrase, the shamisen is more active, doubling the notes against the voice.

Section 4: Hosshi hosshi wa, ki no hashi to

This section begins with three and a half lines unaccompanied in the style of utai (as imitated in jōruri), the shamisen coming in briefly in the fourth line. This is followed by some semi-spoken (iro kotoba) delivery. Wankyū is addressed as a 'priest' (Hosshi, hosshi) who is begging.

Section 5: Chie mo kiryō mo, shindai mo

This section begins in the basic itchū narrative style, but with greater elaboration in the shamisen part, indicating a building up of dramatic tension. The last two lines are close to what is identifiable as urgent narrative in bungo-kei jōruri. The section finishes with a suete cadential pattern, emphasizing pathos.

Section 6: Totemo nuretaru ya, mi naredomo

Commencing with a brief shamisen melody like a flourish, this narrative section calls on the faster narrative patterns characteristic of the second half of a piece. This is a lovesick plaint, but tonally it hovers on the nuclear tones more than intermediate tones, until the phrase 'morete mieshi wa'. The last phrase ends dramatically on the low B, and leads into the kudoki-like following section.

Section 7: Horie no fumi no, tayori sae

This section is a monozukushi of canals (hori, -bori), rivers (kawa) and bridges (hashi, -bashi), forming a verbal journey (michiyuki) around the Osaka landscape. It is at the same time like the conventional kudoki, in a high register, with its lingering phrases on the intermediate tone F, sometimes reaching up to top B; it also has incipient otoshi semi-cadences. It commences with the pattern hachitataki with its religious connotations, reminding us of the close connection between religion and pathos even in romantic narratives.

Section 8: Mayoiyukedomo, Matsuyama ni

The final section brings the verbal narrative to a more removed (objective) third person perspective of pity for this figure of unparalleled misery, whom it is difficult to behold. The final phrase 'fuzei nari' is a conventional statement of resignation used to end a large number of jōruri narratives, literally meaning 'such a scene'. The penultimate phrase (the pattern called tome mae) dwells on the syllables mo and te, with shamisen nagashi emphasizing the tones, then the conventional tone (dangire).

Tokiwazu *Seki no to* (The Snowy Barrier)

Table 6.8   Outline of tokiwazu *Seki no to*

Sections	Text	FMM
(1) Pre-oki Oki (Example 6.2)	Koyoi mo sude ni Furishikiru Yuki no tsubana no, hakaze o mo Oto shizuka ni ya, fukete yuku Masa ni sentei, on-nakiato o Toitatematsuru, goya no dokkyō Nao mo ekō o, wasure mo yarazu Jusuru mo otōto, Yasusada to Kokoro bakari no, tamukegusa.	Hyōshigi, taiko Heike gakari 1 7 2 (3) 7/3 7/3 Declamatory cadence Nagashi on 3rd string Kihon: Oki substyle. Jibushi Reiterative on C Declamatory, iro, nagashi on 7$_{II}$ Reiterative F 4 dan nagashi cadence (suete)

continued

Table 6.8   continued

Sections	Text	FMM
(2)Speech	Oo, sarinagara, chishio ni somishi, kono katasode, mi ni soemotaba, Sentei e no osore ari, ikaga wa sen. O, saiwai naru koto no shita.	
Narrative	Koto no shita hi e, oshikakusu. Sono ma ni oku no, hitoma yori Ippai kigen de, sekimori wa Chōshi sakazuki, tazusaete Ashi mo hyoro hyoro, ayumiide	Urgent (2 lines)
(3) Speech (Sekibei)	Yo no naka ni sake hodo no tanoshimi wa nee no ... Ya, omee wa mada nenee ka. Ya, sa ...	
Narrative Song	Nenu wa son da, basaranda Are wa sa no ei, kore wa sa no ei ya to Koi no fuchi Moshi mo hamaru ki de, yotsu momiji.	Lyric cadence
Speech (Munesada)	Naruhodo, washi wa ite neyō ga, sonata wa kitsui eiyō ja. Abunai zo ya, abunai zo ya. Aa korya, nani o suru e? kore ga futokoro e te o irete dou suru no da? Sa, kore wa ... Sa, dou suru no da yo? Hahahaha, kikoeta. Kono ōyuki ni te ga kogoeta to iu koto ka sa. Sono te o te ni totte kotobuki no.	(unaccompanied)
Song (manzai)	Medeta, medeta no Wakamatsu sama yo Eda mo sakaete, ha mo shigeru Omedetaya sa Chiyo no ko Omedetaya sa, Senshū banzei Banzei banzei banzei banzei. Ahahahaha ...	Urgent (3 lines)
Narrative (semeji)	(Example 6.3) Iza sase tamae to, oshiyarare Shijū o mune ni, Munesada wa Kokoro nokoshite, oku e iru.	2 dan nagashi
(4) Narrative Speech Song Speech Narrative	Ato wa tejaku no, hitorizake Aa sazo, imagoro wa, yai Shigere Matsuyama Ei, aa ee kimi da zo. Korya inochi o kakimushiru wa e. Dore, mō ippai, sake ni utsurō ...	
Narrative (eerie) (Example 6.4)	Hoshi no kage	2 dan nagashi

Sections	Text	FMM
(5) Speech Narrative Aikata (mimetic, sharpening axe) Narrative (urgent)	Hate, kokoroenu … … kono ono o motte tachidokoro ni, doore. Kashikono ishi ni, ono no ha o Oshiate, oshiate, togitatsuru. Oto wa sōsō, dōdō to Yami o teraseru, kanairo wa Tama chiru bakari, monosugoki.	Shamisen ashirai melody (eerie) Hayashi Hayashi Urgent Declamatory nagashi on second string (E)
(6) Speech (Action + dorodoro) Narrative: song like (new scene: Kurozome's voice) Song (niagari) Quasi kudoki (still niagari) (fast, unison)	Kono ono no ha o kokoromiru wa, saiwai naru kono koto … … ayashiki kono sakura. Maboroshi ka Miyuki ni tsumori, sakurakage Ge ni ashita ni wa, kumo to hari Fuzan no mukashi, ma no Atari Sumizome ga tachisugata. Adashi adanaru, na ni koso tatsure Hana no tsubomi no, itoke naki Kamurodachi kara, kuruwa no sato e Negoshite uete, harugoto ni Tomarisadamenu, utakata no Mizu ni chirishiku, nagare no mi.	 Nagashi on 3rd string (B) Niagari song Kudoki-like
(7) Kuruwa-banashi Speech Sugagaki no aikata Nagebushi Narrative / speech Kudoki	Ee, izuku to mo naku minarenu onna … … hanasou ka e. Yuku mo kaeru mo, shinobu no midare … Ma, kore kono yō ni, hajime kara … kore wa natsukashii, kanashii wai na.	 (several sub-sections with otoshi cadences, kan for new section, passionate narrative)

continued

Table 6.8   *concluded*

Sections	Text	FMM
(8) Speech (miarawashi) Tsuzumi uta à	Saizen yori kono katasode ni … nani mono ja e?	
Narrative (urgent)	Aa, nō, sarishi urami no areba koso … Komachi zakura no seikon nari. Ware wa hijō no sakuragi … nasake naya. Furyo no yakizu ni, tama no o mo …	Tsuzumi uta (unaccompanied); taiko dorodoro throughout.
Speech Narrative	On'ani-gimi no … … kakarishi zo ya.	Passionate melismatic
Aikata	Tsuma no katami no, katasode ni hirari hira hira hira	Otoshi iii
Aikata		
(9) Chirashi Pre-dangire Dangire	Tobikou sugata, fubuki no sakura … Amaneku fude ni (kakinokosu.)	Sanjū (pre-dangire) (Dangire omitted)

Text 6.2   *Seki no to*

Text for Example 6.2

1. 今宵もすでに、降りしきる、   The snow has come down hard tonight
Koyoi mo sude ni, furishikiru
2. 雪の翼の、葉風をも   The wind stirring the wing-like flakes
Yuki no tsubana no, hakaze o mo
3. 音静かにや、更けてゆく   And silence attends the deepening gloom.
Oto shizuka ni ya, fukete yuku
4. まさに先帝、御亡きあと   Mourning sutras must be read
Masa ni sentei, on-nakiato o
5. 問い奉る、後夜の読経   For the late emperor from midnight
Toitatematsuru, goya no dokkyō   to morn
6. 尚も回向を、忘れもやらず   Nor must a service be forgotten
Nao mo ekō o, wasure mo yarazu
7. 誦するも弟、安貞と   for Yasusada, beloved brother,
Juzuru mo otōto, Yasusada to
8. 心ばかりの、手向け草   my heart my only offering.
Kokoro bakari no, tamukegusa.

Text for Example 6.3

1. いざさせたまえと、おっしゃられ　　Forced by Sekibei's persistence,
Iza sase tamae to, osshare
2. 始終を胸に、宗定は　　　　　　　Munesada goes within,
Shijū o mune ni, Munesada wa
3. 心残して、奥へ入る　　　　　　　his many doubts still unresolved.
Kokoro nokoshite, oku e iru.

Text for Example 6.4 (CD Track 10)

1. 星の影　　　　　　　　　　　　　(Reflected in the sake is) the shadow of
Hoshi no kage　　　　　　　　　　　the stars.
2. (shamisen aikata with speech) Ha! What's this? I see in this wine cup the glimmering shadow of Saturn, meaning it's four in the morning. If I cut down this 300-year-old cherry tree tonight and use its wood to light invocation fires to the gods at the grave of Prince Hansoku, I'll achieve my grand ambitions. Ah! ... What happiness! Fortunately I've got this axe at hand ... Well, now!
3. かしこの石に、斧の刃を　　　　　On that handy stone he grinds the axe
Kashikono ishi ni, hono no ha o
4. 押し当て、押し当て、研ぎたつる　back and forth till it is razor sharp.
Oshiate, oshiate, togitatsuru.
5. (shamisen aikata)
6. 音はそうそう、どうどうと　　　　Hear the swishes and thuds
Oto wa sōsō, dōdō to
7. 闇を照らせる、金色は　　　　　　as the gleaming blade lights up
Yami o teraseru, kanairo wa　　　　　the darkness
8. 玉散るばかり、物凄き　　　　　　eerily...
Tama chiru bakari, monosugoki

Translations adapted from Brandon and Leiter 2002: 229, 231–2.

Seki no to (Tsumoru koi yuki no seki no to) (The Snowy Barrier) (50′35″) (1784) is a hard historical play (jidaimono), with some contemporary (sewamono) sequences. A full translation of the play can be found in Leiter and Brandon (2004). This narrative is the dénouement of a long complicated drama no longer performed in its entirety. The drama's final two scenes were tokiwazu narrative, and this second part is still frequently performed in kabuki as a dance drama (Furuido 1990: 168–73). Since its first performance in 1784, *Seki no to* has enjoyed continuous popularity, remaining one of tokiwazu's best-known pieces. The most frequently performed second part alone of *Seki no to* is about 50 minutes. Like most narrative music, it is in honchōshi tuning throughout ('basic' tuning: b-e′-b′), as is typical of 'narrative' (katarimono) genres, apart from a quotation song in section 6, in niagari (b-f′♯-b′).

Example 6.2 Tokiwazu, *Seki no to* (1)

Example 6.3 Tokiwazu, *Seki no to* (2)

Example 6.4 Tokiwazu, *Seki no to* (3)

continued

Example 6.4 *concluded*

This piece is set in the liminal space of a barrier check point where guards stop all who pass. It is a place of danger and of questioned identity, the same kind of location as *Ataka* where Yoshitsune and his party were accosted and asked to prove their identity. It is a place where extraordinary things can happen.

A period play (jidaimono) set in the ninth century, the plot concerns a succession dispute after the death of the emperor. The nobleman Yoshimine Munesada has come to a mountain retreat near the Ōsakayama barrier. His political opponent, the famous poet Ōtomo Kuronushi, is also in the area, disguised as the barrier guard Sekibei. A black cherry tree there is blooming weirdly out of season, and the spirit of the tree appears in the guise of a courtesan to confront Sekibei and take revenge on him. This scene anachronistically enacts the encounter between a prostitute and a customer in an Edo-period brothel.

Typically of tokiwazu, much effort is put into conveying the rough (yabo) masculine character of Sekibei, belching and drunk, and the coquettish but devious figure of the courtesan: her laughter, her tears and her passion for revenge.

The piece contains extensive passages of dramatic dialogue (many with atmospheric shamisen backing) and much dramatic interaction. Kabuki dance form –

that is, oki, kudoki and chirashi – is superimposed on narrative form, but there is no odoriji, only a couple of quotation songs interpolated diegetically. The sections of sung narrative are of varying length and style, and are interspersed with dialogue, some brief songs and instrumental interludes. Both kudoki and chirashi have a dramatic function. The kudoki is a play-acting section in which the pair pretend to take the roles of courtesan and customer, though each has ulterior motives and tries to outwit the other. The chirashi depicts a violent showdown between the supernatural force of the tree spirit/courtesan and the guard, really the poet-rebel of the court.

Much more rambling and diffusive than *Wankyū michiyuki*, *Seki no to* is one of the longest pieces in the tokiwazu repertoire.

The oki, kudoki and other neutral narrative sections are part of the legacy from itchū. The two-tone reiterative pattern jibushi is found in the oki section, followed by the sequence of reiterative patterns characteristic of basic soft narrative. However, the piece also contains many narrative sections and sub-styles that do not have clear counterparts in itchū (see, for example, Examples 6.3 and 6.4).

As shown in Table 6.8 and the transcription Example 6.2, the piece starts with a declamatory unaccompanied narrative pre-oki ('Koyoi mo ...'), beginning with the heike-gakari shamisen motive and ending with the shamisen nagashi motive on E. From the second phrase, the oki proper starts ('Yuki no tsubana mo'), displaying the typical features of oki substyle: jibushi focusing on B, against the shamisen reiteration of A-B, followed in phrase 3 with the reiterative pattern on C. Phrases 4 and 5 are an interpolation of declamatory narrative ('Masa ni sentei ...'; referring to the august emperor in solemnity), and from phrase 6 typical oki style resumes with the reiterative phrase focusing on F, which tends towards pathos, underlined by the vocal counterpart positioned in the lower octave than the shamisen, as the narrative mentions Munesada intoning sutras for his dead brother. The oki ends with the 'sobbing cadence' or urei otoshi, or four-step nagashi, even more spectacular than its itchū antecedent.

Section 2 involves interaction between Munesada and Sekibei with speech and sung narrative. Sekibei is depicted as vulgar and drunk, calling forth a strongly contrasting narrative style. In Section 3 Sekibei is enjoying his drink and carousing as he sings a manzai song. Munesada retires. The section concludes with a segment of urgent narrative (Example 6.3) and the narrative cadence (2 step nagashi) at 'oku e iru'.

Section 4 is made up of several short fragments of narrative and speech and a song (manzai). At the end of the section, something eerie happens, as an astral phenomenon is reflected in Sekibei's large sake cup: 'hoshi no kage'. The sung narrative changes to the eerie melismatic substyle, and ends with the narrative cadence (2 step nagashi) (Example 6.4). Track 10 of the accompanying CD starts with this phrase.

Section 5 again alternates between speech and narrative, but is full of action as Sekibei sharpens his axe. The shamisen interlude accompanies his movements here with a bright rhythmic section, and an obligato counter melody.

Section 6 introduces a new mood again, as the spirit of the cherry tree appears in the guise of an Edo-period courtesan. This mood is created with the song in niagari tuning, suggesting the kind of song fashionable in the kuruwa licensed quarters.

Section 7 continues this fiction with banter between Kurozome and Sekibei, as if he is a customer at the brothel. The song nagebushi is again suggestive of this situation. A long, fully developed kudoki about the woman's resentment toward an inconstant lover is the musical heart of the piece.

In Section 8, however, the narrative returns to the reality of the drama in which these two characters are enemies intent on revenge. Instead of an odoriji section, in this heavily narrative piece, further narrative ensues – similar to kudoki style, but more impassioned and threatening: Kurozome expresses her feelings in melismatic passionate narrative style.

The following extended chirashi in Section 8 is a contest between the supernatural power of Kurozome and Sekibei's physical power. The drama ends with Kurozome in an imposing stance (mie), her appearance having been transformed by stage assistants into a demonic figure. The musical narrative draws on the sanjū pattern to create an impressive climax before the subdued dangire final pattern (often omitted in kabuki performance). The text returns to the neutral and authoritative narratorial voice with the final phrase, 'Amaneku fude ni kakinokosu' (This story will be recorded and remain throughout the world).

Shinnai, *Ranchō*

Among the disciples of the infamous Miyakoji Bungo no jō (d. 1740) was one Miyakoji Kagadayū (d. 1757) who went from Kyoto to Edo with Bungo no jō. Kagadayū broke away from the Miyakoji ranks in 1745 after a rift with Mojitayū. He set himself up as Fujimatsu Satsuma in 1746, and his satsuma-bushi had some engagements in kabuki up to 1752. Another follower, Tsuruga Wakasa no jō (1717–86) (founder of tsuruga-bushi and the Tsuruga-ha), appeared in the Morita kabuki theatre in 1758. His disciple Tsuruga Shinnai was acclaimed for his shinnai-bushi in the 1770s and 1780s. A loose conglomeration of related performers including Fujimatsu and others were active in salon entertainment and occasionally in kabuki, and subsequently all were subsumed under the name of shinnai-bushi, after Tsuruga Shinnai. From then, shinnai-bushi included the Tsuruga-ha and Fujimatsu-ha groups. To Tsuruga Wakasa no jō is attributed the composition of *Ranchō*, *Akegarasu* and *Onoue Idahachi*, three of the shinnai classics. A substantial part of the current repertoire is attributed to him and Tsuruga Shinnai: altogether 30 pieces dating from this era are listed in *Ongaku Daijiten* (1983: 1625). In the early nineteenth century, shinnai was again given some kabuki dance scenes. Later in the century much new repertoire was created, particularly that attributed to Fujimatsu Rochū (1797–1861).

The direct genealogical link to itchū via bungo-bushi is obvious in shinnai music, both in its soft basic narrative, and in its emphasis on erotic expression. By shifting its main locus of activity to the salons of the brothel district, this tendency was strengthened: the shinnai singing style is unique in conveying injured lament. Shinnai mainly continued to find a niche in zashiki entertainment in the licensed quarters. Its most characteristic pieces are the sewamono stories of love suicides set in the licensed districts (*Akegarasu, Masayume, Ranchō*), and also the seamy world of mizu shōbai including sumō (*Senryō nobori*). The shinnai repertoire has few pure dance pieces, in strong contrast to tokiwazu and kiyomoto. Odoriji is not, therefore, a common feature of shinnai narratives.

A body of new pieces were created in the twentieth century, most notably by Okamoto Bun'ya (1895–1996), who is said to have created some 200 shinnai pieces. Some are based on modern literary works (such as *Jūsanya*, from the 1895 novel by Higuchi Ichiyō, and *Onna keizu*, from the 1907 novel by Izumi Kyōka); others follow developments in proletarian literature and theatre. He also wrote several books about shinnai. There are a number of shinnai lineages (ryūha) apart from his, however, and currently two Living Human Treasures, Shinnai Nakasaburō (b. 1940) and Tsuruga Wakasa no jō III (b. 1938), both of whom have created new repertoire often crossing over with other genres. Tsuruga, for example, is active in creating new works collaborating with other art forms – such as Hachiōji puppets on wheels (kuruma ningyō), Japanese dance and nō – and taking these performances overseas.

Shinnai shamisen developed a unique practice called shinnai nagashi, a kind of busking with two performers walking along the street and playing without vocal narrative. This was one factor that led to the development of the uniquely shinnai obligato shamisen (uwajōshi) part; elaborating the counter-melody it is played by a second shamisen tuned one fifth higher by using a capo (kase). Another factor in the development of the uwajōshi was that, away from kabuki dance, shinnai slowed down considerably. The doubled shamisen part had the effect of giving a stronger sense of pulse to the narrative, as the beats were delineated and made more rhythmic and metrically regular. Whereas the uwajōshi of nagauta and other kabuki dance music is characteristic of active and virtuoso shamisen interludes (like that in *Seki no to*, the axe-sharpening aikata), in shinnai it complements the very slow 'basic' narrative style, particularly in the kudoki section, bringing a clear pulse to this delivery. This can be seen in Example 6.5, and in the recorded excerpt (CD Track 11).

In fact, the kudoki is what characterizes shinnai music more than anything, so much so that it is quoted in other shamisen music; for example, in *Michitose* and other kiyomoto pieces, whose kudoki features the quotation pattern shinnai gakari.

Shinnai-bushi is like itchū in its limited exposure in kabuki, and its favouring of private (zashiki) performance. Perhaps surprisingly there is an even greater breadth of category of piece than in the other bungo-kei genres. Contrast, for example, the sewamono love stories (*Akegarasu, Masayume*), the comic pieces in the Hizakurige series, the male heroes of the entertainment world (*Ranchō, Senryō nobori*), and even jidaimono (*Ichi no tani*). Ultimately, what distinguishes shinnai style most is the nasal, tear-jerking singing style. Its decisively narrative feature is the absence of the odoriji, and the prominent use of spoken dialogue, emphasizing dramatic interaction. This may have disappeared from contemporary performance of *Ranchō*, but is still central to the comic series of pieces in Hizakurige.

Table 6.9   Outline of shinnai *Ranchō*

Sections	Text	FMM
(1) Maebiki Oki jōruri (no longer performed)	Gagataru … … tōsei no … yakusha no nizura …	Same as maebiki in kiyomoto *Kasane* Opens with jo (ōzatsuma name)
(2) Ranchō is introduced. Classic oki patterns Equivalent of hanamichi	Na ni shi ou, Sumida ni soishi nagare no mi Na ni nagaretaru, Sakuragawa Ranchō to iu tori narade Kono Wakakiya ni su o kumite Itsumo negura to, kayoikuru.	Rōshō; jibushi Reiterative c Reiterative F; nagashi Narrative cadence
(3) Narrative / speech sequence	Funayado no chōchin o … … futari wa tatte, shita e yuku.	(Omitted)
(4) Narrative/ speech sequence Mushizukushi Lovers' quarrel	Ato ni futari wa, suneai no Hateshi nakereba Ranchō wa Mono o mo iwazu zutto tatsu o Konoito hikitomete 'Omae doko e yukinansu?' 'Doko e ikou to okamai nasaru na; ore ga ashi de mukou e de mo, tonari e de mo, suki na tokoro e yukiyasu' to mata tachiagaru o, hikimodoshi 'Hon ni amari mushi ga you arinsu e' … … ichikawa-ryū no kuzetsu nari.	Rōshō To-gaki style narrative Speech + ashirai
(5) Narrative Konoito Yotsuya kudoki	Konoito wa urameshige ni. Otoko no kao o uchimamori 'Omae no soushita …' Imasara iu mo sugishi aki Yotsuya de hajimete outa toki … … kawari wa nai wai na. (… urami namida dōri nari.)	Rōshō / kakari Speech + ashirai (abbreviated)
(6) Kotoba/ narrative Omiya arrives	'Sou ieba sonna mono ja ga …	
(7) Narrative Kotoba Omiya kudoki (CD Track 11 and transcription (Example 6.5) from En de koso to araba koso)	Iwaneba itodo, sekikakaru Mune no namida no, yaru kata nasa 'Ano Ranchō dono to fūfu no naritachi … 'En de koso are, sue kakete Yakusoku katame, mi o katame Setai katamete, ochitsuite Aa, ureshiya to, omouta wa Hon ni ichinichi, araba koso … … Kyō made hi ni wa, iku tabi ka.' Sono urami o, uchisutete Tagai no tame no, shintei-banashi.	Passionate declamatory Speech (heike gakari) Urgent passionate narrative Melismatic passionate narrative 4 dan nagashi (suete)

Sections	Text	FMM
(8) Kotoba	Kore koko o you kikashanse ya ...	Speech + ashirai
Narrative (Fukutake no dan)	Ranchō dono ni mi o tatesase ... ... Mi o shizumetaru Fukagawa take no ukitsutome ... ... hitokoto iute kudasanse to koto o waketaru shinjitsu o kiite dōri ni fushi shiba no.	(kudoki style) 4 dan nagashi (suete)
(9) Kotoba/ Narrative Omiya thanks Konoito	'Mōshi, Omiya san ... ... suru you na' to Mono ga shirasu ka, chi no yukari Hashigo oriru mo, tayo tayo to Chikara naku naku, tachikaeru.	Speech + ashirai Narrative cadence
(10) Narrative / speech	Kakure kiitaru, Ranchō wa 'Kore, Konoito ... ... awarenu wai na' Kore ga konjō no, okao no miosame, You misete kudasanse, to Sugari nagekeba	Speech + ashirai
(11) Narrative / speech	Ranchō wa Oo, nokorazu kite naite ita. Sonnara sonata wa iyoiyo kireru ki ka? ... Hyakuman nen no oinochi sugite ... Iya iya, sore de wa Miya e no ... kikoenu wai nou	Urgent passionate narrative
(12) Narrative	Sonata o koroshite, ore hitori Yo ni nagaraete, hitonaka e Nan to kao ga, mukeraryou. Totemo nagarae hatenu mi o Issho ni yai no to sugaritsuki Idakishimetaru kokoro to kokoro Futari ga inochi mijikayo no Tori mo tsuguru ya, kane no ne mo Asu no ukina ya, hibiku ran.	Chirashi Semeji, chirashi Sanjū (pre-dangire) (dangire)

Source: based on recording by Shinnai Nakasaburō (Teichiku 1976) and with reference to *Nihon Ongyoku Zenshū* and Nakagawa (1911) and other commercial recordings.

Text 6.3   Shinnai, *Ranchō*

蘭蝶	**Ranchō**
1. 縁でこそあれ、末かけて En de koso are, sue kakete	Because of our good fortune, I expected to have a long happy life together
2. 約束かため、身を堅め Yakusoku katame, mi o katame	We promised firmly, and committed ourselves to that life
3. 世帯堅めて、落ち着いて Setai katamete, ochitsuite	We set up a home, and settled down
4. アア、うれしやと、思うたは Aa, ureshiya to omouta wa	Oh, how happy we are, I thought
5. ホンニ一日、あらばこそ Hon ni ichinichi araba koso	But that lasted barely a day…
そりゃたれゆえじゃ、こなさん故 Sorya tare yue ja, konasan yue	Whose fault is that? It is yours.
大事な男を、そそのかし Daiji na otoko o sosonokashi	You dragged away my precious man
夜昼となく、引き付けられ Hiru yoru to naku hikitsukerare	day and night …

Ranchō (1857; attributed to Tsuruga Wakasa no jō I) is a soft or sewamono jōruri, shinjūmono, about a tragic love affair set in the entertainment quarter. Basically, the male entertainer (taiko mochi, or male geisha) Ichikawaya Ranchō is deeply involved with Konoito, a courtesan in the Wakakiya establishment in the brothel district. The first part of the piece depicts their troubled relationship. Ranchō's wife Omiya, also an entertainer, visits Konoito and begs her to stop seeing Ranchō, so he will spend more time doing his job, even start up a small business and become an ordinary husband. Konoito agrees, but after Omiya leaves, Konoito and Ranchō resolve to commit suicide together.[7]

According to texts printed in the late Meiji to early Shōwa era, *Ranchō* was much longer than performed today.[8] Although there is almost no change of scene (downstairs to upstairs of the same establishment) and the time of the narrative might be the same as (or even shorter than) the duration of the sung narrative, because of its unusual length as a narrative it is often conceptualized as consisting of four scenes (dan in the narrow sense): Yotsuya no dan; Omiya kudoki no dan; Fukagawa Take no dan; and Shinjū no dan. One commercially released compact disc (*Shinnai*, Nippon Columbia 2003) reflects this division, by including abbreviated versions of each of the four parts, all by different performers.

---

[7] There is a five-act kabuki play based on this, called *Wakagi no Adanagusa* (1855, Chikugo Shibai, Osaka), in which Ranchō is 'really' a samurai searching for a missing heirloom. In this play he kills Konoito (Leiter 1979: 423).

[8] See Nakauchi (1927) and Nakagawa (1911).

Example 6.5 Shinnai, *Ranchō*

continued

Example 6.5 *continued*

They form a telescoped version of the whole piece. Most recordings focus on just one of the first two scenes mentioned, a trend hardly different from the days of SP records, according to the inventory of the Takeuchi collection at the Tokyo National Institute for Cultural Properties (Iijima 2009).

The most complete commercial recording available is that of Shinnai Nakasaburō (Teichiku 1976). Nakasaburō starts his hikigatari performance with 'Na ni shi ou ...', and includes the mushizukushi. His Yotsuya kudoki is only about one third of the length of the early printed texts, however. The whole performance occupies two sides of an LP record, a total time of nearly one hour. The need to divide the long piece (even longer in earlier times, evidently, judging by the extant texts) into four scenes or dan might make it sound like danmono with multiple episodes. However, the 'action' takes place in less than one hour in 'narrative time' and the scene does not change. This reflects the intensity at the heart of the narrative which distils the essence of the characters' feelings and their emotional and ontological dilemma that can only be solved by suicide.

The opening section (oki) ('Gagataru ...') is heavily Sinitic and refers to broad themes comparing the erotic culture of India, China and Japan; it seems to be no longer transmitted. Current performance starts with Section 2 ('Na ni shi ou ...'), the equivalent of the hanamichi in kabuki dance form, which introduces the main character, Ranchō, an entertainer specializing in kowairo, the art of imitating kabuki actors' dialogue. He frequents the Wakakiya where his lover Konoito lives and works, and makes it his 'nest'. In general, few contemporary shinnai performers actually start so early in the piece. Sections 2 to 5 are the Yotsuya kudoki no dan.

Section 3, omitted in all recordings I have access to, is a roisterous depiction of behind the scenes activity in the Wakakiya establishment, alternating between speech and sung narrative. Section 4 ('Ato ni futari wa ...') relocates the narrative from the public business space to the privacy of Konoito's upstairs room where she and Ranchō are quarrelling. In a facetious punning on insects' names (mushizukushi), Ranchō is rude and cold to Konoito, provoking her famous kudoki, the Yotsuya kudoki. It actually starts with the phrase 'Imasara iu mo sugishi aki' (and this is the point at which a number of SP recordings began) just before the famous line 'Yotsuya de hajimete outa toki ...'. I have placed the start of Section 5 a little earlier, after the definitive cadence 'kuzetsu nari'; Section 5 thus begins with two phrases telling how Konoito looks discontentedly at his face, and her short speech reproaching his temper, before commencing the kudoki.

In the old printed texts, this is a long section, but Nakasaburō among others cut it after about one third, finishing at 'Jitsu ni kawari wa nai wai na'. (Fujimatsu Tsurichiyo on the Nippon Columbia LP [1974] is the same, but the version of Yotsuya no dan by Fujimatsu Sagakichi on the Columbia CD [*Shinnai* 2003] continues for several more phrases which do not appear in the old printed texts, evidence of a separate transmission.)

Section 6 is mainly speech with occasional sung narrative phrases. Ranchō admits that she is right. Then Konoito is called and told that she has a visitor, so Ranchō hides. It is in fact his wife, Omiya, who explains that she has come to appeal to Konoito to stop seeing Ranchō. With an intricate obligato part, this section is like a kudoki.

Section 7 is the so-called Omiya kudoki, one of the most famous passages of shinnai, starting with the phrase 'En de koso'. Only the first few lines are contained in CD Track 11, and are transcribed in Example 6.5. The section starts with very slow melismatic declamatory (rōshō) phrases after the introductory shamisen double stops, in high register. Inexplicably, the kudoki itself begins with the shamisen motive heike-gakari, surprising in the middle of a piece, but perhaps reflecting the fact that this has become one place to begin a performance. In this intense kudoki section, the musical delivery slows right down as the melody expands, as if in slow motion. The number of words per minute is minimal. The pulse, when established, is very slow, while the shamisen obligato (uwajōshi) intricately fills the space between the notes of the main part (honte). The vocal line is highly embellished, in contrast with the skeleton melody delineated by the shamisen honte part and its embroidered uwajōshi. The kudoki generally occupies a high pitch register, but the vocal melody reaches down into lower pitch areas covering a wide range in some phrases, mainly those in declamatory (rōshō) style. Although shinnai basic narrative style has slowed down considerably in the interests of emotional intensity, the shamisen maintains a steady pulse through the device of the elaborate uwajōshi. It is meant to tug at the heartstrings of the addressee in the narrative, and also of the listener.

After her kudoki, in Sections 8 and 9, the so-called Fukagawa Take no dan, there is tearful dialogue between Omiya and Konoito, who is affected by Omiya's appeal and undertakes to separate from Ranchō. There follows more sung narrative, very similar to the kudoki in style and in content, in which Omiya presses her case that separation is the only way Ranchō can focus on work and become a hardworking husband. Following this, more tearful dialogue ensues: Omiya thanks Konoito emotionally, and leaves in tears (nakikaeru).

From Sections 10 to 12, the end of the piece, the pace of the narrative speeds up; there is more urgent narrative, mainly of the urgent passionate narrative type, and the sections are shorter. This is the so-called Shinjū no dan. Section 10 starts with Ranchō coming out of hiding, having heard the exchange between the two women. Rather than going back to Omiya, Ranchō and Konoito decide to die together. The narrative ends with the censorious phrase: their story will echo scandalously.

The overwhelming dominance of kudoki and of related passionate narrative sections in *Ranchō* makes it like one huge kudoki, especially since the more neutral oki section and extended sections of dialogue and action-based narrative have been excised from the early part of the piece. The nasal almost sobbing singing style, indeed fitting the sobriquet of nakibushi attributed to the seventeenth-century forerunner Okamoto Bun'ya, creates the dominant image and characteristic of shinnai narrative, and creates the impression that shinnai is only kudoki and sobbing narrative. However, just as other bungo-kei genres can cover all kinds of narrative territory, so too shinnai has other kinds of piece in its repertoire. The shrinking repertoire in most public performance is largely responsible for this selective perception.

Kiyomoto, *Kasane*

Kiyomoto is the youngest or latest of the bungo-kei jōruri genres, appearing in 1814 when a disciple of Tomimoto Buzendayū II broke away and formed his own group. This was Kiyomoto Enjudayū (1777–1825). Kiyomoto took some of the tomimoto repertoire and built on it and grew in popularity at the expense of tomimoto.

Kasane was premiered in 1823, the opening scene of a drama by Tsuruya Nanboku IV (1755–1829) (Leiter 1979: 176). It derives from legends originating in events of the later seventeenth century, about which many plays and dance scenes were created during the eighteenth century (Tokita 1999). There is a related shinnai piece, *Kasane miuri no dan* and its sequel in which Kasane is disfigured from birth, though in the kiyomoto piece she is a beauty until halfway through the piece. The CD excerpt (Track 12) is the hanamichi section, and is in the kiyomoto basic soft narrative substyle.

Table 6.10   Outline of kiyomoto *Kasane* (CD track 12)

Narrative content	Text*	FMM
(1) Maebiki Oki jōruri	Omoi o mo … *Kokoro mo hito ni*, someba koso Koi to iu gao, *natsugusa no* *Kiyuru majikaki*, sue no tsuyu Moto no shizuku ya, yo no naka no Okiresakidatsu, *futamichi o*	Oki substyle Reiterative f# Kizami-otoshi Haruji Lyric cadence
(2) Hanamichi (CD Track 12) (Example 6.6)	1. Onaji omoi ni, atosaki no 2. Wakachi shidoke mo, natsu momiji 3. Kozue no ame ya, sameyaranu 4. Yume no ukiyo to, yukinayamu 5. Otoko ni chōdo, aohigasa 6. Hone ni naru tomo, nan no sono 7. Ato o ōse no, onnagi ni 8. Kowai michi sae, yō yō to 9. Tagai ni shinobu, nobe no kusa 10. Hazue no tsuyu ka, hotarubi mo 11. Moshi otte ka to, mizukuroi 12. Kokoro seki ya mo, ato ni nashi 13. Kinegawa-zutsumi ni, tsukinikeri.	Aikata; basic substyle Kakari on E+e Reiterative on F♮ Kizami-otoshi Reiterative on F♮ Reiterative on C Lyric cadence Urgent semi-cadence Urgent narrative Reiterative on C Kakari on C Urgent narrative 2-dan nagashi narrative cadence
(3) Speech	Kore, Kasane, omoigakenai kono tokoro e …	Shamisen ashirai melody
(4) Kudoki (Kasane)	Iu kao tsukuzuku, uchimamori Ato iisashite, kuchigomoru.	Kakari: B+E Narrative cadence
(5) Speech	Hate, zehi ni oyobanu … … fubin n mono no kokoro ya na.	Shamisen ashirai
(6) Kudoki (Yoemon)	Fukaki kokoro o, shiratama no … Kawabe ni shibashi, nakiitaru.	Kakari: B Urei otoshi (sobbing cadence)
(7) Narrative Speech Narrative	Fushigi ya, nagare ni, tadayou doku*ro* Nani, Zokumyō Suke … Shibashi arasou orikara ni Kaze ni nagaruru, *hitofushi ni*	Eerie narrative Nagashi on B Shamisen ashirai Urgent narrative Lyric cadence
(8) Song	Yo ya fukete … … shiramu shinonome.	Hauta Lyric cadence
(9) Speech	Aa moshi, omae doko ye yukashansu e? … miseraremai ga na. Chee, omae wa naa	Shamisen ashirai

Narrative content	Text*	FMM
(10) Kudoki (Kasane)	Sore sono yō ni, yoso hoka ni … … aware ni mo mata, ijirashiya.	Kakari: F♮ Pre-narrative cadence; narrative cadence.
(11) Speech Narrative Speech Narrative Speech Narrative	Dōri dōri, shinuru to iu wa, mina itsuwari … Isoiso saki e, tachimachi ni Korya watashi o damashite … Kagami ni utsuseba … Aree? Hoya, ya, ya, ya! Korya ma dōshite kono yō ni Jōbutsu se yo to, muni muzan …	Urgent narrative Eerie narrative Shamisen ashirai Urgent narrative
(12) Kudoki (Kasane)	*Nō nasake na ya, urameshiya* … ikanaru uram ka, imawashi to	Passionate narrative Kakari B, F♮, otoshi Urgent semi-cadence
(13) Narrative	Kudoitsu naitsu, mi o kakimushiri … Omoishire ya to, sukkutachi	Urgent narrative Eerie narrative (melismatic)
(14) Chirashi (extended)	Furimidashitaru, kurokami wa … *Osoroshikarikeru*, shidai nari.	Ōsanjū, dangire

* Italics indicate the extent of the patterns named under FMM.

Text 6.4   Kiyomoto *Kasane* (CD Track 12)

1. 同じ思いに、跡先の
Onaji omoi ni atosaki no
2. 別ちしどけも、夏紅葉
Wakachi shidoke mo natsu momiji
3. 梢の雨や、さめやらぬ
Kozue no ame ya sameyaranu
4. 夢のうき世と、行なやむ
Yume no ukiyo to yuki nayamu
5. 男に丁度、青日傘
Otoko ni chōdo aohigasa
6. 骨になるとも、何のその
Hone ni naru to mo nan no sono
7. あとを逢う瀬の、女気に
Ato o ōse no onnagi ni
8. 怖い道さえ、やうやうと
Kowai michi sae yōyō to
9. 互いに忍ぶ、野辺の草
Tagai ni shinobu nobe no kusa
10. 葉末の露か、蛍火も
Hazue no tsuyu ka hotarubi mo

But with the same intent.

Acting recklessly, the confused, tangled summer maples, the rain falling through the treetops, unceasing.

In this dream world of travail, progress is difficult.
On her way to meet (au/ao) the man, her umbrella is tattered,
worn to the ribs, but she cares not.

Pursuing him, her woman's heart is set on the rendezvous.
Nor heeds she the fearful path.

At last, under cover of dark, they yearn to meet,
like the hare's-foot ferns entwining.
Seeing a light, perhaps the glint of the dew

11. もし追っ手かと、身づくろい	on the leaf tips, perhaps the light of fireflies.
Moshi otte ka to mizukuroi	'What if it should be my pursuers?'
12. 心関屋も、後になし	She girds herself again;
Kokoro Sekiya mo ato ni nashi	with a sense of urgency, rushing,
13. 木下川に、つきにける	Sekiya is now past.
Kinegawa-zutsumi ni tsukinikeru.	She arrives at the bank of the Kine River.

Although a contemporary piece (sewamono), *Kasane* also has elements of the supernatural, and draws on all the narrative resources available to kiyomoto to express widely contrasting moods: lyric scenery in a michiyuki mode, the desire and pain of love and betrayal in four kudoki sections, action drama and violence, and a living ghost that threatens its murderer.

The whole piece takes the form of a journey, one of the oldest narrative themes in Japan, and the hanamichi section is literally a michiyuki in itself. The four kudoki sections progress from mildly reproachful love to angry resentment with plenty of passionate narrative substyle applied. Kasane is transformed into a disfigured victim of the karma of her father's crime, and is then murdered by her lover. She does not then disappear but rises up as a living ghost that haunts its murderer. The chirashi finale section is an oshimodoshi: the dying and then dead Kasane takes on supernatural power and threatens her aggressor with waves of energy which ebb and flow in a prolonged climactic finale.

Like *Seki no to*, this very dramatic piece accumulates a number of purely narrative sections of varying type alternating with sections of dialogue. The sections of kabuki dance form which have a predictable musical style are the oki (opening), hanamichi (entrance), kudoki (entreaty) and chirashi (finale), displaying a dual structural orientation towards both dance music and narrative music, but with a stronger emphasis on the latter.

As well as the dominant basic soft narrative style, there are many short sections of urgent narrative substyle. There are also specialized formulaic narrative sections for certain textual content types, such as the eerie appearance of a ghost, and the oshimodoshi at the end of the piece, or the intensely emotional sections (passionate narrative style). These are ready-made musical resources to be exploited to fit the needs of a particular text.

The formulaic narrative styles are characterized by formulaic phrases both verbal and musical. The hanamichi, for example (Example 6.6), ends with the typical compound verb of motion, conveniently occupying a five-syllable phrase, tsukinikeru (arrived), matched with the narrative cadence, two-step nagashi. The second kudoki section ends with the verb of weeping nakiitaru, again occupying five syllables, with the corresponding 'sobbing cadence' (urei otoshi) or four-step nagashi. In the final two lines of the piece an archaic narrative voice can be picked up, as in most other jōruri, and kōwaka dance dramas. The phrases 'Nochi ni tsutaeshi monogatari / osoroshikarikeru shidai nari' (her story is passed on in later days; what a fearful matter it was) are matched with the spectacular sanjū pattern, followed by the sober final phrase (dangire) that ends every piece.

Example 6.6 Kiyomoto, *Kasane*

continued

Example 6.6 *continued*

Example 6.6 *continued*

Line 1 is kakari on double stop two Es, non-metric unaccompanied vocal phrase on top E (onaji omoi). From the syllable ni, the shamisen joins in with a clear rhythmic pulse in basic soft narrative style, which continues for most of the section. Line 3 ends with the pattern kizami otoshi, usually an oki pattern, dividing the section into subsections. Line 4 then starts with a reiterative pattern on F (urei), moving into a higher register, then line 5 is reiterative on C. Another sub-section is created at the end of line 7 with the lyric cadence (bungo-fū nagashi), and a further sub-section in line 8 with the urgent narrative semi-cadence which should lead into urgent narrative, but doesn't. Instead, soft basic continues, and line 10 has reiterative on C again, with a semi-cadential finish. Line 11 begins with kakari on C and a melismatic vocal line, and a snatch of urgent narrative. Line 13 is the cadence for the whole hanamichi section, ending with the two-step nagashi narrative cadence (arrived). Next is a section of spoken dialogue between Kasane and Yoemon, with the atmospheric shamisen ashirai pattern, repeated as required for as long as the dialogue lasts. This feature of kabuki dance music has no counterpart in gidayū-bushi. Such patterns are not specific to kiyomoto but can turn up in any dance music genre, and even for the dialogue in straight dramas.

One can imagine that, with the formulaic resources indicated above, even in mature kabuki dance music the 'composer' could throw together such a piece without much trouble, given a text to work with. By the time *Kasane* was written (1823), the process of composition for kabuki dance was fixed in the order of text (written by the playwright), followed by music (composed by the shamisen player), and finally the dance by professional choreographers or lead actors. The role of text writer was also bound by the conventions that include formulaic musical material. The conventions of oki, kudoki, chirashi and so on were inseparable in text and music. With such a multiplicity of components and creators involved, there was little scope for composition in performance, but the force of tradition and convention remained even with the pressure for creating new and commercially viable work. The use of fixed melody patterns, some of which go back centuries, was not abandoned. It remains a hallmark of narrative music in Japan.

Conclusion

Jōruri musical narrative was the mainstay of musical expression in both the puppet theatre (bunraku) and the live kabuki theatre. However, gidayū-bushi and the bungo-kei jōruri genres (and nagauta that was heavily influenced by jōruri) have in effect fundamentally different theatrical contexts. The gidayū-bushi narrator and his shamisen partner have full responsibility for the verbal and musical delivery of the drama in the puppet theatre endowing the puppets with life, in equal measure with the puppet manipulators. The kabuki jōruri performers are upstaged by the charismatic live actor-dancers. Puppet jōruri is the musical accompaniment for whole multi-act plays, whereas kabuki jōruri is rarely more than one act or scene of a play – whether a michiyuki or other scene from a long play, or one of a suite of pure dance pieces. Dramatic dialogue is far more central in gidayū, whereas in kabuki performance the dialogue is taken by the actor-dancer. In concert recital, however, the jōruri tayū takes the dialogue as well as the sung narrative. In puppet jōruri, only one singer and one shamisen player present the musical narrative of the drama for most acts, whereas there are several performers onstage in kabuki jōruri. The timbre of both the shamisen and of the voice are very different: gidayū shamisen is the heavy, lower-pitched (futozao), bungo-kei the medium (chūzao), and nagauta the lightest and slightest (hosozao).

Musical analysis has shown that gidayū-bushi has more fluidity in its formulaic musical expression and can switch substyles rapidly and frequently in response to the flow of the narrative text, whereas for the jōruri in kabuki dance the requirements of the kabuki dance form provide a more rigid framework for the musical narrative. This leads to a more clearly defined set of substyles in sections and sub-sections closed with various cadential formulas. The formal elements tend to outweigh the narrative expressive elements, particularly in the pure dance pieces and ceremonial pieces. However, as this chapter has demonstrated, the bungo-kei jōruri genres retain a full battery of narrative resources that are fully exploited in the narrative-dramatic pieces, showing their connection with the broader musical heike-jōruri narrative music tradition.

Chapter 7
Sung Narratives and Kabuki Dance: Nagauta and Ōzatsuma-bushi

Why nagauta?

Nagauta ('long song') is conventionally categorized as lyric or utaimono. A lot of ink has been spilled on the differences between narrative and lyric in Japanese vocal music (Oshio 2002). However, as with most binaries, they are not as mutually exclusive as it might seem. As indicated in Chapter 1, there are lyric aspects in most narrative genres, and narrative aspects in most lyric genres. So-called lyric nagauta is no exception.

The development of nagauta was inextricably entwined with the development of bungo-kei jōruri, in the context of kabuki dance. Nagauta and kabuki jōruri shared a common history of development from the early 1700s. Both groups came to resemble each other over the course of the 1700s, and exerted mutual influence on each other. Thus, their extant repertoires have a common form and common themes.

As we have seen, jōruri narratives came to be used in the kabuki theatre, and interacted with the songs and dance music to form a dance style with a narrative framework. Nagauta is commonly designated as 'lyric', but it was strongly influenced by jōruri narrative. Nagauta and bungo-kei jōruri styles in kabuki share a common structure, a structure that is arguably narrative, with strong doses of song and dance music. Kabuki was the locus for the interaction of song, dance, narrative, drama and instrumental music, and the emphasis on each of these different elements varied at different stages of the form's historical development. As kabuki music, nagauta and kabuki jōruri contain elements of narrative music, dance music, shamisen music, and are musically more diverse than the gidayū-bushi of the puppet theatre.

The literal meaning of nagauta, 'long song', reflects its evolution from a series of kouta (short songs) forming a suite of songs (kumiuta) in the formative onna kabuki period, to an integrated multi-section song, in effect a narrative, like the bungo-kei jōruri narratives.

In the service of kabuki dance and drama, nagauta was infinitely flexible, and came to absorb all sorts of musical influences at different times, including narrative music. It has been said that nagauta has no individual characteristics to call its own. However, despite its highly eclectic chameleon nature, it can be recognized from among other genres of shamisen music.

Most amazingly, nagauta adopted the ailing hard narrative jōruri genre of ōzatsuma-bushi, something that has implications for the nature of transmission of tradition. This aspect of nagauta has no direct counterpart in bungo-kei jōruri. Perhaps it is analogous to Kannami's incorporation of kusemai into sarugaku nō. Nagauta was so accommodating and adaptable that it adopted, absorbed and ingested the whole genre of ōzatsuma-bushi, holus-bolus. Through this feat, nagauta acquired an extensive range of narrative musical resources which it utilized in creating a new dramatic repertoire in the nineteenth century. This further broadened the expressive capacities of nagauta, enabling it to encompass narrative and lyric modes, and may well have contributed to nagauta becoming the most vigorous genre of shamisen music in the twentieth century with the capacity for developing modern repertoire. For comprehensive studies of nagauta, see Malm (1960) and Keister (2004).

This chapter demonstrates the narrative character of nagauta lyric-dance music. It introduces the purely narrative jōruri genre of ōzatsuma-bushi as preserved in nagauta, with case studies of two pieces that have been transmitted in the nagauta repertoire, *Kawazu Matano sumō no dan* (early 1720s), and *Ya no ne* (1729). The chapter then examines a further example from the post-ōzatsuma merger, *Kanjinchō* (1840), as an example of hybrid nagauta, ōzatsuma and nō (matsubame-mono), and as a typical example of mature late nagauta.

What is Narrative about nagauta?

Nagauta's lyric nature is seen in the domination of song and dance sections. The vocal quality and singing style is restrained. The strongly narrative sections are less decisive, especially the kudoki, which can be in sansagari tuning, whereas the jōruri kudoki is always in honchōshi. The centrality of the hayashi ensemble and of odoriji rhythmic dance sections further characterize nagauta in comparison with jōruri, together with the quality of the hosozao shamisen, the virtuoso playing of the shamisen in the many instrumental interludes, and the multiple line-up of players and singers.

However, even though its oldest genetic pool is lyric not narrative, nagauta also has narrative features, enough to make it narrative by adoption. Like jōruri, some nagauta pieces possess strong narrative and dramatic features. As argued in Chapter 6, kabuki dance is intrinsically narrative, and so is its music. Even a centrally non-narrative or lyric piece has some narrative features by virtue of the kabuki dance form and a focus on a dramatic character (dramatis personae). Exceptions are the ceremonial pieces and scenic pieces such as *Azuma hakkei*.

One of the most famous and oldest extant nagauta pieces, *Kyōkanoko musume Dōjōji* (A Maiden at Dōjōji Temple) (1753), well illustrates this point. It is an early example of the adaptation of a nō play to kabuki dance.[1] The narrative-dramatic

---

[1] Translation by Mark Oshima in Brazell (1998: 506–24). See also *Bandō Tamasaburō Buyō-shū 1: Kyōkanoko Dōjōji*. Shochiku Home Video, 2003.

framework of the nō original is still present, but the addition of an extended sequence of songs and dances, one of which is a kudoki (albeit in sansagari tuning), with rapid costume changes is purely kabuki and pure nagauta. The narrative is overshadowed by the spectacle of Kiyohime putting on a dazzling show with multiple rapid costume changes, a variety of musical tunings, rhythmic styles and hayashi accompaniment styles.

This example illustrates how nagauta can take a narrative motif and use it for non-narrative purposes – de-narrativization – and how even this most emblematic of nagauta pieces is framed in narrative, and unfolds in the kabuki dance structure, however loosely.

Ōzatsuma-bushi: nagauta's Adoptive Narrative Heritage

The pre-eminence of gidayū-bushi and bungo-bushi crowded out many other older styles of jōruri. Ōzatsuma was already being edged out from kabuki by the 1740s, when nagauta musicians were being called on to play shamisen for ōzatsuma. As the bungo-kei genres of tokiwazu and tomimoto were re-inventing themselves by incorporating various non-narrative sections – odoriji and songs, with hayashi accompaniment – ōzatsuma apparently was not able to, or did not feel the need to adapt to changing tastes. Instead, it teamed up with nagauta shamisen players. This leads to speculation as to whether the acclaimed shamisen virtuosity of ōzatsuma-bushi preludes and interludes came about from the influence of nagauta shamisen. It is quite unlike the more restrained shamisen playing of other jōruri genres.

The grafting on of a whole narrative genre gave nagauta a battery of powerful narrative resources to call its own. It faithfully preserved and transmitted a body of ōzatsuma repertoire; a small number of purely ōzatsuma pieces which predated the amalgamation are still performed. Furthermore, the musical resources of ōzatsuma (the so-called '48 patterns') have been put to creative use in certain sections of new pieces created after 1826, or in some cases added retrospectively to earlier pieces.

The lineage of Ōzatsuma-bushi can be traced back to the jōruri of seventeenth-century chanter Satsuma Jōun and geki-bushi (Kojima 2008; Wada 1998: 254–60; Dunn 1966; *Ōzatsuma-bushi* record notes, 1968).[2] These Edo styles of jōruri were associated with kinpira-bushi, the bombastic puppet theatre narrative. This is hard narrative, used to narrate exploits of samurai and of superhuman heroes. It developed further in kabuki as the musical accompaniment for the aragoto ('wild acting'; see Kominz 1995: 153–62) style of acting by the Ichikawa Danjūrō lineage of actors. Kominz argues that aragoto, which portrays violence and power, is closely linked to the Soga tradition, and through that to the religious practices of shugendō and mountain ascetics (yamabushi), especially the fierce deity Fudō Myōō.

Ōzatsuma Shuzendayū performed in kabuki rather than the puppet theatre. His name first appears in a kabuki programme in 1720 (*Ongaku Daijiten* 1983: 266).

---

[2] Some geki-bushi patterns were absorbed into katō-bushi. See Machida (1982).

Having begun his career with geki-bushi, Ōzatsuma Shuzendayū probably added to it the most attractive elements of other old styles such as kinpira-bushi and eikan-bushi, and created a style suitable for accompanying the aragoto of the Ichikawa acting family in Edo kabuki.[3] His ōzatsuma-bushi replaced geki-bushi as the accompaniment for aragoto. His first collaboration with Ichikawa Danjūrō II (1688–1758) was *Ya no ne*, 1729. Ōzatsuma-bushi gained popularity with the success of the second and fourth Danjūrō active under this name (1754–1770).

Shuzendayū was at first accompanied by shamisen players Umetsu Shinnojō and Tobaya San'emon, but from 1729 by nagauta shamisen player Kineya Kisaburō.

Although contemporary with bungo-bushi, ōzatsuma-bushi did not take on the features of kabuki dance as did the bungo-kei jōruri genres. Neither did it have the fluid and nuanced dramatic expressiveness of gidayū-bushi. It may be considered a survivor from the era of 'old jōruri'. It has no dance or song, and the musical delivery of its narrative is highly formulaic. Its texts drew on kōwaka narrative.

The apogee of ōzatsuma-bushi was from the 1720s to the 1750s. As aragoto went out of fashion, ōzatsuma lost its popularity too. It was inevitable that this hard genre of ko-jōruri should have fallen out of favour with the public, as tastes became more refined and demanded the more colourful, varied narratives of bungo-kei jōruri and nagauta. Its reliance on nagauta shamisen accompaniment was also a weakness.

The iemoto rights of ōzatsuma-bushi were in 1826 provisionally entrusted to the tenth Kineya Rokuzaemon by their custodian (school head, iemoto) Nakamura Hachibei. They were eventually officially granted to the third Kineya Kangorō in 1868. After that, nagauta performers took separate ōzatsuma names when playing ōzatsuma pieces. For example, the eleventh Kineya Rokuzaemon (later the thirrd Kangorō) under the name of Ōzatsuma Gendayū composed *Tsuna yakata*.

In the Meiji period, new nagauta pieces were composed using ōzatsuma patterns for certain parts of the piece, to give a strong narrative and dramatic or declamatory flavour where appropriate, especially in adaptations of nō plays. By taking on the responsibility of preserving and transmitting a narrative repertoire on the request of the remaining exponents, nagauta was able to draw on those narrative resources to beef up its ability to create powerful pieces. It led to a further hybridization of nagauta and diversified and enriched its repertoire. Ōzatsuma has thus become a sub-set or sub-genre of nagauta, ōzatsuma mono. Of 101 nagauta pieces listed in *Ongaku Daijiten* (1983: 1683–1686), 12 are noted as ōzatsuma (ōzatsuma mono).

---

[3] Aragoto, with its hard musical narrative accompaniment, has a counterpart in wagoto, the effeminate style made famous by Kyoto actor Sakata Tōjūrō, who was particularly noted for his role as Izaemon in Yūgiri plays (Kominz 1995: 107). In kabuki, Yūgiri plays came to be accompanied by the soft narrative of bungo-kei jōruri. See Chapter 6.

Ōzatsuma-bushi: Generic Analysis

Repertoire

Kawazu Matano sumō no dan (date of composition unknown) is the oldest extant piece, but it is no longer performed in kabuki. The Ichikawa family's special repertoire (18-ban as defined in 1832 by Danjūrō VII) includes *Ya no ne* (1729), *Shibaraku, Nue taiji, Fudō* and *Narukami*, all accompanied by ōzatsuma narrative. For such items, the nagauta singers and players are seated on the jōruri style dais on stage left, not at the back like the usual nagauta ensemble, and the performers are listed under ōzatsuma names (*Ōzatsuma-bushi* record notes 1968).

Kabuki goers recognize ōzatsuma in the isolated cases when a singer and player perform ōzatsuma patterns before certain scenes in front of the curtain. For example, *Sanmon Gosan no kiri* (1778) is performed in front of the temporary blue curtain (asagimaku). However, this is not the original ōzatsuma performance format; before the 1830s (Tenpō era) it used to be played in the wings by the kage-bayashi.

The record collection *Ōzatsuma-bushi* (1968) contains a number of nagauta pieces with substantial sections in ōzatsuma: *Kumo no hyōshimai* (Ōzatsuma – Nagauta kakeai; 1781), *Yorinori michiyuki* (also around 1781), *Chikumagawa* (1879), *Fudō* (1821), *Sōjō Henjō* (1831; one of the *Rokkasen* suite of six dance pieces), *Kurama-yama* (1856), *Tsuna yakata* (1868), *Gojōhashi* (1868). It also features nagauta pieces in which the ōzatsuma patterns were applied selectively for special effects in restricted parts. The following fragmentary examples of ōzatsuma also appear in the collection: *Rashōmon, Okina Sanbasō, Hakkenden, Shinkyoku Urashima* (text by Tsubouchi Shoyō), *Sōshiarai Komachi* and *Yoshiwara Suzume*.

Structure

A typical ōzatsuma piece, such as *Kawazu Matano sumō no dan*, has a narrative structure similar to other musical narrative styles like gidayū, itchū and tokiwazu; it consists of the accumulation of a series of short sections (from two to six lines of text), each marked with a cadential formula. The sections do not take on a specific character or 'themes' (musically and textually defined formulaic sections) as in kiyomoto or even gidayū, because they are all 'narrative'. The lines of text – that is, the sung phrases – show a tendency towards 7-5 meter, generally with a kind of musical caesura in the middle of the line.

Formulaic Phrases

In order to commemorate the acquisition of the iemoto rights in 1868, Kineya Kangorō III (1829–77) published the ōzatsuma patterns and called them the '48 holds' (shijūhatte), after sumō terminology, though actually he identified about 52 patterns. He classified them in groups called jo, kakari, ji, te, sanjū, dangire, tataki, otoshi, musubi. Many of these are actually geki-bushi – not ōzatsuma – patterns, but he wanted the number to be 48 (*Ongaku Daijiten* 1983: 266). Awareness of the formulaic nature of ōzatsuma probably existed earlier than this, due to influence of the fushi-zukushi collections of named melody patterns in gidayū.

These named melody patterns of ōzatsuma-bushi, as analysed by Kangorō, were added to by Asakawa Gyokuto, who published them in the record set, *Ōzatsuma-bushi* in 1968. Asakawa called the additional patterns 'quasi ōzatsuma patterns' (junzuru te).

This strong reliance on stock formulas distinguishes this genre from other extant jōruri, and results in the monotonous repetitiveness with which the patterns are used, although opening and closing patterns are differentiated. We can see, however, an affinity between this style and some specific ōzatsuma patterns with the noriji of gidayū and the urgent narrative style of tokiwazu, shinnai and kiyomoto. The opening shamisen motive jo appears under different names in other genres. See for example its use in itchū-bushi, where it is called *sonae* (*Itchū-bushi koten meisakusen*, record notes).

When the factor of variation is removed, Asakawa identifies categories of basic pattern types as laid out in Table 7.1, second column.

Table 7.1   The named patterns of ōzatsuma-bushi

Opening	jo	Patterns for the beginning of a piece; abridged versions also appear at the opening of major sections within a piece.
	kakari	A varied group of patterns for the beginning of a section.
Narrative	ji	A variety of shamisen patterns accompanying the semi-speech Sprechstimme.
	honte	Short shamisen patterns played between lines, or on long, held notes in melismatic passages.
	ukete	Very short shamisen motives punctuating Sprechstimme sections in alternation with ji patterns.
	tataki	Emphatic shamisen phrases using rapidly reiterated notes (nagashi).
Cadential	watarimusubi	Semi-cadential.
	sanjū	Not uniquely ōzatsuma.
	otoshi	Semi-cadential (several types).
	musubinagashi	Semi-cadential.
	dangire	For the end of a piece.
	fushi	Means both cadence and melody (as in gidayū).

The classification centres on the shamisen part, but in all cases except jo and ukete the patterns have a counterpart in the sung narrative, which has more variation than the shamisen part.

In contrast to gidayū and bungo-kei, little of the music is not accounted for by these named patterns. Given the limited range of the patterns, composition in performance (oral composition) in this kind of music may still have been possible in the 1600s (in kinpira jōruri, for example) or even later. However, such improvisation would have been rendered impossible after incorporation into the kabuki theatre, and by the division of labour between shamisen and chanter.

Strangely, Machida (1982) does not treat ōzatsuma patterns systematically, despite their clear formulaic nature and their status as Edo jōruri. They are related to all jōruri in terminology as well as content. The pattern names show a shared concept and nomenclature of ji as the basic all-purpose narrative in jōruri. The many sanjū patterns are a generic jōruri feature. Many other cadential patterns and opening patterns are shared with other jōruri genres, but often with different names. The ōzatsuma opening shamisen motive jo became a generic jōruri pattern.

Substyles

There are basically only two ōzatsuma substyles: spoken delivery (kotoba) accompanied by shamisen and sung delivery. There is no kudoki, but surely this dense rhythmic kind of narrative shares the same origins as the military monologue (monogatari) and of noriji and urgent (semeji) substyles in other jōruri.

We have already noted the substyle affinity of the ōzatsuma sung narrative with the monogatari formulaic section in kabuki dance, and of the Sprechstimme narrative with noriji. At a broader, more fundamental level is the extensive use of nagashi patterns, which links the genre with other jōruri.

The Texts: Links with kōwaka and the Soga Legends

The Tale of the Soga Brothers (Cogan 1987) is a bold and bloodthirsty tale of rivalry, loyalty and revenge at the beginning of the era of warrior ascendancy. It is a mixture of history, legend and fiction, based on historical events surrounding a land feud between relatives in the late twelfth century. The motive for revenge killing is established during a huge outdoor banquet and hunting party. Suketsune has been done out of his lands and wife by his scheming guardian Sukechika. In 1176, Sukechika held a hunting party for his 3,000 warriors. Under cover of the hunt, two of Suketsune's retainers ambush Sukechika and his son Sukeyasu, killing the latter, who leaves a beautiful wife and two small sons, aged five and three. The sons later acquire the names Soga no Jūrō and Soga no Gorō. They never cease to harbour the ambition to avenge their father's death, although their enemy is allied to Yoritomo, the most powerful figure in the land, and all influential warriors refuse to support them. They are unsupported even by their mother. Undaunted, 17 years later they finally kill Suketsune at another hunt in 1193, thus causing their own deaths. The brothers' respective lovers become nuns and devote the remainder of their lives to praying for the repose of their souls and preaching Buddhism (Cogan 1987: xv ff.; Oyler 2006b).

This tale had an enduring influence on the narrative and dramatic arts right up to the nineteenth century, its various episodes forming the material for nō plays, kōwaka dance narratives, puppet plays, kabuki plays and popular fiction. The oldest extant written version of this story is the *Manabon Soga monogatari* (written in a corrupt form of Chinese, hentai kanbun), believed to date from the fourteenth or fifteenth century (Cogan 1987: xxxvi). It was orally conceived and transmitted by many types of itinerant storytellers, before becoming part of the literary canon and dramatic repertoire. It was a major source of kabuki drama, and by the eighteenth century, it was obligatory to have a play on the Soga theme for every New Year production (Kominz 1995).

Episodes were brought together to form a cycle; but after time a decycling and recycling of individual episodes occurred in later performance arts of nō, kōwaka and kabuki.

Like the heike narrative, the Soga tale belongs to the medieval literary genre of the war tale (gunki monogatari), providing a rich body of material for historical drama (Rabinovitch 1986: 62–70). Again, like the heike narrative, there is no 'author' as such, but it is believed that Soga episodes were performed as part of an old religious cult referred to as the propitiation of malevolent spirits (goryō shinkō); through telling the heroic exploits of the dead, their spirits would be placated and would not come back to wreak havoc in the form of natural disaster and pestilence (Cogan 1987: xxxix). As they continued to be told, different story elements accrued to the original events, including messages of Buddhist salvation. The women in the story are assumed to reflect the gender of those who told the story, and their role as quasi-religious shamanic figures as well as entertainers, before the tale was finally written down by literati and appropriated into the literary tradition. Whereas the narrative events of the tale are dated to the twelfth century, the narrative patterns include both ancient mythical ones of malevolent spirits, and later ones such as loyalty, revenge and Buddhist salvation. The prominent role of women in the narrative suggests the role of female religious itinerants in the formation of the narrative cycle.

In textual content, several 'themes' (in the Parry-Lord sense) can be identified in *The Tale of the Soga Brothers* that align it with oral narrative. The hunt, of which there are five in the whole work, is reminiscent of the tournament in European narratives (Cogan 1987: xviii). The theme of tests of strength (chikara kurabe) is connected with medieval concepts of warrior honour. More broadly, we can note the pervasive themes of Confucian loyalty and honour, of Buddhist karma and of Shintō revenge. The theme of pacification of malevolent spirits is common to the heike, and is also frequently found in kōwaka dance narrative, and in bunraku and kabuki stories. Finally we can note the theme of the loyal mother or lover who saves, supports and later prays for the salvation of the soul. This is common in sekkyō narratives and prefigures the sewamono love suicide trope that Chikamatsu developed into a major genre in jōruri.

Ōzatsuma pieces feature some verbal formulas typical of oral narrative which mark it as 'old jōruri', and very similar to the formulaic expression of kōwaka. Found at the beginning of many pieces is the phrase 'saru hodo ni' (in *Matano sumō*, *Ya no ne* and *Tsuna yakata*). In other pieces are found the formulas 'sareba ni ya' (*Noriyori michiyuki* and *Sōjō Henjō*), 'sore ...' (*Kumo no hyōshimai, Shōfudatsuki, Chikumagawa, Sakuramon Gosan no kiri, Kurama-yama, Gojōhashi*) and 'ge ni ya' (*Fudō*). The following are examples of formulaic verbal phrases found at the end of pieces:

a. Mata omoshiroshi to mo mōsu bakari wa nakarikeri (*Matano*);
b. Arigatashi to mo nakanaka mōsu wa nakarikeri (*Fudō*);
c. Yuyushikarikeru shidai nari (*Ya no ne*);
d. Susamajikarikeru shidai nari (*Kumo no hyōshimai*);
e. Isamashikarikeru shidai nari (*Chikumagawa, Gojōhashi*);
f. Kanzenu mono koso nakarikere (*Tsuna yakata*).

The following sections of this chapter introduce three pieces: the first two, *Kawazu Matano sumō no dan* and *Ya no ne*, are episodes with their origin in *The Tale of the Soga Brothers*, while the third, *Kanjinchō*, derives from the world of *The Tale of the Heike*, as developed in *Gikeiki* and nō, and further in kōwaka and kabuki.

Kawazu Matano sumō no dan

The oldest extant ōzatsuma-bushi piece is *Kawazu Matano sumō no dan*. This and *Ya no ne* belong to the world of *The Tale of the Soga Brothers*, but the actual texts are taken directly from kōwaka. This piece is an abridged version of the kōwaka piece *Youchi Soga*, which in turn combines two episodes in *The Tale of the Soga Brothers*: a rock lifting competition (Cogan 1987: 25) and the ensuing wrestling match between pairs of warriors (Cogan 1987: 26–34) at an outdoor banquet after a hunt early in the narrative, setting the scene for the murder which was the cause of the revenge narrative.

Kawazu Matano sumō no dan is a good example of pure ōzatsuma musical style: the only thing that smacks of nagauta are the vocal fushijiri, the standard throwaway flourish at the end of the major cadences. It is straightforward, and responds closely to textual content with forceful declamatory style. The shamisen has a narrow repertoire of fixed patterns as it accompanies Sprechstimme narrative, and only occasionally melodic singing.

On the basis of this piece we can make a generic musical analysis of ōzatsuma-bushi. It consists of several sections, each ending with a cadential formula (most commonly the otoshi types). The first section is all sung. The sections are of very unequal length ranging from two to over a dozen lines.

Musical formulas are conspicuous; the piece is largely made up entirely of formulaic patterns. However, there is not a total correspondence between formulaic sections as indicated by the use of final verb forms (keri, keru) and musical cadential formulas.

Two broad types of sung delivery are used: melismatic, song-like, melodramatically expressive parts (eishō), and syllabic, chant-like narrative or Sprechstimme (rōshō). There is no true spoken delivery, even for those parts of the text that present the actual speech of characters. The Sprechstimme sections are all accompanied with a limited range of shamisen patterns, mainly either a series of basic patterns called ji ('ground') corresponding to the sung narrative, linked with shorter motives called te ('hand'). A strong rise and fall contour is found in the patterns.

The piece begins with an extensive sung narrative section (eishō), and ends in the same style of delivery. Most sections within the piece also end, and usually also begin, with a sung phrase or two. In between, the narrative proceeds briskly with the syllabic Sprechstimme delivery, so characteristic of ōzatsuma-bushi, with its small repertoire of distinctive lively shamisen patterns. While melody in these sections is mostly limited to these shamisen patterns, the rhythmic variety and ingenuity of the vocal part and its interlocking with the shamisen provide considerable interest. The syllabic delivery is basically one beat per syllable, but interspersed with an interesting use of prolonged syllables, creating a syncopation-like effect. The sung and Sprechstimme phrases have a wide pitch range, from falsetto to middle register, giving contour to the phrases.

Ya no ne (The Arrow Sharpener) (1729)

This piece is basically ōzatsuma, into which some nagauta features have been interpolated. It is more elaborate and sophisticated than *Kawazu Matano sumō no dan* and the ōzatsuma sections give the piece weight. This is an innovative use of the hard jōruri narrative of ōzatsuma as an ersatz utai, effectively evoking the medieval period of the Soga incident, even though it is a parody. It contains extended hayashi and shamisen interludes and some other more nagauta-like musical passages. Parts of the text are full of word play and irreverent facetious humour, typical of kabuki rather than jōruri.

Nagauta or kabuki dance features found in the piece:

- hayashi interludes; hayashi accompaniment for some parts;
- shamisen and hayashi interludes;
- section 3 is a blend of ōzatsuma declamatory sung delivery and nagauta rhythm;
- spoken dialogue taken by actors;
- eerie narrative for the dream appearance of Jūrō, like a ghost;
- facetious text in section 3.

Ya no ne is based on the kōwaka *Wada sakamori* (Wada's banquet), but parts of the text are more sophisticated and full of witty parody, in the Edo kabuki style.

The diction retains stereotypical beginning and ending phrases strongly reminiscent of ko-jōruri (such as 'saru hodo ni'), but it also features much Sinified language redolent of samurai culture, producing a hard formal style.

The two Soga brothers, Gorō and Jūrō, have bided their time for 17 years to avenge their father's murder. It is New Year and Gorō is idly filling in time, it seems, sharpening his arrowheads. Kominz (1995) in his study of the Soga motif in Japanese theatre translates and analyses this scene as kabuki drama, but barely refers to the music.

Table 7.2   Outline of ōzatsuma *Ya no ne*

Sections	Text	FMM
(1) Oki jōruri, before the appearance of the actor. Functions as entrance music.	Saru hodo ni ... ya no ne migaite itarikeru.	(aikata) (tobitataki) (jo) (dangiri otoshi) (yose no aikata; shamisen + hayashi)
(2) Equivalent of hanamichi, actor is visible, but is revealed behind a 'wall' in his abode, sharpening his grotesquely large arrow.	Tsutaekiku ... otoraji to	Voice: ōzatsuma. basic; shamisen + hayashi apply nagauta rhythm: dance-like
(3) Facetious text: word play with New Year foods and customs – monozukushi; typical of kabuki dance character scenes.	Tensei ... itarikeru.	Ōzatsuma 'basic'. Long speech from 'Tora no mite ...' Brief speech and sung narrative alternated between musicians and actor. (dangiri otoshi)
(4) New Year visit from Ōzatsuma Shuzendayū; comic short interlude featuring the lead singer.	Toki ni nenshi no ... (Shuzendayū) tachikaeru.	Speech (koto otoshi)
(5) Gorō sleeps, arms held straight and stiff at right angles to his body, resting on the stage assistant's shoulder for a pillow.	Sono toki Gorō ... fushimarobu.	(koto otoshi)
(6) Gorō's vision of Jūrō. This is typical of a kabuki dance ghost scene, though Jūrō is not dead, but a living ghost. He appeals to Gorō to come to his rescue.	Aara fushigi ya ... araware-ide	'eerie narrative'
(7) Jūrō's spoken appeal.	Ika ni Tokimune ... Tokimune	

continued

Table 7.2 *concluded*

Sections	Text	FMM
(8) The 'ghost' disappears.	To iu ka to omoeba ... use ni keri.	(koto otoshi)
(9) Gorō arouses himself and gets ready for action.	Tokimune ... itarikeru.	(koto otoshi)
(10) Gorō postures, his intention to seek out his enemies in the furthest extremities of Japan.	Sate wa muchū ni ... shidai nari.	(koto otoshi) Shamisen aikata sanjū (indicates change of scene)
(11) A ludicrous radish seller leading his packhorse enters along the hanamichi; Gorō struggles to highjack the horse.	Kakaru tokoro e ... hitotsubute	(kakari-ji) (aikata by shamisen and hayashi)
(12) Chirashi = finale	Tazuna ottori ... Kudō no yakata he (omitted in kabuki version) Isogishi wa (omitted in kabuki version) Yuyushikarikeru shidai nari. (omitted in kabuki version)	(interlude features sanjū) No hayashi until 'shidai nari'. (dangire omitted in kabuki version)

Note: Performance time: 28 minutes. The main version referred to is *Nihon Koten Ongaku Taikei*. There are several differences between this nagauta recital version and the kabuki version.

Text 7.1   *Ya no ne*, Section 1 (CD Track 13)

1. 去る程に
Saru hodo ni
2. 曽我の五朗時宗は
Soga no Gorō, Tokimune wa
3. 恵方に向かってふとのっと
Ehō ni mukatte, futo notto
4. 夫れ父の仇には
Sore chichi no, ada ni wa
5. 俱に天箪和合楽
Tomo ni tenpitsu, wagōraku
6. 寿福開円万巻の
Jufuku Kaien mangan no

So it came to pass that

Soga no Gorō Tokimune,

facing in an auspicious direction offers a prayer.

He cannot live under the same

heaven as his father's murderer.

North of the 'Strategy Treatise'

7. 軍書の窓の北面は Gunsho no mado no, hokumen wa	window this morning,
8. 残んの雪のあさ緑 Nokon no yuki no, asamidori	between the remaining patches of snow there is pale green;
9. 春風春水一枝の梅 Shunpū shunsui, isshi no ume	in the breezes and waters of Spring. a branch of plum bursts into bloom:
10. ハット開くや花の春 Hatto hiraku ya, hana no haru	flowery Spring is here.
11. 新しい庵の物事に Atarashii an no, monogoto ni	Although his hermitage has been renewed,
12. 改まれども時宗の Aratamaredomo, Tokimune no	Tokimune
13. 今年も古庵ふる畳 Kotoshi mo furuan, furudatami	begins this year
14. 古井と言っし所にて Furui to isshi, tokoro ni te	in his old hut, at a place called the 'Old Well'.
15. 矢の根磨いて居たりける。 Ya no ne migaite, itarikeru.	He sits, sharpening arrowheads.

Translation adapted from Kominz 1995: 202.

The first part of the CD excerpt (Track 13) is the opening section of the piece, performed by two ōzatsuma singers and two shamisen players seated stage left in jōruri style, before the actor is revealed; the text is solemn and serious. The opening shamisen pattern (jo) is found in other genres as a typical motive at the beginning of a piece. However, from the first sung phrase, 'saru hodo ni', the music is immediately recognizable as ōzatsuma narrative. There is no specific oki style; it is much the same as in sections throughout the piece. This is ōzatsuma basic style. In parts, the shamisen is joined by the hayashi ensemble and brings in a nagauta-like dance rhythm. Musically, this supports the text to create a martial identity with emphasis on the pedigree important in warrior tradition.

The first brief extract is the opening section of the piece, which introduces the hero – alluding to his long-held ambition to avenge – and the time of year, with a lyrical evocation of the emergent spring. Each line of text tends towards the typical Japanese poetic metre of 7-5 syllables, though more often than not it is slightly irregular: 6-5, 8-5, 8-6 and so on, though there is a natural break between a longer and a shorter phrase (which I have indicated with a comma). The phrases are almost entirely a sequence of ōzatsuma patterns: tobitataki – jo-okibushi – honte – watariji – and so on.

As the piece proceeds, however, the theme of heroic revenge is undermined by the tongue-in-cheek wordplay based on vegetables and the typical dishes for New Year celebrations. It is comic and anti-heroic, almost slapstick. In section 3, the pure ōzatsuma basic style returns, and is used antiphonally with brief snatches of spoken delivery by the actor, like a kind of repartee between musicians and actor. This goes on for much longer in kabuki performance than in nagauta concert performance.

Example 7.1 Ōzatsuma, *Ya no ne* (1)

Example 7.1 *concluded*

Gorō is visited by Ōzatsuma Shuzendayū (the name of the accompanying narrative singer!), paying his New Year visit, bringing a gift. Shuzendayū's appearance on stage is a typically kabuki way of breaking down the wall between reality and theatrical artifice. The singer's dialogue is delivered by the onstage musicians, whereas Gorō's words are delivered by the actor.

Gorō then sinks into a post-prandial nap and while slumbering is summoned in a dream-like vision by his brother Jūrō, who is in danger. The musical style is the kind of 'eerie' substyle that is found in other kabuki jōruri when a ghost appears. This leads to section 10, which provides the second part of the CD excerpt (Track 13).

Text 7.2   *Ya no ne*, Section 10 (CD Track 13 continued)

1. さては夢中に兄祐成	So, does that mean that my brother
Sate wa muchū ni, ani Sukenari	Sukenari's thoughts came to me in a dream
2. 念力通じて急難を	and that he told me to save him
Nenriki tsūjite, kyūnan o	from danger?
3. 救ひくれよと我への告げ	
Sukui kure yo to, ware e no tsuge	
4. たとはば祐経天へ昇らば	Even if Suketsune climbs up to heaven,
Tatowaba Suketsune, ten e noraba	
続いてのぼり	I'll climb up after him.
Tsuzuite nobori	
5. 大地へ入らば同じく分け入り	If he enters the bowels of the earth, I'll dig
Daichi e iraba, onajiku wakeiri	my way down to him.
6. 日本六十余州は目のあたり	The sixty-odd provinces of Japan are
Nippon rokujū yo shū wa, ma no atari	before my eyes:
7. 東は奥州外が浜	to Sotogahama of Ōshū in the east,
Higashi wa Ōshū, Sotogahama	
8. 西は鎮西、鬼界ヶ島	to Kikigashima of Chinzei in the west,
Nishi wa Chinzei, Kikaigashima	
9. 南は紀の路熊野浦	to the Kumano shore on the Kii Road in
Minami wa Ki no ji, Kumano ura	the south,
10. 北は越後の荒海まで	to the rough seas of Echigo in the north,
Kita wa Echigo no, araumi made	
11. 人間の通わぬ処	even to where men have never been,
Ningen no kayowanu tokoro	
12. 千里も行け、万里も飛べ	I'll walk 1,000 ri, I'll fly 10,000 ri!
Senri mo yuke, banri mo tobe	
13. いで追掛けむと時宗が	Now for the pursuit! he says.
Ide-okkaken to, Tokimune ga	
14. 勢ひ進む有様は	When Tokimune shows his strength,
Ikioi susumu, arisama wa	
15. 怖ろしかりける次第なり。	he looks terrifying.
Osoroshikarikeru, shidai nari.	

Translation adapted from Kominz 1995: 212, 215.

Example 7.2 Ōzatsuma, *Ya no ne* (2)

Section 10 describes Gorō being stirred to action after being visited in a dream by his brother. He vows to go to the ends of Japan, even the ends of the earth to protect his brother. The bombastic ōzatsuma musical style builds up a picture of epic heroic proportions. It is followed by a comic anti-climax when a radish-seller (again related to New Year cuisine) is accosted to provide him with a horse, which he then mounts and rides off on to the stronghold of Suketsune who is threatening his brother's life.

In the kabuki version of this section, in which Gorō announces his intention to pursue his enemies in every corner of the realm, the first part of the section is delivered as unaccompanied speech by the actor. From 'Nishi wa ...' the singers take up the strain while Gorō concentrates on his posturing (furi), and thereafter actor and singers alternate in repartee style. After the cadential pattern, koto otoshi, an elaborate aikata by shamisen fills in the time needed for stage hands to dress Gorō ready for action. When almost ready one of them nods to the singers, and they start on the ōzatsuma sanjū pattern which signifies a scene change. Some of the extended instrumental interludes (aikata) for this action are omitted in the nagauta-only version.

Kanjinchō

Matsubame-mono: Kabuki Adaptations of nō Plays

In the nineteenth century, as part of the urge to 'improve' kabuki, a fashion developed for dance dramas based on nō and kyōgen plays drawing on the capacities of nagauta in combination with the appropriation of nō texts and music to create a new nagauta sub-genre. These plays were called matsubame-mono because they used as the scenery a replica of the pine image of the fixed nō stage. Examples are also found in tokiwazu and kiyomoto. The nagauta dance drama *Kanjinchō* (The Subscription List; 1840) is an early example of matsubame-mono. It is a relatively faithful adaptation of the nō play *Ataka*. As the last piece to be analysed in this book, *Kanjinchō* links back thematically to heike, nō, kōwaka and old jōruri, in the context of mature nagauta.[4]

Musically, *Kanjinchō* is a hybrid piece, drawing equally on the resources of nagauta, nō and ōzatsuma. The kabuki stage evokes the nō stage with its pine and bamboo, and its entrance curtain, whereby some characters (Togashi and his party) enter; Yoshitsune, Benkei and party, however, enter in kabuki style from the hanamichi. The text to a large extent keeps to the nō original, and much of the musical delivery is an adaptation of utai and nō hayashi accompaniment. However, because the shamisen is the main accompanying instrument, the interpolation of song and dance is quite out of character with nō, making the whole atmosphere resonate with Edo culture. The inclusion of an erotic kudoki contrasts with the nō kuse section, which is more noble in its pathos, and two dance sections give the piece parity with kabuki dance form. The requirements of narrative solemnity are met by calling on the resources of ōzatsuma-bushi patterns, which contrast with the softer nagauta kabuki dance parts in a kind of musical code-switching.

---

[4] The nagauta piece *Ataka no matsu* is thematically related, and calls on the audience's familiarity with the story, and focuses on a lyrical evocation of the first part where Yoshitsune and Benkei's party encounter a group of children and discuss a famous pine tree. Another related kabuki play is *Imoarai*, a version also translated in Brandon and Leiter (2002).

The Kanjinchō Story

The story of how Yoshitsune, Benkei and their party, disguised as mountain monks, crossed the Ataka barrier was introduced in Chapter 4, where a contrastive analysis of nō *Ataka* and kōwaka *Togashi* was provided; here we examine nagauta *Kanjinchō* in comparison with nō *Ataka* on which it was closely based (Parker 2006). Nagauta *Kanjinchō* keeps closely to the text and the musical and plot structure of nō *Ataka*, especially in the opening and closing sections. It makes extensive use of the onstage hayashi ensemble to evoke nō, and retains many of the dramatic structural units of nō (shidai, mondō, otoko mai and so on).

In many kabuki dance pieces (kiyomoto and others), the unaccompanied sung pattern, utai-gakari, specifically evokes nō plays, or at least earlier eras, giving an 'antique' effect. This pattern is used in *Kanjinchō* in the shidai entrance section ('Tabi no koromo suzukake no …'). However, the piece goes far beyond mere evocation of the nō play on which it is so closely based.

Table 7.3   Outline of nagauta-ōzatsuma *Kanjinchō* (CD Track 14) (see also *Kabuki meisakusen: Kanjinchō* DVD; 58 minutes)

Sections	Text (first lines)	FMM*
(1) Togashi and party enter from stage right. Togashi introduces himself, explains situation. Dialogue, Togashi and guard.	Kayō ni sōrō mono wa …	Oki NANORI MONDŌ
(2) Yoshitsune, Benkei and followers enter along hanamichi.	Tabi no koromo wa, suzukake no …	Hanamichi SHIDAI Utai-gakari
(3) Michiyuki journey description.	Tokishimo koro wa … Tsuki no miyako o tachiidete.	Okiuta – ōzatsuma solo voice and solo shamisen
(4) Yoshitsune and his followers enter.	Kore ya kono … yukashikeru.	Aikata + hayashi (yose no aikata) uta jōruri, oki style
(5) The band reaches the main stage.	Namiji haruka ni … tsukinikeri. Iza tōran to, tabigoromo Seki no konata ni, tachikakaru. (no hayashi)	Aikata Sung narrative Hayashi. Cadence: nagashi on f♯, and low b. [MONDŌ] of Benkei, Yoshitsune and followers
(6) Togashi and Benkei debate.		MONDŌ
(7) Declaration of yamabushi identity.	Sore yamabushi to ippa … oshimondari.	NOTTO Ōzatsuma style

continued

Table 7.3   *continued*

Sections	Text (first lines)	FMM*
(8) Togashi asks to see the kanjinchō.	Saki ni … kokoroe-mōshi sōrō.	MONDŌ
(9) After fumbling in his pack, Benkei 'reads' the kanjinchō.	Moto yori … yomiagekere.	Sung narrative
	Sōre tsuratsura … Daion kyoushu … mousu. Ten mo hibike to yomiagetari.	Aikata YOMIMONO Notto-gakari.
(10) Interrogation of Benkei by Togashi about Buddhist teaching (no counterpart in nō). Togashi is overwhelmed, orders gifts for Tōdaiji. Benkei replies.	Kanjinchō chōmon no ue wa … Kanshin shite zo, mie ni keri. Sore shugen no michi zo mōsu … Shisotsu wa … naoshikere	MONDŌ
(11) Togashi makes an offering to Benkei (not in nō), tells them to pass the barrier. One of Togashi's men recognizes Yoshitsune, Togashi stops porter. Benkei responds by chastising and beating the porter. The band is menacing towards Togashi.	On-tōri sorae. Katajikenai soro. Kowa, ureshiya to, yamabushi mo, shizu shizu tate ayumarekeri. Suwa ya wagakimi … tachikaeru. kongouzue o ottotte sanzan ni chōchakusu. Tōre! Tōre to to koso wa nonoshirinu. Katagata wa … mienikeru. Shisotsu o hikizure sekimori ha, kado no uchi e zo, irinikeru.	MONDŌ Long section alternating speech and sung narrative (ōzatsuma).
(13) Yoshitsune expresses gratitude, Benkei his abject apology. The sadness of the warrior life.	Aikata (ashirai, cyclical) Tsui ni nakanu, Benkei mo … torinugui. Yoroi ni soi-shi, sode makura … bakari nari. Tagai ni sode o … orikara ni	MONDŌ Benkei's 'monogatari' (first person sung narrative)

Sections	Text (first lines)	FMM*
(14) Togashi et al. enter with sake for Benkei. (Benkei laughs) (Benkei drinks)	Ge ni, ge ni kore mo, kokoroetari … onna sae. Mayoi no michi no, seki koete … koekaneru. Hito me no seki no, yaruse naya … ukiyo nare	MONDŌ: (Uta) Returns to honchōshi
(15) (Benkei dances)	Omoshiro ya … mai o maou.	Odoriji
(16) Togashi asks Benkei to dance.	Sendachi oshaku ni …	MONDŌ:
(17) Benkei sings and does mai.	Banzei mashimase Banzei mashimase … Moto yori Benkei ha Benkei: Kore naru yamamizu no ochite iwao ni hibiku koso (Chorus) Kore naru yamamizu … naru wa taki no mizu.	Utai Odoriji OTOKO-MAI Hayashi, then with shamisen.
(18)	Aikata + hayashi for dance	Odoriji
(19) Yoshitsune et al. exit on hanamichi. Only Benkei is left on stage. Benkei makes a spectacular roppō exit on the hanamichi, after the curtain has closed.	Naru wa taki no mizu, hi wa teru to mo Tora no o o fumi … Mutsu no kuni e zo (Benkei on hanamichi) Kudari keru.	Chirashi Dangire

* Capitals indicate sections with the same name and style as nō drama.

Text 7.3   *Kanjinchō* (CD Track 14)

1. いざ通らんと 旅衣
Iza tōran to, tabigoromo
2. 関のこなたに 立ちかかる
Seki no konata ni, tachikakaru.
3. それ山伏といっぱ
Sore yamabushi to ippa
4. 役の優婆塞の行儀を受け
En no Ubasoku no gyōgi o uke
5. 即身即仏の 本体を
Sokushin sokubutsu no hontai o,
6. 此処にて打留め給わん事
koko ni te uchitome tamawan koto,

They decide to travel on to the barrier

Here they have reached it.

We are yamabushi

Who follow the teaching of En no Ubasoku.

As his disciples we represent Buddha himself while we are living..

If you kill us here

7. 明王の照覧測りがとう Myō-ō no shōran hakarigatou	Myo-O will guard our destiny,
8. 熊野権現の御罰当らん事 Yuya Gongen no, gobatsu ataran koto,	Yuya Gongen will punish you
9. 立ち処に於て疑いあるべからず tachidokoro ni oite utagai arubekarazu	instantly, there is no doubt.
10. 唵阿毘羅吽欠と on abira unken to	We pray to them for help.
11. 珠数さらさらと 押しもんだり juzu sarasara to, oshimondari	So saying, Benkei rubbed his prayer beads.
12. 先きに承り候は Saki ni uketamawari sōrō wa	(Togashi) You said you were soliciting
13. 東大寺の勧進帳と仰せられ候あいだ Tōdaiji no Kanjinchō to, ōserare sōrō aida	subscriptions for the Tōdai temple,
14. 勧進帳のなきことは候わじ Kanjinchō no naki koto wa, sōrawaji.	So you must have a subscription scroll.
15. 此れにて聴聞申そうずるにて候 Kore ni te chōmon mōsouzuru ni te sōrō.	(Togashi) Let me hear you read it please.
16. 何と、勧進帳を読めと候や Nani to, Kanjinchō o yome to sōrō ya.	(Benkei) What! Read the subscription scroll?
17. 心得申して候 Kokoroe-mōshite sōrō.	(Togashi) That is exactly what I mean!
18. 元より勧進帳のあらばこそ Moto yori Kanjinchō no, araba koso	Of course he has no kanjinchō
19. 笈の内より 往来の巻物 Oi no uchi yori, ōrai no makimono	but taking out a scroll from his box
20. 一巻取り出し ichikan toriidashi	
21. 勧進帳と名付つつ Kanjinchō to nazuketsutsu	he calls it the kanjinchō
22. 高らかにこそ 読み上げけれ takaraka ni koso, yomiagekere.	and pretends to read loudly.

Translation adapted from Scott 1953: 20–28.

Example 7.3 Nagauta-ōzatsuma, *Kanjinchō*

continued

Example 7.3 *continued*

continued

Example 7.3 *concluded*

The solemn narrative parts of the piece are predominantly allocated to traditional ōzatsuma narrative accompanied by shamisen. There are extensive passages, indeed whole sections in ōzatsuma-style hard narrative. Ōzatsuma functions as an ersatz tsuyogin (strong chant), whereas normal nagauta singing can substitute for yowagin.

The dramatic highlights are the same in both nō and nagauta: the reading of the kanjinchō subscription list, the beating of Yoshitsune and getting through the barrier. The denouement of gifts from Togashi and Benkei's felicitous dance are also virtually the same. Of course, the kabuki version has the purely theatrical effects of Yoshitsune and party entering and exiting along the hanamichi, and most spectacularly Benkei's final exit after the curtain closes, doing a roppō leaping run to off-stage geza accompaniment.

The musical and textual differences between the nō and nagauta plays are most apparent in the lyrical sections between passing the barrier and the presentation of gifts. Whereas nō changes from tsuyogin, the hard narrative style that has dominated the play up till then, to tsuyogin soft narrative (as heard in the CD track), in nagauta, after Yoshitsune's (spoken) thanks to Benkei for his quick-wittedness that saved them, Benkei proffers an extended apology with tears, prostrated before Yoshitsune, then bemoans the fate of the warrior. This functions like a kudoki and brings in the structure of kabuki dance. It is the equivalent of the kuse in nō. This exaggerated humbling of Benkei is a foil to his macho aragoto performance toward Togashi as a fearsome mountain priest. Benkei is then forgiven and is encouraged to relax and sing. When the gifts are delivered, he drinks, sings an erotic song from the Edo licensed quarters, and finally the play returns to nō style with the otoko mai to the accompaniment of ōzatsuma narrative.

Implications and Conclusions

The incorporation of the hard ko-jōruri ōzatsuma-bushi narrative into the lyric genre of nagauta is suggestive for the nature of transmission of Japanese music. By being packaged into named melodic formulas, it could be handed over to the ownership of the nagauta musicians and used for new musical productions. It could partially by-pass the normal method of oral transmission. This process of adoption, unlike natural reproduction, was quite different from the normal nature of transmission, and was structurally possible in the context of the iemoto system.

By being incorporated into nagauta, the bombastic ko-jōruri flavour that seemed only fit for crude kinpira puppet plays and aragoto acting was creatively adapted to become a solemn and 'antique'-effect, shamisen-accompanied ersatz utai, particularly useful in the nineteenth-century adaptations of nō plays in kabuki. Although the nagauta (hosozao) shamisen is used, and the nagauta singer uses the nagauta vocal production, what is unique is the vocal sung and Sprechstimme patterns, the energetic shamisen patterns, and the extensive instrumental interludes, highly virtuosic solo passages that always and uniquely attract applause. Hard narrative with its roots in heike and kōwaka military narratives found a place in the musical expression of mature nagauta. It became one of the most musically spectacular aspects of nagauta.

Nagauta was strengthened by its absorption of ōzatsuma narrative; it became a more vigorous musical genre, able to more effectively meet the challenges of modernity and modernization in the late nineteenth century. It was the first genre of shamisen music to develop a rational form of musical notation, the kojūrō-fu in vertical format closely tied to the traditional way of writing the sung texts. It was adapted and borrowed by jōruri genres such as kiyomoto and tokiwazu (asada-fu).[5] It developed a new concert repertoire, and a society of performers who were not connected with the kabuki theatre or nihon buyō world (see Keister 2004). New compositions were generated from this stream, notably by the prolific Kineya Seihō (1914–96). It showed strategic intelligence, and remains the most viable traditional genre of shamisen music.

---

[5] Another horizontal style of notation, bunka-fu, was developed and is widely used.

Epilogue

Japan's literary traditions and theatrical traditions, and to a lesser degree its musical traditions, have been extensively researched. Much less attention has been given to its performed narrative or oral literature, which falls in between literature, theatre and music.

The Japanese literary canon, as enshrined in the various anthologies, from early on included nō plays, Chikamatsu's and other puppet jōruri, and kabuki plays. More recent anthologies have gradually expanded to include more of the performed genres, such as kōwaka mai and sekkyō-bushi. However, still the texts of nagauta and of most other jōruri cannot be found in these sets, though extensive collections of texts of these genres were published independently from the literary anthologies in the Taishō and early Shōwa eras.

Of course, various research associations specialize in performed narrative genres such as kōshiki and heike, but, little research on these has found its way into English publications.

This study has started to fill this gap by approaching one particular stream of Japan's performed narrative, what I have termed the heike-jōruri stream. The study has limited itself to extant genres: three of medieval origin – kōshiki, heike and kōwaka – and six of the many jōruri genres originating in the Edo period – gidayū-bushi, itchū-bushi, tokiwazu-bushi, shinnai-bushi, kiyomoto-bushi and ōzatsuma-bushi.

I have argued for substantial structural continuities across these genres, having examined them from the point of view of the context of the independent performance item, whether temple, private gathering, shrine stage or commercial theatre. Some performance items constitute one part of a multi-movement or multi-act work, whereas others are stand-alone items, though most of the latter are linked thematically to a larger narrative cycle or narrative world. The internal structure of the performance item consists of several narrative units or scenes that make up one unified piece, but musically the basic unit of analysis is a section of indeterminate length with a certain formulaic musical style concluded with a cadential formula.

In the search for continuities in formulaic musical expression, I have developed the concept of musical substyle, arguing that each genre had a range of different musical resources to call on for different parts of a narrative. Neither a structural unit such as a section, nor a phrase-length pattern, the substyle is a style of musical delivery that can be defined in terms of musical parameters such as pitch register, rhythm, and syllabic versus melismatic enunciation of the text. The style is maintained for a certain duration then shifts to another style. So the characterization of these musical narratives as multiple-melody is really multiple-style.

In older genres (kōshiki, heike), the section is coterminous with a particular substyle. In more elaborate genres, specifically those more influenced by dramatic performance, a musical section is often composed of more than one type of musical delivery, and often will contain non-musical dramatic dialogue. One parameter of the musical substyle is the presence of some fixed formulaic phrases (melody patterns, senritsukei), but on the whole the style of a section is not completely formulaic as the often-used but misplaced metaphor of mosaic suggests. The texts of the older genres are prosaic in the sense that they do not follow a regular poetic metre, whereas the later genres tend towards the basic Japanese classical metre of lines of seven plus five syllables. This difference affects the nature of musical formulaism, though the analysis has not dwelt on this.

The present study attempts to elucidate the nature of Japanese musical narrative in a global context, taking a cross-cultural perspective of oral narrative study. It started from the perspective of oral narrative studies that were pioneered by Milman Parry and Albert Lord, to see if their model of theme (formulaic scene or section) and formula (a group of words or formulaic phrase) was applicable. It was found that the heike-jōruri stream of musical narratives did not fit the Parry-Lord model of oral narrative. However, the Parry-Lord concepts of theme and formula were found to have counterparts in the formulaic musical material of these genres. There were musical analogies for themes and formulas. Each genre considered displayed formulaic sections, and formulaic phrases, as well as formulaic substyles.

Although the narratives studied in this book are not primary oral texts, they are indisputably 'oral-derived', and show 'residual orality' in their use of thematic materials and phraseology. Over a period of several centuries, a similar approach to musical narrative can be seen, showing the power of this musical idiom, and its vigour as a tradition. Foley's 'traditional referentiality' is seen here. The narratives draw on pre-existing themes and rework them in new ways for new generations of audiences. The themes of the twelfth-century heike narrative emerge again and again in the ensuing centuries, always with new emphases and twists.

From another global cross-cultural perspective, I considered three models of performed narrative: strophic, stichic and prosimetric. The strophic form of equal length verses with the same melody repeated for each verse, perhaps with a refrain added, is a highly condensed formalized narrative made to fit a song form, showing a development from narrative to song. Japanese performed narratives differ in that the sections of the narrative do not follow the pattern of a fixed number of lines to form verses or sections, and neither do they use the same melody for each section. Some of the genres do not even follow a fixed line length, and in this they are something like prose, although they can still be 'poetic' if not metric.

The stichic form of narrative is probably the oldest form of narrative globally: according to this model, a line of metrically uniform text is declaimed musically to basically the same melody repeated in each line. This is the style of the Southern Slavic narratives that formed the basis of the Parry-Lord theory. Japanese performed narratives differ radically from this model, in that there are multiple melodies used; that is, not only is there not just one line-length melody, there is also a stock of section-length melodic substyles called on to cater for the formal needs of narrative development and to respond to variations in content. The simplistic concepts of hard and soft narrative substyles were evoked in the discussion of most genres to show how different styles of musical delivery respond to narrated content.

Furthermore, the concept of prosimetric narrative was considered. Putting Japanese performed narratives in the context of global prosimetrum studies, it was concluded that if prosimetrum is defined very broadly as narrative that alternates sung and spoken delivery (instead of a more common definition of alternating spoken prose with sung verse), these Japanese genres can be seen as one variant in the spectrum. However, the particular nature of the musically delivered parts of the narrative which formed the focus of the book is in itself complex and goes beyond a simple definition of alternation of musical and spoken delivery. In prosimetric narrative, is the musically delivered part stichic, strophic or something more complex? The study therefore raised the need to problematize the musically delivered narrative.

I have argued for an evolution from stichic to more complex melodic narrative, but have maintained that the stichic basic style is still present in these narratives as a basic starting point. I believe the multiple melody delivery of performed narrative developed from the simple stichic style. Within each genre in this study there exists a basic style which while flexible can look like the repeated melody (stichic) type. It is probable that these multi-melodic narratives all originated in the stichic model, the simple basic melody used again and again, like shojū and nijū in kōshiki, and kudoki in heike. Their diversification came about gradually, first by transposing the basic melodic contour to a register one fourth higher, and then another fourth and so on, following the tonal framework of the music. By moving through the different pitch registers using the same melodic contour the variant patterns developed in the basic style of each genre.

In kōshiki and related Buddhist music, the earliest form was hyōbyaku, virtually stichic, which was the equivalent of what came to be called shojū. It is a simple melody built around the alternation of two tones one second apart. In heike, the simplest melody type is kudoki, the basic style, built on the alternation of two tones one fourth apart. In jōruri, the simplest basic form is the almost unaccompanied declamatory style with minimal shamisen accompaniment, much of it focusing on one tone. In bungo-kei jōruri, this evolved into a steady but simple unobtrusive shamisen underpinning of the non-metric vocal line. So as a general trend we can hypothesize that the multiple melodies developed by transposing the simplest melodies up to a higher pitch range and elaborating them.

The analysis of the reiterative patterns of bungo-kei jōruri in Chapter 6 revealed that most likely this kind of pattern ultimately derived from the simpler narrative styles like the heike kudoki, and the kōshiki shojū and nijū, whose musical development was minimal. In the early stage of development of narrative music, simple stichic narrative with a repetitive melody moved through different pitch registers in melodic blocks (Chapter 2). Jōruri is linked with the practice in kōshiki and heike of calling a melodic type after the pitch register in which it was located.

The case studies and analysis has demonstrated the continuing importance of performed narrative in Japanese culture, and has confirmed the strong ongoing preference for musical storytelling in Japan well beyond the development of its rich theatrical culture, or rather underpinning that culture. This is underlined by the continuing presence and high visibility of the narrator or narrator-singers on the stage together with puppets or live actors. When cinema came to Japan, jōruri narrators even found a role as benshi in silent movie theatres.

Even more remarkable is the birth of new performed narrative genres in the modern era. While outside the scope of the present study, the emergence and prominence of the modern biwa narratives from the provinces of Satsuma and Chikuzen show that the modernizing elites found significance in these arts that seemed to fit the new culture of Meiji Japan. They stem from a regional tradition of biwa narrative which it seems did not directly undergo the influence of kōshiki shōmyō and heike narrative, but are closer to a folk model of sung narrative with less musical complexity.

At the same time, at the proletarian levels of society in modernizing nineteenth-century Japan, the shamisen-accompanied narrative naniwa-bushi surpassed the popularity of the established storytelling genres of rakugo and kōdan, to become the repository of narrative for the working classes. After being appropriated as a propaganda tool by the military state in the 1940s it fell out of favour in the postwar period.

Having focused on musical narrative genres that are still being actively performed in contemporary Japan, I have omitted several genres of shamisen music that fall into the narrative category, including most of the so-called kokyoku – katō-bushi, tomimoto-bushi and ogie-bushi. A late-eighteenth century offshoot from nagauta, ogie-bushi became a viable narrative genre with influence from kiyomoto.[1] In jiuta too there are pockets of katarimono, in the form of a group of shigetayū and handayū pieces. One major genre of jiuta, yamada-ryū sōkyoku, is musically very close to jōruri.

In folk music, the Tsugaru shamisen became commercially popular in the 1980s, but focusing on instrumental pyrotechnics, it almost entirely abandoned the narrative singing from which it emerged.

Another regional narrative style, the shamisen-accompanied goze uta, was referred to in Chapter 1 as an example of stichic narrative, and as such it lies outside the scope of this study, but is still waiting for a detailed sustained treatment in English. For an in-depth study in Japanese, see Groemer (2007 and 2014). Distinct from the heike-jōruri stream of narratives, it belongs to what might be called a saimon stream, including min'yō kudoki, naniwa-bushi, fushidan sekkyō and sekkyō-bushi.

Goze uta is not folk narrative, because it was the monopoly of strict associations of blind women. In this it is like the biwa-accompanied regional narrative from

---

[1] See http://www.japo-net.or.jp/mame2/?p=38 (accessed 9 September 2014).

Kyūshū, zatō biwa (also called higo biwa). This is virtually indistinguishable from mōsō biwa, and has been studied in depth by de Ferranti (2009). In Japanese, Hyōdō's many publications are most significant, the fullest statement being Hyōdō (2000).

Naniwa-bushi (rōkyoku), the non-musical oral narratives of rakugo and kōdan, and the comic duo of manzai are still evolving genres, rather than being classical and fixed. The genres in the present study on the other hand fall in the realm of the classical and as such are valued as part of Japanese traditional culture. They are recognized by the Agency for Cultural Affairs (Bunkachō) in the Ministry of Education through various forms of support including awarding the status of Living National Treasure. Nō, ningyō jōruri bunraku, and kabuki are on the UNESCO list of Intangible Cultural Heritage. All such recognition is highly significant in assuring their respected position in contemporary Japanese culture, and in inspiring conscientious efforts to foster general knowledge and appreciation of these performing arts, through Japanese, English and other language materials.

All the genres in this study are still actively practised, appreciated and studied. Their stories are still being re-told and re-invented for the new age. Stories going back to the twelfth-century Genpei Wars, stories from the nineteenth-century struggle to modernize, even accounts of modern wars find their way into musical narrative. Completely new stories are being narrated in naniwa-bushi. Manzai has used the new modern media of radio and television effectively to develop as a cross-over with modern comic routines. The ongoing power of performed narrative, both live and mediated, is evident in contemporary Japan.

References

Abe, Yasurō. 'Girei no Koe: Nenbutsu no Koe o megurite' [The Voice of Ritual: Calling on the Name of the Buddha]. In *Shiriizu Shisō No Shintai: Koe no Maki*, edited by Hyōdō Hiromi, 100–133. Tokyo: Shinjūsha, 2007.
Agō, Toranoshin et al., eds. *Kōwaka Bukyoku Kenkyū*. Tokyo: Miyai shoten, 1979–2004.
Amano, Denchū. *Tendai Shōmyō: Amano Denchū Chosaku-Shū*. Kyoto: Hōzōkan, 2000.
Anderson, Benedict R. *Imagined Communities: Reflections on the Origin and Spread of Nationalism*. London: Verso, 1983.
Anzako, Iwao. *Kōwaka-Mai, Kabuki, Mura Shibai*. Tokyo: Bensei shuppan, 2000.
Araki, James T. *The Ballad-Drama of Medieval Japan*. Berkeley, CA: University of California Press, 1964.
———. 'Otogi-zoshi and Nara-ehon: A Field of Study in Flux'. *Monumenta Nipponica* 36, no. 1 (1981): 1–20.
Aston, W.G., trans. *Nihongi: Chronicles of Japan from the Earliest Times to A.D. 697*. Rutland, VT; Tokyo: C.E. Tuttle, 1972.
Bender, Mark. 'A Description of "Jiangjing" (Telling Scriptures) Services in Jingjiang, China'. *Asian Folklore Studies* 60, no. 1 (2001): 101–133.
———. *Plum and Bamboo: China's Suzhou Chantefable Tradition*. Urbana, IL: University of Illinois Press, 2003.
Bethe, Monica, and Karen Brazell. *Dance in the Nō Theater*. Cornell University East Asia Papers. 3 vols. Ithaca, NY: China-Japan Program, Cornell University, 1982.
Bialock, David T. 'Nation and Epic: The Tale of the Heike as Modern Classic'. In *Inventing the Classics: Canon Formation, National Identity, and Japanese Literature*, edited by Haruo Shirane and Tomi Suzuki, 151–78. Stanford, CA: Stanford University Press, 2000.
Børdahl, Vibeke, and Nordic Institute of Asian Studies. *The Eternal Storyteller: Oral Literature in Modern China*. Richmond, Surrey: Curzon Press, 1999.
———. *Wu Song Fights the Tiger: The Interaction of Oral and Written Traditions in the Chinese Novel, Drama, and Storytelling*. Copenhagen: NIAS Press, 2013.
Bowring, Richard John. *The Religious Traditions of Japan, 500–1600*. Cambridge; New York: Cambridge University Press, 2005.
Brandon, James R. *Chushingura: Studies in Kabuki and the Puppet Theater*. Honolulu, HI: University of Hawai'i Press, 1982.
Brandon, James, and Samuel Leiter. *Villainy and Vengeance, 1773–1799*. Kabuki Plays on Stage. Vol. 2. Honolulu, HI: University of Hawai'i Press, 2002.

Brazell, Karen and James T. Araki. *Traditional Japanese Theater: An Anthology of Plays*. Translations from the Asian Classics. New York: Columbia University Press, 1998.

Butler, Kenneth D. 'The Heike Monogatari and Theories of Oral Epic Literature.' *Seikei Daigaku: Faculty of Letters Bulletin* 2 (1966): 37–54.

Chibbett, David. *The History of Japanese Printing and Book Illustration*. Tokyo; New York: Kodansha International, 1977.

Clunies Ross, Margaret. *Old Icelandic Literature and Society*. Cambridge Studies in Medieval Literature Vol. 42. Cambridge; New York: Cambridge University Press, 2000.

Cogan, T.J. *The Tale of the Soga Brothers*. Tokyo: University of Tokyo Press, 1987.

de Ferranti, Hugh. *Japanese Musical Instruments*. Images of Asia. New York: Oxford University Press, 2000.

———. *The Last Biwa Singer: A Blind Musician in History, Imagination and Performance*. Ithaca, NY: East Asia Program, Cornell University, 2009.

———. 'Biwa'. *Grove Music Online* Oxford Music Online. Oxford University Press. http://www.oxfordmusiconline.com.ezproxy.lib.monash.edu.au/subscriber/article/grove/music/03169 (accessed 8 September 2014).

Dunn, Charles James. *The Early Japanese Puppet Drama*. London: Luzac, 1966.

Emmert, Richard. 'The Maigoto of Nō: A Musical Analysis of the Chū-no-mai'. *Yearbook for Traditional Music* 15 (1983): 5–13.

Engeki Hyakka Daijiten, edited by Shigetoshi Kawatake and Waseda Daigaku Engeki Hakubutsukan. Tokyo: Heibonsha, 1960/1983.

Erdely, Stephen. 'Music of South Slavic Epics'. In *The Oral Epic: Performance and Music*, edited by Karl Reichl, 69–82. Bamberg: VWB – Verlag fur Wissenschaft und Bildung, 2000.

———. *Music of Southslavic Epics from the Bihać Region of Bosnia*. Milman Parry Studies in Oral Tradition. New York: Garland, 1995.

Foley, John Miles. *The Theory of Oral Composition: History and Methodology Folkloristics*. Bloomington, IN: Indiana University Press, 1988.

———. *Homer's Traditional Art*. University Park, PA: Pennsylvania State University Press, 1999.

Fröhlich, J. *Rulers, Peasants and the Use of the Written Word in Medieval Japan: Ategawa no shō 1004–1304*. Bern: Peter Lang, 2007.

Fujii, Seishin. *Saifubon Heikyoku*. Nagoya: Nagoya-shi Kyōiku Iinkai Heikyoku Hozonkai, 1966.

Fujita, Takanori. 'The Music of the Noh Theatre'. In *The Ashgate Research Companion to Japanese Music*, edited by Alison Tokita and David W. Hughes. Aldershot: Ashgate, 2008.

———. *Kōwaka-mai ni nō o miru: Chūsei Geinō no Dentō to Fukugen Atsumori*. Kyoto: Research Centre for Japanese Traditional Music, Kyoto City University of Arts, 2009.

———. 'Masculinity as Expressed through the Distortion of "Musical" Scale in Japanese Noh Drama Song'. In *Uta to Katari no Kotoba to Fushi no Kenkyū*, edited by Takanori Fujita and Masaaki Ueno, 63–78. Kyoto: Research Centre for Japanese Traditional Music, Kyoto City University of Arts, 2012.

Fukuda, Akira. *Chūsei Katarimono Bungei: Sono Keifu to Tenkai*. Miyai Sensho 8. Tokyo: Miyai shoten, 1981.

Furuido, Hideo. *Buyō Techō*. Tokyo: Shinshindō shuppan, 1990.

Gamō, Mitsuko. 'Chusei Seigaku no Ongaku Kōzō: Katarimono no Kyokusetsukei to Dan'. In Iwanami Kōza, Nihon no Ongaku, Ajia no Ongaku, Vol. 5, 105–28. Tokyo: Iwanami shoten, 1989.

Gamō, Mitsuko and Susumu Kumada. 'Ōe Kōwaka no Ongaku Yōshiki'. In *Kōwaka Bukyoku Kenkyū*, 6, 18–50. Tokyo: Miyai shoten, 1990.

Gerstle, C. Andrew. *Circles of Fantasy: Convention in the Plays of Chikamatsu*. Cambridge, MA: Council on East Asian Studies, Harvard University, 1986.

Gerstle, C. Andrew, Kiyoshi Inobe and William P. Malm. *Theater as Music: The Bunraku Play 'Mt. Imo and Mt. Se: An Exemplary Tale of Womanly Virtue'*. Michigan Monograph Series in Japanese Studies. Ann Arbor, MI: Center for Japanese Studies, University of Michigan, 1990.

Goodwin, Janet R. *Alms and Vagabonds: Buddhist Temples and Popular Patronage in Medieval Japan*. Honolulu, HI: University of Hawai'i Press, 1994.

———. *Selling Songs and Smiles: The Sex Trade in Heian and Kamakura Japan*. Honolulu, HI: University of Hawai'i Press, 2007.

Gorai, Shigeru. *Kōya Hijiri*. Tokyo: Kadokawa shoten, 1975.

Groemer, Gerald. 'The Guild of the Blind in Tokugawa Japan'. *Monumenta Nipponica* 56, no. 3 (Autumn 2001): 349–80.

———. *Goze to Goze uta no Kenkyū*. 2 vols. Nagoya: University of Nagoya Press, 2007.

———. 'Marketing the Performing Arts in Osaka before the Twentieth Century'. In *Music, Modernity and Locality in Prewar Japan: Osaka and Beyond*, edited by Hugh de Ferranti and Alison Tokita, 53–74. Farnham: Ashgate, 2013.

———. *Goze uta*. Tokyo: Iwanami shoten, 2014.

Guelberg, Niels. *Buddhistische Zeremoniale (Koshiki) und ihre Bedeutung fuer die Literatur des Japanischen Mittelalters*. Stuttgart: F. Steiner, 1999.

Gunji, Masakatsu. *Buyō: The Classical Dance*. Translated by Don Kenny. Performing Arts of Japan. New York: Walker/Weatherhill, 1970.

Harris, Joseph, and Karl Reichl. *Prosimetrum: Crosscultural Perspectives on Narrative in Prose and Verse*. Suffolk; Rochester, NY: D.S. Brewer, 1997.

Hattori, Yukio. *Kabuki Seiritsu no Kenkyū*. Tokyo: Kazama shobō, 1968.

Hayashi, Tokiko. 'Kojōruri no Shinfū: Kaga no Jō'. In *Jōruri no Tanjō to Kojōruri*, edited by Bunzō Torigoe, Mikiko Uchiyama and Tamotsu Watanabe. Iwanami Kōza, Kabuki Bunraku, Vol. 7, 157–78. Tokyo: Iwanami shoten, 1998.

He, Xuewei. 'Narrators of Buddhist Scriptures and Religious Tales in China'. In *The Eternal Storyteller: Oral Literature in Modern China*, edited by Vibeke Børdahl, 40–44. Richmond, Surrey: Curzon Press, 1999.

Herzog, George. 'The Music of Yugoslav Heroic Epic Folk Poetry'. *Journal of the International Folk Music Council* 3 (1951): 62–4.

Hirano, Kenji. 'Katarimono ni okeru Gengo to Ongaku'. *Nihon Bungaku* 39, no. 6 (1990): 33–43.
———. 'Katarimono ni okeru Ongaku to Kotoba'. In *Heike Biwa: Katari to Ongaku*, edited by Yukō Kamisangō, 195–212. Tokyo: Hitsuji shobō, 1993.
Hoff, Frank, and Willi Flindt. *The Life Structure of Noh: An English Version of Yohomichi Mario's Analysis of the Structure of Noh*. Racine, WI: Concerned Theatre Japan, 1973.
Honko, Lauri. *Textualization of Oral Epics*. Trends in Linguistics Studies and Monographs. Berlin; New York: M. de Gruyter, 2000.
Hughes, David W. *Traditional Folk Song in Modern Japan: Sources, Sentiment and Society*. Folkestone: Global Oriental, 2008.
Hyōdō, Hiromi. *Katarimono Josetsu: Heike-Gatari no Hassei to Hyōgen*. Heike Monogatari 8 / Shinei Kenkyū Sōsho 8. Tokyo: Yuseidō, 1985.
———. 'Yasaka-ryū no Hassei: Heike Monogatari to Tekusuto ni okeru Chūsei to Kinsei.' In *Ronshū: Chūsei no Bungaku*, edited by Jun Kubota, 23–47. Tokyo: Meiji shoin, 1994.
———. *Taiheiki 'Yomi' no Kanōsei: Rekishi to iu Monogatari*. Kōdansha Sensho Mechie. Tokyo: Kōdansha, 1995.
———. 'Kōshō Bungaku Sōron'. In *Kōshō Bungaku 1*. Iwanami Kōza, Nihon Bungaku-shi, Vol. 16, 1–50. Tokyo: Iwanami shoten, 1997.
———. *Heike Monogatari no Rekishi to Geinō*. Tokyo: Yoshikawa Kōbunkan, 2000.
———. *Biwa Hōshi: Takai o Kataru Hitobito*. Tokyo: Iwanami shoten, 2009.
———. *Heike Monogatari no Yomikata*. Tokyo: Chikuma shobō, 2011.
Idema, Wilt. 'Prosimetric Literature'. In *The Indiana Companion to Traditional Chinese Literature*, edited by William H. Nienhauser Jr. et al., 83–92. Bloomington, IN: Indiana University Press, 1986.
Iguchi, Junko. *Chūgoku Hoppō Nōson no Kōshō Bunka: Katarimono no Sho, Tekisuto, Pafōmansu*. Tokyo: Fūkyōsha, 1999.
Iijima, Mitsuru. 'Kunitachi Ongaku Daigaku Fuzoku Toshokan-zō Takeuchi Dōkei Kyūzō Onban Mokuroku (3)'. *Mukei Bunka Isan Kenkyū Hōkoku* 3 (2009): 193–231.
Illich, Ivan. *In the Vineyard of the Text: A Commentary to Hugh's Didascalicon*. Chicago, IL: University of Chicago Press, 1993.
Inobe, Kiyoshi. *Jōrishi Kōsetsu*. Tokyo: Kazama shobō, 1991.
Ishii, Nobuko. 'Sekkyō-bushi'. *Monumenta Nipponica* 44, no. 3 (1989): 283–307.
Iwasa, Shin'ichi. *Edo Bungo Jōruri-shi*. Tokyo: Kuroshio shuppan, 1968.
Iwata, Sōichi. *Shōmyō no Kenkyū*. Kyoto: Hōzōkan, 1999.
Johnson, Henry Mabley. *The Shamisen: Tradition and Diversity*. Leiden: Brill, 2010.
Kanemitsu, Janet. 'Kinpira'. In *Publishing the Stage: Print and Performance in Early Modern Japan*, edited by Keller Kimbrough and Satoko Shimazaki. Boulder, CO: University of Colorado Center for Asian Studies, 2011.

Kano, Ayako. *Acting Like a Woman in Modern Japan: Theater, Gender, and Nationalism.* New York; Houndmills: Palgrave, 2001.
Kasaya, Kazuhiko. 'Tokugawa Yoshimune no Kyōhō Kaikaku to bungo-bushi torishimari mondai o meguru ikkōsatsu'. *Nihon Kenkyū* 33 (2006): 11–28.
Katō, Yasuaki. *Nihon Mōjin Shakaishi Kenkyū.* Tokyo: Miraisha, 1974 [1984].
Keene, Donald, trans. *Essays in Idleness: The Tsurezuregusa of Kenko.* Tokyo; Rutland, VT: Charles E. Tuttle, 1967.
Keister, Jay. *Shaped by Japanese Music: Kikuoka Hiroaki and Nagauta Shamisen in Tokyo.* Current Research in Ethnomusicology, edited by Jennifer C. Post. Vol. 10, New York: Routledge, 2004.
Kim, Yung-Hee. *Songs to Make the Dust Dance: The Ryojin Hisho of Twelfth-Century Japan.* Berkeley, CA: University of California Press, 1994.
Kimbrough, Keller. *Wondrous Brutal Fictions: Eight Buddhist Tales from the Early Japanese Puppet Theater.* New York: Columbia University Press, 2013.
Kimbrough, Keller, and Satoko Shimazaki, eds. *Publishing the Stage: Print and Performance in Early Modern Japan.* Boulder, CO: University of Colorado Center for Asian Studies, 2011.
Kindaichi, Haruhiko. *Shiza Kōshiki no Kenkyū.* Tokyo: Sanseidō, 1964.
——. *Kokugo Akusento no Shiteki Kenkyū: Genri to Hōhō.* Tokyo: Hanawa shobō, 1974.
Kishibe Shigeo Hakushi Koki Kinen shuppan iinkai. *Nihon Koten Ongaku Bunken Kaidai.* Tokyo: Kōdansha, 1987.
Kitagawa, Hiroshi, and Bruce T. Tsuchida, trans. *The Tale of the Heike.* Tokyo: University of Tokyo Press, 1975.
Kobayashi, Kenji. *Chūsei Geki Bungaku no Kenkyū: Nō to Kōwaka Bukyoku.* Tokyo: Miyai shoten, 2001.
——. 'Oda Nobunaga to kōwaka bukyoku *Atsumori*'. In *Kōwaka-mai ni nō o Miru: Chūsei Geinō no Dentō to Fukugen Atsumori*, edited by Takanori Fujita, 2–3. Kyoto: Research Centre for Japanese Traditional Music, Kyoto City University of Arts, 2009.
Koizumi, Fumio. 'Musical Scales in Japanese Music'. In *Asian Musics in an Asian Perspective: Report of [Asian Traditional Performing Arts 1976]*, edited by Osamu Yamaguchi et al., 73–9. Tokyo: Heibonsha, 1977.
Kojima, Tomiko, ed. *Nihon no Dentō Geinō Kōza: Ongaku*, edited by Kokuritsu Gekijō. Kyoto: Tankōsha, 2008.
Kominz, Laurence Richard. *Avatars of Vengeance: Japanese Drama and the Soga Literary Tradition.* Michigan Monograph Series in Japanese Studies. Ann Arbor, MI: Center for Japanese Studies, University of Michigan, 1995.
Komoda, Haruko. 'Heikyoku no Kyokusetsu to Ongaku Kōzō'. In *Heike Biwa: Katari to Ongaku*, edited by Yūkō Kamisangō, 161–93. Tokyo: Hitsuji shobō, 1993.
——. 'Heikyoku no Ongakushiteki Kenkyū ni Mukete'. In *Heike Monogatari: Hihyō to Bunkashi*, edited by Hiroaki Yamashita, 7, 256–76. Tokyo: Kyūko shoin, 1998.
——. *Heike no Ongaku: Tōdō no Dentō.* Tokyo: Daiichi shobō, 2003.

———. 'The Musical Narrative of the Tale of the Heike'. In *The Ashgate Research Companion to Japanese Music*, edited by Alison Tokita and David W. Hughes, 77–103. Aldershot: Ashgate, 2008.

———. *Heike Monogatari: The Tale of the Heike*. Commentary to a 7 CD and 1 DVD set. English notes by Alison Tokita. Tokyo: EBISU 13~19, 2009.

Konishi, Jin'ichi. *A History of Japanese Literature*. Vol. 3, Princeton, NJ: Princeton University Press, 1991.

Kornicki, Peter F. *The Book in Japan: A Cultural History from the Beginnings to the Nineteenth Century*. Handbuch Der Orientalistik Fünfte Abteilung, Japan. Leiden; Boston, MA: Brill, 1998.

———. 'Bluffing Your Way in Chinese'. In *Sandars Lectures in Bibliography 2008 Lecture 2*. Cambridge University, 2008.

Koyama, Tadashi. *Jōkyoku no Shinkenkyū*. Tokyo: Nihon Gakujutsu Shinkōkai, 1962.

Kwon, Yung-hee Kim. 'The Female Entertainment Tradition in Medieval Japan: The Case of Asobi'. *Theatre Journal* 40 (May 1988): 205–16.

Leiter, Samuel L. *Kabuki Encyclopedia: An English-Language Adaptation of Kabuki Jiten*. Westport, CT: Greenwood Press, 1979.

Leiter, Samuel L., and James R. Brandon. *Masterpieces of Kabuki: Eighteen Plays on Stage*. Honolulu, HI: University of Hawai'i Press, 2004.

Lord, Albert B. *The Singer of Tales*. Cambridge, MA: Harvard University Press, 1960 [2000].

Lu, David John. *Japan: A Documentary History*. 2 vols. Armonk, NY: M.E. Sharpe, 1997.

Lurie, David Barnett. *Realms of Literacy: Early Japan and the History of Writing*. Harvard East Asian Monographs. Cambridge, MA: Harvard University Asia Center; Distributed by Harvard University Press, 2011.

Machida, Kashō. *Shamisen Seikyoku ni okeru Senritsukei no Kenkyū*. Tōyō Ongaku Kenkyū. Vol. 47, Tokyo: Tōyō Ongaku Gakkai, 1982.

Machida, Kashō, and Ryūnosuke Ueda, eds. *Gendai Hōgaku Meikan: Kiyomoto Hen*. Tokyo: Hōgaku to Buyō shuppanbu, 1967.

Mair, Victor. 'Oral Narrative in Chinese Literature'. *Oral Tradition* 3, nos. 1–2 (1988): 106–21.

———. 'The Prosimetric Form in the Chinese Literary Tradition'. In *Prosimetrum: Crosscultural Perpectives on Narrative in Prose and Verse*, edited by Joseph Harris and Karl Reichl, 365–85. Cambridge: D.S. Brewer, 1997.

———. 'Buddhist Influences on Vernacular Literature in Chinese'. In *Encyclopedia of Buddhism*, edited by Robert E. Buswell, 1, 154–7. New York: Thomson-Gale (Macmillan Reference USA), 2004.

Malm, William P. *Nagauta: The Heart of Kabuki Music*. Rutland, VT: Charles E. Tuttle, 1963.

———. 'A Musical Approach to the Study of Japanese Joruri'. In *Chushingura: Studies in Kabuki and the Puppet Theater*, edited by James R. Brandon, 59–110. Honolulu: University of Hawai'i Press, 1982.

Maruya, Saiichi. *Chūshingura to wa nani ka*. Tokyo: Kodansha, 1984.
Masumoto, Kikuko. 'Shingi Shingon (Buzan-Ha) no Kōshiki ni tsuite: Ongaku no Sokumen kara'. In *Record Notes for Shiza Kōshiki*, edited by Nobuyoshi (Engi) Shida, 76–81. Tokyo: Nihon Columbia, 1977.
Matisoff, Susan. 'Reflections of Terute: Searching for a Hidden Shaman-Entertainer'. *Women & Performance: A Journal of Feminist Theory* 12, no. 1 (2001): 113–34.
———. 'Barred from Paradise? Mount Koya and the Karukaya Legend'. In *Engendering Faith: Women and Buddhism in Premodern Japan*, edited by Barbara Ruch, 463–500. Ann Arbor, MI: Center for Japanese Studies, University of Michigan, 2002.
Matsumoto, Ryūjin, ed. *Otogi zōshi*. Shinchō Nihon Koten Shūsei. Tōkyō: Shinchōsha, 1980.
McCullough, Helen Craig, trans. *The Taiheiki: A Chronicle of Medieval Japan*. Tokyo and Rutland, VT: Charles E. Tuttle, 1959.
———. *Yoshitsune: A Fifteenth-Century Japanese Chronicle*. Unesco Collection of Representative Works. Stanford, CA: Stanford University Press, 1966.
———. *The Tale of the Heike*. Stanford, CA: Stanford University Press, 1988.
McLaren, Anne. *Chinese Popular Culture and Ming Chantefables*. Leiden: Brill, 1998.
Miner, Earl Roy, Hiroko Odagiri, and Robert E. Morrell. *The Princeton Companion to Classical Japanese Literature*. Princeton, NJ: Princeton University Press, 1985.
Mitsui, Tōru, and Shūhei Hosokawa. *Karaoke around the World: Global Technology, Local Singing*. Routledge Research in Cultural and Media Studies. London; New York: Routledge, 1998.
Morioka, Heinz, Miyoko Sasaki, and Harvard University Council on East Asian Studies. *Rakugo: The Popular Narrative Art of Japan*. Harvard East Asian Monographs. Cambridge, MA: Council on East Asian Studies. Distributed by Harvard University Press, 1990.
Mulhern, Chieko Irie. 'Otogi-zōshi: Short Stories of the Muromachi Period'. *Monumenta Nipponica* 29, no. 2 (1974): 181–98.
Muroki, Yatarō. *Mai no Hon: Eboshi-ori*. Osaka: Izumi shoten, 1982.
———. *Katarimono: Mai, Sekkyō, Ko-Jōruri no Kenkyū*. Tokyo: Kazama shobō, 1992.
———. 'Jōruri Hime Monogatari: Katarimono-shi o Fukumete'. In *Jōruri no Tanjō to Ko-jōruri*. Iwanami Kōza, Kabuki Bunraku, Vol. 7, 3–26. Tokyo: Iwanami shoten, 1998.
Nagatomo, Chiyoji. 'Jōruribon: Sono Juyō to Kyōkyū'. In *Ōgonjidai no Jōruri to Sono Go*. Iwanami Kōza, Kabuki Bunraku, Vol. 9, 257–69. Tokyo: Iwanami shoten, 1998.
Nakagawa, Aihyō. *Shinnai*. Tokyo: Iroha shobō, 1911.
Nakamura, Kyōko. 'Kiyomoto-bushi no ongakuteki tokuchō'. Unpublished Masters thesis, Tōkyō Geijutsu Daigaku, 1967.

Nakauchi, Chōji, and Nishio Tamura. *Tomimoto oyobi Shinnai Zenshū*. Nihon Ongaku Zenshū. 11 vols. Vol. 8, Tokyo: Nihon Ongyoku Zenshū Kankōkai, 1927.

——, eds. *Kiyomoto Zenshū*. Nihon Ongyoku Zenshū, Vol. 3. Tokyo: Nihon Ongyoku Zenshū Kankōkai, 1928.

——, eds. *Tokiwazu Zenshū*. Nihon Ongyoku Zenshū, Vol. 8. Tokyo: Nihon Ongyoku Zenshū Kankōkai, 1929.

Nelson, Steven G. 'Buddhist Chant of Shingi-Shingon: A Guide for Readers and Listeners'. In *Shingi Shingon Shōmyō Shūsei, Gakufu-Hen, Dainikan, Nika Hōyō-Shū (Ge) / Buddhist Chant of Shingi-Shingon: Neumes and Transcriptions 2*, 458–503. Tokyo: Shingon-shū Buzan-ha Bukkyō Seinenkai [Youth Association of the Buzan Branch of the Shingon Sect], 1998.

——. 'Court and Religious Music (2): Music of Gagaku and Shōmyō'. In *The Ashgate Research Companion to Japanese Music*, edited by Alison Tokita and David W. Hughes, 49–76. Aldershot: Ashgate, 2008.

Nihon denki densetsu daijiten. Tokyo: Kadokawa shoten, 1986.

Nishino, Haruo. 'Kannami no Nō'. In *Nō no sakusha to sakuhin*. Iwanami Kōza, Nō Kyōgen, Vol. 3..Tokyo: Iwanami shoten, 1987.

Nishino, Haruo and Hisashi Hata (eds). *Nō Kyōgen Jiten*. Tokyo: Heibonsha, 1999.

Nishiyama, Matsunosuke. *Gei no Sekai*. Tokyo: Kōdansha, 1980.

Okamoto, Bun'ya. *Shinnai Kyokufu-kō*. Tokyo: Dōseisha, 1972.

Okuhara, Rieko. '"Deja Lu or Deja Entendu"?: Comparing a Japanese Fairy Tale with European Tales'. *The Lion and the Unicorn* 24, no. 2 (2000): 188–200.

Omote, Akira, and Mario Yokomichi. *Yōkyokushū*. Vol. 41. Tokyo: Iwanami shoten, 1963/1981.

Ong, Walter J. *Orality and Literacy: The Technologizing of the Word*. New Accents. London; New York: Methuen, 1982.

Ongaku Daijiten. Tokyo: Heibonsha, 1981–1983.

Oshio, Satomi. 'Nagauta ni okeru Katarimonosei'. In *Nihon no Katarimono: Kōtōsei, Kōzō, Igi*, edited by Alison Tokita and Haruko Komoda. Nichibunken Sōsho, 231–47. Kyoto: International Research Centre for Japanese Studies, 2002.

Ōyama, Kōjun. *Bukkyō Ongaku to Shōmyō*. Osaka: Tōhō shuppan, 1989.

Oyler, Elizabeth. 'The Heike in Japan'. *Oral Tradition* 18, no. 1 (2003): 18–20.

——. 'Daimokutate: Ritual Placatory Performance of the Genpei War'. *Oral Tradition* 21, no. 1 (2006a): 90–118.

——. *Swords, Oaths, and Prophetic Visions: Authoring Warrior Rule in Medieval Japan*. Honolulu, HI: University of Hawai'i Press, 2006b.

Parker, Helen S.E. *Progressive Traditions: An Illustrated Study of Plot Repetition in Traditional Japanese Theatre*. Brill's Japanese Studies Library. Leiden; Boston, MA: Brill, 2006.

Philippi, D.L. *Kojiki*. Tokyo: University of Tokyo Press, 1968.

Pigeot, Jacqueline. *Histoire de Yokobue (Yokobue No Sōshi); Étude sur les récits de l'époque Muromachi*. Paris: Presses universitaires de France, 1972.

Pihl, Marshall R. *The Korean Singer of Tales*. Harvard-Yenching Institute Monograph Series. Cambridge, MA: Council on East Asian Studies; Distributed by Harvard University Press, 1994.
Plutschow, Herbert E. *Chaos and Cosmos: Ritual in Early and Medieval Japanese Literature*. Brill's Japanese Studies Library. Leiden; New York: E.J. Brill, 1990.
Pollack, David. *The Fracture of Meaning: Japan's Synthesis of China from the Eighth through the Eighteenth Centuries*. Princeton, NJ: Princeton University Press, 1986.
Quinn, Shelley Fenno. *Developing Zeami: The Noh Actor's Attunement in Practice*. Honolulu, HI: University of Hawai'i Press, 2005.
Rabinovitch, Judith N. *Shōmonki: The Story of Masakado's Rebellion*. Tokyo: Monumenta Nipponica, Sophia University, 1986.
Reichl, Karl, ed. *The Oral Epic: Performance and Music*. Intercultural Music Studies, Vol. 12. Berlin: VWB - Verlag fuer Wissenschaft und Bildung, 2000.
Reischauer, A.K., trans, 'Genshin's Ōjō Yōshū: Collected Essays on Birth into Paradise'. In *Transactions of the Asiatic Society of Japan*, 2nd series, 7 (1930): 16–97.
Rubinger, Richard. *Popular Literacy in Early Modern Japan*. Honolulu, HI: University of Hawai'i Press, 2007.
Ruch, Barbara. 'Origins of the Companion Library: An Anthology of Medieval Japanese Stories'. *The Journal of Asian Studies* 30, no. 3 (1971): 593–610.
——. 'Medieval Joungleurs and the Making of a National Literature'. In *Japan in the Muromachi Age*, edited by J. Whitney Hall and Takeshi Toyoda, 279–309. Berkeley, CA; Los Angeles, CA; London: University of California Press, 1977.
Saeki, Junko. *Yūjo no Bunka-shi: Hare no Onnatachi*. Tokyo: Chūō Kōronsha, 1987.
——. *Bishōnen-zukushi*. Tokyo: Heibonsha, 1992.
Sakaguchi, Hiroyuki. 'Kojōuri'. In *Nihon no Dentō Geinō Kōza: Ongaku*, edited by Tomiko Kojima and Kokuritsu Gekijō Chōsa-yōseibu, 294–305. Kyoto: Tankōsha, 2008.
Satō, Michiko. 'Hōyō no Keishiki to Naiyō'. In *Shōmyō Jiten*, edited by Mario Yokomichi and Gidō Kataoka, 27–51. Kyoto: Hōzōkan, 1984.
Sawada, Atsuko. 'Shōmyō to Heikyoku'. In *Heike Gatari: Dentō to Keitai*, edited by Masaaki Kajiwara. Anata ga yomu Heike Monogatari 5, 55–66. Tokyo: Yuseidō shuppan, 1994.
——. 'Bukkyō Girei ni okeru Katarimono no Ongaku Kōzō: Hyōbyaku, Kōshiki o Rei to shite'. In *Nihon no Katarimono: Kōtōsei, Kōzō, Igi*, edited by Alison Tokita and Haruko Komoda, 181–93. Kyoto: International Research Centre for Japanese Studies, 2002.
Saya, Makito. *Heike Monogatari kara Jōruri e*. Tokyo: Keiō Gijuku Daigaku shuppankai, 2002.
Scott, A.C. and Gohei Namiki. *Kanjincho: A Japanese Kabuki Play*. Tokyo: Hokuseido Press, 1953.
Sekiyama, Kazuo. *Sekkyō no Rekishiteki Kenkyū*. Kyoto: Hōzōkan, 1973.
——. *Sekkyō no Rekishi: Bukkyō to Wagei*. Tokyo: Iwanami shoten, 1978.

Shimazu, Hisamoto. *Yoshitsune Densetsu to Bungaku*. Tokyo: Meiji shoin, 1935.
Shively, Donald. 'Tokugawa Plays on Forbidden Topics'. In *Chūshingura: Studies in Kabuki and the Puppet Theater*, edited by James R. Brandon, 23–57. Honolulu, HI: University of Hawai'i Press, 1982.
——. 'Popular Culture'. In *The Cambridge History of Japan*, edited by John W. Hall and James L. McClain, 706–69. Cambridge: Cambridge University Press, 1991.
Smith, Henry D. 'History behind Chushingura'. 1990. http://www.columbia.edu/~hds2/47ronin.htm (accessed 7 September 2014).
Sieffert, René, ed. and trans. *Histoire de demoiselle Jôruri*. [Paris]: Publications Orientalistes de France, 1994.
Squires, Todd Andrew. 'Reading the Kōwaka-Mai as Medieval Myth: Story-Patterns, Traditional Reference and Performance in Late Medieval Japan'. PhD thesis, Ohio State University, 2001. http://images.lib.monash.edu.au/er/theses/squires.pdf (accessed 8 September 2014).
Strippoli, Roberta. 'Dancing through Time: Transformations of the Gio Legend in Premodern Japanese Literature and Theatre'. PhD, Stanford University, 2006.
Suda, Etsuo et al., eds. *Kan'ei (1624–1643) Ban Mai no Hon*. Tokyo: Miyai shoten, 1990.
Suzuki, Takatsune. *Heikyoku to Heike Monogatari*. Niigata Daigaku Jinbun Gakubu Kenkyō Sōsho. Tokyo: Chisen shokan, 2007.
Takeda, Izumo, Miyoshi Shōraku, Donald Keene and Namiki Senryū. *Chūshingura: The Treasury of Loyal Retainers*. New York: Columbia University Press, 1971.
Takei, Kyōzō. 'Wakashū Kabuki, Yarō Kabuki'. In *Kabuki no Rekishi 1*. Iwanami Kōza, Kabuki Bunraku, Vol. 2, 1–33. Tokyo: Iwanami shoten, 1997.
Takenouchi, Emiko. 'Koshibai'. In *Nihon no Katarimono: Kōtōsei, Kōzō, Igi*, edited by Alison Tokita and Haruko Komoda, 269–84. Kyoto: International Research Center for Japanese Studies (Nichibunken), 2002.
Takeuchi, Michitaka. 'Shamisen Ongaku no Denshō to Ryūha: Bungo-Kei Jōruri no Baai'. In *Denshō to Kiroku*, edited by Satoaki Gamō et al. Iwanami Kōza, Nihon no Ongaku Ajia no Ongaku, Vol. 4, 125–59. Tokyo: Iwanami shoten, 1988.
Takeuchi, Yūichi, ed. *Shishōhon no Sekai: Kinsei no Utahon, Jōruribon no Shuppan Jijō*. Kyoto: Research Centre for Japanese Traditional Music, Kyoto City University of Arts, 2008.
Tanaka, Yumiko. 'Gidayū-bushi Kihonji no Seiri: Bunrui Shian'. *Gakugekigaku* 8 (2001): 39–68.
——. 'Itchū-bushi no Senritsukei Bunseki: Shodai Miyakodayū Itchū no Sakuhin o Chūshin to shite'. *Tōyō Ongaku Kenkyū* 67 (2002): 1–22.
Tokita, Alison. 'Mode and Scale, Modulation and Tuning in Japanese Shamisen Music: The Case of Kiyomoto Narrative'. *Ethnomusicology* 40, no. 1 (1996): 1–33.
——. *Kiyomoto-Bushi: Narrative Music of the Kabuki Theatre*. Studien zur Traditionellen Musik Japans. Kassel: Baerenreiter, 1999.

———. 'The Reception of the Heike Monogatari as Performed Narrative: The Atsumori Episode in Heikyoku, Zatō Biwa and Satsuma Biwa'. *Japanese Studies* 23, no. 1 (2003): 59–85.

———. 'Music of the Kabuki Theatre: More Than Meets the Eye'. In *The Ashgate Research Companion to Japanese Music*, edited by Alison Tokita and David W. Hughes, 229–60. Aldershot: Ashgate, 2008.

Tokita, Alison, and David W. Hughes. *The Ashgate Research Companion to Japanese Music*. Aldershot; Burlington, VT: Ashgate, 2008.

Tokita, Alison McQueen. 'The Nature of Patterning in Japanese Narrative Music: Formulaic Musical Material in Heikyoku, Gidayū-Bushi, and Kiyomoto-Bushi'. *Musicology Australia* 23, no. 1 (2000): 99–122.

Tyler, Royall. 'One Million'. In *Granny Mountains: A Second Cycle of Nō Plays*, translated by Royall Tyler. Cornell University East Asia Papers, 117–29. Ithaca, NY: Cornell University East Asia Program, 1978.

———. *Before Heike and After: Hōgen, Heiji, Jōkyūki*. San Bernadino, CA: Arthur Nettleton, 2012a.

———. *The Tale of the Heike*. London: Viking, 2012b.

Uchiyama, Mikiko. 'Geki no Tanjō'. In *Kabuki to Bunraku no Honshitsu*. Iwanami Kōza, Kabuki Bunraku, Vol. 7, 187–206. Tokyo: Iwanami shoten, 1997.

Varley, H.P. *Warriors of Japan as Portrayed in the War Tales*. Honolulu, HI: University of Hawai'i Press, 1994.

Wada, Osamu. 'Yamamoto Kakudayū'. In *Jōruri no Tanjō to Kojōruri*, edited by Bunzō Torigoe, Mikiko Uchiyama and Tamotsu Watanabe. Iwanami Kōza, Kabuki Bunraku, Vol. 7, 179–200. Tokyo: Iwanami shoten, 1998.

Wakita, Haruko. *Josei Geinō no Genryū: Kugutsu Kusemai Shirabyōshi*. Kadokawa Sensho. Tōkyō: Kadokawa shoten, 2001.

———. *Women in Medieval Japan: Motherhood, Household Management and Sexuality*. Translated by Alison Tokita. Clayton, Vic.; Tokyo: Monash Asia Institute; University of Tokyo Press, 2006.

Watson, Michael. *A Narrative Study of the Kakuichi-bon Heike Monogatari*. PhD Thesis, University of Oxford, 2003.

Yamada, Chieko. 'Gidayū-Bushi no Katari ni okeru Kihan to Henkei: Jiai no Ongakugakuteki Kenkyū'. PhD Thesis, Osaka University, Department of Musicology, 2003.

———. 'Gidayū-Bushi: The Music of the Bunraku Puppet Theatre'. In *The Ashgate Research Companion to Japanese Music*, edited by Alison Tokita and David W. Hughes, 197–228. Aldershot: Ashgate, 2008.

Yamada, Chieko and Mariko Ōkubo (eds). *Shamisen Ongaku no Senritsukei Kenkyū: Machida Kashō o megutte*. Kyoto: Kyoto City University of Arts, Research Report No. 9, 2015.

Yamada, Shōzen. 'Kōshiki: Sono Seiritsu to Tenkai'. In *Shōdō no Bungaku*, edited by Hiroyuki Itō. Bukkyō Bungaku Kōza, 11–53. Tokyo: Benseisha, 1995.

Yamaji, Kōzō. 'Ayatsuri Jōruri no Seiritsu'. In *Jōruri No Tanjō to Kojōruri*, edited by Bunzō Torigoe, Mikiko Uchiyama and Tamotsu Watanabe. Iwanami Kōza, Kabuki Bunraku, Vol. 7, 27–50. Tokyo: Iwanami shoten, 1998.
Yamamoto, Kichizō. *Kutsuwa no Oto ga Zazameite: Katari no Bungei-kō*. Tokyo: Heibonsha, 1988.
Yamane, Tameo. 'Fushizuke to Hanpon'. In *Chikamatsu no Jidai*. Iwanami Kōza, Kabuki Bunraku, Vol. 8, 19–40. Tokyo: Iwanami shoten, 1998.
Yamashita, Hiroaki. *Heike Monogatari no Seiritsu*. Nagoya-shi: Nagoya Daigaku shuppankai, 1993.
Yano, Christine Reiko. *Tears of Longing: Nostalgia and the Nation in Japanese Popular Song*. Cambridge, MA: Harvard University Asia Center; Distributed by Harvard University Press, 2002.
Yasuda, Kenneth. 'The Dramatic Structure of *Ataka*, a Noh Play'. *Monumenta Nipponica* 27, no. 4 (1972): 359–98.
Yasuda, Tokiko. 'Gunyū Kakkyo no Jidai'. In *Jōruri no Tanjō to Kojōruri*, edited by Bunzō Torigoe, Mikiko Uchiyama and Tamotsu Watanabe. Iwanami Kōza, Kabuki Bunraku, Vol. 7, 97–118. Tokyo: Iwanami shoten, 1998.
Yokomichi, Mario. *Shōmyō Jiten*. Kyoto: Hōzōkan, 1984.
———. *Nōgeki no Kenkyū*. Tōkyō: Iwanami shoten, 1986.
———. *Nihon no Gakugeki*. Tokyo: Iwanami shoten, 2011.
Yoshida, Kōzō. 'Shōmyō Gaku Gairon'. *Tōyō Ongaku Kenkyū* 12–13 (1954): 5–100.
Zeami, and Thomas Blenman Hare. *Zeami, Performance Notes*. Translations from the Asian Classics. New York: Columbia University Press, 2008.

Audio/Videography

Ataka: Kanze-ryū yōkyoku hyakuban-shū 87. 1 cassette tape. King CNT-815. no date.
Bandō Tamasaburō Buyō-shū 1: Kyōkanoko Dōjōji. Shochiku Home Video, 2003.
Biwa hōshi no sekai, Heike monogatari: Imai Tsutomu [The world of the biwa hōshi, Heike monogatari: Imai Tsutomu]. 3 CDS and 1 DVD. Ebisu EBISU-13~19. 2009.
Bungo-kei no jōruri. 6 LPs. Victor SJ-3011/1~3, SJ-3012/1~3. 1964.
Gidayū-bushi no kyokusetsu [Melody patterns of gidayū-bushi]. 6 LPs. Produced by Shuzui Kenji and Nagao Sōichirō. Victor SJ-3016/1~3, SJ-3017/1~3. 1967.
Goze uta. From *Jōetsu-shi Hossoku 20-shūnen kinen*. 5 CDs. Produced by the Jōetsu City 20th Anniversary Committee. ACD-907~911. 1991.
Heike monogatari no ongaku. CD. Performed by Imai Tsutomu. Produced by Hirano Kenji. Nippon Columbia COCF-7889. 1991.
Heike Monogatari: The Tale of the Heike. 7 CDs and 1 DVD. Performed by Imai Tsutomu. Produced with commentary by Komoda Haruko; English notes by Alison Tokita. EBISU-13~19. 2009.
Hōgaku Taikei. Tokyo: Chikuma shobō, 1970–1972.

Itchū-bushi koten meisakusen [Selection of itchū-bushi classic masterpieces]. 6 LPs. Performed by Miyako Ichiiki. Teichiku GM-6019~6024. 1982.
Kabuki meisakusen: Kanjinchō [The best selection of kabuki: Kanjinchō]. 1 DVD. NHK DVD NSDS-7860. 2004.
Kanadehon Chūshingura. 7 CDs. King KICH-2148~2154. 1994.
Kiyomoto Shizudayū Zenshū: kiyomoto gojūban [Collected works of Kiyomoto Shizudayū: kiyomoto top fifty]. 30 LPs. Produced by Eishi Kikkawa et al. Victor SJ-3020~3029. 1970. Re-issued as 21 CDs. VZCG-8085~8104, VZCP-1026. 2000.
Kōwakamai: Ataka, Atsumori. 1 CD and 1 DVD. Kyoto City University of Arts Research Centre for Traditional Japanese Music. 2010.
Nihon Geinō Taikei (Oto to Eizō ni yoru). Tokyo: Victor, 1991.
Nihon Koten Ongaku Taikei: 1,000 Years of Japanese Classical Music. 80 LP records. Kōdansha-Victor, 1981–83.
  Vol. I: Gagaku, Shōmyo, Biwa.
  Vol. II: Nō, Kyōgen.
  Vol. III: Sōkyoku, Jiuta, Shakuhachi.
  Vol. IV: Nagauta.
  Vol. V: Gidayū.
  Vol. VI: Kokyoku.
  Vol. VII: Tokiwazu, Tomimoto, Kiyomoto, Shinnai.
  Vol. VIII: Hauta, Utazawa, Kouta.
Ōzatsuma-bushi. Victor SJ-3018. 1968.
Ranchō, Akegarasu. LP. Fujimatsu Tsurichiyo and Kaga Koteru. Nippon Columbia SJL-76. 1974.
Shinnai. Hōgaku Meikyoku Selection 20. CD. Nippon Columbia COCJ-32447. 2003.
Shinnai Nakasaburō: Shinnai no miryoku, shinnai nagashi. 2 LPs. Teichiku PP-6101~2. 1976.
Shiza Kōshiki. 6 LPs and commentary. Performed by Aoki Yūkō. Produced by Shida Engi. Nippon Columbia GL–7003~08. 1978.
Shōmyō Taikei. 12 LPs. Produced by Yokomichi Mario and Kataoka Gidō. Hōzōkan. 1984.

Index

Page numbers in **bold** refer to tables and examples.

ageuta 99–100
Ainu yukar 11
Akashi, Kakuichi 61
Amano, Denchū 34
Anzako, Iwao 95
Aoki Yūkō 28, 39, 45
aragoto acting 235, 236
Araki, James T. 97, 98, 100, 105, **106**, 106
Asakawa, Gyokuto 238
Ataka (nō) 100, 123, 127–8
    compared to *Togashi* 120, 122
    Kanjinchō adaptation 252, 253
    outline **124–6**
    text 126–7
auspicious narratives 9, 182

Bender, Mark 16
Bethe, Monica 96–7
biwa hōshi
    heike 53
        guild 57, 58
        originators 60
        ritual appeasement 57
        texts 58
    influence on kōshiki 51
    origins 60
    shamisen playing 136
    status loss 62
biwa hōshi tradition 66, **66**, 68, 70
biwa lute
    compared to shamisen 138
    description 59–60
    heike 7, 66, 68, 69, 89, 95
    jōruri 137
    neo-traditional genres 8
blind storytellers/musicians
    goze uta 11, 266
    kengyō 62, 138 n6
    loss of status 3
    musical development 62, 138, 139
    theatre's impact 13
    zatō biwa 11
    see also biwa hōshi
boys 7, 92–3, 98, 129
Brazell, Karen 96–7
Buddhism in Japan
    Chinese texts 29
    fund-raising 5–6
    introduction 25, 29
    Japanization 25
    personal devotionalism 30
    popularization 30
    rituals 29
    salvation narratives 5
    shōmyō (musical liturgy) 29–30
    state religion 30
    visual expression 29
    see also kōshiki
bungo-bushi 10, 148, 173, 174, 175, 176, 235
bungo-kei jōruri 171
    cadences 186, 188, 189, 190, 191, 192–3
    compared to gidayū-bushi 176–7, 232
    compared to nō drama 171
    dan 180–181
    dance in 173, 175–6, 177, 179, 182, 183, **184**, 184–5
    development 173
    genres 174, 174–5, 178–9
    itchū-bushi, *see* itchū-bushi
    kabuki dance form **184**, 184–5
    kiyomoto-bushi, *see* kiyomoto-bushi
    kudoki 182, **184**, 184, 188–9, 191, 192, 193, **194**, 215
    miyazono-bushi 174, 175, 179

modern day performance 177
musical formulaism 178–9, **180**, 226
musicians 174
and nagauta music 175–6, 233
patterns 185–6, 186–92, **192**, **194–5**
phrases **180**, 190–192, **192**
piece types 180–183, **181**
sections 179, **180**, **184**, 184–5
shigetayū-bushi 174, 266
shinnai-bushi, *see* shinnai-bushi
simplest melody type 265
soft jōruri 176
structure 179, **180**, 181
substyles **180**, **194**, **194–5**
   cadences 192–3
   kihon substyle 186–9
   rōshō substyle 190–192, **192**
   semeji substyle 186, 189–90
   special effects 193
tokiwazu-bushi, *see* tokiwazu-bushi
tomimoto-bushi, *see* tomimoto-bushi
bunraku (puppet theatre), *see* puppet theatre (bunraku)
Butler, Kenneth 11, 60

cadences 18, 20, 192–3
   bungo-kei jōruri 186, 188, 189, 190, 191, 192–3
   gidayū-bushi **145**, 148, 167, 168, 169, 179
   heike **64**, 65, 66, 68, 69
   kōshiki 34, 36–8, 50
   ōzatsuma-bushi 237, **238**, 239
chigo mai 7, 92–3, 98, 129
Chikamatsu, Monzaemon 9, 141, 143, 173, 178, 195, 240
China 4, 15–16, 25, 29
Chinese culture 4–5, 12, 15–16, 30
chirashi dance section 145, 180, 182, 184, **184**, 189–90, 193, 194, 198, 206, 213, 214, 217, 225, 226, 231, 244, 255
Chōken 32
The Chronicle of Yoshitsune (Gikeiki) 22, 53, 136
chūon
   heike **66**, 66, **67**, 68
   kōshiki 36, **37**, 37, 49, 51, **67**

Chūshingura stories/plays 54, 153; *see also Kanadehon Chūshingura*

dance
   boys 7, 92–3, 98, 129
   and bungo-kei jōruri 173, 175–6, 177, 179, 182, 183, **184**, 184–5
   chirashi dance section 182, 184, **184**, 189–90
   development 95
   furi dance 95, 171, 172, 173
   and gidayū-bushi 147
   kabuki dance form **184**, 184–5
   and kiyomoto-bushi 175
   mai dance 7, 91, 92, 95–8; *see also* kōwaka mai
   men 97, 98, 130–131; *see also* kōwaka mai
   in nō drama 7, 95–8, 171
   odori dance 95, 130, 172
   odoriji dance section 173, 175, 182, **184**, 184, 193, 215, 234
   oki section 182, 184, **184**, 186, 187, 188, 191, 192, **194**
   patterns 96–7
   shosagoto dance 95, 171, 172, 173, 184; *see also* kabuki
   and tokiwazu-bushi 174, 175
   and tomimoto-bushi 175
   types 95, 97
   women 7, 91, 92–3, 95, 97, 98, 130
   see also kabuki
debayashi ensemble 172

eishō delivery 20, 185, 242
Engeki Hyakka Daijiten 95
enka ballads 3
epic tradition 6
Erdely, Stephen 14

flutes 121, 172; *see also* hayashi ensemble
Foley, John Miles 3
formulaism 264
   musical 3, 10, 12, 16, 18, 19, 20, 21, 263, 264
      bungo-kei jōruri 173, 176, 178, 179, **180**, 188, 189, 196, 203, 216, 224, 226, 231, 232

Index

gidayū-bushi 148, 149, 150, 151, 154
heike 54, 63, 65, 67, 68, 69, 71, 78, 79
jōruri 137, 141–2
kōshiki 34, 35, 41, 50
kōwaka 107, 123, 129
ōzatsuma-bushi 236, 237–9, **238**, 241–2, 243, 253, 261
sections 20
Parry-Lord formulaic theory 10, 11, 15, 18–19, 264
verbal 18, 21
heike 63
jōruri 241
kōshiki 33
kōwaka 102, 120
Fröhlich, Judith 12
Fujimatsu, Satsuma 214
Fujita, Takanori 92, 95, 97, 98, 100, 104
Fukuda, Akira 6, 60
fund-raising (kanjin) 5–6
furi dance 95, 171, 172, 173
fushi
in gidayū-bushi 149
in kōwaka 103, **104**, 105, 106, **106**, 111, 120, 128
fushi-zukushi collections 21, 148, 238
fushidan sekkyō 8, 29

Gamō, Mitsuko 103, 105
geki-bushi 235, 236, 237
Genji clan, *see The Tale of the Heike*
Genshin 30, 32
gidayū-bushi 169
acts and scenes 146–7
authorship 144
cadences **145**, 148, 167, 168, 169, 179
compared to bungo-kei jōruri 176–7, 232
dance in 147
dialogue 145
emergence 141–2, 171
formulaism 149–50
fushi 149
hard genre 10
Kanadehon Chūshingura, see Kanadehon Chūshingura
kotoba 150–151

kudoki 148, 150, 163–4
musical formulaism 148, 149, 151
musical notation 144
musical sections 148
narrative segments 144, 147–8
orality and textuality 143–4
patterns 148–50
phrases **145**, 147–50
plays 146
prominence 175
sections **145**, 147–8
structure **145**
substyles **145**, 150–151
transitional phrases 147–8
Gidayū, Takemoto 141, 171
gingata (chant style) 122
ginshō delivery 20, 185
Go-Shirakawa 55, 92
goze uta 11, 266–7
Guelberg, Niels 30, 31–2, 51
Gunji, Masakatsu 95

Hamaide **101**, 101, 102, 104
hanamichi section **184**, 184, 223, 226, 231
Harris, Joseph 15
Hashimoto, Toshie 62
Hattori, Yukio 130
hayashi ensemble
kabuki 95, 172, 177, 182, 184
nagauta music 234, 253
nō drama 91, 96, 99, **121**, 123
ōzatsuma-bushi 242, 245, 253
Ya no ne 245
Heike clan, *see The Tale of the Heike*
heike-jōruri stream of narratives 8
formulaism 18–19, 264
hard and soft strands 9–10
literacy 11–12
models of performed narrative 264–5
multiple performers 12–13
musical aspect 12
orality 11–12, 264
patterns 265–6
phrases 20, 21
and prosimetric narratives 16–17
sections 20, 264
structure 19–20, 20–21
substyles 20–21, 263–4

theatrical context 12
thematic continuities 9
Heike mabushi 59, 62, 65, 67–8, 78
heike narrative
    cadences **64**, 65, 66, 68, 69
    categories 64–5, **65**
    chapters 64
    chūon **66**, 66, **67**, 68
    compared to jōruri 136–7
    compared to kōshiki 67
    hiroi 64, **66**, **67**, 69, 80, 81–3
    history 53–4
    kamiuta 69
    and kōshiki 51
    kudari 84, **87–8**
    kudoki 66, **66**, 67, **67**, 73, **75–6**, 265
    melody types 65, 66–9, **67**
    metre 16
    musical analysis 63
    musical formulaism 63, 65, 68
    Nasu no Yoichi, see *Nasu no Yoichi*
    oral origins 9
    orality 63
    orikoe 69, 74, **76–7**
    patterns 63, 64–70, **65**, 66, **66**, **67**
    phrases 63, **64**, 69
    piece types 64–5, **65**
    sanjū 68, 83, **85–7**
    sashikoe 68, **77**
    sections and substyles **64**, 64, 65–6, **66**, 67, 67–9
    shimouta 69
    shirakoe 67–8
    shojū 68
    simplest melody type 265
    structure 64, **64**
    themes 10
    under Tokugawa shogunate 61–2
    verbal formulaism 63
    vertical structure **64**, 64
    Yokobue, see *Yokobue*
    see also *The Tale of the Heike*
Herzog, George 14
Hirano, Kenji 20, 21, 185
hiroi substyle 64, **66**, **67**, 69, 80, **81–3**
hiroimono pieces 10, 64–5, **65**, 69;
    see also *Nasu no Yoichi*
Homeric epic narrative 14, 60

Hosshin kōshiki (Jōkei) 32
Hyakuman 94
hyōbyaku section 25, 26, 31, 33, 34, 36, 39, 265
Hyōdō, Hiromi 6, 11, 57, 61, 64, 70, 84, 267

Ichikawa, Danjūrō II 236
Idema, Wilt 16
identity, Japanese 1, 23
iemoto rights 236, 237
iemoto system 21, 173–4
Iguchi, Junko 16
Ihara, Saikaku 196
Imai, Tsutomu 62
Inoue, Harima no jō 141
instruments
    biwa lute, see biwa lute
    debayashi ensemble 172
    flutes 121, 172
    hayashi ensemble, see hayashi ensemble
    shamisen, see shamisen
    tsurigane gong 130, 172
    tsuzumi drum 92, 95, 104
itchū-bushi
    bungo-kei genre 174
    character 178
    compared to tokiwazu-bushi 176, 177, 178
    emergence 171–2
    piece types **181**, 183
    reiteration 186, 187
    'speech' 185
    structure **180**, 184
    substyles 186, 188, 189, 190, **194**, **194–5**
    Wankyū michiyuki, see *Wankyū michiyuki*
itinerant singers/storytellers 1, 5–6, 30, 56, 61, 74, 92, 135, 240
Iwata, Sōichi 34
Izumi ga jō **101**, 102, 104, 105–6

ji narrative
    bungo-kei jōruri 185–6
    gidayū-bushi 150–151
    ōzatsuma-bushi 237, **238**, 239
jiuta music 62, 137, 138, 139, 174, 192, 266
jōruri narrative 169
    compared to heike 136–7

emergence and development 7–8, 130, 134, 135–6, 139–41, 171
genres 140, 173, 175
and kabuki, *see* bungo-kei jōruri
and kōwaka 129
as meta-genre 137
metre 137
modernization 134
musical formulaism 16, 20, 21
musicians 174
and nagauta music 172–3, 233
'old jōruri' 174
orality and textuality 143–4
overview 133
ōzatsuma-bushi, *see* ōzatsuma-bushi
patterns 137
phrases 21, 137
printed books 101, 130, 135, 142–3
and puppet theatre 139, 141–2; *see also* gidayū-bushi
quotation sections 17
shamisen 137–8
simplest melody type 265
structure 137
substyles 21

kabuki
bungo-kei jōruri, *see* bungo-kei jōruri
dance 95, 172, 173
dance form **184**, 184–5
development 172
emergence 130, 133–4
formulaism 179
hayashi ensemble 95, 172, 177, 182, 184
and jōruri 134, 171, 172, 232, 233; *see also* bungo-kei jōruri
Kanjinchō, *see Kanjinchō*
Kasane, *see Kasane*
and kōwaka 129, 130–131
Kyōkanoko musume Dōjōji 234–5
matsubame-mono plays 252; *see also Kanjinchō*
men's 130–131, 172
mimesis 95, 172, 173
nagauta music 172–3, 233
Okuni's 130
ōzatsuma-bushi 235–6

pieces 180–181, **181**, 182–3
and puppet theatre 133–4, 142, 145, 169, 171, 176–7
Ranchō, see Ranchō
sections 184–5
Seki No To, see Seki No To
structure 179, **180**
substyles 185–93, **192**, **194**, **194–5**
The Tale of the Soga Brothers 240–241
Wankyū michiyuki, see Wankyū michiyuki
women's 130, 172
Ya no ne, see Ya no ne
kabuki dance form **184**, 184–5
Kadensho (Zeami) 98
kakari phrases
in bungo-kei jōruri 190–192, **192**
in kōwaka **104**, 105, **106**, 111, **112–13**, 115, **117**
in ōzatsuma-bushi **238**
kakeai repertoire 175
Kakuichibon text 54, 58, 59, 61, 63
Kakyō (Zeami) 97
kamiuta melody 69
Kanadehon Chūshingura 152–3
  Act VI 164, 167
  Act VI musical analysis 167–9
  Act VI musical examples **158–9**, **160**, **162**, **165–6**
  Act VI outline **154–6**
  Act VI texts 156–7, 159–60, 161, 163–4
  outline **152**
Kanjinchō 252, 253, 260–261
  musical example **257–60**
  outline **253–5**
  text 255–6
Kannami 7, 92, 93, 94, 99, 102
karaoke 3
Kasane 223, 226, 231–2
  musical example **227–31**
  outline **224–5**
  text 225–6
katari (narrative) 6
katarimono (musical performed narratives)
  bungo-kei jōruri, *see* bungo-kei jōruri
  continuity 2, 3
  cross-cultural comparisons 13
  prosimetric model 15–17

stichic model 14–15
strophic model 13
factors 12–13
form and structure
   delivery types 17
   musical substyles 18
   repeated melody 17–18
gidayū-bushi, *see* gidayū-bushi
heike-jōruri stream, *see* heike-jōruri stream of narratives
heike narrative, *see* heike narrative
importance 266
intertextuality 54
Japanese categories 6
jōruri, *see* jōruri narrative
kabuki, *see* kabuki
kokyoku 266
kōshiki, *see* kōshiki
kōwaka mai, *see* kōwaka mai
and literacy 2
literacy 11–12
models 264–5
modern period 3, 8, 266
and music 1, 8
nagauta music, *see* nagauta music
and national identity 1
nō drama, *see* nō drama
orality 10, 11–12
ōzatsuma-bushi, *see* ōzatsuma-bushi
recognition 267
research 10–11
research methodology 18
revenge tales 7
salvation narratives 5
setsuwa tales 5–6
twentieth-century 3
vitality 2–3
vs. oral narrative 12–13
war tales (gunkimono) 6–7
Kawatake, Mokuami 173
Kawazu Matano sumō no dan 237, 241–2
Keene, Donald 61, 99
Ki no Kaion 141, 196
kihon (soft) substyle 186–9, **194**
kindai biwa 8
Kindaichi, Haruhiko 28
Kineya, Kangorō III 237–8
Kineya Kisaburō 236

kinpira-bushi 139–40, 143, 235
kiyomoto-bushi
   bungo-bushi offshoot 174
   bungo-kei genre 175
   character 178
   kabuki dance scenes 175
   Kasane, see Kasane
   kudoki 215
   latest jōruri genre 171
   modern day performance 177
   piece types **181**, 183
   reiteration 187
   Sanja matsuri 181
   structure 179, **180**
   substyles 188, 189, 190, **194**, **194–5**
   themes 196
Kobayashi, Kenji 95, 100
kōdan storytelling 3, 7, 267
Kojiki 4–5, 23, 26
Kojima Hōshi 7
kokyoku (old music) 174, 266
Kominz, Laurence Richard 173, 235, 243
Komoda, Haruko 59, 62, 64, 66, 68, 69
Korea 17, 25, 29, 31
Korean Singers of Tales (Pihl) 3
kōshiki
   biwa hōshi, influence of 51
   cadences 34, 36–8, 50
   chūon subsection 36, 37, **37**, 49, 51, **67**
   compared to heike 51, **67**
   development 29–31
   emergence 5, 25
   historical development 51
   hyōbyaku section 25, 26, 31, 33, 34, 36, 39, 265
   indigenous influences 30–31
   literature review 28
   metre 16, 20
   modern day performances **27**, 28
   musical formulaism 35, 50
   musical literacy 50
   narrative 50
   Nehan kōshiki, see Nehan kōshiki
   orality and literacy 30–31
   overview 26–7
   patterns 34–9, **35**, **37**, **38**, **67**
   phrases 33, 38

pitch areas **35**, 35–7
prosimetric model 51
recordings 28
sections 33, 34–40
Shiza kōshiki 39
simplest melody type 265
structure 34–7, 68
substyles **35**, 35–40, **37**, **38**, 50, 68
tetrachords **38**, 38–9
texts 31–2
textual features 32–3
tone 34
transitional subsections **37**, 37–8
types 32
verbal formulaism 33
kotoba substyle
  in bungo-kei jōruri 185, 186, **194**
  in gidayū-bushi 150–151
  in kōwaka 104, **104**, 105, **106**, 106,
    110–111, **112**, 114, 115, 128
  in ōzatsuma-bushi 239
kōwaka mai
  amateur performance 100
  authorship 102
  character 10
  compared to nō drama 128
  delivery types 104–5
  development 91
  formulaism 102–3
  fushi substyle 104, **104**, 105, **106**, 106,
    111, **113–14**, 120, 128
  and jōruri 129
  and kabuki 129, 130–131
  kakari phrases **104**, 105, **106**, 111,
    112–13, 115, **117**
  kotoba delivery **104**, 104, 105, 106,
    106, 110–111, **112**, 114, 115, 128
  kudoki 105, **106**
  legacy 129–31
  mai dance 95–8
  masculinity 7, 91, 93
  melody types **106**, 106
  metre 20
  mimesis 98
  musical formulaism 129
  and nō drama 7
  orality and literacy 102–3
  origins 92, 93
  overview 92–3
  patterns 104–6, **106**, 120
  phrases **103**, **104**, 105, **106**, 111,
    112–13, 115, **117**
  pieces 104
  popularity and decline 129–31
  sections **103**, 104–6
  structure **103**, 103
  substyles **103**, **104**, 104–6
  Tenmangū shrine performance 103
  texts 100–102, **101**
  Togashi, see Togashi
  tsume 115–16, **117–19**, 128
  verbal formulaism 102, 120
  war tales (gunkimono) 92, 93, 100
kudari pattern 66, 84, **87–8**
kudoki
  bungo-kei jōruri 182, 184, **184**, 188–9,
    191, 192, 193, **194**, 215
  gidayū-bushi 148, 150, 163–4
  heike 66, **66**, 67, **67**, 73, **75–6**, 265
  kōwaka 105, **106**
  nagauta 234
  nō drama 99, 123
Kumada, Susumu 105
kuri 126
kuse section 94, 98, 99, 123, 127
kusemai 91, 92, 93, 95–6, 98, 122
Kusumi, Taiso 62
kutsu 37, **37**, 49, 50
kyōge 31
kyōgen 94, 97–8, 122
Kyōkanoko musume Dōjōji 234–5
kyokusetsu 35, 63, 64, 105
Kyūshū narratives 89, 93

Lady Jōruri tale 134, 135–6
literacy 2, 4–5, 11–12, 50, 63, 142, 144
Lord, Albert B. 3, 10, 14, 264; *see also*
    Parry-Lord formulaic theory

Machida, Kashō 18, 149, 187, 239
mad character stories 195–6
mai dance 7, 91, 92, 95–8; *see also*
    kōwaka mai
maimai 7, 91, 92, 98, 130
manzai 9, 64, 267
Masumoto, Kikuko 28

Matsu no hagoromo 175
matsubame-mono plays 252; *see also*
    Kanjinchō
Matsuya, Seishichi 144
men
    control of public stage 13, 172
    eroticism 131
    holy men (hijiri) 5–6
    kabuki 130–131, 172
    mai dance 97, 98; *see also* kōwaka mai
miko 5, 7, 92
mimesis
    kabuki 95, 172, 173
    mai dance 96, 98
    nō drama 91, 98–100
min'yō 3, 36, 38, 39
Miyakodayū Itchū 171, 177, 195
Miyakoji Bungo no jō 171, 174, 175
Miyakoji Kagadayū 214
Miyakoji Mojitayū 176
miyazono-bushi 174, 175, 179
Miyoshi, Shōraku 153
modern biwa narratives 8, 266
monogatari (literary tales) 6
monomane 91, 92, 94, 95, 98–100
Muroki, Yatarō 96, 101, 129, 130, 135
musical formulaism, *see* formulaism, musical
musical narrative delivery types 20
musical notation 59, 144, 261
Myōe 32, 51

nagauta music
    and bungo-kei jōruri 175–6
    development 233
    emergence 172
    evolution 233
    flexibility 233
    hayashi ensemble 182, 234
    jōruri's impact 171
    and kabuki 233
    kabuki dance form 184
    Kanjinchō, *see Kanjinchō*
    kudoki section 188
    Kyōkanoko musume Dōjōji 234–5
    lyric and narrative natures 23, 233, 234–5
    modern day performances 177
    musical formulaism 172–3

musicians 174
Ninin Wankyū 186
ōzatsuma-bushi, *see* ōzatsuma-bushi
piece types 183
timbre 232
Ya no ne, *see Ya no ne*
Namiki, Shōzō 153
naniwa-bushi 8, 266, 267
narratives, performed, *see* katarimono
    (musical performed narratives)
Nasu no Yoichi 64, 70, 84, **101**, 102, 104
    compared to *Yokobue* **89**
    formulaism 102
    musical examples **81–3**, **85–8**
    outline **78–9**
    texts 80, 83–4
Nehan kōshiki 39–41
    analysis 45
    dan hyōbyaku 39
    dan 1 40, **41–2**, 42–5, **46–9**
    dan 2 40
    dan 3 40
    dan 4 40
    dan 5 41
    frequency and distribution of melodic material 49–50
    text 42–5
neo-traditional genres 8
Nihongi 5, 101, **101**, 102, 104
nijū 34, 35, **35**, 36, 37, 38, 39, 42–3, 49
Nijūgo sanmai shiki (Genshin) 32
Nishino, Haruo 102
nō drama 91
    Ataka, *see Ataka* (nō)
    compared to bungo-kei jōruri 171
    dance types 97
    instruments 121
    kabuki adaptations 252
    literacy 102
    mai dance 95–8
    mimesis/monomane 96, 98–100
    narrative elements 98–100
    orality 103
    origins 7, 93–4
    performers 92
    phrases **121**
    pieces/plays 10, 121–3
    sections and substyles **121**, 122–3

singing style 99
structure 19, 121, **121**, 123
texts 100, 102
verbal styles 99

Oda, Nobunaga 93, 97, 100, 129
odori dance 95, 130, 172
odoriji dance section 173, 175, 182, **184**, 184, 193, 215, 234
'Ōe-bon' 105
Oka, Seibei 143
Okamoto, Bun'ya 18, 188, 215, 223
oki section 182, 184, **184**, 186, 187, 188, 191, 192, **194**
Okuni 130
Ong, Walter J. 11–12
Ongaku Daijiten 105, 195, 214, 236
onna sarugaku 93
oral composition 11, 14, 239
oral-formulaic theory, *see* Parry-Lord formulaic theory
orality 2, 10–11, 11–12, 264
  gidayū-bushi 143–4
  heike 59, 63
  kōwaka 102–3
  nō drama 103
orikoe substyle 64, 66, **66**, **67**, 69, 74, **76–7**
Orikuchi, Shinobu 6, 84
otogi zōshi 93, 134
Ōyama, Kōjun 29
Oyler, Elizabeth 54
Ōzatsuma, Shuzendayū 235–6
ōzatsuma-bushi 234
  cadences 237, **238**, 239
  delivery types 242
  development 235–6
  hayashi ensemble 242, 245, 253
  ji narrative 237, **238**, 239
  kabuki 235–6
  kakari phrases **238**
  Kanjinchō, *see* Kanjinchō
  Kawazu Matano sumō no dan 241–2
  kotoba delivery 239
  musical formulaism 237–9, **238**, 241–2
  nagauta, adoption into 261–2
  phrases/patterns 237–9, **238**
  repertoire 237
  sections 237

shamisen 235
structure 237
substyles 239
The Tale of the Soga Brothers 241
Ya no ne, *see* Ya no ne

Parry-Lord formulaic theory 11, 15, 18, 19, 63, 264
Parry, Milman 3, 10, 264; *see also* Parry-Lord formulaic theory
patterns 19, 21, 264
  bungo-kei jōruri 185–6, 186–92, **192**, **194–5**
  dance 96–7
  gidayū-bushi 148–50
  heike 63, 64–70, **65**, **66**, **67**
  jōruri 137
  kōshiki 34–9, **35**, **37**, **38**, **67**
  kōwaka 104–6, **106**, 120
  kudari pattern 66, 84, **87–8**
  ōzatsuma-bushi 237–9, **238**
  reiterative 186–8, 189, 191–3, **192**, 213, 265–6
  shamisen 138, 148–9
  see also cadences; formulaism; substyles
phrases 264
  bungo-kei jōruri **180**, 190–192, **192**
  gidayū-bushi **145**, 147–50
  heike 63, **64**, 69
  jōruri 21, 137
  kōshiki 33, 38
  kōwaka **103**, **104**, 105, **106**, 111, **112–14**, 115, **117**
  nō drama **121**
  ōzatsuma-bushi 237–9, **238**
  unit for analysis 20
  see also formulaism; patterns; substyles
Pihl, Marhsall 3
pitch areas 17–18
  heike 68
  kihon (soft) substyle 186, 187
  kōshiki 34, **35**, 35–7, 50
  kudoki substyle 189
  rōshō substyle 190–191
  semeji (hard) substyle 190
preaching (sekkyō) 5, 16, 25, 29, 30–31; *see also* kōshiki

printing 59, 93, 101, 130, 135, 142–3
proselytizing (shōdō) 5, 25, 29–31;
    see also kōshiki
prosimetric narrative 15–17, 29, 50–51,
    185, 265
puppet theatre (bunraku)
    development 133–4, 139–42
    and jōruri 134; see also gidayū-bushi
    and kabuki 142, 145, 169, 171, 176–7
    Kanadehon Chūshingura,
        see *Kanadehon Chūshingura*
    kinpira-bushi 235
    narration 134
Pure Land faith 30–31, 56

Rakan kōshiki 28, 49, 50
rakugo storytelling 3, 266, 267
Ranchō 214–15, 218, 221–3
    musical example **219–21**
    outline **216–17**
    text 218
Reichl, Karl 15
reiterative patterns 186–8, 189, 191–3,
    192, 213, 265–6
revenge tales 7, 22, 54, 153; see also
    The Tale of the Soga Brothers
ritual narratives 7, 9, 53, 93, 95; see also
    kōshiki
Rokudō kōshiki 32, 39
romantic narratives 9–10
rōshō delivery 20, 149, 185, 186, 190–192,
    192

sageuta 99–100
salvation narratives 5, 9–10, 56, 58;
    see also kōshiki
sanjū
    bungo-kei jōruri 192
    heike 51, **67**, 68, 83, **85–7**
    kōshiki 35, **35**, 36–7, 38, 39, 43, **48**,
        49, **67**
    ōzatsuma-bushi **238**
sashi substyle **104**, 126–7
sashikoe substyle 66, **66**, **67**, 68, **77**
Satō Michiko 28
Satsuma Jōun 235
Sawada, Atsuko 34
Saya, Makito 95

sections 19, 264
    bungo-kei jōruri 179, **180**, **184**, 184–5
    gidayū-bushi **145**, 147–8
    heike 64, **64**, 65
    kōshiki 34–40
    kōwaka **103**, 104–6
    nō drama **121**, 122–3
    ōzatsuma-bushi 237
    unit for analysis 20
Seki no to 181, 207, 212–14
    musical examples **208–9**, **210**, **211–12**
    outline **203–6**
    text 206–7
Sekiyama, Kazuo 25, 31
sekkyō, see preaching (sekkyō)
sekkyō-bushi 5, 29, 30, 134
sekkyō jōruri 29
semeji (hard) substyle 186, 189–90, 193, **194**
senritsukei, see patterns
setsuwa tales 5–6, 53, 56, 100; see also
    The Tale of the Heike
shamisen 133, 266
    accompaniment styles 151, 169, 185,
        186, 187, 189, 190, 191, 232
    introduction 137–8
    in kabuki 172
    in nagauta music 234
    notation 144
    in ōzatsuma-bushi 235, **238**
    patterns 138, 148–9
    physical description 138
    popularity 7–8
    in shinnai-bushi 215
Shari kōshiki **27**, 28, 49, 50
shigetayū-bushi 174, 266
shinnai-bushi
    bungo-bushi offshoot 174
    bungo-kei genre 175
    character 178
    Kasane miuri no dan 223
    modern day performances 177
    piece types **181**, 183
    Ranchō, see *Ranchō*
    reiteration 187
    structure 179, **180**
    substyles 188, 189, 190, **194**, **195–6**
shinnai nagashi 215
Shinnai, Nakasaburō 215, 221

Shintō 30, 92, 128
shirabyōshi 92, 98
shirakoe 65, **67**, 67–8
Shiza kōshiki 27, **27**, 28, 32, 39, 49;
   see also *Nehan kōshiki*
shogunate 53, 55, 61–2
shojū 265
   heike 51, **66**, 66, **67**, 68
   kōshiki 34, 35, **35**, 36, 37, **37**, 38–9,
      42, 44, 49, **67**
Shōmonki 6–7, 61
Shōmyō Jiten (Yokomichi) 28
shōmyō (musical liturgy) 25, 28, 29–31,
   34, 51; *see also* kōshiki
Shōmyō Taikei (Hōzōkan) 28
shosagoto dance 95, 171, 172, 173, 184;
   see also kabuki
Singers of Tales (Lord) 3
Slavic narratives 14–15
Smith, Henry D. 153
Soga monogatari, see *The Tale of the Soga Brothers*
special effects substyles 186, 193, **194**
stichic narrative 13, 14–15, 17, 36, 264–5
strophic narrative 13, 264
substyles 263–4
   bungo-kei jōruri **180**, 185–93, **192**,
      194, **194–5**
   gidayū-bushi **145**, 150–151
   heike 65–6, **67**, 67–9
   kōshiki **35**, 35–40, **37**, **38**
   kōwaka **103**, **104**, 104–6
   nō drama 122–3
   ōzatsuma-bushi 239
   unit for analysis 20–21
suicide plays 9, 146, 173, 174, 215

Taiheiki 7
Taira clan, see *The Tale of the Heike*
Takadachi **101**, 102, 104
Takano, Tatsuyuki 93
Takeda Izumo II 153
Takenouchi, Emiko 175
The Tale of the Heike
   grand narrative 6
   history and legend 55
   kōwaka pieces 104
   Kyūshū narratives 89

multiple texts 57–9, **58**
musical analysis 63
musical notations 59
musicality 63
orality 2, 11, 63
origins 7, 53, 54, 57, 89
performance traditions
   biwa hōshi 60
   extant traditions 62
   history 60–62
   instruments 59–60
   research 89–90
   as romantic and religious tale 56–7
   transmission 57–8
   see also heike narrative
The Tale of the Soga Brothers 2, 7, 54, 104,
   122, 144, 153, 239–41; *see also*
   Kawazu Matano sumō no dan; *Ya no ne*
Tanabe, Hisao 28
Tanaka, Yumiko 149, 150, 176, 184, 190
Tateyama, Kōgo 62
Tateyama, Zennoshin 62
television 3, 89
tetrachords **38**, 38–9
themes in formulaic theory 10, 15, 18–19,
   63, 151, 240, 264
Tobaya, San'emon 236
Tōdō guild 57, 58, 62, 174
Togashi 114–15, 120
   musical examples **112–14**, **117–19**
   outline **107–10**
   texts 110–111, 115–16
Tokita, Alison 187
tokiwazu-bushi
   bungo-bushi offshoot 174
   bungo-kei genre 175
   character 178
   compared to itchū-bushi 176, 177, 178
   demand for 177
   emergence 176
   kabuki dance scenes 174, 175
   mad characters 196
   Matsu no hagoromo 175
   modern day performance 177
   and nagauta music 184
   piece types **181**, 183
   reiteration 187

scenes 181
Seki No To, see Seki No To
structure 179, **180**
substyles 188, 189, 190, **194–5**
Tokiwazu, Mojitayū 176
Tokugawa, Ieyasu 133
Tokugawa shoguns 61, 130, 133
tomimoto-bushi
 bungo-bushi offshoot 174
 bungo-kei genre 175
 character 178
 kabuki dance scenes 175
 structure 179, **180**
 substyles 190
Toyotomi, Hideyoshi 93, 97, 100
traditional referentiality 3, 264
tsume substyle 105, 106, **106**, 115–16, **117–19**, 128
Tsurezuregusa 57, 61
tsurigane gong 130, 172
Tsuruga Shinnai 214
Tsuruga Wakasa no jō 214
Tsuruga Wakasa no jō III 215
tsuyogin chant 10, 94, 122, 127, 128, 182
tsuzumi drum 92, 95, 104

Uchiyama, Mikiko 102
Uji Kaga no jō 140, 143
Umetsu, Shinnojō 236
utai 96, 99, 123, 191

Varley, H.P. 6
verbal formulaism, *see* formulaism, verbal
vocal delivery types 20

Wankyū michiyuki 188, 195–6, 198–9
 musical example **199–201**
 outline **196–8**
 sections 201–3
 text 198
war tales (gunkimono) 6–7, 9, 10, 92, 93, 100; *see also* heike narrative; *The Tale of the Heike*

Watson, Michael 64
women
 banning from public stage 13, 97, 172
 dance 91, 95, 97, 98
 holy women (miko) 5–6, 7, 240
 kabuki 130, 172
 kusemai 92
 Lady Jōruri tale 135–6
 maimai 130
 miko 92
 onna sarugaku 93
 shirabyōshi 92
 see also itinerant singers/storytellers
writing, development of 4–5, 12

Ya no ne 236, 242–3, 245, 248, 251–2
 musical examples **246–8, 250–251**
 outline **243–4**
 text 244–5, 249
Yamada, Chieko 147, 149–50, 151
Yamada, Shōzen 30–31, 32
Yamamoto, Kakudayū 141
Yamamoto, Kichizō 11
Yanagita, Kunio 6
Yashima **101**, 102, 104
Yashirobon 58
Yōkan 32
Yokobue 64, 68, 70, 74, 78
 compared to *Nasu no Yoichi* **89**
 musical example **75–7**
 outline **71–2**
 texts 73–4
Yokomichi, Mario 18, 19, 91, 122, 123
yomikudashi kanbun 31, 32
Yoshimitsu 61, 93, 98
Youchi Soga **101**, 102, 104, 241
yowagin chant 10, 94, 122, 128
Yūgiri plays 178–9, 195, 236
Yuiseki kōshiki 49, 50
Yukinaga 61

zatō biwa 11, 136, 137, 138
Zeami 5, 7, 92, 93–4, 97, 98, 102, 103